NEW MEXICO GUIDE

YOUR PASSPORT TO GREAT TRAVEL!

CRITICAL ACCLAIM FOR OPEN ROAD TRAVEL GUIDES!

Whether you're going abroad or planning a trip in the United States, take Open Road along on your journey. Our books have been praised by ***Travel & Leisure, The Los Angeles Times, Newsday, Booklist, US News & World Report, Endless Vacation, American Bookseller, Coast to Coast****, and many other magazines and newspapers!*

Don't just see the world – experience it with Open Road!

ABOUT THE AUTHOR

Larry H. Ludmer is a professional travel writer whose other books include *Arizona, Colorado & Utah; The Northern Rockies*; *The Great American Wilderness: Touring America's National Parks*; and *Cruising Alaska*. He is currently at work on another Open Road publication, *Arizona Guide*, due out Fall 1997.

NEW MEXICO GUIDE

YOUR PASSPORT TO GREAT TRAVEL!

LARRY H. LUDMER

OPEN ROAD PUBLISHING

Special thanks to my brother David, who contributed so much to the writing of this book. As we take our travels together he is in a unique position to be a second set of eyes in case I miss something. Moreover, his comments and suggestions almost always find their way into my work. The value of his assistance has been immeasurable in every book I have written and New Mexico Guide will not be an exception.

1st Edition

Library of Congress Catalog Card No. 96-72604
ISBN 1-883323-50-9

Front and back cover photos by Kimberly Grant, Boston, MA . Maps by Rob Perry.

TABLE OF CONTENTS

CONTENTS

MAPS

CONTENTS

SIDEBARS

1. INTRODUCTION

If you're looking for a place with the exotic appeal of a foreign country but feel more comfortable staying right here in the United States, then consider New Mexico. It has something for everyone, regardless of your preference in travel destinations. For those who are fascinated by large cities, there's Albuquerque. Seekers of smaller towns filled with history will simply be delighted by Santa Fe, Taos, and scores of others. Those of you who relish the beauty of nature will find the mountains, deserts, and unusual geological formations of New Mexico second to none. Add to all of that the intriguing blend of cultures and you have the perfect vacation destination.

New Mexico is a big state. You can spend a lot of time here and still not be able to see it all. Yet, with its excellent system of roads, you can take in the highlights from north to south and from east to west within a couple of weeks. Or you could plan several visits, perhaps establishing a different base each time to venture out and explore in detail all that a particular region of New Mexico has to offer. While the summer months are the most popular with the majority of visitors, New Mexico's climate makes it possible to visit most areas of the state at just about any time.

Regardless of your major interests and availability of time, this book has all the information you will need to plan a vacation that you'll never forget. For New Mexico is much more than cities and towns, history and scenery. It's a way of life that's true-blue American on the one hand and very different on the other. This other side of New Mexico is reflected in its architecture, shops, and cuisine.

So read on. Get comfortable with New Mexico as I share with you the state's best known treasures, as well as some places off the beaten track. I'll show you unique places to stay and where to unwind from busy days of seeing the sights. And best of all, it can be done no matter what your travel budget is, for New Mexico caters to the economical visitor as well as the one who seeks luxury at every turn.

2. EXCITING NEW MEXICO! - OVERVIEW

Have you ever noticed that every state in the Union has a motto or slogan? Some of them are good and some aren't so hot. The best ones are those that ring the truest. And none hits the mark on this score better than the official New Mexico slogan – *The Land of Enchantment.*

There's something very special about New Mexico. It has as much in the way of colorful history as any part of America. As the southernmost of the Rocky Mountain states it has its share of wonderful mountain scenery. Add to that the beautiful solitude of vast desert regions, rushing rivers, and incredible caverns and you have a nature lover's paradise. But what makes New Mexico especially "enchanting" is its unique way of life. As you read on you'll discover details of the differing cultures that have made New Mexico what it is and how they all blend together to create an atmosphere that simply cannot be found anywhere else in these great United States.

New Mexico is a land of wide open spaces. It's been attracting hordes of visitors to fill up those spaces since early in this century. Some come for the scenery, some for the history, and some for the culture. You may well find yourself especially attracted to one of those aspects. I have found through my many trips into New Mexico that it is the blend of all these features that makes New Mexico what it is – the Land of Enchantment.

Because New Mexico is so large and is filled with so many different things to see, even the experienced traveler needs some help in planning how to see it. In this chapter, I'll briefly describe the major touring areas and what they offer. Having whetted your appetite, I'll move on to a discussion of how to use this book to select exactly what you want to see and do and help plan your itinerary (full itineraries are detailed in Chapter 3, *Suggested Itineraries*).

COLORADO
ARIZONA
OKLA.
TEXAS
MEXICO
Farmington
Raton
ENCHANTED CIRCLE
Taos
Los Alamos
Bandelier N.M.
Santa Fe
25
Gallup
Las Vegas
40
Tucumcari
El Malpais N. M.
Albuquerque
Rio Grande
Clovis
25
Roswell
Truth or Consequences
Silver City
White Sands N.M.
Alamogordo
Hobbs
Deming
Las Cruces
Carlsbad Caverns National Pk.
Carlsbad
10
N
NEW MEXICO

ALBUQUERQUE

New Mexico's largest city combines the features of a modern metropolis with the rich and colorful history of the area's many cultures. **Old Town**, just steps away from high-rise office buildings and contemporary residences, is like taking a walk back in time. A number of well-preserved adobe structures, picturesque tree-filled plazas, and the aromas of Mexican cooking will delight all the senses. Adjacent to Old Town are some of the state's best museums, while the majestic scenery of New Mexico's mighty **Sandia Peak** is only minutes away.

Because Albuquerque is the most cosmopolitan locale in the state you'll find the largest variety of places to eat, regardless of your preference. Fine continental restaurants are as easy to find as the many small cafes that feature outstanding regional selections. And while Albuquerque isn't known for its after-dark entertainment scene, you'll discover that there is a more diverse range of activities here than elsewhere in New Mexico.

SANTA FE & LOS ALAMOS

Perhaps no other city in New Mexico presents a more definitive snapshot of the multi-cultural heritage of the region than **Santa Fe**, the small state capital. The historic **Plaza of the Governors** contains several excellent museums and is filled with Native Americans selling their wares spread out upon blankets in front of the low adobe buildings that line each side of the Plaza. If you were suddenly transported from your home to the middle of the Plaza, it would take you awhile to realize that you weren't in a foreign country. This is the great appeal of Santa Fe. The rest of the city is similarly filled with historic treasures and it has become equally famous for its fine shopping. The number of art galleries and places selling unusual southwestern items will simply astound you.

Nearby **Los Alamos** is another study in contrast. Here, too, you'll find much evidence of the past, but Los Alamos is very much a city of the present. You'll discover the vital role of Los Alamos in the development of nuclear weapons as well as the peaceful use of the atom. Los Alamos is as much as a "scientific colony" as Santa Fe is an artists' colony! Within a short drive of Los Alamos is the incredible **Bandelier National Monument**, a combination of beautiful scenery and a historic journey back in time to the era of the cliff-dwelling native peoples of the region.

TAOS & THE ENCHANTED CIRCLE

Taos, like Santa Fe, is another journey back into a time long passed by in most places; to a time where a much simpler way of life prevailed. Smaller than Santa Fe, but extremely crowded with visitors during the summer, Taos is most famous for the Indian pueblo of the same name, where the Native Americans have chosen to forsake modern conveniences and live their lives as their ancestors did. While the northern portion of New Mexico contains many pueblos and native cultures, Taos is one of the largest and most easily reached. Even though the Indians generally try to maintain their privacy, several colorful festivals are open to the public and draw throngs annually.

Taos was an art colony even before Santa Fe. Many artists settled here in the early part of the twentieth century and through their paintings spread the word of the beauty that was to be found not only within Taos, but in the surrounding countryside. So lovely is this area that a loop road from Taos has been dubbed the **Enchanted Circle**. It's a popular day trip for those staying in Taos.

Visitors to Taos will be delighted by the nature of the accommodations. Although high prices are common, there are many beautiful inns and lodges in the area that feature the distinctive architecture of the southwest. Some of the best combine this southwest designs with outstanding European-style hotel service. Excellent restaurants can be found throughout Taos, in numbers completely out of proportion to what one would expect to find in such a small community.

THE NORTHWEST: NATIVE AMERICAN COUNTRY

A beautiful region of mountains, plateaus, abundant forests and volcanic rock formations, the **northwest** was and remains home to many of New Mexico's Native Americans. Most of the states largest Indian reservations fall within this quadrant of New Mexico and include several that are of special interest to visitors, such as the **Zuni Pueblo** and the surrealistically beautiful **Sky City** at **Acoma Pueblo**.

While much of this area is easily accessible from an interstate highway, there are dozens of back-country routes reaching into the historic and fascinating geologic regions of the interior. The interesting **Chaco Culture National Historic Park** and the unusual **Bisti Badlands** are just a couple of examples of what awaits the adventurous visitor. One of New Mexico's most famous landmarks, **Shiprock Peak**, is also to be found in the northwest corner of the state along with several easy to reach remains of past civilizations, like the **Salmon Ruins** and **Aztec Ruins National Monument**, both near Farmington.

Farmington is one of the bigger communities in the northwest, along with **Gallup** and **Grants**. All are gateways to the nearby Indian reservations and historic sites that make this Native American Country an ideal place to spend time in New Mexico either by itself or as part of a more ambitious tour throughout the state.

THE NORTHEAST: CROSSROADS OF CULTURES

Served by a network of highways and good secondary roads, the **northeast** is where the blending of New Mexico's cultures is in some ways the most evident. Settlers heading west used one of several trails into this area, including the **Santa Fe** and **Cimmaron Trails**. Modern Interstate 25 parallels the historic Santa Fe Trail through this region, and you can see history come alive in such communities as **Raton**, **Las Vegas**, and a number of national historic monuments.

The northeast quarter of the state is an extension of the Great Plains. To the west the **Sangre de Cristo Range** of the Rockies forms an impressive backdrop. But the area is not without its own natural beauty – such places as the **Capulin National Monument**, a volcanic remain, lure visitors in search of natural splendor.

Visitors in search of recreation will find this area to their liking, too, for some of New Mexico's largest lakes are to be found in the northeast. Major lakes and state recreation areas lie close to the communities of **Tucumcari** and **Santa Rosa**, both on the main east-west route leading to Albuquerque.

ALAMOGORDO

One of the larger towns in the southern half of the state, **Alamogordo**, like Los Alamos, has had its most significant historical epoch only in very recent times. Nearby sites were important in the development of World War II's **Manhattan Project** that produced the first two atomic bombs, and the continued presence of **Holloman Air Force Base** is vital to the economy.

But visitors will find Alamogordo of interest because of its interesting museums, the stark beauty of the **White Sands National Monument**, and the proximity of nearby mountain resorts and recreation areas.

THE SOUTHEAST: DESERT LANDSCAPES & NATURAL WONDERS

Carlsbad, **Roswell**, **Clovis**, and **Hobbs** are the only large towns in the southwestern quarter of the state, which is New Mexico's most sparsely populated region. But visitors don't come to this wonderland to see the towns. They come for the solitude that only the desert can provide and to visit one of the great wonders of the natural world – **Carlsbad Caverns National Park**. You could spend several days exploring Carlsbad, which would be time well spent, but there are other areas of this region that deserve some of your attention as well. These include vast ancient **lava fields** and numerous remains of **petroglyphs** – drawings made on rock by ancient native cultures.

Given the large desert areas in the southeast, you may also be surprised to find clusters of higher ground where green forests and cooler air prevail. In fact, winter brings with it great **skiing** in the mountainous areas around **Ruidoso**, less than an hour's drive from the flat, hot desert terrain to the east. But it is just that kind of diversity that makes the southeast, like the rest of New Mexico, so appealing.

NEW MEXICO PROFILE: FACTS AT A GLANCE

Sometimes you can tell a lot about a place just by looking at some statistics. In the case of New Mexico, it only tells a small part of the story. But it's interesting and it could help you win a trivia game with your friends.

Entered the Union: *January 6, 1912, becoming the 47th State*
Area: *121,666 square miles, ranks 5th*
Number of Counties: *33*
Number of State Parks: *37*
Population: *1,653,521 (official 1994 Census Bureau estimate), ranks 36th*
Population Growth *(1990-1994): 9.1%*
Population Density: *13 people per square mile (US average is 72 per square mile)*
Largest localities *(1995 estimates): Albuquerque 384,619; Las Cruces 62,360; Santa Fe 56,357; Roswell 44,260; South Valley 35,701; Farmington 33,997; Rio Rancho 32,515; Clovis 30,954; Hobbs 29,121; Alamogordo 27,596 (South Valley and Rio Rancho are both Albuquerque suburbs)*
Nickname: *Land of Enchantment*
Motto: *Crescit Eundo (It grows as it goes)*
State Flower: *Yucca*
State Bird: *Roadrunner*
State Tree: *Piñon*
State Vegetable: *Chile and Pinto Beans*
State Song: *"O, Fair New Mexico"*
Highest Point: *Wheeler Peak, 13,161 feet*
Lowest Point: *Red Bluff Reservoir, 2,817 feet*
Tourism Industry: *$2.8 Billion*
Major farming activities: *Hay, wheat, cattle, milk*
Largest natural resources: *Natural gas, petroleum, coal*
Largest manufactured products: *Electronic equipment*

THE SOUTHWEST: THE RUGGED WILDERNESS

Interesting towns like **Deming**, **Las Cruces**, and **Truth or Consequences** are scattered throughout the southwestern quarter of New Mexico. Here, too, you'll find forested mountain areas as well as desert. Much of the best of what this region has to offer is located close to the historic town of **Silver City**. Besides the fascinating history of the mining era, nearby attractions include the mysterious **Gila Cliff Dwellings** and a wonderful walk through a beautiful gorge known simply as the **Catwalk**.

Between Silver City and Deming is the unusual **City of Rocks**. Nearby, several **ghost towns** invite visitors to use their imagination a little bit to take a journey back into another era.

HOW TO USE THIS BOOK

The next several chapters have general information, beginning with some suggested itineraries of varying lengths for those of you who don't feel comfortable with planning your own day-by-day activities. Do-it-yourself readers will still find the itineraries useful as a means of checking their own plans to make sure nothing important has been left out from the area or areas that you have chosen to visit. After a brief history and geography lesson, I'll go on to the important chapter on planning your trip, which contains the detailed nuts and bolts of vacation planning information. While some will apply no matter where you are headed, now or in the future, other portions relate specifically to New Mexico. You'll also find chapters on New Mexico's cuisine and my picks for the best places to stay throughout the state.

DIAL 505 FOR NEW MEXICO

Remember, the area code for the entire state is **505**. *Throughout this book, I've only listed the local number, so if you're dialing from home (or anywhere else in New Mexico outside local limits), don't forget to dial 1/505 first!*

Once you've gone through these chapters, you'll reach a series of chapters on each of New Mexico's major cities and larger towns or an historical or geographical region. These chapters correspond to the eight previous headings in this overview. Each of these chapters will contain a detailed look at what to see and do within a specific area.

In addition, a listing of places to stay and where to eat is given for each city or major town, and I even throw in a couple of places in some out of the way spots for those of you who don't always want to stay in town. Each destination chapter also lists places to camp and hook up an RV under Where to Stay.

THE BEST OF NEW MEXICO

Like almost everyone else, I'm kind of fond of compiling "Best" lists for just about everything I see and do. After spending so much time in New Mexico and pondering the many wonderful sights and experiences, I've come up with my favorites. You may concur or disagree with my choices after your own journey, but I think most people would have to include most of them on their list. You should attempt to include as many of these as possible in your itinerary. Any such list is subjective because, among other things, it's very hard to compare a beautiful mountain with a great museum of art. Therefore, the following list is not in any particular order.

- ***Carlsbad Caverns National Park**, including the Bat Flight*
- *A walk through historic **Santa Fe***
- ***Sandia Peak Aerial Tramway***
- ***Bandelier National Monument** OR the **Gila Cliff Dwellings National Monument***
- ***Pueblo de Taos***
- ***White Sands National Monument***
- ***Enchanted Mesa** area (Acoma and Sky City/El Malpais)*
- ***Jemez Mountain Trail** (the red rocks and mountain scenery, pueblos and historic missions)*
- ***Albuquerque's Old Town museums***
- ***Museum of New Mexico** (Santa Fe)*

3. SUGGESTED ITINERARIES

The possibilities and combinations for touring New Mexico are limited only by your imagination and, alas, the amount of time you have. In this chapter I'll give you some ideas to follow day-by-day whether you have just a few short days or a couple of weeks. Don't feel constricted by my suggestions. Read through the rest of the book and add to or subtract from any of the itineraries that follow.

There are ten different itineraries in all, the first five of which use a "base" to operate from as described in the section below. The remaining five, all of which are longer trips, explore regions or all of the state, spending nights in different places.

While there is bus service connecting cities and major towns, most of these trips are only practical if you have a car. Exceptions are those involving only Albuquerque, Santa Fe, and Taos. But even with those, the flexibility provided by your own car or a rental will allow you to venture further afield and see so much more.

USING ALL THE BASES

As you read through the chapters on each major tourist region, you'll probably begin to visualize your itinerary taking shape. Depending on how much time you have and what you want to see, your New Mexico adventure will take one of two forms.

The first is a continuous journey in the form of a loop that begins and ends at the same particular point (most likely in Albuquerque) and winds through the state so as to reach every destination that you wish to see. The other possibility is to make a base in one or more localities and venture out from the base each day to see the sights before returning to the same place each night. This works especially well if you plan to concentrate only on specific regions. If you use this method, then planning an itinerary from each chapter will be a breeze. For the areas discussed, I suggest the following "bases" in the table on page 22:

COLORADO
ARIZONA
OKLA.
TEXAS
MEXICO
Farmington
Raton
Taos
ENCHANTED CIRCLE
Los Alamos
Santa Fe
Las Vegas
Gallup
Albuquerque
Tucumcari
Rio Grande
Clovis
Roswell
Truth or Consequences
Alamogordo
Silver City
Hobbs
Deming
Las Cruces
Carlsbad
N
15
16
17
14
13
19
20
17
25
40
40
25
10
10
NEW MEXICO TOURING REGIONS
The numbers on the map correspond to these regional touring chapters:
Chapter 13—Albuquerque
Chapter 14—Santa Fe & Los Alamos
Chapter 15—Taos & the Enchanted Circle
Chapter 16—The Northwest: Native American Country
Chapter 17—The Northeast: Crossroads of Culture
Chapter 18—Alamogordo
Chapter 19—The Southeast: Desert Landscapes and Natural Wonders
Chapter 19—The Southwest: The Rugged Wilderness

TOURING REGION	BASE
Albuquerque	*Albuquerque*
Santa Fe & Los Alamos	*Santa Fe*
Taos & the Enchanted Circle	*Taos*
The Northwest	*Gallup or Farmington (Santa Fe also possible)*
The Northeast	*Las Vegas or Raton (Taos or Santa Fe also possible)*
Alamogordo	*Alamogordo*
The Southeast	*Carlsbad*
The Southwest	*Silver City or Truth or Consequences*

You can visualize the various regions better by referring to the accompanying map which gives you a better picture of the above.

You can also use base cities to explore parts of different regions. Albuquerque, Santa Fe, Taos, and Alamogordo are the best cities to stay in if you want to stay in one hotel for the entire length of your trip. Here's a list of other places you can reasonably expect to reach as a day trip from each of those four base cities:

- **Albuquerque**: Santa Fe, Los Alamos/Bandelier National Monument and the Jemez Mountain area; the Zuni-El Moro loop (to Gallup and back).
- **Santa Fe**: Los Alamos/Bandelier and the Jemez Mountains; Chama; Taos and the Enchanted Circle; Las Vegas/Santa Fe Trail attractions.
- **Taos**: Santa Fe, Los Alamos/Bandelier and the Jemez Mountains; Chama; Las Vegas/Santa Fe Trail; Cimarron, Raton and Capulin Volcano National Monument.
- **Alamogordo**: White Sands, Las Cruces; Ruidoso and Lincoln National Forest.

THE SANTA FE AREA

(5 days/4 nights)

This tour will interest those who wish to concentrate on the attractions of Santa Fe itself, as well as the immediately surrounding area.

Day 1

Arrive in Albuquerque and drive to Santa Fe. There will be time to see some of the sights in town.

Day 2

A full day for continuing to explore historic Santa Fe, with time for browsing the many shops for unique local arts and crafts.

Day 3

A short drive from Santa Fe takes you to the interesting sights of Los Alamos. Then it's on to the wonderful canyon scenery and fascinating ruins of Bandelier National Monument; return to Santa Fe.

Day 4

Today you drive south and, less than a half hour out of Santa Fe, make the first of many stops on the Pueblo Route. Among the Pueblos you'll see are Santo Domingo, Cochiti, San Felipe, Santa Ana, Zia, and Jemez. The Coronado State Monument is another feature of this excursion as is the lovely scenery, dominated by vividly colored red rocks, along the state highway that connects many of these pueblo areas.

Day 5

Time for a little last minute sightseeing or shopping in Santa Fe before returning to Albuquerque and making connections for your return home.

ALBUQUERQUE & BEYOND

(6 days/5 nights)

This short trip concentrates on the sights of New Mexico's largest city but includes time for side trips to some of the most famous of the state's Indian and historic communities.

Day 1

Arrival in Albuquerque. There will be time to explore the Old Town area as well as some of the many museums located in or close to Old Town.

Day 2

Not everything of interest in Albuquerque is in Old Town. Today you can explore some of Albuquerque's modern sections with the highlight of the day being the ascent of Sandia Peak on one of the world's longest aerial tramways.

Day 3

A day trip to Santa Fe. It's only a little over an hour each way from Albuquerque to Santa Fe, so you can plan on spending a minimum of six hours exploring New Mexico's capital and most historic city.

Day 4

The Turquoise Trail is one of New Mexico's most scenic roads, slowly threading its way through a number of small, quaint communities. You can also ascend Sandia Crest via the good auto road and get a beautiful but different perspective than from the aerial tramway.

Day 5

Today you take an excursion to Los Alamos and Bandelier National Monument. There'll be time to stop at a couple of pueblos along the way if you get an early start.

Day 6

You can use the morning to finish up any Albuquerque sightseeing or shopping that you didn't have time for previously before heading home.

SANTA FE EXPLORER

(7 days/6 nights)

This trip is essentially an expanded version of the first itinerary for those who have a few extra days to spare.

Day 1

Arrive in Albuquerque and then drive to Santa Fe. Time for some sightseeing in town.

Day 2

Take a full day to explore the wonders of this remarkable community. Don't forget to allow some time for shopping.

Day 3

A circle route following the many attractions and natural wonders found along State Routes 4 and 44. These include visiting Los Alamos, the Bandelier National Monument, and several pueblos and state historic sites before returning to Santa Fe. A day jam-packed with beauty of all types.

Day 4

Follow the Turquoise Trail south for more great scenery. If you don't mind a little mountain driving, ascend the Sandia Crest.

Day 5

About a ninety minute drive north of Santa Fe, via a good road traversing pleasant scenery, you'll come to Taos, second only to Santa Fe in attracting visitors to New Mexico. You'll have at least five hours to explore the town's sights and shops as well as visiting famous Pueblo de Taos.

Day 6

Leave Santa Fe early this morning for the two-and-a-half hour journey to Chama. Here you'll take an exciting ride on the scenic Cumbres and Toltec Railway. It can be a whole day journey if you don't mind getting back to Santa Fe late. Otherwise, the railroad offers a half-day trip.

Day 7

Sleep in this morning before heading back to Albuquerque for your connections home.

THE TAOS AREA

(7 days/6 nights)

This week-long trip features Taos as its highlight but allows plenty of time to explore the surrounding countryside.

Day 1

Arrival in Albuquerque. It's less than a three hour drive to Taos, so you may even have some time to explore and shop on the first day.

Day 2

Taos is not as large as Santa Fe so you can fully explore its history, architecture and shopping opportunities in a single day.

Day 3

Today will be devoted to a loop drive from Taos known as the Enchanted Circle. You'll pass through beautiful forests with views of mountains, broad valleys, and lakes. A number of small resort communities are along the Enchanted Circle and make interesting stops where you can shop in their unique boutiques and visit historic attractions.

Day 4

You'll head down to Santa Fe for a half-day of exploring that city. But in one direction you'll take the slower and more scenic route through the Sangre de Cristo, stopping at the Picuris and Nambe Pueblos.

Day 5

Cross the Rio Grande River, stopping at the suspension bridge for a breathtaking view of the gorge before preceding to the town of Antonito for the full-day excursion on the Cumbres and Toltec Scenic Railway. Note that the Antonito terminal is actually in Colorado just above the New Mexico line, but a good portion of the train ride is in New Mexico.

Day 6

Today you head south to Las Vegas and Fort Union National Monument. You'll be exploring the historic path of the Santa Fe Trail before returning to Taos for a final evening.

Day 7

An early departure from Taos will enable you to make a timely connection in Albuquerque to anywhere in the country. If you have a later flight, you'll probably have time to stop for the tramway up to Sandia Peak.

ALBUQUERQUE, SANTA FE, & THE NORTHEAST

(9 days/8 nights)

Our first longer trip covers the entire northeastern portion of the state, with the highlights being the time spent in Albuquerque and Santa Fe.

Day 1

Arrival in Albuquerque with time for exploring Old Town before settling in for the evening.

Day 2

Take the short ride this morning to your next overnight destination – Santa Fe. You'll have just about the entire day to explore the many sights and shops.

Day 3

Leaving Santa Fe this morning, you'll stop at the Tesuque Pueblo before visiting Los Alamos and wonderful Bandelier National Monument. A final stop can be made at the Ghost Ranch Living Museum in the small town of Abiquiu before arriving for the night in Chama.

Day 4

A full day is devoted to the beautiful scenery aboard the Cumbres & Toltec Scenic Railway. After your rail ride, drive west to your overnight stop in Farmington.

Day 5

The Aztec Ruins and Shiprock are the morning's major sights before you head south to Gallup. If more difficult driving conditions don't faze you, then you can reach Gallup via either the Bisti Badlands or Chaco Culture National Historic Park. Either way that won't allow time for exploring Gallup itself. The choice is yours.

Day 6

Heading south from Gallup today, you'll first explore the Zuni Pueblo and the forbidding landscapes of El Moro National Monument and the Mal Pais Lava Beds. The overnight stop is in the community of Grants.

Day 7

The Acoma Pueblo and unique Sky City are on the agenda for this morning. Heading east now through a series of Indian reservations will bring you back to Albuquerque. Visit the Petroglyphs National Monument on the west side of the Rio Grande before checking into your Albuquerque accommodations for the final two nights of your trip.

Day 8

The sights of Albuquerque outside of Old Town are your objectives for today. The main thing to do: take the aerial tramway up to Sandia Peak.

Day 9

Depending upon what time you have to depart Albuquerque, you should still have some time for final sightseeing or shopping. Or maybe you just want to sleep late today.

THE WEST

(10 days/9 nights)

This journey covers the entire western half of New Mexico and combines historic, cultural, and natural highlights in Albuquerque, Santa Fe, and the Silver City area.

Day 1

Arrive in Albuquerque and immediately head towards Santa Fe, where you should have a couple of hours to sightsee before checking in.

Day 2

Spend the morning in Santa Fe. This afternoon you'll head north, stopping at the Ghost Ranch Living Museum before arriving at your overnight stop in Chama.

Day 3

The entire day is devoted to a trip on the Cumbres and Toltec Scenic Railway. Then head west for your overnight stay in Farmington.

Day 4

Visit the Aztec Ruins National Monument and see famous Shiprock Peak before arriving in Gallup where you'll spend overnight.

Day 5

Today will take you on a fascinating jaunt through the Zuni Pueblo, the El Moro National Monument and Mal Pais Lava Beds, and then make a final stop at Acoma Pueblo's Sky City before arriving in Albuquerque.

Day 6

Tonight will also be spent in Albuquerque after allowing for a full day to see the sights of Old Town as well as the rest of the city, including Sandia Peak.

Day 7

A three hour drive south on the Interstate through Socorro and Truth or Consequences brings you into an area associated with the mining days of the late 19th and early 20th century. Stop at a ghost town before arriving for your overnight stay in Silver City. You'll have time to explore this quaint old town.

Day 8

Leave the mountains behind as you descend into flatter and more arid country. Visit the unusual City of Rocks State Park and explore the town of Deming, your overnight destination. Take a short jaunt south of town to explore colorful Rock Hound State Park.

Day 9

Start making your way back towards Albuquerque, stopping first to visit the sights in Las Cruces and Truth or Consequences, your overnight destination.

Day 10

Your departure time from Truth or Consequences for the drive to Albuquerque will depend upon your flight connections.

THE NORTH

(11 Days/10 nights)

For visitors whose primary interest lies in the historical and cultural aspects of New Mexico, this journey is a good choice, for it is in the north that these characteristics are at their best. There's also plenty of good mountain scenery.

Day 1

Arrival in Albuquerque with time for seeing Old Town and some museums.

Day 2

Finish up with some city sights and the Sandia Peak Tramway before heading north. Pass through several Indian reservations and beautiful red rock countryside before arriving in Los Alamos, your overnight stop.

Day 3

A morning visit to Bandelier National Monument gets the day off to a great start. Then a short drive brings you to Santa Fe in the early afternoon, giving you plenty of time to sightsee and shop.

Day 4

You'll have the morning to continue your exploration of the many wonders of Santa Fe. Your overnight stop will be in Raton, but before reaching there via the Interstate highway you can make some touring stops in historic Las Vegas and Fort Union.

Day 5

Heading west through scenic Cimarron Canyon, you'll reach the beautiful Enchanted Circle at the town of Eagle's Nest before arriving in Taos by late afternoon. Visit the Pueblo de Taos and explore the historic sights and shops in the Plaza area.

Day 6

Give yourself a few more hours to continue exploring Taos before heading out across the famous gorge of the Rio Grande. At day's end settle into the small town of Chama.

Day 7

Take either the half or full-day trip on the Cumbres & Toltec Scenic Railroad. Upon completion of the ride head toward your next overnight stop in Farmington. If you only took the half-day train ride there will be time to make a short detour just before Farmington to the Aztec Ruins National Monument.

Day 8

Take a stroll through historic Farmington this morning before departing. En route you'll view the famous Shiprock Peak and travel through a large stretch of the Navajo Indian Reservation before arriving in Gallup.

Day 9

An interesting day awaits as you visit the Zuni Indian Reservation and the fantastic formations of the El Moro National Monument and the Mal

Pais Lava Beds. Overnight is in Grants, a bustling town along the Interstate.

Day 10

Visit the beautiful Pueblo of Acoma (Sky City) and drive through the Laguna Indian Reservation before returning to the Albuquerque area. The interesting Petroglyphs National Monument on the west side of the Rio Grande are worth a stop before checking in.

Day 11

Maybe you'll have some time to shop or do some additional sightseeing in town before heading home with fantastic memories of your adventure through northern New Mexico.

THE SOUTH

(11 Days/10 Nights)

If you're more interested in seeing the desert, one of the world's greatest caves, and in learnng about the history of the mining era, this adventure through the southern half of the state will be just right for you.

Day 1

Arrive in Albuquerque and immediately head south, making your first overnight stop in Ruidoso, situated in the natural splendor of the Lincoln National Forest. On your way, a brief stop should be made to view the volcanic rocks in the Valley of Fire Park outside of Carrizozo.

Day 2

Explore the town of Ruidoso this morning before continuing your journey. A mid-day stop will allow you to visit the sights in Roswell before the final leg of the ride to Carlsbad, your overnight stop for tonight and tomorrow. Visit the interesting Living Desert State Park.

Day 3

About a half hour drive from Carlsbad are the indescribable sights of Carlsbad Caverns National Park. You'll need at least the entire day to properly visit the caves. Be sure to stay around for the dusk bat flight.

Day 4

Soon after leaving Carlsbad you'll make a detour into the Guadalupe Mountains to discover lovely Sitting Bull Falls, an unexpected sight so close to the desert. Then drive along a series of sparsely traveled roads until you suddenly arrive back in "civilization" at Alamogordo. Visit the excellent Space Center.

Day 5

Upon leaving Alamogordo it's only a short ride to an outstanding natural attraction – the beautiful White Sands National Monument. Continuing your journey westward, make a brief stop to explore Las Cruces before reaching your next overnight locale, Deming. You'll have time to look around town and explore Rock Hound State Park, a short jaunt south of town.

Day 6

Today you'll be entering a region where the mining of silver played an important part in the development of New Mexico. First, however, is a stop at the weird City of Rocks State Park, one of many natural attractions that grace southern New Mexico. Next pay a visit to the authentic ghost town of Santa Rosa, close to your home for the next two nights – Silver City. This town is rich in history and you'll have time to explore it today upon your arrival.

Day 7

An exciting adventure is in store for you today. Head north from Silver City for about an hour through the Sitgreaves National Forest until you reach the end of the road at the Gila Cliff Dwellings National Monument. You'll be fascinated by the sights and the history of this ancient culture. Returning to Silver City in the afternoon, you'll have some time to relax or continue exploring. Perhaps you'll want to see one of the area's open-pit copper mines.

Day 8

Arriving in the late morning in Truth Or Consequences, you'll have plenty of time to explore the town's sights and relax along the shore of Elephant Butte Reservoir in the state park of the same name. Continue on to your overnight stop in Socorro.

Day 9

You'll arrive in Albuquerque before lunch time, giving you most of the day to see the city's many sights. Overnight in Albuquerque both tonight and tomorrow.

Day 10

Today you'll be able to finish seeing the sights in town and have plenty of time to shop as well. You should also be sure to take the ride on the Sandia Peak Aerial Tram.

Day 11

Your southern New Mexico adventure comes to a close today as you head home.

THE NEW MEXICO SAMPLER

(13 Days/12 Nights)

With so much to see and do in diverse New Mexico, it's natural to want to see it all. This trip allows you to take in many of the state's more famous attractions, concentrating on the most important.

Day 1

Arrive in Albuquerque and spend the afternoon exploring the city. Concentrate on the Old Town area.

Day 2

Ride up to Sandia Peak on the aerial tram before heading through the Indian reservations and roadside state historic sights and monuments in the red rocks area before arriving at Los Alamos, your overnight stop.

Day 3

Tour fantastic Bandelier National Monument and visit the Bradbury Science Museum in Los Alamos before embarking on the short ride to Santa Fe, which you'll reach in late afternoon.

Day 4

Take the entire day to see the many sights of Santa Fe and sample the goods available in the endless shops.

Day 5

An early morning drive from Santa Fe north to Chama where you'll board the Cumbres & Toltec Scenic Railroad for the full day trip. Tonight will be spent in quaint Chama.

Day 6

This morning you'll drive across the suspension bridge over the deep gorge of the Rio Grande River before arriving prior to mid-day in Taos, your stop for the next two nights. You'll have plenty of time to explore the historical and cultural treasures of Taos and the Pueblo de Taos.

Day 7

Yesterday was for history, culture, and shopping. Today is scenery. Your route, begins and ends in Taos and covers the wonderful Enchanted Circle.

Day 8

Heading south through the Sangre de Cristo mountains, you'll pay a brief stop at Las Vegas, part of the old Santa Fe Trail before descending into the desert. Overnight in Roswell.

Day 9

In less than two hours drive from Roswell you'll be at the fantastic Carlsbad Caverns National Park, which will take the entire day to see. Watch the sunset Bat Flight before turning in for the evening in the town of Carlsbad.

Day 10

Visit the Living Desert State Park before making the drive to Alamogordo, your overnight stop and site of an outstanding space museum.

Day 11

This morning is highlighted by a visit to the White Sands National Monument. Then head west to Deming and then north into Silver City. On the way, stop at the City of Rocks State Park. Overnight is in historic Silver City.

Day 12

An hour's drive east from Silver City brings you to the Interstate Highway, from where an easy three hour drive brings you back to Albuquerque. You'll have most of the afternoon available to see the sights before your journey's final night arrives.

Day 13

Some last minute touring before making connections for home.

NEW MEXICO ADVENTURE

(14 days/13 nights)

This final and longest trip also includes New Mexico's most important highlights – Santa Fe and Taos, Carlsbad Caverns, and Albuquerque. But you'll find several different items from the preceding itinerary.

Day 1

Arrive in Albuquerque and head for your first overnight destination – Los Alamos. En route you'll visit several historic pueblo sites and pass through country containing beautiful red rocks.

Day 2

Visit the Bradbury Science Museum in town and nearby Bandelier National Monument. By early afternoon you'll be in Santa Fe, your home for tonight. Use the remainder of the day to browse the art and craft shops and to see the many interesting historic and cultural sites of New Mexico's capital city.

Day 3

A ninety minute drive brings you from Santa Fe to Taos. This will give you almost a full day to explore the Taos area, perhaps including part of the Enchanted Circle. Overnight is in Taos.

Day 4

Drive this morning through the Cimarron Pass before reaching Raton. Nearby you'll visit eerie Capulin Mountain National Monument. Overnight tonight is in Las Vegas.

Day 5

Today starts in the mountains and ends in the desert at Roswell. En route you'll visit the volcanic formations of the Valley of Fire.

Day 6

The day is highlighted by a visit to Carlsbad Caverns National Park, complete with breathtaking rock formations and millions of bats! Spend the night in Carlsbad.

Day 7

Visit the Living Desert State Park and then drive to Alamogordo where you'll visit the Space Museum and spend the night.

Day 8

On the agenda for today is the unusual beauty and solitude of White Sands National Monument. Other stops are in Las Cruces and the Rock Hound State Park. Overnight is in Deming.

Day 9

Visit the City of Rocks State Park, a ghost town in Santa Rita, and the interesting mining heritage of Silver City, your overnight stop.

Day 10

Heading north through the Apache Sitgreaves National Forest, stop at a fantastic natural attraction known as The Catwalk – a journey through a beautiful gorge. The afternoon will consist primarily of a ride to your next overnight destination, Gallup. However, take some time to visit the Zuni Pueblo before arriving in Gallup.

Day 11

Today you'll be traveling through the Navajo Indian Reservation and will see the famous Shiprock Peak before arriving in Farmington, your next overnight stop. Visit the Aztec Ruins National Monument in the adjacent town of Aztec.

Day 12

From a point about 12 miles east of Farmington, State Route 44 is a scenic route that will take you back to Albuquerque where you'll spend tonight and tomorrow night. Before reaching Albuquerque, however, make interesting stops at the Jemez and Zia Indian Reservations and pueblos, and the Coronado State Monument. On the way into Albuquerque you'll also have time to take a ride on the Sandia Peak Aerial Tramway.

Day 13

Today you'll have a full day to explore the many sights of Old Town and the rest of the city.

Day 14

You can return home satisfied in the knowledge that you've covered every corner of the state of New Mexico and seen so many remarkable sights.

TRAVELING NEW MEXICO'S SCENIC BYWAYS

Another interesting way to create an itinerary for a fabulous New Mexico trip is to make use of some of the nearly 20 routes that have been officially designated by the state as ***Scenic Byways****. Actually, they often contain much more than just scenery – history and culture will also be found along the route on many of the byways.*

I will provide you with a detailed description of the following byways in later chapters, either as a sidebar or as part of the sightseeing section:

- ***Wild Rivers Byway*** *(see the sidebar under Taos)*
- ***Enchanted Circle Byway*** *(see Taos)*
- ***Jemez Mountain Trail*** *(see Santa Fe/Los Alamos)*
- ***Sandia Crest Byway*** *(see Albuquerque)*
- ***Gila Cliff Dwellings Byway*** *(see Silver City)*
- ***Sunspot Byway*** *(see Alamogordo)*
- ***Old Route 66*** *(see sidebar under Planning Your Trip)*

Some other byways, most of which are at least partially described, are the Billy the Kid Trail, the Geronimo Trail, the Camino Real, and the Santa Fe Trail. Many of the byways are in close proximity to one another or even cross paths at some point. This makes it easy to plan a trip combining several trails. Some of the byways are long enough that you can plan a trip of a week or more. The Santa Fe Trail and the Camino Real are two such examples. In fact, the Camino Real, which follows an old Spanish trade route that connected Santa Fe with Mexico City, traverses more than three quarters of New Mexico from north to south.

Many of the shorter byways cover well under a hundred miles, making them an excellent choice as an excursion from some of New Mexico's more popular destinations. The greatest number of byways are located along a corridor connecting Albuquerque, Santa Fe, and Taos.

4. A SHORT HISTORY

THE INDIGENOUS CULTURES

Archaeological evidence indicates that the San Juan River basin in the northwestern quarter of the state has been inhabited for more than 10,000 years. These primitive Stone Age settlements slowly progressed to what is now known as the **Anasazi** culture in the millennium up to around 1000 A.D. The Anasazi disappeared for unknown reasons and were eventually replaced by the **Pueblo** Indians around 1300 A.D.

The Pueblo developed an advanced society that was concentrated in almost 25 different communities spread out along the Rio Grande from the site of present-day Taos to an area south of Albuquerque. The Pueblo were known for their beautiful arts and crafts, especially their finely crafted pottery and skillful weaving. They lived in sturdy adobe structures, some of which were as high as five stories. The modern **Hopi** Indians also claim to be direct descendants of the Anasazi. For more information on the Anasazi, see the sidebar on the next page.

The peaceful life of the Pueblo was to be shattered around the year 1400 A.D. by the arrival of the nomadic **Navajo** and **Apache**. The latter tribes raided Pueblo towns. The struggle between Pueblo, Navajo, and Apache was to last for almost 400 years and would soon be joined by another outside force that was to change the history of the region forever.

THE ERA OF THE SPANIARDS

The first European to make contact with the native cultures of what is now New Mexico was the Spanish Franciscan Priest, **Marcos de Niza**. He visited the Zuni in the year 1539. In the following year **Francisco Coronado** explored the Rio Grande River valley. The Spaniards were searching for gold that was reputedly to be found in seven cities (obviously Anasazi settlements). The early explorers failed to find any gold. The initial short-sightedness of the Spaniards is evident from the fact that several leaders of these early expeditions were court-martialed upon their

MYSTERY OF THE ANASAZI

The ancient ***Anasazi*** *developed an advanced civilization as far back as 10,000 years ago. They occupied a vast area covering portions of what are now the states of New Mexico, Arizona, Utah, and Colorado. However, it was in New Mexico where the greatest number of Anasazi sites have been found and explored. It is generally agreed that the Anasazi, like all native American tribes, can trace their origins to Asiatic peoples that crossed the Bering land bridge in prehistoric times. However, information concerning the beginnings of their civilization in this region are just as obscure as was their sudden demise.*

Archaeological evidence indicates that the Anasazi were a peaceful, agricultural civilization. Anthropologists classify them as hunters and gatherers. Their main crops were maize, beans, and squash. Anasazi building took two main forms. The first were adobe structures built on the ground. These could be large and elaborate or small and simple. The latter type were often built in fields and occupied only during the summer growing season.

The more famous Anasazi structures are the massive dwellings carved out of cliffs, often beneath large, natural rock overhangs. This, along with an outer wall, provided a great deal of protection to the community. The larger "apartment" buildings often had several hundred rooms and the largest had as many as 2,000. In many cases, the cliff dwellings did not require construction of a roof since they were often built up to the very overhang of the cliff. The most important building in any Anasazi community was the great ceremonial structure known as a ***kiva****. It was the centerpiece of an Anasazi community. The Anasazi were also masters of irrigation, a vital necessity in the mostly arid environment in which they lived.*

The exact reasons for the demise of the Anasazi are not known, although it is believed that nomadic Indian invasions beginning about 1300 A.D. played at least a part. Evidence also indicates that there was massive drought at around that time that probably was an even more important factor. The Pueblo Indians are direct descendants of the Anasazi.

Today's visitor to New Mexico can easily find remains of Anasazi architecture and culture in the northwestern quarter of the state. The best examples are ***Bandelier National Monument*** *(near Los Alamos), the* ***Aztec Ruins National Monument*** *(near Farmington), portions of the* ***El Morro*** *and* ***El Malpais National Monuments*** *(both between Gallup and Grants), and the* ***Puye Cliff Dwelling*** *(near Espanola). The more difficult to reach* ***Chaco Culture National Historic Park*** *(between Gallup and Farmington) has extensive remains of the Chaco, a subgroup of the Anasazi.*

return for not having found the expected riches. Despite these early "setbacks," the Spaniards did follow up over the next century with a succession of military and religious expeditions. These established control over the vast territory with the objective of converting the natives to Christianity.

They met with mixed success. Indian resentment grew as the Spaniards increasingly repressed the native culture and religion. Conflict was inevitable. In the **Pueblo Rebellion of 1680**, most of the Spaniards were driven out. However, reconquest began in 1692 with the occupation of Santa Fe. The Spanish completely subdued the natives by 1696, but agreed to recognize Pueblo Indian ownership of their ancestral lands. The settlement of Albuquerque began in 1706.

The Navajo and Apache, however, were not yet subdued. They continued their raids not only on the Pueblo, but now on the Spaniards as well. These tribes were now joined by a third raiding Indian nation, the **Comanche**. Despite these difficulties, the Spaniards continued to expand their settlements throughout the 18th century.

MEXICAN & ANGLO CONTROL

The great empire of Spain that had developed over the past two centuries was crumbling by the early 19th century. In 1821, Spain was forced to forgo most of its North American possessions and the area came to be part of the newly established nation of Mexico. While the Spaniards had barred virtually all trade with Americans and strongly discouraged settlement by the "Anglos," Mexico encouraged both. Thus, to the native and Spanish cultures was added a third ingredient. Just as the other two had clashed, conflict seemed to be inevitable once again.

The opening of the **Santa Fe Trail**, also in 1821, led to a huge influx of American pioneers. With continued Anglo settlement, the true Spanish ethnic group had become a minority by the 1840s. Nonetheless, Spanish culture was still the predominant force. Attempts by the short-lived Republic of Texas in 1841 to seize New Mexico failed. However, just five years later the United States declared war on Mexico. **General Stephen Kearny** invaded New Mexico. He seized Santa Fe without firing a shot and all of New Mexico fell under American control on August 18, 1846.

At that time of the official proclamation of the **New Mexico Territory** in 1848, the area included what is now the state of Arizona. Every resident of the Territory became a United States citizen, but the Pueblo strongly resented and resisted American control. Another Indian revolt at Taos resulted in the death of Charles Bent, the Territorial Governor. The revolt was put down and it was only very slowly that American-Indian tensions lessened. During the Civil War, the Confederacy attempted to control the Southwest and California and succeeded in capturing Santa Fe. Southern forces advanced well up the Rio Grande before being defeated at the **Battle of Glorietta Pass** in March 1862. Congress separated Arizona from the New Mexico Territory in the following year.

The post-Civil War era saw the slow submission of the Navajo, Apache, and Comanche by the US Cavalry in the late 1860s. The "pacification" of the Indians was accomplished only through further bloodshed and the forced relocation of most of the native population onto reservations. Economic and social progress on the reservations was generally mismanaged by the Bureau of Indian Affairs that the government had established to "help" the native population. It is only in recent years that the negative effects of reservation life have begun to be overcome.

It was the submission of the Indians, however, along with the coming of the railroad and extensive mineral discoveries that was to lead to an unprecedented era of tremendous growth in the final quarter of the 19th century. That growth was not without its own problems and violence. Landowners, ranchers, and other interests clashed during the 1870's for economic control of the territory. This culminated in the so-called **Lincoln County War** of 1878. The "war" was actually a five day battle that involved many famous names of the American West, including **Billy the Kid**.

MODERN NEW MEXICO

By 1900, the outlaw age of New Mexico had virtually come to a halt. It was at the turn of the century that artists' romantic depictions of the Taos area began the tourism industry that has become so vital to the economy of New Mexico. Despite the growth and the influx of more settlers as well as visitors, New Mexico remained a Territory. Opposition to statehood came from many residents because they didn't want the higher taxes that accompanied becoming a state.

Just as important was Congressional opposition. Many in that institution felt that democracy just wouldn't work in a Spanish-speaking land. (It's interesting to note that it wasn't until 1898 that English began to be taught in the public schools.) Opposition by Congress and the residents of the territory slowly weakened, however, and New Mexico was admitted to the Union as the 47th state in 1912.

The 20th century has seen almost constant growth. New Mexico's population is one of the fastest growing in the nation and the economy has kept pace. This has been fueled not only by its attractive climate and life style but by several economic factors. Among these have been the discovery of important natural resources such as oil, gas, and uranium.

However, it was a secret project taking place during World War II that is most responsible for New Mexico as we know it today.

The sleepy little town of Los Alamos, isolated and difficult to reach, seemed the perfect place to work on the development of the atomic bomb. The **Manhattan Project** brought the greatest scientific minds and thousands of military personnel to the area. New Mexico's even more isolated Jornado del Muerto Mountains, about 60 miles north of Alamoagordo in the southern part of the state, proved to be an excellent site to test the bomb that was developed at Los Alamos.

These events, of course, changed the world. But they changed New Mexico even more. For the elaborate facilities and many people associated with the project were to remain in the state. As a result, New Mexico became a leader in high tech industries and especially in scientific research. Today, the research at the **Los Alamos National Laboratory** and in Albuquerque's **Sandia National Laboratory** continue to churn out useful information in nuclear energy, space exploration, and other scientific fields.

Growth has, unfortunately and unavoidably, brought with it some problems. There is concern about pollution resulting from a larger population and an influx of new groups of people who are far different than those who lived here before. Despite these difficulties, New Mexico seems more capable of housing a multi-cultural population in greater harmony than many other American locales. Perhaps it is the strong traditions that pervade life in New Mexico. Perhaps it is the beauty of the state that so many residents, both old and new, want to protect. Whatever the reason, New Mexico is anxious to welcome the millions of visitors who are anxious to share, even for a short time, the things that make it the Land of Enchantment.

WHAT IS A KIVA?

*I'll be using the term **kiva** quite often in later chapters so you might as well become familiar with it. A kiva is a round, underground (or at least partially underground) chamber that the Pueblos and the Anasazi before them used for ceremonial and religious purposes.*

5. LAND & PEOPLE

THE LAND

New Mexico is the southernmost of the Rocky Mounain states. It covers 121,661 square miles, making it the fifth largest state in the nation. Except for a couple of blips on the southern edge, New Mexico is almost shaped like a square. It measures approximately 390 miles from north to south and about 350 miles from east to west.

Elevations in New Mexico range from a low of 2,817 feet above sea level at the Red Bluff Reservoir near the southern border with Texas to a high of 13,161 feet at Wheeler Peak. The average elevation of 5,700 feet is one of the highest in the nation. New Mexico is bordered by Texas and Mexico on the south, Texas and the Oklahoma panhandle on the east, Arizona on the west and Colorado on the north. However, the northwestern corner is unique in that it is the only place in the United States where four states come together. Utah joins Arizona and Colorado in sharing with New Mexico the spot known as the **Four Corners**.

Geographically, New Mexico can be divided into three main areas. These are the **Colorado Plateau**, the **Basin and Range Region**, and the **Great Plains**. Let's take a closer look at each of them.

Colorado Plateau

The Colorado Plateau area covers a roughly triangular shaped area in the northwestern portion of the state. This is a region of high, flat-topped mountains called **mesas**. They are filled with narrow and often deep canyons as well as numerous wide valleys and small plains. The colorful rock formations of this region are closer to those found in Utah and northern Arizona than the rest of New Mexico.

Basin and Range Region

The single biggest portion of New Mexico is the Basin and Range Region which covers the entire central portion of the state from Colorado to Mexico. Here are located the tall peaks of the **Sangre de Cristo**

Mountains, the southernmost range of the Rocky Mountains. **Wheeler Peak** is located here, as are numerous other mountains whose summits exceed 12,000 feet. The **Nacimiento Mountains**, to the immediate west of the Sangre de Cristos, are generally lower. Both mountain ranges dominate the north. The elevations lower dramatically as you travel south through the Basin and Range region. The southern half of this region contains broad valleys and large desert basins interspersed with higher, forested mountain areas. The deserts of New Mexico aren't like those you see in movies depicting the Sahara. Most of them are rocky and covered with growth of shrubs and cactus.

TRACKING THE CONTINENTAL DIVIDE THROUGH NEW MEXICO

Sometimes known as the Great Divide, the ***Continental Divide*** *derives its name from the fact that it separates waterways that flow west toward the Pacific from those that flow to the east. Following the crest of the Rocky Mountains, it is generally the highest or nearly the highest point in the areas that it cuts across. Extending all the way from Alaska through Mexico, the Divide cuts an irregular path through New Mexico.*

Entering the state from Colorado approximately ten miles west of Chama, it heads south and then southwesterly to a point about 30 miles east of Gallup. Becoming part of the Zuni Mountains as it zig-zags south into the San Francisco Mountains, it passes west of the Gila Cliff Dwellings and practically through Silver City. Finally, continuing on a curving southerly course through the Cedar and Animas Mountains, it exits into Mexico about 20 miles east of the point where Arizona, Mexico, and New Mexico meet.

The attraction of the Continental Divide is the generally great scenery from its summits. This is especially true in the higher elevations which, in New Mexico, are in the northern part of the state. Major road crossing points in New Mexico (from north to south) are:

- *US 64 west of Chama*
- *NM 44 northwest of the town of Cuba*
- *I-40 near milepost 48*
- *US 60, 20 miles west of the town of Datil*
- *NM 12, 24 miles northeast of the town of Reserve*
- *North of Silver City on NM 15 or west of town on US 180*
- *I-25 near milepost 55.*

One of the main features of the Basin and Range region is the **Rio Grande River**, which runs the entire north/south distance of the state before turning towards the east where it serves as the border between the United States and Mexico. The Rio Grande is New Mexico's largest and most important river. There are a few other major waterways, although these also either originate in or are located entirely in this same region. The **Pecos** and **San Juan** rivers are the two next most important rivers and both are tributaries of the Rio Grande. The **Canadian River**, which runs eastward into the Great Plains, is the only other significant river. There are relatively few lakes of note but the state does contain several large man-made reservoirs.

Great Plains

The eastern third of New Mexico is an extension of the Great Plains. It can be subdivided into two sections. The northern portion is known as the **Llano Estacado** (the High Plains). This area shows much evidence of erosion among its mesas and buttes as it blends into the Rockies in the western portion.

To the south of the Llano Estacado are the true Great Plains. Here are found the lowest elevations in the state. Much of the land is suitable for farming with proper irrigation, but there is also extensive desert area.

THE PEOPLE

Like most of the southwest, New Mexico is growing rather fast. The 1994 population was estimated to be 1,654,000 people, an increase of 10 percent from the 1990 census. Even so, this ranks only 37th in the nation. Considering the size of New Mexico, this means that there are plenty of wide open spaces.

Albuquerque, with almost 400,000 people, is far and away the state's largest city. In fact, no other locality in New Mexico has as many as 100,000 residents. Other "cities" in the top ten are Santa Fe, Las Cruces, Roswell, Farmington, Clovis, Hobbs, Carlsbad, Alamogordo and Gallup. The corridor from Albuquerque through Santa Fe is the most heavily populated and contains about half of the state's total population. Almost three-quarters of New Mexico's people live in urban areas.

The term "Anglo," which I introduced to you in the history section, is still commonly used in New Mexico, even by the Anglos themselves. The Anglo population represents about 70 per cent of the total, while about 10 percent is Native American. The remainder of the population is mostly of Mexican or Spanish origin, although a significant number of the Anglo residents list their background as being at least partially Hispanic. With the large number of Hispanic residents it should come as no surprise that the largest religious group in New Mexico is Roman Catholic. However, in the larger urban areas you'll find houses of worship for just about every major religion.

Many of New Mexico's residents are bilingual (English and Spanish). Indian languages are primarily confined to the more reclusive of the reservations. Colorful Mexican festivals are common throughout the state and are enjoyed by both residents and visitors, Hispanic or otherwise.

Despite the pervasive influence of Hispanic culture, the majority of visitors are, not surprisingly, most interested by the Native American population. While many have assimilated into the general population (especially those of mixed parentage), a large number still live on reservations. In fact, the total Native American population is well in excess of 150,000 people, with approximately 134,000 still residing on one of 25 different reservations throughout the state.

Except for the Mescalero Apache in the south-central region, the majority of reservations are located in the north. A significant number are Navajo and Apache but the single largest Indian group are the Pueblo. Only Arizona, California, and Oklahoma have larger Native American populations than New Mexico. However, as a percentage of the total state population, New Mexico's Indians are in first place. They comprise almost nine percent of the state's residents (while second place Oklahoma stands at around eight percent).

While the Spanish influence is perhaps the most evident of all cultural influences to visitors to New Mexico, the Indian heritage is a close second. A good example of the importance placed on that heritage is the state flag, which features the traditional Zia Indian sun symbol on a yellow field. Except for a few of the smaller and most conservative Pueblos, the Native American population dresses and acts like any typical American on any given day. It is only on tribal feast days or other important occasions, however, when the colorful old costumes and traditional customs prevail. Of course, many tribes also cater to tourists by holding regularly scheduled performances throughout the year that feature tribal dress and customs. These performances may not have any particular religious or other significance to the Indians, but they are authentic in every detail.

Don't expect to see wild Indians on the warpath, whooping it up and carrying tomahawks. It isn't helpful to perpetuate half-true stereotypes. Approach your contacts with the Native American population as a learning experience and you'll enjoy it that much more. It's very important that anyone who is planning on visiting a pueblo be familiar with the rules of behavior, which I've included in the sidebar on the following page.

CLOSE ENCOUNTERS OF THE PUEBLO KIND

There is hardly a visitor to New Mexico who is not at least somewhat fascinated with the very unique culture of the Pueblo Indians. There are more than 20 Pueblo communities in existence today throughout New Mexico and almost all of them welcome tourists, at least to some degree. The so-called **Eight Northern Pueblos** *(in the past they were sometimes called the Eight Civilized Tribes) are clustered between Santa Fe and Taos. These are the Tesuque Pueblo, Pojoaque Pueblo, Nambe Pueblo, San Ildefonso Pueblo, Pueblo de Santa Clara, San Juan Pueblo, Picuris Pueblo and Pueblo de Taos. Other major pueblos not in this group are Acoma (Sky City) Pueblo, Jemez Pueblo, Pueblo de Santo Domingo, and the Zia and Zuni Pueblos.*

I'll tell you more about each of these in the touring sections, but some general instructions about how to behave when visiting an Indian pueblo are in order.

Indian reservations are governed according to tribal law, which takes precedence over most state regulations and even some federal laws. This means that you have to abide by their rules, just as you would have to if you were visiting any sovereign nation. Please respect their traditions by following the few rules they impose on visitors. These generally include not taking photographs or videos, using a tape recorder or sketching what you see without their permission. Never enter a home without the owner's permission (which is often granted on feast days). Always expect to have to pay a fee for that privilege when it is extended to you. It may be easier to understand this by remembering that you aren't visiting a museum or an amusement park when you're on a reservation. These are people's everyday homes. I'm sure you wouldn't be amused if a tourist barged into your home and began taking pictures or examining your furniture. Certainly you too would want to be compensated if this were to occur on a regular basis.

Some other important rules are to always be quiet during any dances or ceremonies that you are allowed to observe. Never go into ceremonial sites without permission and don't tread on ruins. Leave everything where you found it. Finally, alcohol or drugs should never be brought onto an Indian reservation.

Now, that isn't so very difficult, is it? Just by following these simple steps you'll be able to meet Native Americans close up and have a most enjoyable visit. It is sometimes natural for small children to have difficulty in understanding the need for these rules. Your best bet is to keep a tight rein and a close watch on your little darlings when visiting the pueblos. My own observations, however, lead me to believe that most children will not present a problem and will usually wind up enjoying their visit.

6. PLANNING YOUR TRIP

BEFORE YOU GO

WHEN TO VISIT

Since the climate of New Mexico has been one of the main drawing cards to the recent influx of easterners and many others, it shouldn't surprise you when I say that almost any time of the year can be the right time to plan a vacation. There are some exceptions, however, because the weather in mountainous areas can be down-right cold during the winter. This includes Santa Fe and Taos. Of course, if you're coming to experience the great skiing, then that's a plus.

Sunshine is abundant throughout the state during every season. The average minimum amount of annual sunshine is in excess of 70 percent, with many locales being even higher. It's no wonder that New Mexico was, like Florida, referred to as the Sunshine State before adopting its much more catchy Land of Enchantment moniker.

The climate does vary because New Mexico is so large and the differences in altitude are so great. Most of the state is dry or semi-arid. Even the wettest areas receive only about 25 inches of precipitation per year. As you can see from the chart below, you probably won't have to worry much about rain interrupting your activities. Most of the already light rainfall comes in the form of afternoon thunderstorms during the summer. Some of these can be quite heavy, but they usually don't last long.

While most of the state receives little or no snowfall, some areas in the northern mountains can receive as much as 300 inches. Humidity levels are generally quite comfortable, especially in the summer when you need them to be lower. Most areas of the state have a summer humidity in the 30s, although some of the southern desert areas are much lower.

Although New Mexico is a year-round playground, the majority of visitors do come during the summer months. Santa Fe and Taos, especially, are extremely crowded during those months. Prices rise accordingly during the peak visitor season so you may want to consider a shoulder period such as May or late September. Generally you shouldn't be risking too much of a problem with colder weather interfering with outdoor activities. Peak winter periods in the Taos area also see much higher prices because of all the ski activity, but this is less so in Santa Fe.

In Albuquerque (and most other areas except for the aforementioned Santa Fe/Taos corridor and the resorts around Ruidoso) the price of a room is consistent throughout the year, with the exception of brief rises during special events such as Native American festivals, fairs, and major holiday periods.

AVERAGE TEMPERATURE & ANNUAL PRECIPITATION

The numbers below are given as High/Low in Farhenheit.

	Jan.	*April*	*July*	*Oct.*	*Annual Precip.*
Alamogordo	57/28	78/44	95/65	78/46	11"
Albuquerque	46/28	69/42	91/66	71/45	9"
Carlsbad	59/29	80/46	96/67	80/49	15"
Farmington	43/17	69/34	92/57	71/36	8"
Las Cruces	56/25	77/41	94/65	78/44	9"
Roswell	56/27	73/40	88/66	79/46	12"
Santa Fe	42/18	62/33	85/56	65/38	14"
Silver City	49/24	67/37	87/59	70/41	17"
Taos	40/10	64/29	87/50	67/32	12"

WHAT TO PACK

New Mexico is a highly informal state, just as most of the mountain states are. You won't find much of a need for fancy clothes as even most of the better restaurants have rather permissive dress codes. There are some exceptions and you'll find those indicated in the sections on dining.

The key to proper packing is to take what's appropriate for the time of year and the types of activities you'll be undertaking during your vacation. Your sightseeing activities will almost certainly involve a great deal of time outdoors, so you have to take into consideration the temperature and sunshine.

Summer clothing should be lightweight regardless of what part of the state you'll be in. A hat to protect you from the bright sun is an absolute must, even in the mountains where the cooler air might make you think that the sun isn't so strong. Believe me, it is! A sweater or light jacket is appropriate for the evenings, both in the mountains and the desert where the temperatures can drop sharply once the sun goes down. Comfortable shoes are also a must; sneakers are great. Both men and women might want to bring along a dressier pair of shoes as well to change into at dinner time, although sneakers will be acceptable in most places. Don't wear sandals for outdoor activity – they simply don't provide enough support on rough terrain that you'll almost certainly encounter. While you probably won't see too much rain during your visit, having an umbrella with you can be handy.

"YES, VIRGINIA. THERE IS A STATE CALLED NEW MEXICO"

One would think that every American realizes that New Mexico is a state just like every other state. Surprisingly, that's not the case. Maybe it's the name and maybe it's the foreign atmosphere that is so easily found that causes the confusion. A lot of people think that New Mexico is part of Mexico!

The New Mexico State Tourism Office reports that many people inquire as to whether they require a passport to enter New Mexico. The answer, of course, is absolutely not. Many potential visitors also are concerned because they don't speak Spanish and are afraid they will have a hard time making themselves understood. Again, no problem. Informed readers may laugh at all of this because the thought of New Mexico being anything other than American seems silly to them. Apparently, however, the state of New Mexico does take it rather seriously. Seriously enough to have their automobile license plates read "New Mexico USA" instead of just having the name of the state, as is the case in every other part of the country.

My favorite story, though, concerns an attempt by a New Mexico resident to obtain tickets for the 1996 Olympic Games. It seems as though a certain amount of tickets were allocated to each state. Unfortunately, when the ticket clerk on the phone plugged the New Mexican's zip code into the computer it showed no such place. They refused to send him tickets. When he inquired as to how he might resolve this problem, it was suggested that he seek the assistance of the Mexican Embassy! Well, the computer glitch was finally settled and the man got his tickets, but it is typical of what can happen when talking about the Land of Enchantment.

For those of you who will be hiking or climbing in the mountains, make sure you have the proper equipment for those undertakings, particularly a good pair of hiking boots. Dress in layers to be prepared for the sudden changes in weather that can occur at higher elevations.

Everyone should consider using sunglasses and sunscreen. It may seem a bit obvious to tell you to make sure to pack your medications, eyeglasses, toothbrush and other personal items, documents (which include tickets, pre-paid vouchers, identification, copies of credit card and/or travelers check numbers, copies of prescriptions), film and cameras, but you would be surprised how many people manage to forget one or more of these things. I suggest you make a checklist of things to take well before you're ready to pack and add things as they come to mind. This way you won't leave anything out when the big day arrives.

FOR OUR FOREIGN VISITORS' EYES ONLY

Americans are not the only ones who have discovered the Land of Enchantment. Almost a quarter of a million foreign visitors will see New Mexico this year. American customs regulations and formalities are generally quick and easy. The American embassy or consulate in your home country can familiarize you with the exact requirements, which vary from one country of origin to another. They can also fill you in on limitations on what can be brought into or taken out of the United States. However, you will always need a passport except if you are a citizen of Canada or Mexico. An international driver's license is required (Canada and Mexico are, again, the exceptions to the rule) if you plan on driving.

Keep in mind that the United States does not use the metric system of weights and measures. This can be rather confusing, so you should get a good conversion chart to make things simple. Perhaps the most important thing to always remember, though, is that one kilometer is equivalent to about 6/10 of a mile. So, those 55 mile-per-hour speed limits aren't as slow as you might first think – its equivalent to about 90 kilometers-per-hour.

NEW MEXICO TOURISM INFORMATION

While you should definitely be able to plan your entire New Mexico trip from the information in this book, I would be remiss if I didn't tell you about at least one other good source of information. The **State of New Mexico Department of Tourism** publishes a lot of brochures, both general and specific, relative to vacationing in New Mexico. Their helpful staff can be contacted by calling *Tel. 1-800/SEE NEWMEX (1-800/733-6396)*. You can get a lot of information on specific areas by contacting local chambers of commerce or visitor bureaus. These are listed in the Practical Information section of each city or regional chapter. Many have toll-free numbers.

One essential item that everyone needs is a good road map (unless you're going to be limiting your trip to places like Albuquerque, Santa Fe, and Taos). The Department of Tourism has good maps, as does the American Automobile Association (for members). You can also find decent maps put out by major map publishers like Gousha or Rand McNally in the travel section of many larger book stores.

NEW MEXICO TOURISM ON THE NET

There's no doubt that the world of high-tech has hit the tourism industry. For those who like to get their information by computer the Department of Tourism has two addresses. First, for E-mail, use ***enchantment@newmexico.org****. The World Wide Web address is:* ***http://www.newmexico.org/****.*

Those of you who'll be driving into New Mexico will find an official visitor information center within a few minutes drive of the border on all four sides of the state, right along the major Interstate highways.

BOOKING YOUR VACATION

Some people like to suddenly arrive at a destination and take their vacation on a "let's see what happens" basis. Although there may be something to be said for such flexible travel plans, I have always strongly recommended doing some solid advance planning for several reasons. First of all, the planning process can be a lot of fun. It serves as an appetizer for what is to come. More important, however, are the practical reasons. Most of us only have a limited time to take a vacation and we want to make the best of it. Planning allows you to do exactly that. Also, in popular areas such as New Mexico you cannot always expect to have a hotel room available just because you show up and say "I'd like a room for tonight." Running around trying to find a place to sleep at the last minute is definitely not fun – even if you have a lot of time. And finally, advance planning can save money. We all like to do that.

This section will give you guidance on what to book in advance and how to go about doing it. Then I'll delve into some of the finer points on transportation, lodging, and getting around New Mexico.

After you've come up with an itinerary, the things that need to be booked in advance are (1) air transportation (or whatever form of common carrier you're going to use to get to New Mexico), (2) lodging, and (3) car rental within New Mexico. Your first decision regarding all of these is whether you should book on your own or use a professional travel agent.

Do You Need a Travel Agent?

The answer depends upon you. There's nothing difficult about getting and reading airline schedules or contacting various hotels and car rental companies to get rates and making the reservation yourself. Many people feel uncomfortable doing that because they think that a travel agent can do it better. That's true in some cases but not always. If you are going to use a travel agent, make sure that it is a reputable firm. They should, at a minimum, be a member of the American Society of Travel Agents (ASTA). Ask friends and relatives about their experiences with a particular agent. You can even contact the local Better Business Bureau if you have any doubts about an agent.

Regardless of which travel agent you choose, their services should be free of any charge to you. They get paid commission by the airlines, hotels, etc. The only fee you should ever have to pay a travel agent is if they do special individual planning for you, which is commonly known as F.I.T. Travel agents have access to on-line systems that should result in your getting the best rate. I have always found that even if you do use an agent its a good idea to make some calls on your own to the airlines and others to secure a rate. Sometimes you can do better. Or by telling a travel agent what you've already found they may be able to save you even more.

It is sometimes difficult if not impossible to, as an individual, book a reservation on organized tours. These are often exclusively handled through travel agents. If this is the type of trip you're planning to take then you should immediately go to a travel agent. Organized tours usually include air options.

Individual Travel vs. Organized Tours

I almost always opt for travel on my own instead of being herded into a group. Many tourists do like the group situation for its "people interaction" and the expertise of the guides. However, there are a lot of shortcomings. The first one is that you are on a schedule that someone else sets. And that schedule has a lot of built in down-time to accommodate what will be the slowest person in the group. Organized tours generally dictate where and when you will eat, which is not always to everyone's liking. Careful reading of an organized tour itinerary will show that you do not always spend a lot of time seeing what you want to see. In fact, finding an itinerary that suits your interests can be a major problem.

While you may feel uncomfortable on your own in some exotic foreign destination, remember that New Mexico only seems foreign. It's the good-ol' USA and you don't have to feel that you're in a strange place. You can get around as easily as in your home town.

In short, organized tours in a place like New Mexico aren't necessary for most people. The primary exception is for people who do not drive – in such a case an organized tour is certainly better than the alternative of public transportation. Another possible reason for group travel is if you are traveling alone. That's not often the most enjoyable way to take a trip, so that is another instance where I would consider a tour.

Many airlines offer individual travel packages that include, besides airfare, hotel and car rental. Sometimes these can save money but often you can still do better arranging everything separately. But do figure the costs both ways. Be careful about how restrictive these "fly-drive" packages are. Some are quite flexible but others have a lot of rules regarding which cities you can stay in or minimum number of nights required. If they fit into your plans, fine; if not, simply build the pieces of your trip block by block.

Tour Operators

Having said all this, I will give those readers who are going for organized tours a few suggestions. Travel agents, of course, will be able to provide you with brochures on lots of itineraries that go to New Mexico. The absolute best bus tour operators in North America are **Tauck Tours** and **Maupintours**.

Tauck has an eight day/seven night tour that departs from El Paso (spending most of the first day there and in neighboring Juarez, Mexico) and ends in Albuquerque. Among the highlights are White Sands, Cloudcroft, Santa Fe, Bandelier, Taos and Albuquerque. A side trip to Carlsbad Caverns has been added for 1997. For anyone who doesn't drive it's certainly not a bad itinerary. The trip is offered on a weekly basis from mid-April to late October. *Contact your travel agent or Tauck at Tel. 1/800-468-2825.*

Maupintours offers an eight day New Mexico trip from May through October that begins and ends in Albuquerque. Highlights include White Sands, Carlsbad Caverns, Santa Fe, Taos, and Bandelier National Monument. Although I believe that the Tauck trip makes better overall use of the time available, Maupintours does hit all the high spots and stays longer at Carlsbad Caverns. Two other Maupintours also visit parts of New Mexico. The 11-day Southwest Indian Lands Trip covers the Four Corners region and also originates and ends in Albuquerque. New Mexico sights on the itinerary are Santa Fe, Bandelier National Monument, and Taos. Another 11-day trip, the Rockies By Rail (Denver to Albuquerque) spends a few days in New Mexico and does the Cumbres & Toltec Scenic Railroad, Taos, Santa Fe and Albuquerque. *Maupintours can be reached at Tel. 1/800-255-4266.*

Both companies stay at first class hotels and the prices are quite high.

If you are looking for a custom designed F.I.T. vacation in New Mexico you should consider one of the following reputable organizations:

- **Blue Sky Tours/New Mexico**, *Tel. 1/800-453-4407*
- **Tourservice/Custom Travel Experts Ltd.**, *Tel. 1/505-989-5072*

Both companies will gladly handle individual requests. There are others but they cater mainly to groups. If you go to New Mexico on your own without automobile transportation, you should take advantage of some of the many day tours operated by **Gray Line of Albuquerque**, *Tel.*

1/800-256-8991. The name is misleading since many of their trips are in the Santa Fe and Taos areas and other places.

Getting the Best Airfare

Even travel agents have trouble pinning down what the best airfare is on a given flight on a given day. The crazy airlines aren't much better in figuring it out. You can get ten different answers to ten separate inquiries to the question "I want to go from A to B on July 10th in the afternoon. What will it cost?" Such is the state of the airfare game. There are, however, a couple of things to keep in mind about getting a good rate.

Midweek travel (Tuesday through Thursday for sure, but may include Monday afternoon and Friday morning depending upon the airline) are lower priced than weekends. Holiday periods are higher. Night flights are considerably less than daytime travel if you don't mind arriving on the "red-eye" special.

Advance confirmed reservations, paid for prior to your flight, are almost always the cheapest way to go. The restrictions on these low fares also vary. In general you must book and pay for your tickets at least seven to 30 days in advance. They usually are non-refundable or require payment of a large penalty to cancel or make a change in flight itinerary. So be sure when and where you want to go before reserving.

You can sometimes find big bargains by taking the opposite strategy – waiting for the last minute. If the airline has empty seats they're often willing to fill it up for an unusually small price. Problem is you don't know if there will be an available seat at the time you want to go. If you have definite reservations for everything else this can be a dangerous game to play. If you do get a ticket it can also wind up being at a very high price.

In this era of deregulation, airfares from one airline to another can sometimes be radically different. Some of the low-cost carriers are as good as the major airlines. Since you're going to New Mexico, you should definitely be aware of **Southwest Airlines**, *Tel. 1/800-435-9792* – a low cost operator with an excellent reputation and a loyal following. They happen to also have a lot of service to New Mexico. More about the carriers going to New Mexico a bit later.

Finally, I know that those accustomed to first class air are going to squirm in their seats at this, but the cost of first class is simply not worth it – you're only going to be on the plane for a few hours. This isn't a week long cruise where you want to be pampered every minute. Go coach, bring along a good book, and enjoy the flight.

FLYING TO NEW MEXICO

Although there are commercial airports in a number of localities throughout New Mexico, the only practical place to fly into is Albuquerque. The biggest carrier in Albuquerque is discount **Southwest Airlines**, *Tel. 1/800-435-9792*. They have the most non-stop service, including Dallas, El Paso, Houston, Kansas City, Las Vegas, Los Angeles, Phoenix, St. Louis, San Diego and San Francisco. One-stop or change of plane service is available to their entire network of cities throughout the southwest and some in the east.

America West, *Tel. 1/800-235-9292*, has non-stop service several times a day from Phoenix. That city is America West's hub, so you can make easy connections to dozens of cities in the America West route system, mostly in the west but going to the east coast as well.

Continental Airlines, *Tel. 1/800-525-0280*, flies non-stop to Houston. There you can connect to their extensive system which covers every portion of the country.

Other airlines with Albuquerque service include American (non-stop service to Dallas); Delta; Northwest; TWA; United; and USAir. Reno Air, another low-cost carrier operating in the western United States, provides daily non-stop service to Los Angeles and Reno.

ALTERNATIVE TRAVEL

Over the past few years, a new industry has grown up within the overall travel industry. Going under various different names, I refer to it as alternative travel. It covers an enormously large range of possibilities – everything from special trips for gays, seniors, or any other number of "special" groups to people interested in specific aspects of travel such as the environment, social history of various ethnic or national groups, and so forth.

I don't pretend to be an expert in the needs and interests of all these special groups and, frankly, in most cases don't even see a great need for "alternative travel." A broad-based vacation experience provides more than enough opportunity for intellectual improvement. However, the Native Americans of New Mexico have a long-standing tradition of being "as one" with nature. Therefore, it is appropriate to include in this guide something about environmentally friendly or other "holistic" based travel. Oddly, considering that alternative travel is so individualistic, it's easier to find opportunities for it with larger groups rather than as an individual.

Here are some alternative travel options I'd recommend:

- **Access Adventure Tours**, *Tel. 1/800-821-1221*. Specializing in photographic "safaris" to New Mexico and other places.
- **Explora Tours**, *Tel. 1/800-MEX-TREX*. Trips of from one to eight days highlighting one or more of the following: cultural history; minerals and mining; archaeology; pueblo culture and others.

- **International Universities**, *Tel. 1/800-547-5678*. Seminar type tours emphasizing cultural and historical aspects of New Mexico.
- **South Mountain Wilderness Tours**, *Tel. 505/281-9638*. A variety of outdoor based trips designed for women only.
- **Nambe Pueblo Tours**, *Tel. 505/820-1340 or 1/800-94-NAMBE*. Offers nine different tours concentrating on the Northern Pueblos. What makes the tours different is that they are given by Native American guides who welcome you into their communities.
- **Pathways Customized Tours**, *Tel. 505/982-5382*. Famous Santa Fe and Southwestern guide Don Dietz will prepare an itinerary based on your special interests and personally escort you. One of the few that can be done on a truly individual basis.
- **Recursos de Santa Fe**, *Tel. 505/982-9301*. A large operator that gives you the opportunity to select from either a variety of specialized tours or customized trips for groups of ten or more people.
- **Santa Fe Detours**, *Tel. 1/800-DETOURS*. One of the largest specialty tour operators in the state, covering the Santa Fe area as well as other regions. Unfortunately, like Recursos de Santa Fe, you have to be part of a group that satisfies their minimum size requirement.

ACCOMMODATIONS & DINING

NEW MEXICO LODGING

Selecting the place or places to stay on a vacation is, for a large number of people, one of the single most important aspects of your trip planning. Even if you aren't very fussy about where you plop yourself down for the night, a bad hotel experience can be a real downer. New Mexico has an awesome number and variety of places to stay. From simple bed and breakfasts, to convenient roadside motels, to big city high-rise hotels, or to extravagant resorts – New Mexico has it all.

Of the great number of lodging establishments of every type and price range throughout the state, I'll give a detailed description and mini-review of a hundred of them. These represent the ones that I believe deserve your most serious consideration. They will each be described in the appropriate geographic sections that follow.

The informal atmosphere characteristic of New Mexico extends to most lodging establishments, even "fancy" resorts. I find it refreshing that both hotel operators and most visitors want their stay in New Mexico to be relaxing and fun. The smug attitude of keeping up with and outdoing "the Joneses" that prevails at many resorts, including the majority in nearby places like Scottsdale, Arizona, is happily an exception in New Mexico.

Regardless of where you stay it is important to have advance reservations in all popular areas. Even those places that are more off the beaten track often fill up fast during the summer months, so I urge you to not try to arrive in New Mexico without having all of your hotel reservations confirmed.

Most chain properties do not require that you pay in advance so long as you arrive before 6:00pm. However, its a good idea to guarantee a late arrival with your credit card. Many times they will ask for this information. Smaller, independent establishments and many resort properties require that you pay in advance, at least for the first nights' stay. Be sure you understand and comply with payment regulations at the time you make your booking.

Reservations can be made in a number of ways. All major chains and many independent hotels accept reservations made through travel agents. You can make reservations on your own by contacting the hotel directly or via a chain's central reservation system. Many independent places belong to associations which handle reservations through a toll-free number. Reservations for many hotels throughout New Mexico can be made free of charge by contacting **New Mexico Central Reservations**, *Tel. 1/800-446-7829*.

UNDERSTANDING HOTEL RATES & TERMS

It used to be easy to make a hotel reservation. Give them a date and they would tell you if a room was available and how much it would cost. Plain and simple. But life has gotten complicated in every aspect of travel. Some hotels have as many rate variations as the airlines and car rental companies. So getting the best rate isn't always an easy task. There isn't much standardization within the hotel industry for rate terms. One important term, though, is something universally known as the **rack rate**. In plain English, rack rate refers to the normal full price for a room on an ordinary evening. Of course, special events often involve prices higher than the rack rate. Most of the time you can get a better price than the rack rate.

In all of the listings in this book, the price will be the so-called rack rate during the summer season, essentially Memorial Day through Labor Day. This is the **high season**, referring to the time of the year when prices are at their highest (except for short term special events) throughout most of New Mexico. The biggest exception is in winter resort areas – they have "high season" when ski conditions are at their best. In Taos, for example, rates are frequently higher in the winter, especially for lodging establishments located away from town and in the ski areas. On the other hand, many New Mexico hotels and motels away from the most popular tourist areas have the same or similar rates year round.

Quoted prices will always refer to the room (not the per person) rate but are based on double occupancy. Single person rates are usually not much, if at all, less than for a double room. Hotel policies concerning additional charges, if any, for children in the same room vary considerably. If you plan to have your children stay in the same room with you, inquire with the individual hotel as to the charge.

All prices listed in this book are for the room only (no meals) unless otherwise indicated. Most hotels in New Mexico charge on such a basis, known as the **European Plan**. Where another plan is involved it will be indicated. A **Continental Plan** includes a small breakfast consisting primarily of pastry and beverage. Depending upon the hotel and your appetite, this may or may not be sufficient to satisfy your morning hunger pangs. Some continental breakfast spreads send me hunting for a place to get a bigger breakfast and sacrifice the fact that the continental is included in the hotel rate. **Breakfast Plan** includes a full breakfast. The **Modified American Plan** (or **MAP**) includes full breakfast and dinner and is rarely found these days outside of resort facilities, although some hotels offer it as an extra option. An all-inclusive three meal per day plan is almost entirely restricted to full-service resorts where guests hardly leave the property. On-premise restaurants will be briefly described unless there is a separate listing for it in the *Where to Eat* section. All hotels listed have private baths in every room so no mention will be made of this in the individual listings, except for a few bed and breakfasts that have shared baths.

Although the press-time price will be given for each hotel, all hotels will be grouped according to their price category, either Very Expensive, Expensive, Moderate, or Budget. For quick reference, the price range for each class is as follows:

- **Very Expensive**, *Over $150 per night*
- **Expensive**, *$100-$150 per night*
- **Moderate**, *$66-$99 per night*
- **Budget**, *$65 or less per night*

Because many facilities have a wide variety of accommodations, price ranges will often overlap two or even three categories. I determined the price category to list the hotel in by the rate for a standard room. Although hotel prices have been going up fast in recent years, it's usually still relative to their category. As time goes by, the dollar amount for each category may rise, but a hotel rarely changes from one category to another.

MAJOR HOTEL CHAINS

In each destination chapter, you will find many suggested places to stay. Although some are affiliated with major chains, the majority are independent. Some people like the convenience of making reservations with nationwide hotel companies and the "no surprises" rooms and facilities of these chains. I myself often use them. The following are nationwide chains that have a strong presence throughout New Mexico:

- **Best Western**, *Tel. 1/800-528-1234*. Upgraded in both facilities and prices over the past several years, Best Western is a mid-price chain that features properties that aren't all in the same cookie-cutter mold. Local architectural styles are popular. Best Western has 41 properties in 25 different New Mexico localities.

- **Choice Hotels**. Consisting of **Quality Inn**, *Tel. 1/800-228-5101*, **Comfort Inn**, *Tel. 1/800-228-5150*, the more upscale **Clarions**, *Tel. 1/800-CLARION*, and budget **Sleep Inns**, *Tel. 1/800-62-SLEEP*, Choice is represented in 14 New Mexico cities and towns and has 21 total locations.

- **Days Inn**, *Tel. 1/800-329-7466*. Like Best Western, Days has improved the quality of their properties in recent years. Still relatively low priced, you can find 24 Days Inns in 21 New Mexico locations.

- **Holiday Inn**, *Tel. 1/800-HOLIDAY*. Featuring regular Holiday Inns, lower priced Holiday Inn Express, and expensive Holiday Inn Crowne Plazas, there are 21 properties in 15 cities and towns.

Other chains that have a significant number of locations in New Mexico are **Econo Lodge** (part of the Choice chain), **Travelodge**, and **Super 8**. All three chains are in the budget to moderate price categories. Within the city of Albuquerque, you'll also find representatives of the more pricey and fancy chains such as Radisson, Hyatt, Marriott, and others. The same, to a lesser extent, is true for Santa Fe.

DINING

Vacation meals can be a fun part of your trip, especially if you like to sample regional cuisine. Each destination chapter lists many restaurants in a variety of price categories. The price range is for a dinner entree exclusive of alcoholic beverages, tip, and taxes. The descriptions are geared towards dinner, but if a place is especially suitable for lunch I will certainly say so. All three meals are offered unless indicated otherwise in the opening information section on each restaurant. The budget category usually encompasses what is termed "family" dining, but also is generally good for lunch.

Fast food chains aren't mentioned but you can almost always find one for lunch in all big towns and along the major interstate highways. Likewise, nationwide sit-down restaurant chains aren't generally listed, but can be found throughout New Mexico, especially in Albuquerque, which brings up one last point: The choice of restaurants in New Mexico (and reflected in my personal suggestions) is greatest by far in the Albuquerque-Santa Fe-Taos corridor, just as is the case with lodging.

I don't pretend to be familiar with every restaurant in the state. So when in small towns don't hesitate to try a place simply because it may not look like what you expect a good restaurant to look like from the outside. More often than not you'll be pleasantly surprised. Then you can write and tell me about it so I can include it in the next edition. Asking hotel employees about good places to eat is almost always an excellent way to find out about unusual dining places, so don't hesitate to ask them. *Bon appetite!*

GETTING AROUND NEW MEXICO

BY AIR

Flying from one location within New Mexico to another is solely by commuter airlines. Fares aren't that low and, with the time you spend getting to and from airports, frankly doesn't make a whole lot of sense.

But, for those who opt for this method of travel, the best bet is **Mesa Air**, *Tel. 1/800-MESA-AIR*. Mesa operates small planes between Albuquerque and Alamogordo, Carlsbad, Roswell, and Santa Fe, among others.

BY CAR

Whether you're driving to New Mexico with your own car or renting at the airport, there's no substitute for an auto if you want to see New Mexico. It provides convenience and flexibility that simply cannot be matched by any other means of transportation. Driving in New Mexico is generally a breeze. Both the major highways and back roads will usually be free of traffic congestion. In fact, on one of my trips to New Mexico we kept track of the number of vehicles coming in the other direction versus the mileage. There were several instances where over a stretch of time we traveled 15 or so miles and saw only about a dozen cars. Of course, it isn't always that empty.

Albuquerque is a big enough city to have traffic problems, but these are primarily limited to rush hours on the freeways. Santa Fe, Taos, and some other popular tourist destinations weren't built to handle the big crowds and the narrow streets can often become congested. However, this isn't a big problem, since you should be doing most of your sightseeing on foot and only have to contend with the traffic on your way into or out of town.

Some special considerations need to be addressed. While most roads are excellent there are some mountain roads that are narrow and twisting. Exercise caution and there shouldn't be any problem. I'll let you know in the sections that follow if any particular road might be "scary" enough to discourage novice drivers. Desert driving calls for paying attention to potential dust storms. If you encounter one it is best to pull completely off the road and wait it out. Severe storms of this type are relatively rare and you most likely won't encounter any.

You should take a 15-minute break from driving for every two hours you travel. That will help keep you alert. Try to schedule your itinerary with some minor stops to keep down the amount of time you spend driving. There's plenty of scenery to be observed from the car, especially in the north, so make sure that you are always paying attention to the road. If something looks very nice and you want to take a better look, use roadside pullouts where available.

Cars rented in Albuquerque should be adapted to the high altitude and climate and you won't have to do anything special. If driving to New Mexico, check all hoses and fluids as well as tire pressure before embarking on your trip to make sure everything is in tip-top shape.

If you recall an earlier sidebar, you'll be informed enough to know that as part of the United States, New Mexico's driving rules are the same as where you live. You won't have any trouble deciphering road signs. However, let's take a brief orientation of New Mexico's road system.

There are two main **Interstate highways** (which will be designated in the rest of this book with the prefix "I"). **I-25** runs from north to south, arriving in New Mexico from Colorado at Raton and running to Las Cruces in the south. **I-40** travels from east to west a little above the middle of the state from Texas to Arizona. The two highways cross in Albuquerque only a few blocks from the heart of both downtown and Old Town. **I-10**, a third Interstate in the south, runs from the state line at El Paso north to Las Cruces (intersecting with I-25) and then west to the Arizona border.

Major **United States highways** (preceded by the prefix "US") crisscross the entire state. The most important north/south route is **US 285** from north of Santa Fe to Carlsbad. In the east/west category are **US 64** in the north, **US 60** in the center, and **US 70** in the south. **New Mexico State highways** (designated "NM") also provide access to important sights and towns. These will be introduced to you when reading about particular localities.

Finally, you should always plan to leave your destination each morning with a full tank of gas. Much of New Mexico is wilderness and you won't always find a gas station when you need one. Plan ahead. If you're going to be traveling through sparsely populated areas (and I include everything except the Albuquerque-Santa Fe-Taos corridor in this category), start looking for a gas station when your tank is only half empty. It could avoid problems later on.

ROUTE 66 LIVES!

The American love affair with the open road is nowhere better exemplified than by the lure of the old ***US Route 66*** *that traversed the western United States, covering a total distance of over 2,400 miles. New Mexico played a part in this piece of Americana. Back in 1926, US 66 twisted its way through the northern portion of New Mexico for 501 miles. Some modifications were made prior to World War II, but the route stayed essentially as it was in the old days until it was replaced by the completion of I-40. There are still a couple of sections of the old road that exist near Tucumcari and a gravel portion around Moriarty.*

Nostalgia lovers will be thrilled to see that along many parts of the old 66 you can still find some of the roadside restaurants and businesses that catered to the westward migration when US 66 was "the" road to travel. Some of the communities on 66 (now usually renumbered as a New Mexico route if it has any number at all) still reflect the hey-days of the 1950s and early 1960s. Time stands still both in architecture and pace of life. There's even a ***New Mexico Route 66 Association****. If this type of nostalgia attracts you, try contacting them through the Grants/Cibola Chamber of Commerce. Their number is Tel. 1/800-748-2142.*

CAR RENTALS

Rules, regulations, and rates for car rentals are almost as confusing as those promulgated by the airlines. You definitely have to shop around for the best price. A one-way rental (that is, returning the car to the original renting location) is always cheaper than dropping it off at another location. If you're going to be covering all or most of the state, a New Mexico trip can add up the miles. Therefore it would probably be wise to look for a rental that provides unlimited mileage. A low base rate with a big surcharge for mileage won't wind up as the bargain you think it is.

All of the major car rental companies are available at the Albuquerque airport. These companies and their airport office telephone numbers are:

- **Avis**, *Tel. 842-4080; nationwide toll-free reservations: Tel. 1/800-331-1212*
- **Budget**, *Tel. 768-5900; nationwide toll-free reservations: Tel. 1/800-527-0700*

- **Dollar**, *Tel. 842-4235 (1/800-800-4000)*
- **Hertz**, *Tel. 842-4235 (1/800-654-3131)*
- **National**, *Tel. 842-4222 (1/800-227-7368)*

Local or regional car rental firms are often less expensive than the majors. They almost always require returning the car to the same location, which if you're flying to and from Albuquerque should present no problem. Worth looking into in the Albuquerque market are:

- **Advantage**, *2200 Sunport SE, Tel. 247-1066*
- **Alamo**, *2601 Yale SE, 842-4057 Tel. 1/800-327-9633*
- **Enterprise**, *1820 Lomas NE, Tel. 764-9100*
- **Thrifty**, *2039 Yale SE, Tel. 842-8733*
- **USave**, *500 Yale SE, Tel. 265-0787*

The five companies above are all within minutes of the airport and provide free transportation to their location and back to the airport upon returning the car.

NEW MEXICO DRIVING DISTANCES

	Alamo.	Albuq.	Carlsbad	Gallup	Santa Fe	Taos
Alamogordo	–	213	145	351	272	351
Albuquerque	213	–	277	138	59	138
Carlsbad	145	277	–	415	268	347
Deming	124	238	269	298	297	376
Farmington	393	180	457	112	214	206
Gallup	351	138	415	–	197	276
Hobbs	233	315	69	453	309	388
Las Cruces	65	225	210	363	284	363
Las Vegas	221	123	275	261	64	77
Raton	349	236	382	374	177	98
Roswell	117	201	76	339	193	272
Ruidoso	45	191	147	329	250	329
Santa Fe	272	59	268	197	–	79
Santa Rosa	176	115	209	253	130	143
Silver City	176	250	321	266	309	388
Taos	351	138	347	276	79	–
T or C	138	172	283	310	231	310
Tucumcari	235	174	268	312	170	183

BY PUBLIC TRANSPORTATION

I've already mentioned that it isn't an easy task to visit New Mexico if you're going to rely on public transportation. An escorted tour would probably be easier. However, I'm sure there are some of you out there who won't be put off by the difficulties and will want information on how to do it. This section is for you.

Amtrak has two routes running through New Mexico, one in the north through Albuquerque and one in the south through Lordsburg and Deming. Unfortunately, they don't connect. The main route, which has stops in Gallup, Albuquerque, Lamy (connecting bus service to Santa Fe), Las Vegas, and Raton has one train per day in each direction. So it becomes kind of difficult to arrange a schedule around theirs. The southern route runs only several times a week, making it even harder. However, Amtrak does offer a number of rail/drive and rail/bus excursions. *If this interests you, contact Amtrak at Tel. 1/800-USA-RAIL.* Amtrak has been making service cuts in recent years due to budget problems. Although neither of the New Mexico routes was slated to be hit by these cuts at press time, it would be wise to confirm that there aren't any changes scheduled prior to your making plans to travel by rail.

Greyhound operates a network of routes, mostly through the Texas-New Mexico-Oklahoma Bus Line, that connects Albuquerque with all of the major towns and cities. Service varies from once a day to several trips between Albuquerque and Santa Fe and a few other routes. Many of the smaller towns aren't served every day. *For information on schedules, routes and fares, call 1/800-231-2222.*

BY RECREATIONAL VEHICLE & CAMPING

Camping sites or places to hook up an RV are in demand as much as hotel rooms. So, once again, early advance planning is an absolute must. Reservations are not always accepted for camping within public lands. Inquire as to whether they operate on a first come, first served or reservation basis. Campsites and RV facilities range from back to nature "roughing it" to, in some commercially-run establishments, facilities that have almost as many amenities as some motels. Most campgrounds are open only between May and September, so check with the owner about availability if traveling at other times.

Aside from commercial RV parks that are often located near natural areas, you'll find both camping sites and RV facilities in almost all national park facilities. Campsites are a part of every New Mexico state park (except those few that are designated as "day use" areas) and about two-thirds of them also have RV hookups. Many sites are also located in the national forests in every part of New Mexico. Only a small fee is charged in these places.

However, while you can just show up at sites within national forests, a **permit** is required for camping in national parks and in most state parks. The permits are free and can be obtained at the visitor center of the park you're visiting. *General information on camping and RV hookups in state parks can be obtained by calling the agency which runs the parks at Tel. 505/827-7465.* For national parks it is best to contact each facility directly. The **Carson National Forest** is one of the most popular areas in the state for campers and RV enthusiasts. *They can be reached at 1/800-283-CAMP.* Almost as popular is camping in the **Santa Fe National Forest**; *for information on campsites within the latter, call 505/988-6940.*

For a sampling of commercially operated sites at major localities throughout the state, see the listings in each regional chapter. Major chain operators of campgrounds, such as KOA, offer nationwide directories.

7. BASIC INFORMATION

HEALTH

Most people don't have to take any special health precautions for a trip to New Mexico. There aren't any weird local diseases affecting the average tourist and the quality and availability of health care is good throughout the state. However, you should be aware of two special situations. The first concerns health risks associated with high altitude and the second affects visitors who will be camping out or hiking in the wilderness.

New Mexico's **high altitude** is both healthful and invigorating. However, for people who are not accustomed to living in such lofty places, it can result in a condition called **Acute Mountain Sickness** (AMS) when the altitudes are in excess of about 8,000 feet. The condition manifests itself with difficulty in breathing, dizziness, disorientation, and can be very serious or even fatal in extreme cases. Most people adapt quickly to the change in height. It's a good idea to slowly work your way into higher altitudes by spending a day in an area for each thousand foot rise in elevation.

If you don't follow that guideline, at least limit strenuous activity until you become accustomed to the altitude. Eat lightly and definitely avoid alcohol for the first few days. If you suffer from heart or respiratory conditions or you are very elderly, consult your physician before undertaking any trip to high altitude areas. Should you start experiencing the symptoms of AMS, the solution is simple – return to lower altitudes immediately. That will effect a quick cure.

Visitors who spend a lot of time in the back country are exposed to specialized hazards. The first is possible **water contamination**. Even the cleanest looking mountain stream can contain dangerous micro-organisms. Be sure to boil all water or use filtration or purification equipment. Also, dress properly to prevent **hypothermia** which can be caused by wearing wet clothing or sudden drops in temperature which can occur in the mountains. Clothing should also provide protection against insect bites and stings. Finally, there have been cases of **bubonic plague** and **rabies** in remote areas of the state resulting from animal bites. Avoiding contact with animals in the wild, even if they appear tame, is of paramount importance. Such simple precautions can almost ensure that you won't have any problems.

A final health consideration during the hot summer months is **dehydration**, something that children are especially prone to. You should drink plenty of water and other non-alcoholic beverages. Because road-side services can be widely scattered in many rural areas of the state, its a good idea to carry drinking water with you in a canteen or in several large "sports" bottles. If you can fill them with ice in the morning that's even better, as the water or beverage can remain cold and refreshing for several hours. At a minimum, you should be prepared to stop at facilities where drinking water or other beverages are available and take a long drink.

INDIAN GAMING

The spread of gambling nationwide has also reached New Mexico, but only in the form of gaming on Indian reservations. This is not Las Vegas by any stretch of the imagination. However, if you're interested in parting with a few dollars on the tables during your New Mexico visit, you should be aware that gambling is offered in many locations throughout the state. As of press time, gambling is available at Acoma Pueblo, Isleta Pueblo, on the Jicarilla Indian Reservation near Dulce, the Pojoaque Pueblo, Sandia Pueblo, Santa Ana Pueblo, and Tesuque Pueblo.

During the past year, there has been a significant dispute between the various Indian tribes and the government over the regulation of Indian gaming. At the heart of the problem is whether the compacts that allow the casinos to operate are legal. The dispute has already forced the Mescalero Apache tribe to cease (at least for the time being) gaming operations at its Inn of the Mountain Gods near Ruiodoso. It is not possible for me to predict what the final outcome of all this will be, but if you are planning to go out of your way to gamble at an Indian casino, it would be wise to check in advance on their current operating status.

NEWSPAPERS & MAGAZINES

Local publications are always a good source of information on current events, cultural attractions, and entertainment. Most lodging establishments will provide visitors with a weekly or monthly magazine detailing what's going on in their area. This is especially true in larger cities (i.e., Albuquerque) and in major tourism areas such as Santa Fe, Taos, and Ruidoso. Daily newspapers (or even weekly in the case of more rural areas) will usually have a section on what's going on.

New Mexico Magazine is an excellent monthly publication that has interesting features on various aspects of the state. They also put out a number of specialty publications. While it would be silly to take out a year's subscription to the magazine, you may find that a sample issue will be of some use. *You can write to the publisher at PO Box 12002, Santa Fe NM 87504, or call them toll-free at Tel. 1/800-898-6639.*

NIGHTLIFE & ENTERTAINMENT

A lot of Americans wrongly think that New Mexico is populated by "cowboys and Indians," neither of which have a lot of culture and nothing fancy in the way of nightlife. Nothing could be further from the truth, especially regarding culture. (The Indians, by the way, have a lot more to offer in the way of culture than you would think from stereotyped western movies.) For a state with a relatively small population and few cities, the variety and quality of the performing arts is quite extraordinary. On the other hand, nightlife in the form of fancy discos and similar glitzy entertainment spots are in comparatively short supply. This is solely because of the lack of major population centers. You can find them in Albuquerque and the most important tourist destinations such as Taos and Santa Fe.

Elsewhere, plan on turning in early after a busy day of sightseeing. The individual city and regional chapters will describe the highlights.

PHYSICAL DISABILITIES

If you are physically challenged, you'll be glad to hear that most facilities in New Mexico have your ease of access in mind. Of course, a lot of the outdoor activity for which the state is so popular can present problems. You must know your own limitations.

There are several excellent brochures available that address the needs of the handicapped visiting New Mexico. You can get them by calling the **Developmental Disabilities Planning Council**, *Tel. 1/800-552-8195*. When making hotel reservations, however, you should make inquiry concerning the availability of handicapped rooms and other special facilities.

SAFETY

New Mexico's crime rate is lower than most places in the United States, but that doesn't mean you should throw caution to the wind. Tourists in any place in the world are always a potential target because criminals know that tourists may be carrying a lot of money and are often distracted due to their hectic schedules. In fact, confusion aids thieves greatly. Although there will be times you aren't sure where you are or what to do next, minimize looking like an easy target by always having a firm plan as to what you're doing next. Plan your routes in advance whether they be on foot or by car. Don't carry much cash. Use credit cards or travelers checks whenever possible. Record credit card and travelers check numbers and keep them in a separate place. Don't leave valuables lying around exposed in your car, even for a short time. Cars with trunks that hide luggage completely are better than hatchbacks where you can see into the storage compartment.

Hotel security is also important. Keep your door locked and don't open it unless you are sure about the identity of the person seeking entry. Also be sure to familiarize yourself with the location of fire exits. If you must have expensive jewelry with you, inquire as to the availability of safe deposit boxes in the hotel. All safety rules are especially important in Albuquerque.

TAXES

The New Mexico state sales tax is **5.75 percent**. Localities have the option of imposing up to an additional 1.5 percent. Special lodging taxes can increase the amount even more. It's not uncommon for the total tax on hotels to be up around 11% in the more popular tourist areas.

TELEPHONES

The **area code** for all of New Mexico is **505**. From this point forward, the 505 area code designation will be omitted for all in-state numbers. However, if you are going to make a long distance call within the state, it requires dialing a "1" and 505 before the number in order for you to be able to complete your call.

TIME OF DAY

All of New Mexico is on **Mountain Time**, one hour later than on the west coast and two hours earlier than the east coast. Daylight savings time is observed throughout the state.

TIPPING

I don't like to make hard and fast rules regarding tipping, because it is a personal decision. Do always remember, though, that most people in the hotel and restaurant industries don't get big salaries and rely on tips for a good part of their income. The same rules on tipping that are used throughout the United States certainly apply to New Mexico, the norm being15 percent for restaurants, 10 percent for taxis, and $1-2 per night for maid service in hotels. If you hire a guide, for a jeep tour or some other excursion, a tip of any amount you deem worthy is in order if you enjoyed yourself.

TRAVEL EMERGENCIES & ROAD CONDITIONS

Hopefully you won't ever have to use this section, but information on who to contact should always be available quickly should the need arise. Throughout New Mexico, the best way to receive coordinated emergency services is by dialing *911*. This will automatically reach the nearest public safety office to you. In each touring chapter, I have also listed a local number for hospitals and police in case of non-emergency needs (i.e., not feeling well but nothing life threatening, or you lost something).

If you are going to be traveling in areas where road conditions could be poor due to weather (primarily snow during the winter months), the state of New Mexico maintains a 24-hour toll-free **Highway Assistance Hotline**, *Tel. 1/800-432-4269*.

TRAVELING WITH CHILDREN

The rich cultural tapestry and outstanding scenery of New Mexico may not have the same appeal to children as Disney World. But that doesn't mean you should let the kids sit this one out. New Mexico has many attractions that children of all ages will enthusiastically enjoy, even if it's not necessarily for the same reasons as they might appeal to adults. Planning for a trip with the kids requires some thought in three areas. These are what to do with the little ones when you want to be alone, keeping the kids busy (and quiet) while traveling long stretches of open road, and finding attractions and activities that they can enjoy with you.

Let's talk about baby sitting services first. Just as you wouldn't want to trust your children's well being at home to someone that you blindly pick out of the yellow pages, you shouldn't follow that route when on vacation. When staying in the more popular tourist areas at a hotel that offers first class service (those establishments with a concierge, for example), hotel personnel can frequently give you a good referral. Within Albuquerque, you can contact **Professional Nannies of New Mexico**, *Tel. 505/291-1818*. They are associated with many good care givers who will gladly come to your hotel to watch the little ones while you take in a show or go dancing. The organization has strict standards, including a thorough background check on all of their employees. They can also often put you in touch with other reputable child care organizations throughout New Mexico. A few hotels have comprehensive programs for children. Among the best is the one at **The Bishop's Lodge** in Santa Fe.

Road activities need not be a major problem. You know best what will occupy your children while riding in the car, be it coloring books, hand-held computer games, a favorite doll or toy, or whatever. Besides bringing things along to keep them busy, you can get them involved in simple little games that make the time go by faster. For example, keeping track of license plates from various states can be both fun and an education in geography.

The following list is just a sampling of places and activities that I think will be of special interest to children. I haven't included the obvious children's diversions such as amusement parks, zoos, and the like. Each of the regional touring chapters also makes special mention of what should appeal most to children.

Highlights of good kid-friendly places include:

- Many of Albuquerque's **museums** (especially the Albuquerque Children's Museum, the Museum of Natural History, and the Rattlesnake Museum).
- Any of the colorful **Northern Pueblos** will delight most children. However, you are responsible for making sure that your children understand proper behavior on Indian property. This was discussed in greater detail previously in a sidebar.
- A **balloon fiesta**. The bigger the better, but almost any fiesta should do.
- Ascending the ladders and climbing into small cliff dwellings in **Bandelier National Monument**.
- Exploring the dimly lit **Carlsbad Caverns**. This will be especially popular with the boys, but be aware that very young children could be frightened by the massive cave.
- The **Space Center** in Alamogordo.
- The **Sandia Peak Aerial Tramway** ride.

8. SPORTS & RECREATION

New Mexico is a mecca for the outdoor enthusiast. Even visitors who come primarily to see the sights will, however, likely get caught up to some degree in the widespread availability of recreational opportunities. The residents certainly do. In fact, a study by the federal Centers for Disease Control released in August 1996 indicated that more than 35 percent of New Mexico's adult population took part in some regular form of exercise. This was the second highest amount of any state.

I'll provide you with an introduction to some of the most popular activities in this chapter. For more detailed information, including a selective list within each category, consult each city or regional chapter.

BALLOONING

Most people, including myself, aren't adventurous enough to get themselves to climb into the basket of a **hot air balloon**. If you just like watching these colorful vessels, New Mexico offers plenty of that and will be described later. But, if you are that type, you'll be happy to know that rides are offered in many localities throughout the state. Your best bet is to contact the local chamber of commerce. The Albuquerque area is especially popular for this activity due to favorable climatic conditions. It is less available in the southern deserts or in the most mountainous regions.

BICYCLING

Droves of bikers traverse the highways and back roads of New Mexico during the spring, summer, and fall. Unpaved roads, especially in the many national forests, are also popular places to ride a bike. The terrain in the latter areas is much more difficult, so inexperienced bikers should plan on staying in lower altitudes on flatter roads.

The **New Mexico Touring Society**, *Tel. 505/298-0085*, is happy to provide information to visitors who plan to bicycle extensively. Bicycle rentals are available in Albuquerque, Santa Fe, Taos and most other major communities. If you plan to bring along your own bike on a fly/drive trip, be sure to find out the restrictions imposed by the airline.

BOATING & SWIMMING

Many of New Mexico's state parks offer the best choice for water-based recreation. **Boating** is available at the following state parks: Bluewater Lake; Brantley Lake; Caballo Lake; Clayton Lake; Conchas Lake; Elephant Butte Lake; El Vado Lake; Fenton Lake; Heron Lake; Morphy Lake; Navajo Lake; Santa Rosa Lake; Storrie Lake; Sugarite Canyon; Sumner Lake; and Ute Lake.

All of the aforementioned and several others offer **swimming**.

FISHING

The warmer lakes and streams of New Mexico are the home to bass (largemouth and smallmouth as well as white bass), walleye, stripers, bluegill, crappie and catfish. Colder waters have several varieties of trout: rainbow, brown, brook, and lake. You can also find some kokanee salmon.

A fishing license is required on all state lands. The one exception to this is that no license is required on Indian reservations. However, you are required to obtain permission from the tribal authorities. This can be accomplished on the day of your visit to the reservation. Information on getting a state license plus other regulations is available from the **New Mexico Department of Game & Fish**, *Tel. 505/827-7911*. You can also get prerecorded information on current conditions and other topics of interest to anglers by dialing *1/800-ASK-FISH*.

GOLF

The climate of most of New Mexico is ideal for year round **golfing** pleasure. Your best choice is to play on a course belonging to the **Sun Country Amateur Golf Association**, *Tel. 505/897-0864*. There are more than 60 courses spread throughout the state that belong.

For your convenience, all of the golf courses listed under each destination chapter in this book are open to the vacationing public – no membership is required even if the course is privately owned.

HORSEBACK RIDING/DUDE RANCHES

Dozens of stables are located in New Mexico, mainly in the areas of national forests where extensive riding trails can be explored. Day riding trips have been joined by overnight to week-long stays at dude ranches as a popular way of experiencing the old west and taking in some of New

Mexico's wonderful scenery. Information on both can be obtained by contacting **Equus USA** in Santa Fe, *Tel. 505/982-6861.*

HUNTING

Visitors planning to hunt are required to secure a license from the **Department of Game & Fish**. The game to be found depends upon the portion of the state. In the mountains you'll find elk, bear, and bighorn sheep. Deer and antelope grace the lower hillsides and plains areas. Bird hunters will find quail, turkey, hawks and grouse throughout the year. Migrating birds include doves and ducks. As was the case with fishing, Indian reservations don't require licenses but you still have to get permission.

A good source of information on equipment and outfitters are local sporting goods stores. If bringing your own hunting weapons, be sure they are properly disassembled and packed to airline specifications.

OFF-ROAD & FOUR-WHEEL DRIVE VEHICLES

The possibilities for exploring the back country of New Mexico are virtually unlimited. Recent years have seen tremendous growth in this type of recreation. Dirt roads and no road areas range from easy to the most challenging. National Forest areas are among the most popular for four-wheel drive enthusiasts. Each area's Forest Supervisor can provide you with maps showing the roads and other areas that can be traveled on. Another good source of information is the **New Mexico Four Wheelers**, *Tel. 505/891-0296.*

Jeep rentals are available throughout the state but are especially popular in the Red River area where an annual **Jeep Jamboree** takes place. Also popular in the northern part of the state are rentals of so-called mountain bikes.

RAFTING

Some of the best **white-water rafting** in the country is available in many rivers of New Mexico's mountainous north. Every rafting operator listed in this book has been certified by the **Bureau of Land Management** (BLM) as having met strict safety standards. If you select another operator you can verify their level of expertise by contacting the BLM at: *224 Cruz Alta Road, Taos NM 87571, Tel. 505/758-8851.*

It is standard operating procedure in this industry for the price to include all protective gear and transportation to and from either their office or local hotels to the raft launch site. Trips can range from an hour or two to overnight. Full-day and longer trips usually include appropriate meals. Most New Mexico rafting trips are white-water. If you're hesitant about being able to handle it, here are a few things to keep in mind. White-water is officially designated by "class," or the degree of white-water. Class I is the most gentle, with it becoming progressively wilder through Class V.

Some operators also offer **float trips**. These involve tame stretches of river and sometimes throw in a short segment of near-Class I level rapids. Float trips tend to be for an hour or two although some longer ones exist. When planning your rafting adventure, don't be afraid to ask the operator as many questions as you need to determine if it's the right one for you. It's a good idea to have advance reservations for rafting trips and to confirm departure information. It is sometimes necessary for operators to cancel trips when the river conditions aren't good – either too much or too little water!

Some of the better rafting trips are described in the regional touring chapters that follow.

SKIING

The mountains of New Mexico provide some of the greatest **skiing** in the west, even though they may not be as famous as those in neighboring Colorado or Utah. Perhaps people don't associate sunny New Mexico with snow. But many mountains soaring above 12,000 feet and containing drops of more than 2,500 feet provide for world class skiing. Novices will find plenty of less challenging slopes.

Some areas open as early as Thanksgiving, but you can't count on good conditions until the middle of December. Most of the state's ski resorts and facilities are located within a relatively small geographic area centered around Taos. However, other good areas do exist, including Sandia Peak right outside of Albuquerque and to the south around Ruidoso. Major ski resorts and their telephone numbers are listed by region in the appropriate touring chapter.

Up to date information on ski conditions is available via the **Ski New Mexico Snow Phone**, *Tel. 505/984-0606*.

TENNIS

Another popular diversion that's played year round in most places in New Mexico, **tennis** courts are usually standard in the major resort properties. Non-guests are sometimes allowed to play for an additional fee. However, if you want to get in a game at more reasonable rates, then try one of the many public courts in parks located in all major communities and even many smaller ones. Since there are tennis courts in resorts throughout the state (and municipal tennis courts in almost every community of any significance), I won't bother to list selective courts. The yellow pages is a good source of information, or call the **Southwest Tennis Association**, *Tel. 520/947-9293* for event information.

ADVENTURE TRAVEL

Along with "alternative travel," **adventure travel** *has also become a major force in the travel industry over the past several years. A lot of people simply aren't satisfied with keeping their feet planted solidly on the ground and walking or riding by car from one sightseeing attraction to the other. If you like to get involved in the action and aren't frightened by vigorous activity and sometimes very unusual modes of transportation, then you're ready for adventure travel. And New Mexico has a lot of it.*

Adventure travel includes a widely (and wildly) diverse number of activities, such as rock or mountain climbing, river running, mountain biking, horseback trips, overnight camping (and not in a comfortable RV) and much more, all of which is readily available in New Mexico. Why, you can even take an all day or extended expedition through the mountains on a llama! Also included in this category are the fast growing dude ranches where guests actually get involved in the operations of the ranch. The hilarious motion picture City Slickers helped to popularize this travel genre. Reputable operators can be found under specific categories in the various regional chapters. The greatest opportunity for adventure travel in New Mexico is in the mountainous north.

9. SHOPPING

While many well-known department and other chain stores can be found in malls in Albuquerque and other large population centers, this is not the type of shopping that brings people to New Mexico. Whether you are looking for a gift to bring back to friends or relatives, a personal memento of your trip, or something beautiful or exotic to grace your home, New Mexico has something special.

Native American arts and crafts are the single most popular item that tourists look for. Other Southwestern-style items are similarly in demand. Another category is paintings, produced and sold in great numbers by many artists who make Santa Fe, Taos, and other areas of the state their permanent homes. Many other artists from all over the United States and, indeed, the world sell their wares in New Mexico's galleries, which have established an international reputation.

The unique New Mexico shopping experience is best exemplified by Santa Fe and, to a lesser extent, Taos and the surrounding resort communities. In these places shopping, or at least browsing, is an integral part of a vacation trip for many visitors. Consequently, I have included a lot of information on where to shop and what to look for in the chapters on Santa Fe and Taos as well as some other localities.

The major categories of shopping and some of the best known items in each of those categories are:

- **Indian crafts**: jewelry, pottery, hand-woven blankets, custom tin items.
- **Southwestern**: pottery, home furnishings. Some people go so far as to furnish their entire homes in Southwestern style with authentic furniture and decorative items made in New Mexico.
- **Western**: clothing (boots, belts and buckles, beaded jackets); silver jewelry
- **Fine Arts**: paintings of all genres with the greatest emphasis on Native American and southwestern themes, sculptures.
- **Food**: the unique ingredients of Southwestern cuisine are being discovered throughout the country. You can purchase some of these special

herbs and spices as well as chile peppers in many locations. Most can stay fresh during your journey, or you can have them shipped directly to your home.

When purchasing Native American items you want to be sure of their **authenticity**. This can be verified in the case of Navajo or Pueblo crafts (the two with the most beautiful work and best quality) by an indication of authenticity on the product. If the item is being sold on an Indian reservation you can be reasonably certain of the authenticity. Where you have to more careful is in popular tourist spots where one gift shop after another competes for your attention. You should note that authentic Navajo and Pueblo goods are not inexpensive. Of course, high price doesn't always guarantee the real McCoy either.

Most businesses have fixed prices for their goods just as they do in your own home town. However, Native Americans who are selling their wares in the public plazas of Santa Fe and Taos, in bazaars or flea markets, or on Indian Reservations are usually willing to reach an accommodation on price. In fact, it's not ordinary practice for the buyer to accept a first price in such instances unless you have an idea of what you're willing to pay by having gotten prices on similar goods from other vendors.

The streets of Santa Fe, Taos, and parts of Albuquerque are filled with expensive boutiques and other fine shops selling everything from the ordinary to the extraordinary. It's very possible that you'll find something in these places that you've been looking for in other cities that has eluded you. Just be prepared to pay top dollar for what you want.

And, finally, a few words on shopping for paintings. I'm by no means an art expert, but I can offer you a couple of tips. Paintings, especially those with Southwestern themes, are available for sale in an overwhelming number of places throughout New Mexico. The fact that one is selling for very little on the street doesn't mean it's of lesser quality than one far more expensive in a famous gallery – it usually means that the artist isn't known.

If you're just looking for something that is pleasing to your eye and will do something for a wall of your home, you're better off looking in the Indian markets and old town plazas. Art experts, who want authenticated quality or who are looking for possible price appreciation will, obviously, be better off in the fashionable galleries of Taos and Santa Fe.

10. ANNUAL EVENTS & FESTIVALS

There always seems to be something special going on all over New Mexico throughout the year. It would be impossible to list even a tenth of these events without this chapter going on ad infinitum. I will attempt to list the most important events and the ones that will have the broadest interest for visitors.

The New Mexico State Department of Tourism as well as local chambers of commerce will be happy to provide more information on special events. Certain events that take place regularly (i.e., either on a weekly or monthly basis) are described in the regional tours and will not be listed below. Also, this main list doesn't include Hot Air Balloon events, but see the sidebar at the end of this chapter for more information on that topic.

JANUARY

New Year's and **Kings' Day** celebrations are held at almost all of the Eight Northern Pueblos as well as the Zia Pueblo. These festive events combine the beautiful colors and traditions of Indian ceremonies with aspects of Christian and modern secular society. The result is a joy to see.

The **Western Winter Carnival** in Red River celebrates the snow season with races, entertainment, and other special events.

FEBRUARY

Angel Fire Winterfest, in the town of the same name, is a week-long event that has many fun-filled activities, including a chile cook-off and imaginative displays of snow sculptures.

Mardi Gras in the Mountains, another Red River event, is highlighted by a parade and festive dancing. The Mardi Gras theme includes Cajun cooking.

MARCH

The **Fiery Food Show** is a popular annual show held at the Albuquerque Convention Center. Visitors may learn about and, of course, sample products made from chiles. Be prepared for a hot time!

APRIL

Easter celebrations at every one of New Mexico's pueblos are another chance to view the interesting combination of native and Christian rites that has become the standard practice of Pueblo Indians. Proper decorum is especially important at these times.

Trinity Site Public Tour is a semi-annual event (also held in October) when the public can enter the White Sands Missile Range to see the site at Alamagordo where the first atomic bomb was detonated. An unusual and educational experience.

The **Farmington Pro Rodeo** is a three-day event and is one of the largest rodeos in the state.

The second half of April is the time for the **Taos Spring Arts Celebration**. Running into early May, the celebration is the largest art show on the Taos calendar and is combined with an outdoor festival and open houses in many of the city's galleries.

American Indian Week is celebrated at the Indian Pueblo Cultural Center in Albuquerque. The event pays tribute to the culture and traditions of Native Americans, with emphasis on the Pueblo.

Natives from more than 700 tribes throughout North America are represented at the annual **Gathering of Nations Pow Wow**. Traditional dancing and singing are among the activities that are open to the public.

MAY

The **Shiprock Marathon** is held each year in early May on the Navajo Indian Reservation.

New Mexico's important Hispanic heritage is celebrated with the exciting **La Fiesta de Colores** in Grants. Mariachi music and other forms of entertainment supplement the arts and crafts fair. This event usually coincides with **Cinco de Mayo** celebrations in several localities, especially Las Vegas.

A **Re-enactment of the Civil War Battle of Glorietta Pass** occurs in La Cienega. History buffs will especially enjoy this event.

The **New Mexico Wine and Chile War Festival** in Las Cruces is a colorful and tasty experience. Novices to real chile cooking beware!

JUNE

An annual open house is held at Alamogordo's **Holloman Air Force Base**. Visitors are able to see different types of aircraft and learn about the base's operations.

The **Aztec Fiesta Days** (in the town of Aztec) kicks off the summer season with a major parade and many carnival activities.

Fort Sumner plays host to **Old Fort Days**. There's a rodeo and arts and crafts shows plus the famous **Billy the Kid Tombstone Race**.

A **Western Roundup** in Cloudcroft celebrates the area's 19th century western heritage. An old fashioned barbecue is held, as are a western parade and street dance. There's also the **Wild, Wild West Pro Rodeo** in Silver City.

The annual **New Mexico Arts and Crafts Fair** in Albuquerque's State Fairgrounds is one of the largest events of its type in the state. You can find just about anything here.

NEW MEXICO: THE HOT AIR BALLOON CAPITAL

Who is not mesmerized by the sight of hundreds of huge, colorful balloons slowly lifting skyward and drifting off into the horizon carrying their passengers in small buckets? While I don't pretend to be a brave soul – flying in a basket isn't for me – I do, like millions of other people, love to watch the mass ascensions of the balloons. Many places claim to be "the capital" of many things, but New Mexico can truly claim to be the world's hot air balloon capital. A combination of frequent clear skies, light winds, and other atmospheric conditions makes New Mexico's sky so suited to ballooning. I think there's something else, too – the Land of Enchantment atmosphere. The colorful balloons against a brilliant New Mexico setting sun are the perfect combination.

There are many balloon festivals throughout the state all through the year. Listed below are some of the best:

- *May: **Farmington International Balloon Festival**.*
- *July: **Santa Fe Trail Balloon Rally** (in Raton); **Wings Over Angel Fire**. In addition to the balloons, this Angel Fire spectacular also showcases birds of prey, helicopter rides, and airplane shows.*
- *September: **Hot-Air Balloon Invitational** (at the White Sands National Monument).*
- *October: The **Kodak Albuquerque International Balloon Fiesta**. The mother of all balloon events, this spectacle attracts more than 600 balloons (for more information, I've given the event its own sidebar in the Albuquerque chapter); **Taos Mountain Balloon Rally**.*

JULY

The **Rodeo de Santa Fe** is one of the state's oldest and largest rodeo events.

Independence Day celebrations are celebrated in a variety of ways. Most feature daytime parades, entertainment and craft shows, and fireworks at night. The biggest and best celebrations are held in Carlsbad, Farmington, Santa Fe, Eagle Nest, Moriarty, Red River and Alamogordo.

A beautiful event is the **Nambe Waterfall Ceremonial** at the Nambe Pueblo. A number of dance performances are given by visiting tribes at the Pueblo.

Mid-July sees the annual **Taos Pueblo Pow-wow**, a very colorful and tradition-filled event.

Santiago's Day festivities are held at the Sky City Acoma Pueblo and the Santa Ana Pueblo.

AUGUST

Culture lovers can enjoy **Shakespeare in the Park** in an outdoor theater on the campus of Santa Fe's St. John's College.

One of the year's more unusual events is the annual **Bat-Flight Breakfast** at Carlsbad Caverns National Park. Visitors enjoy a buffet breakfast while watching the spectacular return of the bats to their cave home. (Actually, while most visitors watch the evening bat-flights, you can do this any morning. However, the Park Service promotes it with this once yearly event to remind people that the bats do come back early each morning.)

The last week of August (through Labor Day) sees the world famous **Music From Angel Fire** classical and chamber music event.

SEPTEMBER

Nights Under the Stars presents Indian legends, story-telling, and dancing at the Indian Pueblo Cultural Center in Albuquerque.

Running most of the month, the **New Mexico State Fair** in Albuquerque is one of the largest state fairs in the country. There's a rodeo, rides, arts and crafts, as well as entertainment by big-name country and western recording artists.

OCTOBER

The **Shiprock Fair** in Shiprock is an annual event featuring a celebration of the Navajo nation. Besides the usual fair events you'll witness traditional Navajo songs and dancing.

NOVEMBER

Around Thanksgiving time or shortly after a number of communities hold **Christmas Tree Lighting** ceremonies. Raton and Eagle Nest have two of the most beautiful. Other related events include boat tours along the Pecos River in Carlsbad and an electric light parade in the town of Lovington.

DECEMBER

Yuletide In Taos covers the first half of the month and features a host of southwestern traditions that have been blended into the celebration of Christmas.

Christmas at the Palace is held at the Palace of the Governors in Santa Fe. This is a beautiful and stirring event celebrating the holiday as it was done hundreds of years ago.

Angel Fire has a **Torchlight Parade and Fireworks** to celebrate the holidays.

11. FOOD & DRINK

There is a restaurant to suit every taste in New Mexico. You might well be surprised by the cosmopolitan nature of the New Mexico dining scene. New York steaks, fresh seafood, and continental cuisine are all easily found. So is more simple fare like fast food or finger-lickin' western barbeque foods. However, a true culinary experience is in order for those seeking the special regional fare that abounds in almost every New Mexico community. Perhaps no other area of the United States, except Louisiana with its Cajun and Creole cooking, has such unique local dishes as does New Mexico.

New Mexico's own cuisine is often thought by the non-initiated to be Mexican. It's not. And it would be even more incorrect to characterize it as "Tex-Mex." It's usually referred to simply as **Southwestern cuisine**. To many Americans, the closest they get to Southwestern style is the salsa sauce they have with their chips. While other examples of Southwestern cooking are relatively new to American taste buds, New Mexico's people have been blending this savory style for hundreds of years.

New Mexico cuisine is a blend of both Hispanic and Native American dishes. The primary ingredients in most Southwestern dishes are tortillas, pinto beans, cheese, and, of course, the ubiquitous chile pepper. Note that New Mexicans use the Spanish spelling with the "e" when writing chile. You can learn more about chile by reading the accompanying sidebar below.

Common breakfast dishes include a special type of burrito, tortillas stuffed with scrambled eggs, potatoes, and spiced sausage. The famous **huevos rancheros** are a corn tortilla with fried eggs, cheese, chile, and beans. Dinner dishes can include various types of chile stew or **carne adovada**, strips of pork marinated in a chile sauce and baked until tender. You might also want to sample authentic Native American dishes. The **Navajo** are considered to be the culinary stars of the many different native groups. You'll like their **open-faced taco** as well as a sweet bread called **pan dulce**.

OH, THOSE CHILE PEPPERS!

So you have visions of biting into a chile pepper and feeling the smoke pouring out through your nose and ears? Well, chile can be real hot, but it can also be mild. There are more than 2,000 different varieties of chile pepper. They take many different shapes, sizes, and colors, although green and red are most common, especially when the chile is made into a sauce. How "hot" a pepper is depends on a combination of factors including the type of pepper and the conditions under which it was grown. A type of chile pepper called **habaneros** *is one of the hottest, so you may want to avoid it if really spicy foods don't agree with you. A tentative stomach, however, is not a reason to avoid chile altogether.*

Chile is prepared in many different ways. It can be fried, roasted, cooked, or stewed, the latter being my personal favorite. It tends to leave some of the heat without making it painful. Oh, yes, you can eat it fresh, too. Like a fruit. Actually, the chile is a fruit, although most people think it's a vegetable. Should you sample a chile dish and find it a bit too strong for your tastebuds, the heat can be lessened by eating sweets or dairy products. Do not try to cool it off with a beverage, especially alcohol. That will pour fuel on the fire, so to speak. While many New Mexican dishes are high in fat, chile is very low in fat and cholesterol. It's actually quite good for you, so don't feel guilty when you devour a big bowl full.

I suggest you start with milder versions of chile and as you acquire a taste for it, then slowly work your way into stronger versions. Restaurant staff will happily comply with requests to temper their chile to your liking.

Sopaipillas are delicious flaky pastries that are light yellow in color. The shapes can vary but are generally rectangular in a form somewhat akin to a pillow. Sometimes they're triangular. Deep-fried, sopaipillas are served with butter and honey as a side dish. They can also be used as an entree when stuffed with such fillings as meat, cheese, beans, or onions. No matter which way you have them, they're absolutely delicious.

Over the year's good chefs have found that the best way to make great New Mexican and Southwestern foods is to use vegetables, herbs, and spices that are organically grown. They seem to do a better job of bringing out some of the delicate flavors associated with this type of cuisine. Many of the better restaurants in New Mexico do organically grow a lot of the ingredients for their dishes. And there are many stores that sell organic foods.

THE WINES OF NEW MEXICO

If any one American state is most associated with wine it would surely be California. You would, however, be surprised to know of the many regional wines that are grown in most parts of the United States. New Mexico is no exception. In fact, wine making has grown to be a fairly important industry in parts of the state and the local wineries produce a fine product whose reputation has yet to be spread far and wide. Like Southwestern cooking, it's only a matter of time.

New Mexico's wine growing region is centered between Albuquerque and Taos and is one of the oldest in the nation. There are 19 different wineries in the state, many of which welcome visitors for tastings and purchasing of their products. New Mexico wines are featured at many of the better restaurants throughout the southwest. Some of the bigger wineries are listed in the regional chapters. However, for general information you can call the **New Mexico Wine Country**, *Tel. 1/800-374-3061.*

LEARN TO COOK NEW MEXICO-STYLE!

If you are really excited about New Mexican and Southwestern cuisine and want to learn more, there are places you can go to satisfy your appetite, so to speak. The **Santa Fe School of Cooking**, *116 W. San Francisco, Tel. 505/983-4511,* has courses of varying lengths that will teach you everything you need to know to bring this type of cooking skill back home. Realizing that tourists make up a large part of their student body, new courses are generally offered each week. Located right off Santa Fe's central plaza, the school also has an adjacent market that sells cookbooks, hard to find cooking utensils and equipment, and all the fresh ingredients you'll need to make your own New Mexican delicacies. Courses start as low as $25 per person and include a delicious meal.

Guests at Santa Fe's **La Fonda Hotel** have for years been trying to pry cooking secrets from the chef of the hotel's fine restaurant. Well, the hotel finally decided in 1996 that they should share some of those secrets. They began offering cooking classes *a la La Fonda Hotel* style and, from what we hear, intend to continue the practice. *Call the hotel for details at Tel. 982-5511.*

In Albuquerque, **Jane Butel's Southwestern Cooking School** has both week-long and weekend classes offering full student participation. Classes are about 2 1/2 hours each day and you can choose between regular and low-fat cooking styles. Jane Butel is a renowned chef, the author of 14 different cookbooks. On the premises is an excellent spice shop where you can purchase premium ingredients for making those authentic Southwestern dishes at home. *Contact the school for fees and schedules at: 800 Rio Grande Boulevard NW (Old Town area), Tel. 1/800-472-8229.*

THE BEST OF NEW MEXICO DINING

Despite the small-town flavor of New Mexico, there are many great restaurants to choose from. I've listed well over a hundred in the regional touring chapters. As a compulsive list maker I couldn't resist the temptation to cull through them one more time and pick out the ten best. What follows is an alphabetical listing of the top ten with the city and type of cuisine also shown.

- ***Anne-Michelle's Restaurant*** *(Ruidoso): Italian and Swiss*
- ***Anthony's at the Delta*** *(Espanola/Santa Fe area): Southwestern*
- ***Casa Cordova*** *(Taos): Southwestern*
- ***The Bishop's Lodge Restaurant*** *(Santa Fe): Southwestern and American*
- ***The Bull Ring, A Prime Steak House*** *(Santa Fe): American*
- ***Maria's New Mexican Kitchen*** *(Santa Fe): New Mexican/Southwestern*
- ***Maria Teresa Restaurant and 1840 Bar*** *(Albuquerque): New Mexican/Southwestern*
- ***Rancher's Club of New Mexico*** *(Albuquerque): American*
- ***Tio Tito's Original Mexican Grill*** *(Albuquerque): Mexican*
- ***Villa Fontana*** *(Taos): Italian*

An honorable mention is in order for Santa Fe's **La Plazuela** *and* **Rebecca's** *in the resort of Cloudcroft.*

12. THE BEST PLACES TO STAY

With so many places to choose from, picking a "best" list is a very difficult task. It is, to say the least, subjective, but it's also something that readers always ask for. And, I've already admitted to my own list compulsion. In making my selections I evaluated several different factors. First of all, the property must have something that is unique about it. I consider it very important for the property to possess qualities that best exemplify the style and atmosphere of New Mexico. Architecture, for instance, is something to be considered. A New Mexico lodging establishment is not unique, in my opinion, if something entirely like it can be found elsewhere.

Other important considerations are the levels of comfort, luxury, and service. All must be first class in order to make the cut. Given the standards I set you're probably beginning to say "uh, oh, I won't be able to pay the price." That shouldn't be the case. I also consider affordability to be important. While the places listed tend to be mostly in the upper price range you will find some relative bargains as well. They certainly aren't all in the most expensive category.

Every hotel listed in this book already represents the results of a considerable weeding out process. I have further narrowed that selection to nine places (excluding one that is separately described in a sidebar) for this chapter. I would have preferred that they be in nine different geographic locations. However, that proved impossible because New Mexico's best lodging is concentrated in the most popular tourist areas. Therefore, you'll find this chapter heavily weighted towards the Santa Fe and Taos areas.

Now you know how I made my selections. Without further ado, I present the best places to stay in the state of New Mexico. They are listed in alphabetical order rather than ranked. Once you get to this level there isn't that much difference between them. I am confident in telling you that they are all great places to stay. You will also find reviews of these establishments in their respective destination chapters, with some additional directions for locating each place with ease. As I mentioned in Chapter 7, *Basic Information*, all phone numbers are in area code 505.

THE BISHOP'S LODGE

Bishop's Lodge Road, Santa Fe. Tel. 983-6377, Fax 989-8739. Rates: $205-255; Deluxe rooms and suites $295-355; MAP Available for about $75 additional per night. 106 Rooms. Major credit cards accepted. Toll-free reservations 1/800-732-2240.

What was once the sumptuous private retreat of a wealthy and distinguished public figure is now a world-class resort. Everything that is unique and beautiful about New Mexico can find representation at the fabulous Bishop's Lodge. Whether it be the colorful adobe architecture, native and Southwestern decorative arts, or just the beautiful scenery of the northern mountains, it's all here for guests to enjoy and savor. Located on a sprawling thousand acres of land just north of Santa Fe, the Lodge occupies the former private estate of Bishop Jean Baptiste Lamy, who was an instrumental figure in the growth of the area. Part of the estate is listed on the National Register of Historic Places. A new honor has been added to The Bishop's Lodge impressive list of tributes. In November 1996, the Lodge was granted memebership in the prestigious Historic Hotels of America Program operated by The National Trust for Historic Preservation.

In 1918, the property passed to the possession of the Thorpe family who have operated it with loving care since that time. An oasis of lush green lawns and magnificent old trees, the Lodge is magnificently situated in a very private valley in the foothills of the Sangre de Cristo Mountains. The scenery is gorgeous in every season, a panorama of ever changing hues.

All of the guest rooms, from standard to deluxe are marvelous, although rooms at the lower end of the scale are not that large. But you'll be surrounded by authentic Southwestern furnishings and many Native American decorative crafts that add both beauty and warmth to the rooms. Ancient pueblo style *kiva* fireplaces and private patios are some of the features in deluxe rooms and suites. Staying at the Bishop's Lodge goes way beyond simply getting a room to sleep in. Amenities and first class service are an important part of the package. Such things as terry bathrobes, nightly bed turndown, and a morning newspaper at your door make you feel like a guest, not a customer.

Dining and entertainment are also first class at Bishop's. The Bishop's Lodge Restaurant offers outstanding cuisine with a New Mexican flair. Or for a less formal atmosphere try the attractive El Rincon patio bar for lunch and a drink. The view from the bar is great, especially at sunset. Bishop's Lodge also offers outdoor cookouts on the patio, room service, or will even prepare a box lunch for you for out on the trail.

No other hotel in the Santa Fe area offers quite as many recreational opportunities as The Bishop's Lodge does. Besides a 1,800 square foot heated pool, there's a Jacuzzi, saunas, and fully equipped exercise facility. You can even arrange to have a professional massage. Four tennis courts, a resident tennis pro, and shop is only the tip of the iceberg as far as sports are concerned. There's skeet and trap shooting, fishing (the Lodge has its own trout pond for children but serious anglers can arrange trips into the surrounding mountain streams) and horseback riding. The Lodge also conducts supervised children's programs.

Whether you use Bishop's as simply a place to stay between days of sightseeing and shopping, or as a complete resort destination, you won't be disappointed.

CASA BENAVIDES

137 Kit Carson Road, Taos. Tel. 758-1772, Fax 758-5738. Rates:$85-195. Includes full breakfast. 30 Rooms. Most major credit cards accepted.

Containing 30 rooms, Casa Benavides is fairly large for a Bed & Breakfast inn. So much the better because with so many individualized rooms there is a great deal more to offer guests. There's a bit of history involved in this beautiful adobe home. It was once the home of Tom Lewis, a prominent local artist. In 1988 it was purchased by Tom and Barbara McCarthy, former schoolteachers who have found the operation of the inn to be a labor of love. They considerably enlarged the original home but remained true to the original architectural style.

Casa Benavides translates as the House of Good Life and it certainly is that. The wonderful rooms are furnished in traditional New Mexico style. This includes polished dark floor tiles, primitive style furniture and native pottery. The McCarthy's have added various antiques from their families' own considerable inventory. What strikes the guest is the overall effect of the rooms – it doesn't look at all like a hotel. It's like a room in your own home that has grown up through the years with the addition of another piece of pottery or a change of curtains. It's luxury without being fancy. It's livable.

Rooms are grouped in five separate buildings and each room has its own name. In the Main Building are six units. I especially like the oversized canopy bed in the Rio Grande room and the El Vaquero room with its stately French doors opening out onto the patio. In the Artist's Studio are two rooms. The El Mirador unit has an upstairs room where Tom Lewis painted. The Benavides Home's six rooms includes the Garden Room, the original house built by Carlos Benavides for his new bride. The Miramon house (six rooms) and the Back Buildings (eight rooms) continue the lovely parade of varied accommodations with fanciful room names such as Sunshine Valley, Blue Lady, Chimayo, and Painted Desert.

Each morning guests are treated to a bountiful and delicious breakfast prepared by Barbara McCarthy in an open kitchen facing the attractive breakfast room with its Mexican pottery and distinctive pink and purple table clothes. Summertime brings breakfast outside onto the sun drenched patio. Homemade granola, muffins, jalepeño salsa, waffles and pancakes highlight the extensive menu. In the afternoon tea and homemade cookies are served.

On the National Register of Historic Places, a stay at Casa Benavides for one night or a week is not like checking in at most hotels. It's an event and an experience.

INN AT THE DELTA

304 Paseo de Onate, Espanola. Tel. 753-9466, Fax 753-9446. Rates: $100-150, including Continental Breakfast. 10 Rooms. Most major credit cards accepted. Toll-free reservations 1/800-995-8599.

A delightful place by any standard, the Inn at the Delta incorporates features of architecture and service that have been time tested in New Mexico for hundreds of years. It began when Augustine Garcia built the Delta Bar (so called because the shape of the building resembled the Greek letter delta) in 1949. It grew into a full service restaurant over the years and the accommodations facility was added only relatively recently. Located amid the Eight Northern Pueblos, the small Inn is authentic Southwestern in every detail. The adobe structure is considered by many architectural experts and ordinary people alike as one of the most stunning buildings in New Mexico. The main house has a beautiful lobby with brilliant white walls decorated with pottery, Navajo rugs, and other native crafts. It's also the location for a generous Continental breakfast.

Each of the ten unique rooms (it would be more proper to call these spacious units suites, because every room has a sitting area that is distinct and separate from the sleeping area) is done in beautiful and classic Spanish Colonial style. Both furnishings and art represent the work of local artisans. All rooms feature a whirlpool tub, *kiva* fireplace, and queen bed. Only the San Antonio Room and Santiago Rooms have two queen beds – the remaining eight have one. Some rooms have tiled floors throughout while others combine carpeting in some areas and tile in others. The San Ysidro and San Teresita have double size Jacuzzi tubs. However, it really doesn't matter which room you get – they're all simply wonderful.

So much can be said about the fine dining facility called Anthony's at the Delta (listed later in the *Where to Eat* section of the Santa Fe chapter). For now I'll just tell you that dining at Anthony's is like eating in a beautiful Garden of Eden. Fresh flowers on the tables, skylights, huge Spanish tables and chairs are some of the atmospheric considerations, while expertly prepared steaks and seafood are menu staples.

The Garcia family takes great pride in their facility and they will be there to personally greet you and tend to your needs. Feel free to ask them questions about seeing the sights, as they're native to the area and know more than just about anyone. They're very pleased to share their experience with their friends (that is, their guests).

INN OF THE ANASAZI

113 Washington Avenue, Santa Fe. Tel. 988-3030, Fax 988-3277. Rates: $230-260. 59 Rooms. Major credit cards accepted. Toll-free reservations 1/800-688-8100.

Within a brief walk of the historic Santa Fe Plaza, the Inn of the Anasazi offers luxury accommodations in a setting that befits its striking and unique surroundings. The exterior of this massive adobe structure is darker in color than many other of Santa Fe's adobe buildings. Massive wooden beams jut out from the front like some old fortress, surrounding the huge hand carved doors. As you walk through those doors you enter a different world – that of the traditional Southwest. Sandstone walls with Indian blankets and many paintings hanging from them, cactus plants in tremendous terra cotta pots, and so many other decorative touches are all meant to convey the spirit and essence of the three cultures that have shaped Santa Fe over nearly four centuries. A two-story waterfall drops along one wall adding immeasurably to the already tranquil atmosphere with its soothing sound and motion.

The Inn's 59 rooms and suites feature fireplaces (gas lit), charming four-poster beds, and wooden ceilings. Everything, including the complimentary toiletries, are all environmentally sound in keeping with the long-standing tradition of the Native Americans who have always been at peace with nature.

The fine restaurant serves Southwestern foods of each of the three cultures in an atmosphere of elegance highlighted by first-class service and a beautiful interior of wood floors, handwoven textiles, and wrought-iron sconces. There's an extensive wine list and an adjacent lounge that's great for an intimate chat. Speaking of intimacy, the Inn also has a "library," complete with fireplace and a large collection of books on local history and culture. And finally, there's the "Living Room" where guests gather to talk, have a refreshing drink, or play a game of cards.

If you're seeking the Southwestern lifestyle that's made New Mexico and especially Santa Fe world famous, you need look no further than the beautiful and highly distinctive Inn of the Anasazi.

INN OF THE MOUNTAIN GODS

Carrizo Creek Road, Mescalero (in the Ruidoso area). Tel. 257-5141; Fax 257-6173. Rates: $90-145. 253 Rooms. Major credit cards accepted. Toll-free reservations 1/800-545-9011.

A uniquely beautiful mountain retreat, the Inn of the Mountain Gods sits along a tranquil lake surrounded by perpetually snow-capped peaks. The luxurious resort of the Sacramento Mountains covers about 150 acres and is but a small part of the larger 463,000 acre Mescalero Apache Indian Reservation. Owned and operated by the Apache tribe, guests are treated to a delightful array of accommodations and recreational facilities. Among the 253 rooms are three Honeymoon Suites, ten "Bizaayi Suites," and ten Parlor Suites. All rooms feature full amenities and have a modern modified Southwestern decor.

Even more important than the rooms at the Inn is the atmosphere and activities. The serene and secluded sight is a great place to take a break from the sometimes hectic pace we set for ourselves when traveling. Guests will find a championship 18-hole golf course, tennis, volleyball, basketball and badminton. There's also boating on the lake (whose shore is dotted with tepees to remind you that you are on Mescalero Apache ground), fishing, and swimming. A wonderful gift shop and boutique are also on the premises. Children of all ages will enjoy the extensive video arcade.

Wining and dining at the Inn of the Mountain Gods is also a very pleasing experience. The Dan Li Ka Dining Room serves outstanding cuisine. Few places can match the bountiful spread of their famous Sunday brunch. For lighter meals or just a drink, then try the Apache Tee Bar and Grill. This room's huge picture windows overlook the beautiful lake with its backdrop of vast forest. Two other lounges, Nas Tane and Gos Kan, are also good spots for a drink or to enjoy some evening entertainment.

If you really want to get away from it all but still want to retain all the comforts and conveniences you've gotten so used to, then Inn of the Mountain Gods should be high on your list. While a resort like this can best be appreciated in a multi-night stay, you shouldn't pass up the opportunity to experience it even if you're only going to be in the Ruidoso-Mescalero area for a single night.

LA FONDA

100 E. San Francisco Street, Santa Fe. Tel. 982-5511, Fax 988-2952. Rates: $174-189, suites $200-250. 153 Rooms. Major credit cards accepted. Toll-free reservations 1/800-523-5002.

Located amid the historic structures of the world famous Plaza, La Fonda is itself an historic attraction. Long known as "the inn at the end of the Santa Fe Trail," it occupies a site that has contained an inn since 1610, the year of Santa Fe's founding. La Fonda, in fact, means The Inn. A member of Historic Hotels of America, the Inn is a large and colorful adobe structure, looking much like an old mission or fortress with its many towers, sections of differing heights and wooden interior beams protruding from the front facade. More than a hotel, La Fonda is almost a museum piece and many visitors to Santa Fe make it a point to visit the place even if they aren't staying there. Both its unique architecture and its status as an art center displaying the rich cultural traditions of Santa Fe make it a special place.

Every guest room is also a unique work of art. Hand painted wooden furniture and wall accents painted by Pueblo Indian artists create a warm atmosphere. Doorways are frequently arch shaped with two half doors beneath a keystone-less row of bricks. Many rooms have fireplaces. If all this weren't enough to capture your fancy, the views of the mountains or of the Plaza from some of the upper stories is fantastic.

A visit to the hotel's lobby is like stepping back in time. It's the hub of many activities and facilities throughout La Fonda. The lobby bar has some of the best margaritas to be found anywhere. But not everything else of interest is in or off the lobby. A bar on the top floor and a cafe on the third floor are both among the best spots in town to savor Santa Fe. The fifth floor Bell Tower Bar is located on the west side of the hotel and offers one of the most memorable views of the Sangre de Cristo Mountains from anywhere in Santa Fe. The outdoor bar is partially beneath a large open tower that, in the old mission days, would have contained a bell. La Terraza on the east side is a great place for either lunch or a snack at any time of the day. An open-air cafe, it provides a most remarkable view of the St. Francis of Asis Church. It almost seems as if you're a part of that famous building.

La Fonda has long rightly prided itself on the high level of service that it offers to guests. Everyone gets personal attention. If you have any questions or problems be sure to ask the Concierge for help. The hotel even publishes a quarterly newsletter that has lots of useful information about the hotel and Santa Fe. Visitors will often find out through the newsletter about special classes or tours that La Fonda may be giving from time to time.

LA POSADA DE ALBUQUERQUE

125 Second Street NW, Albuquerque. Tel. 242-9090; Fax 242-8664. Rates: $102. 114 Rooms. Major credit cards accepted. Toll-free reservations 1/800-777-5732.

A beautiful hotel with old-world elegance, La Posada was originally called the Territory Hotel when built in 1939 by the late Conrad Hilton (of Hilton Hotel fame). It's listed on the National Register of Historic Places and, after undergoing extensive restoration and renovations in 1986, is once again a true classic on the Albuquerque scene. The gorgeous main lobby is simply marvelous and is something you definitely won't see in modern construction. Two stories high, it is topped by massive carved beams. Lowering your eyes you'll then gaze upon the wooden balustrades of the balcony surrounding the entire lobby and the old western style chandeliers. The graceful arched portals leading off the lobby enclose an area that is casual and elegant at the same time. Brilliantly polished Mexican tile floors, a beautiful fountain, and murals on the walls complete the picture.

The guest rooms maintain the same sort of atmosphere and refinement. Again, Mexican tile floors are a common feature throughout the building. An extra bit of charm is added by the old-fashioned wooden shutters on the windows. Yet, every modern amenity awaits you, whether in standard rooms or deluxe rooms and small suites. Some of the latter two even have fireplaces.

For dining and entertainment guests can go to a very good full-service restaurant called Conrad's Downtown or the cozy and friendly lobby bar. Add all this to the excellent downtown location that's within minutes of Old Town as well as the personalized service offered by La Posada, and it's easy to see why it ranks as one of New Mexico's best.

THE LODGE AT CLOUDCROFT

One Corona Place, Cloudcroft (near Alamogordo). Tel. 682-2566; Fax 682-2715. Rates: $75-125. 60 Rooms. Major credit cards accepted. Toll-free reservations 1/800-395-6343.

Set amid the lush forest at an elevation of more than 9,000 feet above sea level, The Lodge at Cloudcroft combines history and scenery with Victorian elegance and a world-class level of service. The wooden structure, with generous use of giant windows is both charming and romantic. In the evening, it takes on a dream-like appearance that anyone could easily fall in love with and not want to leave. Rich wood moldings, exquisite furniture from the turn of the century, and beautiful antique fixtures all combine to create a very special atmosphere in both public areas and guest rooms.

The huge hunting-lodge type lobby features mounted game specimens and big paddle fans that turn as slowly as the dignified Victorian lifestyle at The Lodge. The majestic copper domed tower, called the observatory, provides magnificent views of the surrounding country. In fact, with a range of more than 150 miles on the many clear days here, you can see all the way to White Sands and beyond. Visits to the dome, by the way, are only during guided tours by hotel personnel. Other parts of the vista include the lush forests of spruce, pine, and golden aspen. Guests who wander the grounds are likely to catch glimpses of elk or even bear.

Accommodations in the 47-room main building include regular rooms as well as the Honeymoon Suite, Governor's Suite, and several Parlor Suites. All feature the aforementioned stately old furniture (reconditioned to look like new) and antiques in the best traditions of Victorian interior decorating. There is also a separate building called the Pavilion, a bed and breakfast facility containing ten rustic rooms with knotty-pine walls. Some have stone fireplaces. A completely separate four bedroom home with dining and family room contains hand-hewn railroad beams in the ceiling. Called The Retreat, it's more than affordable (at about $300) if two or more couples are traveling together. Recreational facilities include an outdoor heated pool, spa, and sauna, and both nine and 18-hole golf courses with beautifully verdant fairways surrounded by towering trees. It's one of the highest golf courses in America.

The Lodge has an interesting history. Originally built in 1899 to provide a get-away for railroad workers, it burnt to the ground only ten years later. Within two years it was rebuilt on an adjacent but more scenic site. Although renovated and modernized, the exterior of the main lodge appeared then as it does today. A more fascinating bit of history (although how much of it is true remains to be seen) is connected with Rebecca's, the hotel's outstanding restaurant.

Legend has it that Rebecca was a beautiful young maid at The Lodge. She mysteriously disappeared after she was found by her lover with another man. The staff maintains that she's never been seen since, although it is rumored that she wanders around the building in search of another lover. How will you know if you meet her? Simple – just look at her portrait which hangs prominently in the lounge.

SAGEBRUSH INN

On Paseo del Pueblo Sur, Taos. Tel. 758-2254; Fax 758-5077. Rates: $60-140. 100 Rooms. Full breakfast is included. Major credit cards accepted. Toll-free reservations 1/800-428-3626.

The Sagebrush is a part of Taos' history. It was built in 1929 to serve mainly the rich people who traveled between New York and Arizona. Originally called the Chamisa Inn (which means Sagebrush), it was changed so that English speaking folks would find it easier to remember the name. Constructed in the attractive adobe Pueblo mission style, workers carried huge *viga* logs from the surrounding mountains to use as ceiling beams, while 24-inch thick adobe walls rose from bricks that were then stuccoed over.

Since that time, the Sagebrush has seen many famous people pass through its doors. The famous painter Georgia O'Keefe stayed here for six months. Located a few miles south of the Taos Plaza, the Sagebrush Inn is close enough to the center of the action to be convenient while being far enough away to allow a sense of tranquility and privacy.

You can almost feel the "real" New Mexico as soon as you see the beige colored building with dozens of *viga* beams protruding. A walk around the property reveals many graceful architectural features such as portals, patios, and balconies. The large central courtyard, with its attractive garden, puts the building in the foreground of a magnificent view of the Sangre de Cristos.

Lodging is divided into five categories. These are standard rooms, rooms with fireplace, deluxe rooms (also with fireplace), small suites and executive suites. No matter which class you take you'll find great charm. Features such as Mexican tiles, hand-carved furniture, Native American rugs and pottery lamps create a beautiful and authentic Southwestern atmosphere.

The lobby in the main building is a showcase for Southwestern arts and crafts. Massive wooden beams highlight the architecture in this area and the purposely dim lighting evokes an earlier era. The lobby lounge has nightly entertainment and has, over the years, become one of the most popular nightspots in all of Taos. Off of the lobby area are the Inn's two restaurants. One is attractively casual, especially good for breakfast and lunch, while Los Vaqueros is an elegant room featuring fine service and excellent cuisine.

A VERY SPECIAL PLACE

***The Lodge at Chama**, Tel. 756-2133; Fax 756-2519, is one of several lodging establishments in the state that is owned by the Jicarilla Apache Indian tribe. It occupies a 32,000 acre ranch in the gorgeous San Juan Mountains of northern New Mexico. It is one of the world's most exclusive and awarded hunting lodges. The Lodge caters to a select clientele from all around the world – people looking for privacy, top-notch hunting and fishing, and a place to simply relax and get away from it all.*

The average person will be put off by room prices that start at $200 a day (just for the room) and at $375 when meals and lodge facilities are included. Those prices don't include hunting and fishing fees. Also, if you aren't a hunter, you may not feel very comfortable either during the day or at night in the expansive western-style Great Room, where guests gather to discuss the day's hunt. The Lodge does offer photo safaris for those who wish to do their hunting with camera only. I'm sure that I (since I don't hunt) could nicely fill up a day or two just exploring the beautiful countryside on horseback or foot.

The Lodge is constructed of native timber and stone. The Great Room features a cathedral ceiling and a 20-foot wide fireplace. Guest rooms are typically Southwestern in decor (in keeping with the surroundings, they aren't nearly as opulent as you might expect, especially in view of the prices). Fine Southwestern Ranch cuisine highlights the expertly prepared meals.

While definitely not for everyone, a stay at The Lodge at Chama is most definitely the experience of a lifetime.

13. ALBUQUERQUE

With a population of more than 400,000 people, and still growing rapidly, **Albuquerque** is more than six times as large as the next biggest city in New Mexico. In fact, about a third of the state's population lives in the greater Albuquerque area. That's pretty impressive when you consider the city's rather inauspicious origins.

First settled in the middle of the 17th century, the original town was abandoned as a result of the 1680 Pueblo Rebellion. In 1692, about 30 families from nearby Bernalillo resettled the site although the city wasn't officially founded until 1706. It was named for the Viceroy of New Spain, the Duke of Albuquerque. (To this day the minor league baseball team carries the nickname of Dukes.) At that time the name was spelled *Alburquerque*. Growth was almost constant after that point due to the settlement's strategic location on the Rio Grande and the Camino Real trade route connecting Santa Fe and Mexico.

With the coming of the railroad in the 19th century, the town moved a few miles eastward, taking the name Albuquerque with it. The original settlement remained, though, calling itself **Old Town**. It wasn't until 1949 that Old Town merged with the new city of Albuquerque.

Albuquerque has a large number of high-technology industries and is a major research center. The government, especially the military, is also a major employer, as are the University of New Mexico and other educational institutions. Whether it's because of the interesting blend of different cultures or the combination of its historic attractions and contemporary lifestyle, I think that you'll soon agree that Albuquerque is a uniquely charming large city.

ARRIVALS & DEPARTURES

By Air

Albuquerque International Airport is a convenient place to fly into. It's modern in every respect but doesn't often have big crowds and the attendant delays found in many major city airports. Car rentals and other services are plentiful. What's more, Old Town and the heart of the city are less than five miles away. Even during rush hour you can be downtown in a matter of minutes after leaving the airport.

Should you not be renting a car, there are two methods to get from the airport to the city center – taxi or bus. Plenty of cabs are available right outside the terminal. The approximate fare to downtown is about $12. If you want to get a cab to the airport, your best bet is to call the **Checker Airport Express**, *Tel. 765-1234*. Municipal bus routes number 14 and 50 both serve the downtown area from the airport.

Since most people will be picking up a rental car, here's some simple directions to get to either downtown or Old Town, two areas with a lot of hotels. Upon leaving the airport's exit road, turn left on Gibson Boulevard. From there it's about 1 1/2 miles to I-25. Take that road north. Use Exit 225 westbound (Lomas Blvd.). That street will soon bring you into downtown and, just beyond it, to the Old Town area.

By Bus & Train

The **Greyhound Bus Depot** is located downtown at the intersection of 1st and Silver Streets. The **Amtrak station** is less than a block away from there, off of 1st between Gold and Silver. From either one you can easily get to other portions of the city by public transportation. Rental car agencies can also be found downtown.

By Car

The two aforementioned Interstates will be the route that just about everybody takes into Albuquerque if you're driving in from out of state. Your exact route will, of course, depend upon the location of your hotel or first sightseeing stop. However, for convenience sake, I'll assume that most of you will be initially heading for the Old Town area. Motorists from both east or west should leave I-40 at Exit 157 (Rio Grande Boulevard) which provides direct access to Old Town, located immediately to the south of the highway. North-South travelers can either take the Interstate to I-40 and proceed as above, or use Exit 225 and take Lomas Boulevard west directly into Old Town.

Parking in Albuquerque is generally not a big problem unless you plan to park on the street in the central business district or Old Town, where it ranges from difficult to nearly impossible. In busy areas most on-street parking, when you can find it, is regulated by meters and isn't that convenient if you're going to be spending a lot of time in one area. However, many major attractions have free parking on the premises. The Old Town and downtown areas have numerous municipal lots where plenty of inexpensive parking is available. Many Old Town visitors, especially if you'll be visiting the museums, will find it more convenient to leave their cars at the ample parking facilities of the major museums.

ORIENTATION

Spreading out across a broad valley between the **Sandia Mountains** on the east and the high plateau to the west, Albuquerque covers a large geographic area. Most of the city is located on the flat terrain of the east side of the **Rio Grande**, but a small portion as well as a number of suburban communities are on the bluffs of the west bank. New Mexico's two Interstate highways intersect close to the heart of the city: **I-40** runs through the entire east-west width of the city and **I-25** does the same in a north-to-south direction. This conveniently divides Albuquerque into four quadrants for our purposes.

You should also be familiar with a few other main thoroughfares. **Central Avenue** roughly parallels I-40 but is somewhat to the south. It cuts through the heart of downtown. **Lomas Boulevard** is another such street that begins at Central near Old Town and runs to the east between Central and the Interstate. Besides I-25, some primary north-south streets are (from nearest the Rio Grande and heading eastward) **4th Street**, **University Boulevard**, **San Mateo Boulevard**, and **Wyoming Boulevard**. **Tramway Boulevard** (an upside down L-shaped road also designated as NM 556) begins near the eastern edge of the city at I-40 and goes past the base of the Sandia Peak Aerial Tram before turning west and reaching I-25 in the northern part of the city.

Many attractions are located in the southwest quadrant. This portion of Albuquerque contains both **Old Town** and the downtown business district. The Rio Grande serves as the western boundary of this quadrant. The river also forms the west edge of the northwest quadrant. The two eastern quadrants cover the biggest portion of the city but has, relatively speaking, fewer places of interest to the visitor.

Portions of Albuquerque (primarily Old Town and vicinity) lend themselves to walking tours. However, many of the city's attractions are far-flung and require a car or public transportation to get there and back.

GETTING AROUND TOWN

As you'll soon see, I have arranged your sightseeing in Albuquerque in convenient chunks to avoid having to run back and forth without a logical plan of attack. Except for the area around Old Town, a car is the best way to get around. You can get to most attractions by bus or taxi. However, the former is often inconvenient and the latter can be expensive. Directions for getting places by foot, car, and bus (where appropriate) will be given in each of the described tours.

Municipal bus service is provided by **Sun-Trans**. They operate a fleet of buses connecting all parts of the city with the central business district and Old Town. *For route and schedule information, call them at Tel. 843-9200.*

Two routes that are especially important are the number "10" line which travels east to west along Lomas virtually from one end of the city to the other and route "11" which does the same thing north to south on 4th Street.

WHERE TO STAY

Commensurate with its status as New Mexico's most populous city, Albuquerque also has the most hotel rooms. However, unlike places such as Santa Fe and Taos, lodging properties here, for the most part, lack the authentic Southwestern style, atmosphere, and ambiance found elsewhere. In short, "enchanting" isn't how I would describe most Albuquerque hotels. This doesn't mean, however, that there aren't very nice places to stay. The better chain hotels are represented in Albuquerque and offer the best in modern accommodations.

For your convenience, lodging listings are in two divisions. The first is Old Town & Downtown, while the second section contains the remainder of Albuquerque.

OLD TOWN & DOWNTOWN

Very Expensive

CASA DE SUENOS, *310 Rio Grande SW. Tel. 247-4560. Rates: $175 including breakfast. 15 Rooms. American Express, VISA and MasterCard accepted. Toll-free reservations 1/800-242-8987. Located one block from Old Town.*

An award-winning bed and breakfast, the Casa de Suenos provides guests with an unforgettable experience. Relive the serene atmosphere and outstanding service of another era in an historic adobe building within minutes of the center of a modern metropolis. The exact setting, so close to Old Town, is enhanced by the open green spaces of the adjacent golf course. The owners like to call their B&B the "House of Dreams in the Land of Enchantment" and so it is. A veritable garden of delight in the middle of the city.

The guest rooms are all *casitas* (literally, little houses), each with a private courtyard, kiva-style fireplace, hot tub and kitchen facilities. They're quite large and exquisitely furnished in antique furniture with original Southwestern art gracing every unit as well as the public areas. The bountiful breakfast is served in a sun drenched room that is called the Artist's Studio.

Like most B&Bs, Casa de Suenos is a place to stay – to relax and soak up the tranquil comforts of home, rather than for the extensive facilities associated with a large hotel. It's pleasantly surprising, therefore, that this establishment has a resident masseuse and full concierge-type services for its guests.

HYATT-REGENCY ALBUQUERQUE, *330 Tijeras NW. Tel. 842-1234, Fax 842-1184. Rates: $160. 395 Rooms. Major credit cards accepted. Toll-free reservations 1/800-233-1234. Located in the heart of downtown on Tijeras between Third and Fourth Streets.*

You'll find all of the beauty and luxury that guests of the Hyatt chain have come to expect over the years from these well-run establishments. The 20-story high Southwestern style tower is something of an architectural landmark in Albuquerque with its brilliant reflective glass and rose-hued granite walls. It's right in the middle of the downtown core, adjacent to the convention center and within a few minutes of Old Town's many attractions.

The large number of rooms includes 14 deluxe suites. However, the overwhelming majority of rooms are standard and all feature designer furnishings in a Southwestern motif. Some rooms have hair dryers and bathrobes. You can arrange for evening bed turndown service but only on request. Many rooms on the upper floors have panoramic views of either the city or mountains.

While the Hyatt is one of Albuquerque's main business locations (it has meeting facilities for up to a thousand people), vacation travelers will also find a lot of facilities to fit their needs. These include an outdoor swimming pool, full service health club with gym, sauna, exercise equipment and massage; as well as a gift shop and beauty salon. McGrath's Restaurant boasts an exhibition-style kitchen. Two lounges are located in the lobby. Parking is available for guests but there is an additional charge.

Expensive

LA POSADA DE ALBUQUERQUE, *125 Second Street NW. Tel. 242-9090, Fax 242-8664. Rates: $102. 114 Rooms. Major credit cards accepted. Toll-free reservations 1/800-777-5732. Located downtown opposite the Convention Center at Copper Street.*

Constructed in 1939 by famous hotelier Conrad Hilton, the former Territory Hotel is now on the National Register of Historic Places. It was completely renovated in 1986 and renamed La Posada. The traditional Southwestern style was retained and majestically restored. The two story lobby is especially brilliant, with its carved beams and balcony, tiled fountain, and plenty of murals decorating the walls. Bathed in a warm yellow glow from antique style chandeliers, it exudes the atmosphere of an earlier era.

Guest rooms keep the Southwest theme going strong. Mexican tile floors and wooden shutters are just two of the accents that I find most delightful about rooms at La Posada. You won't be roughing it, however, since all rooms are filled with modern amenities. There are also a small number of suites and rooms with fireplaces.

There's a good restaurant called Conrad's Downtown on the premises as well as a lobby bar. The restaurant's menu features Spanish and Mexican dishes as interpreted by Conrad's untraditional American chef. La Posada is known locally for its lively jazz performances on Friday and Saturday nights. You'll also find a small but excellent gift shop off the lobby.

Selected as one of my Best Places to Stay (see Chapter 12 for more details).

Moderate

DOUBLETREE HOTEL, *201 Marquette NW. Tel. 247-3344. Rates: $79-94. 294 Rooms. Major credit cards accepted. Toll-free reservations 1/800-222-TREE. Adjacent to the downtown Convention Center.*

This modern 16-story high rise hotel in the center of Albuquerque's financial district also strives to maintain the flavor of New Mexico with its Southwestern style decor. The very attractive lobby features a two-floor high waterfall and comfortable seating areas.

All of the guest rooms are large and very comfortable. Quite a few have good views. Extra amenities vary depending upon the price. The better rooms have such things as wet bars or refrigerators and coffee makers. All rooms feature modern Southwestern furnishings and decorative items.

There's a small swimming pool which is okay as long as you're not trying out for the Olympics. Not that the weather often presents a problem in Albuquerque, but the hotel is connected to a large shopping center and the Convention Center by an underground passageway. The Doubletree offers the La Cascada restaurant and a cocktail lounge with live entertainment for those not wishing to venture out in the evening. The elegant restaurant specializes in contemporary Southwestern dishes as well as continental cuisine and is adjacent to the lobby waterfall. And, of course, like all Doubletree hotels nationwide, guests are greeted upon their arrival with those famous and delicious chocolate chip cookies! That's almost reason enough for me to stay there.

SHERATON OLD TOWN HOTEL, *800 Rio Grande Boulevard NW. Tel. 843-6300, Fax 842-9863. Rates:$89. 190 Rooms. Major credit cards accepted. Toll-free reservations 1/800-237-2133. Located immediately to the north of Old Town.*

This is a nice hotel but nothing really special. However, it has three outstanding features, as they say in the real estate business – location, location, location. You can be at Albuquerque's best museums and the center of Old Town within a five minute walk. The 11-story building is in somewhat of a Southwestern style. At least the color is right.

The same attempt is made at Southwestern room decor, which is only partially successful. Large pieces of furniture dominate but they're actually too large for the average size rooms. Some rooms have wet bars or refrigerators. Public facilities include a heated pool, whirlpool, and complete exercise room. For dining, you can select between the Customs House Restaurant, with decor based on the days of sailing ships or, for lighter meals, an attractive coffee shop. There are also two lounges, one of which has entertainment.

WILLIAM E. MAUGER ESTATE BED & BREAKFAST, *701 Roma Avenue NW. Tel. 242-8755, Fax 842-8835. Rates: $79-140, including full breakfast. 9 Rooms. Major credit cards accepted. Located on the edge of downtown south of Lomas Street.*

Nestled on a quiet street just south of downtown and not too far from Old Town, the Mauger (sometimes referred to as the Britannia and W. E. Mauger Estate B&B) is a huge, classic Victorian era house built in the Queen Anne style in 1897. Every inch of the place exudes the old fashioned luxury of that era. You'll feel as if you're staying in the sumptuous home of some 19th century mining tycoon (or perhaps in a museum). As the name implies, it was once the centerpiece of a rambling estate belonging to one of Albuquerque's richer citizens, Mr. William Mauger and his wife Britannia.

The guest rooms are mostly large and also feature high ceilings, brass fixtures and marvelous antique furnishings. There aren't any phones and rooms contain only a small black and white television. How's that for old-fashioned! All rooms, however, have such modern amenities as air conditioning, coffee makers, and hair dryers while a few feature refrigerators. Be aware when booking your reservation that the inn is three stories high but doesn't have an elevator.

My favorite rooms are the Victorian with its brick fireplace and private doors opening onto the front porch; the Talbot with a queen-sized sleigh bed and an old desk that rightly belongs in a museum; and the Britannia, which is the largest room, with three huge windows, separate sitting area and an immense brass bad. The other rooms are the Garden, Wool, Boston Sleeper, Tuers, Graystone and Edwardian and each is distinctive.

A sumptuous three course breakfast is served daily in the combination indoor/outdoor dining room. Although no other meals are available, wine, cheese and snacks and other refreshments are served early each evening. Numerous restaurants are located within a short distance. Guests at the Mauger Estate receive free privileges at a neighboring health club. A great way to cap off the day is to relax in wicker furniture on the inn's 30-foot front porch. Or you can listen to music in the sitting room or watch a movie from their laser disc collection in the library. Your hosts,

Valerie (an architectural designer) and Alan (a lawyer), will see to your every need and help make your stay a most charming experience.

OTHER AREAS

Expensive

ALBUQUERQUE HILTON, *1901 University Boulevard NE. Tel. 884-2500, Fax 889-9118. Rates: $99-139. 262 Rooms. Major credit cards accepted. Toll-free reservations 1/800-274-6835. Located near I-25/I-40 Interchange at Menaul Boulevard, close to downtown and Old Town.*

The contemporary 12-story hotel is typical Hilton, which means business class levels of luxury and comfort. The decor is modified Southwestern. Guest rooms, many of which provide scenic views, are large and feature many convenient amenities such as an iron and ironing board. Some have refrigerators. The upper end rooms are on a separate "luxury level" which provide, among other things, better security.

The Hilton has an enormous amount of facilities, which you would expect for a hotel that caters mainly to business travelers. Two swimming pools (one indoor), a sauna, whirlpool, two tennis courts and a health club all invite your participation. On the gastronomic side, the Hilton features three restaurants of varying cuisine and style including the elegant Rancher's Club. Socializing and entertainment can be found in one of two cocktail lounges.

ALBUQUERQUE MARRIOTT HOTEL, *2101 Louisiana NE. Tel. 881-6800, Fax 888-2982. Rates: $134. 411 Rooms. Major credit cards accepted. Toll-free reservations 1/800-228-9290. Located one block north of I-40, Exit 162 ("uptown" area).*

Of all the top quality hotel chains, Marriott's properties are probably the most consistent. To some people that's good, while others don't like the relative sameness. One cannot deny, however, that the standard of comfort and service at Marriott is excellent. That certainly applies to this modern 17-story facility that is located adjacent to two large shopping centers.

The guest rooms are all large and attractive if somewhat lacking in imagination. A number of rooms have refrigerators. The Marriott boasts both indoor and outdoor swimming pools, a sauna, whirlpool and exercise room. Nicole's is a very good restaurant choice or you can opt for the less formal Allie's American Grille, with its bistro atmosphere and good selection of salads and wonderful desserts. The hotel offers Breakfast plans and a variety of package deals.

AMBERLY SUITE HOTEL, *7620 Pan American Freeway NE. Tel. 823-1300, Fax 823-2896. Rates: $120-130, including full breakfast. 170 Rooms. Major credit cards accepted. Toll-free reservations 1/800-333-9806. Located on I-25 frontage road, north of Exit 231; near Balloon Fiesta Park.*

A modern three-story all-suite facility, the Amberly is well located for jaunts either into Old Town and downtown to the south or to Sandia Peak to the north. You can select from either one-bedroom mini-suites or two-bedroom units. All have full kitchens (including a microwave, coffee makers, and a wet bar). There's plenty available in the way of recreation, too. A swimming pool, sauna, and spa are complemented by a fully equipped fitness center.

On the eating front, a very good buffet breakfast is served (sometimes on the outdoor patio) and a manager's cocktail reception with hors d'oeuvres is held nightly. You can choose from Watson's Restaurant or a quick meal in Amberley Suite's Cafe and Deli. The latter offers an all-you-can-eat breakfast buffet and patio dining. There's also a convenience store right on the premises if you want to prepare all or some of your meals in your own room. The lounge has entertainment.

HOLIDAY INN PYRAMID, *5151 San Francisco Road NE. Tel. 821-3333, Fax 828-0230. Rates: $100-140. 365 Rooms. Major credit cards accepted. Toll-free reservations 1/800-544-0623. Located by the Paseo del Norte (I-25, Exit 232) at the Journal Center.*

This striking ten-story high architectural masterpiece is one of Albuquerque's most beautiful and better hotels. It's certainly among the most unusual and ranks among the best in the Holiday Inn family. At first glance you might consider the style to be ultra-modern. But think about it for a moment and you realize that it was designed to resemble the magnificent pyramids of the ancient Aztec people of Mexico. Dark glass alternates with sandstone colored walls to create a beautiful effect. Notice especially the frieze that runs along the entire front of the building above the first floor. Inside is a lovely atrium lobby (best viewed from the glass elevators) dominated by a five-story high waterfall.

Room accommodations are quite varied, from standard rooms to executive type units to suites. All are large, comfortable and have many amenities to go with the attractive Southwestern decor. Coffee makers and refrigerators are available in some rooms. Guests can opt from one of two fine restaurants. The Terrace Restaurant is located in the middle of the atrium and is best known for its excellent lunch buffet and sumptuous Sunday brunch.

There's also a piano bar and lounge as well as a dance club. A combination indoor/outdoor pool, two saunas, and a large health club provide ample opportunity to recharge your batteries for another day of activity.

Moderate

LAS PALOMAS INN, *2303 Candelaria Road NW. Tel. 345-7228, Fax 345-7328. Rates: $85-125, including full breakfast. 11 Rooms. MasterCard and*

VISA accepted. Toll-free reservations 1/800-909-DOVE. Located less than two miles from Old Town via Rio Grande Boulevard to Candelaria, then right.

For the price, this is definitely one of my highly recommended places to stay in Albuquerque. Located on a former estate and covering three acres, Las Palomas is an historic adobe style house set amid a wonderfully beautiful landscape. Spacious lawns, colorful and fragrant gardens, and even fruit orchards grace the property and are literally at the doorstep of your room. The service level is extremely high and the Stone family proprietors take a strong personal interest both in how the Palomas is maintained and the comfort of their guests.

All of the guest rooms are large and nicely furnished with authentic Southwestern furniture and decorative items. A delicious and hearty breakfast is served in an attractive room overlooking the gardens. There are quite a few other facilities for a B&B. One is an outdoor hot tub surrounded by nature's beauty and providing a relaxing experience that you'll have a hard time duplicating elsewhere. There's also a single tennis court, but with only 11 rooms you shouldn't have trouble getting court time. Finally, a stroll on the short but lovely nature trail that winds through the grounds is a great way to begin or end the day.

LE BARON INN AND SUITES, *2120 Menaul Boulevard NE. Tel. 884-0250, Fax 883-0594. Rates: $72-88, including Continental Breakfast. 200 Rooms. Major credit cards accepted. Toll-free reservations 1/800-444-7378. Located near the I-25/I-40 Interchange, just east of University Boulevard.*

Constructed in a style that combines contemporary and Southwestern architectural features, this attractive property surrounding a nicely landscaped central courtyard is a quiet oasis that is convenient to all parts of the city. The courtyard contains a large swimming pool amid the greenery of bushes and trees that partially obscure the nearby buildings.

Guest rooms are either one or two-bedroom suites each containing a refrigerator, microwave oven, and bar area. Two-room units have two bathrooms. Some of these spacious units even have four-poster beds. There isn't any restaurant on the premises but plenty of dining spots are located within a short walk or ride in any direction. The continental breakfast is on the sparse side but adequate for those who just need a morning fix of juice or coffee and some sweets.

LeBaron is part of a small but growing chain with several locations in the southwest. You'll find that all of them have similar high standards to the Albuquerque location.

PINNACLE HOTEL FOUR SEASONS, *2500 Carlisle Boulevard NE. Tel. 888-3311, Fax 881-7452. Rates: $84-105. 368 Rooms. Major credit cards accepted. Toll-free reservations 1/800-545-8400. Located just north of I-40, Exit 160; near downtown.*

Albuquerque's newest major hotel is another Four Seasons extravaganza. With so many rooms you would probably expect it to be another modern high rise. Well, its definitely not. Instead, the rooms are in low buildings spread out on nicely landscaped extensive grounds. Inside, the lobby and public areas are spacious and open, providing an airy elegance.

While all of the rooms are large and extremely attractive, the types of amenities vary considerably. The higher the room rate, of course, the more features it will have. The list includes coffee makers, wet bars, and Grecian baths. There are also some suites with balconies and a few have direct private access to the swimming pool. Oh yes, I almost forgot the most important thing – all rooms have a built-in Nintendo video game system. How could you leave home without that? Seriously, though, it is a good feature if you're taking the kids with you.

There are two swimming pools (indoor and outdoor), a health club, and whirlpool. The restaurant, called Maxie's, is a decent family style coffee shop but is nothing special considering the generally excellent level of the other facilities. For entertainment, the lounge has nightly karaoke. I mention that only because there seem to be quite a few people these days who go for that sort of thing. For myself, I'll stick to the Nintendo.

WINROCK INN, *18 Winrock Center NE. Tel. 883-5252, Fax 889-3206. Rates: $72. 173 Rooms. Major credit cards accepted. Toll-free reservations 1/800-866-5252. Rates include breakfast. Member of Best Western Hotels. Located off of Louisiana Boulevard exit (#162) of I-40 adjacent to the Winrock Mall shopping center.*

This first class two-story motor inn is located near two major shopping malls. The grounds are among the nicest of any Albuquerque lodging establishment. Most of the guest rooms surround a large and carefully manicured garden as well as a private lagoon. The lagoon has a small duck population which is very popular with guests of all ages. A tranquil and lovely setting by day, the grounds are delicately illuminated in the evening and are striking. In fact, at sunset it's one of the best views in the city!

Rooms are very big and all have either a patio or balcony. Some have refrigerators. There's a nice swimming pool. Complimentary beverages are served each evening in the lobby. It's surprising that an inn of this size doesn't have a restaurant on the premises but quite a few in all price ranges are within a reasonable distance. In the morning, however, you're certainly going to enjoy the large and delicious buffet breakfast that is included in the room rate. Guests receive privileges at a local health club. This is an extremely nice property at a relatively good price value.

WYNDHAM GARDEN HOTEL, *6000 Pan American Freeway NE. Tel. 821-9451, Fax 858-0239. Rates: $94. 152 Rooms. Major credit cards accepted. Toll-free reservations 1/800-WYNDHAM. Located at San Mateo Boulevard, Exit 230 of I-25, about half-way between downtown and the Balloon Fiesta Park.*

This five-story Southwestern style lodge features an attractive central atrium that all of the interior corridors look out on. The guest rooms are very large and comfortably furnished. All of them feature coffee makers and safes for your valuables. Many have refrigerators and hair dryers. Both an indoor and outdoor swimming pool, as well as a sauna, whirlpool, and fully equipped exercise room are available for your recreational needs. There's also a restaurant called the Garden Cafe that features a breakfast buffet, and a cocktail lounge on the premises.

The Wyndham is a modern and fairly luxurious hotel; I can't find anything to complain about. On the other hand it doesn't strike me as having anything special either, which is probably why I consider the preceding Winrock to be a considerably better choice.

Budget

TRAVELERS INN, *411 McKnight Avenue NW. Tel. 242-5228, Fax 766-9218. Rates: $48, including Continental Breakfast. 99 Rooms. Major credit cards accepted. Toll-free reservations 1/800-633-8300. Located north of Old Town via Exit 159A of I-25 (between 2nd and 4th Streets).*

If you're looking for a low-priced place to stay in Albuquerque, there are certainly a number of low priced chains that you can find, including Super 8 and Luxury Inn, to mention just two. However, we all know what those places are like, so I decided to fill you in on a nice, low priced independent motor inn. It's located in an unattractive industrial area, which may turn off some people, but it's not far from Old Town and the city's other major attractions.

Nice size rooms feature queen beds. Some rooms have refrigerators and several multi-room units with living room and wet bar are also available at a slightly higher price ($69). There isn't any restaurant but you can easily find many places to dine within a short ride. Considering that you're in the "big" city, Travelers Inn represents a very good value for your money.

CAMPING & RV SITES

- **Albuquerque Central KOA Kampground**, *Tel. 96-2729*
- **Albuquerque North KOA**, *Tel. 867-5227*
- **Albuquerque West RV Park and Campground**, *Tel. 831-1912*
- **American RV Park of Albuquerque**, *Tel. 831-3545*
- **Turquoise Trail Campground and RV Park** (four miles north of Cedar Crest), *Tel. 281-2005*
- **Wes Winters Resort**, *Tel. 345-3716*

WHERE TO EAT

OLD TOWN & DOWNTOWN

Expensive - $21-30

MARIA TERESA RESTAURANT AND 1840 BAR, *618 Rio Grande Boulevard NW. Tel. 242-3900. Major credit cards accepted. Lunch Monday to Saturday, dinner nightly; Sunday brunch. Reservations suggested.*

Located in a beautifully restored adobe inn that was built in 1840, Maria Teresa's is one of Albuquerque's most historic restaurants. Cozy dining rooms with period furnishings create a warm atmosphere - one that makes you feel that you've been invited to dinner at someone's home rather than being at a restaurant. The chef has created many delicious New Mexican dishes, but you can't go wrong with the excellent aged beef or fresh seafood. There's a children's menu available for the little ones.

SEASONS ROTISSERIE AND GRILL, *2031 Mountain Road NW. Tel. 766-5100. Major credit cards accepted. Lunch on weekdays only, dinner served nightly.*

A quaint and charming multi-level facility, Seasons has a dignified air of elegance despite being comfortably informal. That, and great food, makes it one of the city's more popular dining spots. The exhibition-style kitchen is clearly visible from just about every table. Among the things in the kitchen that capture the rapt attention of the "audience" are an old fashioned wood-fired grill and a huge rotisserie for roasting meats. While dining is indoors, those seeking the al fresco experience can have their appetizers and drinks on the rooftop patio and bar. The bar serves a wonderful selection of unique beers and excellent margaritas. Seasons also has a tremendous wine list from their own cellar.

Moderate - $11-20

THE ARTICHOKE CAFE, *424 Central Avenue SE. Tel. 243-0200. Major credit cards accepted. Lunch on weekdays, dinner nightly except Sunday. Reservations suggested.*

A very attractive dining room offering a good variety of regional and American cuisine, the Artichoke also has outstanding service. Locals have rated it as one of the best restaurants in the city for several years running. Considering all that it has going for it, the prices are quite reasonable. The wine list is not overly large. No other alcoholic beverages are served besides wine and beer.

McGRATH'S, *330 Tijeras NW (in the Hyatt Regency). Tel. 842-1234. Major credit cards accepted. Reservations suggested.*

This award-winning restaurant provides diners with pleasingly comfortable surroundings. The service is very attentive and efficient without being overly stuffy. The menu includes a good variety of American and continental dishes with just enough Southwestern influence to make sure that you don't forget that you're in New Mexico. The attractive bar is a popular place to gather before having dinner.

MYSTERY CAFE, *125 Second Street (in La Posada de Albuquerque Hotel). Tel. 237-1385. Discover, MasterCard and VISA accepted. Dinner on Friday and Saturday nights only. Reservations are required.*

If you're looking for something a bit out of the ordinary, then the Mystery Cafe might just be your dinner ticket. A very funny murder mystery requires the assistance of the audience to find the guilty party. The cast acts surprisingly well, especially considering that they're busy with other things – such as serving your meal. Perhaps the only problem with the Mystery Cafe is that the food seems to get lost in the action. Actually, the four course dinner isn't bad. It's not the best food in town but better than you might expect at one of these affairs. The choice is limited to a few entrees. Alcoholic beverages are served.

RIO GRANDE CANTINA, *901 Rio Grande Boulevard NW. Tel. 242-1777. Most major credit cards accepted. Lunch and dinner; also Sunday brunch.*

Featuring all the traditional New Mexican dishes, as well as a good selection of American fare and fresh seafood for those not hooked on Southwestern cuisine, the Rio Grande Cantina is a popular establishment that successfully combines excellent food with good times. The salsa here is a good as it gets. You can have it mild or burning hot. In fact, at the Rio Grande everything tends toward the fiery version, so if you're not up to it be sure to ask for mild. While the Rio Grande prides itself on having one of the biggest selections of tequila and authentic Mexican beers north of the border, it is most famous within Albuquerque for the "Margarita Grande." If you have only one margarita while in the Southwest, it might as well be from the Rio Grande's excellent bar.

The atmosphere at Rio Grande is also well above average. During the warmer months you can choose to dine either in an attractive and peaceful indoor dining room or outside on the usually crowded and noisier patio. The outdoor area has its own fireplace so it is often used even during cooler evenings. Between the warmth of the fireplace, the food, and the guests working up some heat of their own, you probably won't notice if it is chilly.

TIO TITO'S ORIGINAL MEXICAN GRILL, *2017 Menaul Boulevard NE. Major credit cards accepted. Lunch and dinner.*

After finishing singing the praises of the Rio Grande, I have to admit that Tio Tito's is just as good food-wise and equally enjoyable. Tito's has won numerous awards and is considered by many astute judges to be one of the best Mexican restaurants in the nation. What makes its claim more legitimate is that some of its many awards come from people who should know best, like *Hispanic Magazine*. Excellent service from a friendly and active staff complements the experience.

The menu is certainly one of the biggest in any restaurant. It numbers a staggering 150 items, including a large selection of vegetarian choices for those who won't eat meat or just want to conserve a few calories on a given night. More than 20 types of salsa are made fresh daily on the premises to go along with ten Mexican beers and a dozen types of margaritas. If you're adventurous, try one of the house specials – "Tia Rita" or the "Big Kahuna." But be sure you're sitting down when you have them! Food portions are as generous as the selections. As a final touch, excellent Mexican entertainment enhances the enjoyment of your meal.

Budget – $10 or less

MILAGRO COFFEE COMPANY, *40 First Plaza Galeria (located downstairs in the Galeria shopping area adjacent to the Convention Center). Tel. 242-2555. No credit cards. Breakfast and lunch only.*

With its central downtown location, Milagro's is a good place for lunch on the go during a busy day of sightseeing. As the name would suggest, a variety of gourmet coffees are available, including Espresso, cappuccino, and latte, as well as many other types of hot and cold beverages. Delicious homemade soups and a decent choice of sandwiches provide more substance. Excellent muffins and mouth-watering pastries complete the menu picture.

ZANE GRAZE, *308 San Felipe NW. Tel. 244-3030. No credit cards. Breakfast and lunch only.*

In the middle of Old Town, Zane Graze is an equally good choice for lunch. I hope you are amused by the name without me having to tell you why you should be. (Remember the great western novelist Zane Gray?) Like Milagro's, there's a good selection of coffees and beverages. But the choice of soups, salads, and sandwiches as well as homemade deserts is better. Even if you don't have lunch here, this is one of many places where you can get some of the best tasting ice cream in America – the Taos Cow brand.

OTHER AREAS

Expensive – $21-30

HIGH FINANCE RESTAURANT, *40 Tramway Road (on the top of Sandia Peak). Tel. 243-9742. Major credit cards accepted. Lunch and dinner. Reservations suggested.*

Dining with a view is the specialty of the house. Atop 10,378-foot high Sandia Peak, there are few restaurants that can provide a better panorama while enjoying your meal. Beautiful in the daytime, it becomes a magical wonderland at night with the lights of Albuquerque twinkling below in the distance. What could be more romantic? Reduced admission on the tramway is given to guests who have advance reservations.

Now for the restaurant itself. Elegant but somewhat casual, the staff deftly serves high quality American cuisine prepared in an imaginative and unique manner. Like most restaurants of this class, the portions aren't overly big (but they're adequate), which may be an advantage at this altitude, especially if you're new in town. There's also a classy looking full service bar.

LE MARMITON, *5415 Academy NE. Tel. 821-6279. Major credit cards accepted. Dinner only, Monday through Saturday. Reservations suggested.*

A small and intimate restaurant, Le Marmiton presents expertly prepared and served traditional French cuisine. The atmosphere is romantic and the menu selections also suggest a sophistication that means this is not a family type restaurant. An excellent wine list (beer is also served) is available and the staff will be glad to help you pick just the right one to best complement your meal.

RANCHER'S CLUB OF NEW MEXICO, *1901 University Boulevard NE (in the Albuquerque Hilton). Tel. 884-2500. Major credit cards accepted. Lunch on weekdays, dinner daily. Sunday brunch. Reservations suggested.*

One of Albuquerque's most elegant and sophisticated restaurants (although dress is surprisingly casual), the Rancher's Club successfully recreates the atmosphere of a private salon where cattle barons of a bygone era gathered. Here they could come swap conversation with their peers while sampling the best meats available from their respective ranches. In keeping with that theme, Rancher's offers prime quality steaks and beef served in several varieties. This is done by grilling the meat on one of several different types of hardwoods. Each aromatic wood lends a different flavoring to the final product. Some are sure to be unique tastes for you. Rancher's menu also has a small number of fish and seafood items. There's live piano music on Thursday through Saturday nights.

Moderate – $11-20

AUSTINS STEAKS AND SALOON, *5210 San Mateo Boulevard. Tel. 888-7674. American Express, MasterCard and VISA accepted. Lunch and dinner.*

The poor man's Rancher's, Austins has an excellent selection of steaks and prime rib dishes that will please even the most demanding beef eater. Ribs, chicken, and seafood items also appear on the menu. If you're interested in lighter fare, there's a nice selection of salads and sandwiches to choose from. You can even get some of the best burgers in town. Portions are very generous and the service is excellent. The atmosphere is casual, on the style of an old-time western road house. A late afternoon happy hour at the bar is popular with the locals before sitting down to a hearty meal.

THE COUNTY LINE OF ALBUQUERQUE, *9600 Tramway Boulevard NE. Tel. 856-7477. Most major credit cards accepted. Dinner only.*

Along with New Mexican/Southwestern cuisine and great steaks, barbecue shares the top of the bill when it comes to popularity in the state's restaurants. The County Line is one of the best of its genre, offering a wide selection of barbecued steaks, chicken, and ribs. The sauces are authentic Southwestern, adding a zesty flavor that will probably be quite different from what you may be used to. All entrees are served with delicious homemade bread. Ice cream and great cobblers highlight the desserts. The atmosphere is extremely casual as the building that houses County Line is a 1940s vintage road house. Located only a couple of minutes from the base of the Sandia Peak tram, County Line also has good mountain views and even more outstanding views of the city lights. I highly recommend County Line.

EL PINTO AUTHENTIC NEW MEXICAN RESTAURANT, *10500 4th Street NW. Tel. 898-1771. Most major credit cards accepted. Lunch and dinner.*

The cuisine may be New Mexican, but you'll swear that you just entered Mexico itself when you dine at El Pinto. There are both indoor and outdoor dining rooms. Warm fireplaces, attractive gardens, and even a lovely waterfall create a pleasing atmosphere conducive to fine dining. Live Mexican entertainment and a lively happy hour are also featured. There's an excellent selection of New Mexican dishes all carefully prepared in-house by the talented chef.

GARDUNO'S OF MEXICO. *4 locations. 10551 Montgomery NE. Tel. 298-5000; 2100 Louisiana NE. Tel. 880-0055; 5400 Academy NE. Tel. 821-3030; 8806 4th Street NW. Tel. 898-2772. Major credit cards accepted. Lunch and dinner; also Sunday brunch.*

Garduno's has grown to encompass, besides the four Albuquerque locations, a place in Santa Fe. The authentic Mexican cuisine is excellent – far better than what we've come to expect from chains that mass produce their meals. The enchiladas are especially tantalizing and are best washed down by one of Garduno's huge and strong margaritas. Live Mariachi music (Thursday through Saturday evenings and Sunday afternoon) has become a Garduno trademark and makes for a festive and very enjoyable dinner. Children's menu available.

NICOLE'S, *2101 Louisiana NE (in the Albuquerque Marriott). Tel. 881-6800. Major credit cards accepted. Dinner only. Reservations suggested.*

Considering the elegance of the surroundings, its fancy Marriott location, and the superb continental cuisine offered, it's a real pleasant surprise to be able to include Nicole's in the moderate price category (although a few dishes do push perilously close to expensive). The menu features beef, lamb, and seafood entrees, all creatively prepared and made extra delicious with the chef's own imaginative sauces and vegetable combinations. The desserts are absolutely sinful, so be sure to leave some room in your tummy less you leave without savoring one of the best reasons to dine at Nicole's. The service is simply outstanding without being overdone. There is a dress code (that means tie and jacket for men and dresses for the ladies), which is kind of rare in New Mexico, even in the finer restaurants.

SCALO, NORTHERN ITALIAN GRILL, *3500 Central Avenue SE, Suite J. Tel. 255-8781. Major credit cards accepted. Lunch Monday to Saturday, dinner nightly.*

Owned by the chef, Scalo is a very attractive restaurant that recreates a piece of Italy to go along with the fine northern Italian cuisine. There's an open kitchen where you can watch the delicious food being prepared. Pasta dishes are a staple but there's also meat and fish on the menu. Portions are of average size and there's a limited dessert menu. A full-service bar is on the premises. Children can select meals from their own menu.

TRATTORIA TROMBINO, *5415 Academy NE. Tel. 821-5974. Major credit cards accepted. Lunch on weekdays, dinner nightly.*

A lively place that seeks to make guests feel like they're eating with an Italian family (how much more lively can you get?), the Trombino's friendly staff and Mediterranean atmosphere will put you in just the right mood for eating Italian style. A large menu includes, besides the requisite pasta, ample selections of seafood, chicken, and veal. Alcoholic beverages are served and there is also a children's menu.

TUMBLEWEED STEAKHOUSE, *10205 Central Avenue NW. Tel. 836-2903. Major credit cards accepted. Breakfast and lunch on Sunday only; dinner nightly except Monday. Reservations suggested.*

It's hard to put the Tumbleweed in any particular category of restaurants except highly unusual. The huge menu includes some very common items as well as things that you've probably never encountered in a restaurant anywhere. The ordinary part of the menu – although the taste certainly isn't ordinary – features steaks ranging in size from petite to 22-ounce giants fit for the heartiest appetites. Then there's ethnic fare, including Mexican, of course (this *is* Albuquerque), and Italian. Now, if you're in the mood for something on the exotic side, how about buffalo or ostrich steak? Not that hungry? You can get either of those in burgers, too. And if that's still not far out enough the chef highly recommends an appetizer of either rattlesnake or alligator. While some readers will definitely be turned off by the way these things "sound" to your taste buds, don't be put off unless you try them. They're delicious.

Tumbleweed is on the western edge of the city and the dining room has good views of both the city and the mountains. It's also a place where you can combine entertainment with your food. There's music to listen to or you can get up and take a few swings around the large dance floor. As you might expect from all of this, there is a full-service bar.

Tumbleweed is a fun experience, one you'll happily tell the folks at home all about upon your return from vacation.

Budget – $10 or less

CRACKER BARREL OLD COUNTRY STORE AND RESTAURANT, *5200 San Antonio NE. Tel. 821–8777. Most major credit cards accepted.*

This chain restaurant is spreading throughout the country. However, if you're not from the southeast or haven't traveled there, you may not be familiar with it. It borders on the moderate price category. Okay, this isn't gourmet food or elegant surroundings by any means. But what do you expect for the price? Actually, you'll get great value.

The large family style dining rooms are filled with antiques and oddities. Ample portions of very tasty food (meat, fish, and poultry are always on the menu) are served, including many American favorites such as roast turkey or chicken fried steak. The best desserts are fruit pies or a great warmed deep-dish apple cobbler smothered with rich ice cream. Service is friendly and extremely efficient considering that every Cracker Barrel I've been to always seem to attract big crowds.

The "country store" part of each Cracker Barrel is a recreation of a large old-fashioned general store filled with interesting items, including many useful things for the home. Both the store and the restaurant are fun places, and are especially good for families traveling with children.

66 DINER, *1405 Central Avenue NE. Tel. 247-1421. Most major credit cards accepted. Reservations suggested.*

While there may not be physically too much left of the old Route 66, it lives on in the minds and hearts of thousands of Americans – and at Albuquerque's 66 Diner. It was and is the typical roadside diner from the fifties or early sixties and will surely bring a tear to every nostalgia buff's eye. The food isn't fancy but you can count on a big menu of home-style cooked goodies, including burgers and chicken fried steak. Be sure to check out the daily blue plate specials that the cook works up. For dessert, I can think of nothing more appropriate than an ice cream soda from the old fashioned soda fountain. Beer and wine are served.

I suggest reservations because it has become an "in place" to be in Albuquerque – back in the 60s you could probably walk in and get a seat at any time of the day. Now its an eating icon at very reasonable prices.

SEEING THE SIGHTS

I've divided Albuquerque itself into four different sightseeing tours. The most important is Tour 1, so concentrate on that if you're short on time. With a little bit of extra time you can also combine portions of the other tours that most interest you.

Tour 1 is a walking tour. You can get away without transportation on Tour 2 but the others are best suited to using a car. You can, however, do all or portions of some of the other tours by foot if you've used some sort of vehicle to get to their starting points. Because Old Town (the visitors' heart of the city) is in a corner of Albuquerque, it isn't convenient to use it as a base or starting point for touring most other sections of the city.

Tour 1: Old Town & The Museum District

Approximate duration by foot including sightseeing time is 5 hours. Begin at Old Town Plaza, located off of Rio Grande Boulevard, one block north of Central Avenue.

In the shadow of the modern downtown located only a couple of miles away, **Old Town** is like taking a walk back in time to the early days of Albuquerque. The atmosphere is of a bustling small town, not a large and contemporary American city. The architecture is reminiscent of both Spain and Mexico. Several buildings are more than two hundred years old. The entire area has been designated a historic district. The **Plaza** itself is a large grassy area with, among other things, an attractive gazebo and an old cannon. Artisans, especially Native Americans, frequently sit behind their creations waiting for visitors to come and bargain over price.

There are a number of small streets (actually, back alleys would be a more appropriate term) that branch off of the plaza to the north and east where you can find many shops, art galleries, and numerous eating places. The latter feature southwestern and Native American dishes. Most are more appropriate for a casual lunch, although there are some sit-down restaurants as well.

The centerpiece of the Plaza area is the **San Felipe de Neri Church** located on the northwest corner. Built in 1792, this fine structure contains elements of Adobe and other architectural styles.

While you'll probably want to explore the Old Town Plaza and surrounding areas on your own (you can get a free map showing all of the little side streets at the information booth located opposite the Church), another option is to take a free guided one-hour walking tour. This tour departs from the nearby Albuquerque Museum.

Two of New Mexico's finest museums are located just footsteps away from the edge of the Old Town Plaza. From the Plaza, proceed north on Rio Grande Blvd. to the next corner, which is Mountain Road. Turn right

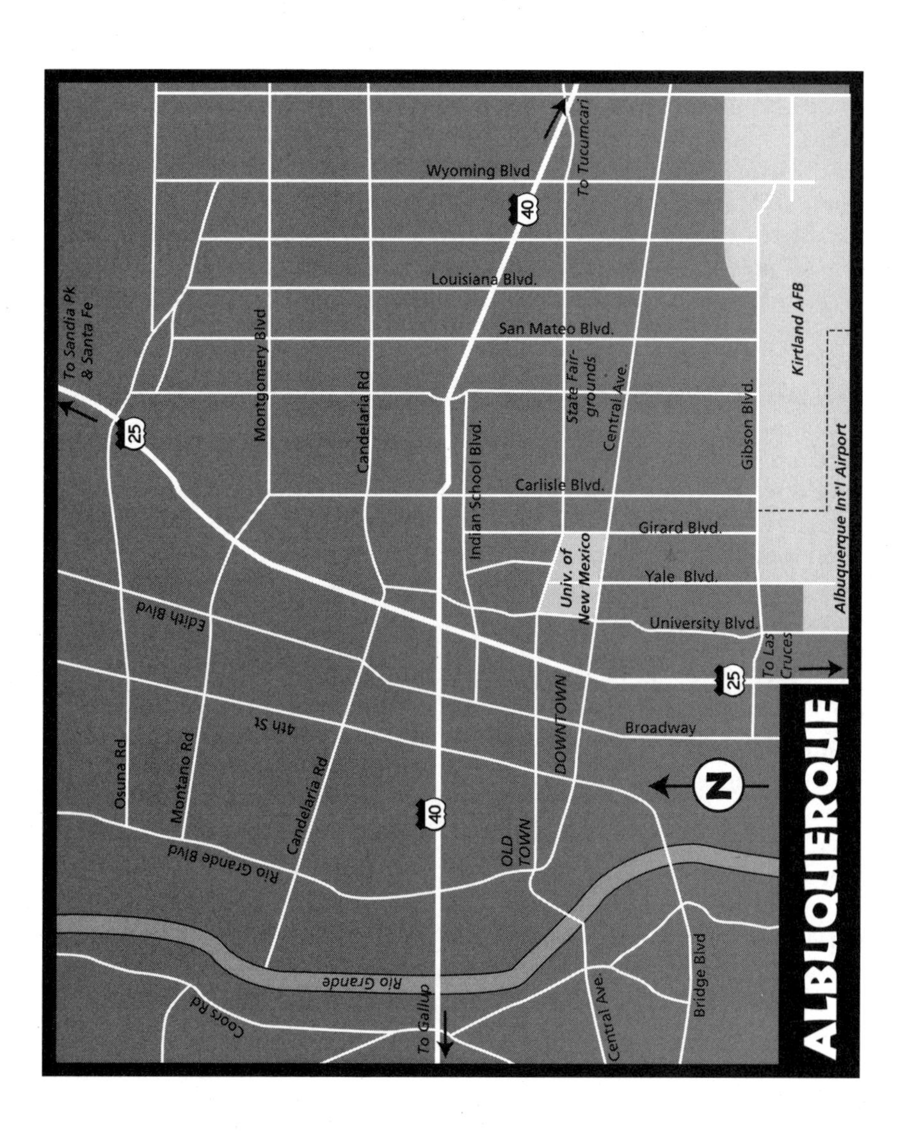
ALBUQUERQUE
To Sandia Pk & Santa Fe
To Tucumcari
To Gallup
To Las Cruces
Wyoming Blvd
Louisiana Blvd.
San Mateo Blvd.
Montgomery Blvd
Candelaria Rd
Indian School Blvd.
State Fair-grounds
Central Ave.
Gibson Blvd.
Kirtland AFB
Albuquerque Int'l Airport
Carlisle Blvd.
Girard Blvd.
Yale Blvd.
Univ. of New Mexico
University Blvd.
Edith Blvd
4th St
Broadway
DOWNTOWN
OLD TOWN
Osuna Rd
Montano Rd
Rio Grande Blvd
Rio Grande
Coors Rd
Bridge Blvd
25
40
N

and you'll be at the entrance of the **Albuquerque Museum**, *Tel. 243-7255.* Housed in an ultra-modern building that contrasts sharply with the surrounding area (the museum is one of the few solar-heated museums in the country), the entry plaza has several unusual western sculptures that are worth taking a look at. Then pick up a self-guiding brochure upon entering.

The museum contains extensive exhibits on art, history, and science, with the emphasis on the Rio Grande Valley. The huge central display portrays four centuries of life in the valley. A gallery on the Spanish era contains America's largest collection of Spanish Colonial artifacts. *The museum is open from 9:00am until 5:00pm Tuesday through Sunday. Closed on legal holidays. Admission is free but donations are greatly appreciated. Free Old Town walking tours are offered from the middle of April through the middle of November at 11:00am on days that the museum is open.*

One block further east on Mountain Road is the equally modernistic **New Mexico Museum of Natural History**, *Tel. 841-8837.* Unlike many museums of this type which can be rather staid and unexciting, this museum involves the visitor from the moment you enter. I have found it to be one of the most enjoyable natural history museums anywhere. The exhibits follow a sequential 12 billion-year journey depicting the natural development of New Mexico from the beginning of the universe until the present day. Quite a task. It does so through such exhibits as life-size models of dinosaurs, a cave from the ice age, and even a volcano that visitors can walk through. A "time machine" called an Evolator takes you on a journey back in time where, of course, something goes wrong and you have to escape from an encounter with powerful beasts. I'm happy to report that everyone returns safely.

Another excellent feature is a large living forest and 3,000 gallon aquarium with sharks. Sharks in New Mexico? Yes, it was a tropical environment 75 million years ago. Among other diversions in the museum are the Dynamax Theater (films on natural history topics), a cafe, special areas for children to discover natural history, and an excellent museum shop. *Open daily from 9:00am until 5:00pm. Admission is $4, those aged 3-11, over age 59 or students with ID are admitted for $3. Additional charge for Dynamax Theater (45 minute shows) is $4 with same discount provisions. Combination tickets are $7 and $5, respectively.*

If you are traveling with children, you might be interested in adding one more museum to this collection. The **Albuquerque Children's Museum**, *Tel. 842-1537* (also at the Rio Grande Boulevard/Mountain Road intersection) has, among other things, a bubble play area and puppet theater. Children older than eight will not be much amused.

If you have some additional time there are a couple of other small but very unusual museums located a couple of blocks south of the Plaza. The first is the **Turquoise Museum**, *2107 Central Avenue, off of Rio Grande Boulevard, Tel. 247-8650.* It has interesting displays about the common mineral and hundreds of specimens from around the world. There's also a replica of a turquoise mine tunnel. People who plan to buy turquoise (a popular souvenir in New Mexico) may do well to come to this museum to view the education area which tells you how to properly select turquoise. *The museum is open daily from 9:00am to 5:00pm and from noon on Sunday, except on New Year's, Thanksgiving and Christmas. Admission is $2 for adults, and $1.50 for children and senior citizens.*

A few blocks away is the **American International Rattlesnake Museum**, *202 San Felipe, a block below South Plaza at the corner of Old Town Road, Tel. 242-6569.* Well, if you can have a museum devoted to turquoise, why not one for rattlesnakes? The museum is dedicated to the conservation of our slithery friends and the collection houses more species of rattlesnakes than the ten largest zoos in America combined. That's a lot of snakes. The snakes are displayed in carefully constructed natural habitats. The exhibits are quite interesting and you may be surprised at the variety of the species and in some cases, their beauty. *The museum is open daily from 10:00am to 5:00pm and charges $2 for adults and $1 for children.*

Tour 2: Downtown & The Rio Grande Zoological Park

Approximate duration including sightseeing time is 3 1/2 hours. Begin at the Civic Plaza, four blocks north of Central Avenue between 3rd and 4th Streets.

The central business district of Albuquerque has a small but modern skyline. There isn't a great deal to see in the heart of downtown which may strike some visitors as kind of unusual for a city of Albuquerque's size. One reason is that downtown is relatively new. There isn't nearly as much history here as in Old Town. However, the large **Civic Plaza** is bounded by a number of buildings that are at least worth taking a brief look at. These include the City Hall, Convention Center, Court House, and Main Library, all of which flank the Plaza. As the Plaza itself is a broad open space, it also is a good place to get a view of the Albuquerque skyline, such as it is.

The Albuquerque **visitors' bureau**, *121 Tijeras Street, runs along the south side of the Plaza.* The new **Explora Science Center**, *at the intersection of 2nd Street and Martin Luther King NW (in the First Plaza/Galeria), Tel. 842-6188,* contains hands-on and interactive exhibits designed to stimulate scientific interest in youngsters. However, many of the exhibits will also appeal to adults.

Two other places of interest in the vicinity are the **Telephone Pioneers of America Museum**, *Tel. 245-5883*, and the **Madonna of the Trail Monument**. The former has interesting exhibits about the history of the telephone. An 1876 telephone is on display and so are fiber optic cables. The monument, four blocks north of the Plaza on 4th Street, is both religious and historical art. It represents the faith of the early settlers. *The museum is located at 201 3rd Street and is open from Monday to Friday from 10:00am until 5:00pm. It is closed on major holidays and offers free admission.*

ALBUQUERQUE'S BALLOON FIESTA

Since this is a short-term annual event (as is the State Fair), I'll tell you about it in a sidebar because it doesn't fit into any of the tours. Great things just can't be forced to conform to neat categories.

Although hot air balloons have been around for a couple of centuries, their popularity has seen explosive growth in the past two decades. There are hundreds of mass balloon ascensions all over the world. If you've been to any you know they're colorful, fun, and exciting. But none, absolutely none, can possibly compare with the world's biggest and best – the ***Kodak Albuquerque International Balloon Fiesta*** *as it's officially known. Locals simply call it "The Big One," a name that has been trademarked. Ideal weather conditions in the valley have helped make the Fiesta a perennial success.*

Spanning a nine day period in October at the ***Balloon Fiesta Park*** *which was built specifically for this event, the Fiesta has become increasingly popular. It will soon attract a million visitors a year. More than 600 balloons now participate. It isn't just the number which dwarfs other balloon events (a hundred or so is considered to be a sizable mass ascension). The Fiesta attracts the world's most famous and unusual balloons which come in a variety of sizes and colors, not to mention unusual shapes such as shoes, elephants, houses, or just about anything else that you could imagine.*

The mass ascensions usually begin around 7:00am, but most people begin arriving as early as 5:00am to wander around the balloons as they are stretched out on the ground and are slowly filled with hot air and come to life before lifting off. In fact, many balloon crews often look for volunteers among the early arrivals to help get things ready. Some are even invited to come along for the ride. But whether you participate isn't important. The Fiesta is an unforgettable event even for those who just come to watch the color and spectacle or to go from one food booth or souvenir stand to another sampling the tasty delights and goods for sale.

To get to Balloon Fiesta Park take I-25 north to either Exit 231 (Paseo del Norte) or 233 (Alameda Blvd.). The Park is located about 3/4 of a mile west of the highway. There is a fee for parking and traffic can be murderous. The Fiesta also runs shuttle bus service from various downtown locations. Call ***1/800-733-9918*** *for exact dates, ascension schedules (including one that usually occurs at sunset rather than in the morning), and transportation alternatives.*

From downtown you can make your way by car or city bus (or foot if you're ambitious) along Central Avenue until reaching 10th Street. Then turn left until you reach Iron Avenue and the entrance of the **Rio Grande Zoological Park**, *Tel. 843-7413*, on the banks of the river. This is the highlight of Tour 2 in terms of probable enjoyment and amount of time. The zoo is thoroughly modern. It doesn't have any cages – rather, animals are housed in outdoor habitats that roughly approximate their native surroundings.

It's a good size zoo, having more than 1,300 animals representing about 300 different species. The zoo is noted for its in-house breeding program. It's been successful enough that they haven't had to "import" any animals. Endangered species are given special attention. The animals cover a broad geographic spectrum, ranging from Africa to the prairie of New Mexico. Bird shows are offered in the summer. *The zoo is open daily from 9:00am until 5:00pm throughout the year. On weekends from June through August the zoo remains open till 6:00pm. It is closed on New Year's Day, Thanksgiving and Christmas. Admission is $4.50 but senior citizens and children aged 3 to 15 pay only $2.50.*

Tour 3: The Northwest Quadrant

Approximate duration including sightseeing is 4 hours. Begin at the Indian Pueblo Cultural Center, 2401 12th Street NW.

It's time to get into your car since bus service conveniently reaches only the first few sights on this particular tour. If coming from downtown, you can reach the first point of interest by heading north on 12th Street. Otherwise, use I-40 and take Exit 158, which is 12th Street. A block north of the exit is the **Indian Pueblo Cultural Center**, *Tel. 843-7270*. Primarily a museum, the center is designed to educate visitors about the 19 different Indian pueblos throughout New Mexico. Both the history and culture of the pueblos are featured, a big task considering that the displays cover about 18,000 years of Pueblo development. Among the exhibits are a humorous look at the typical Pueblo tourist – maybe you'll see yourself and get a good laugh. An impressive circular gallery features exhibits on each individual pueblo.

The Center, which houses numerous special events throughout the year, also has one of the finest Native American gift shops to be found anywhere. You can find anything from the cheapest souvenirs to true works of art costing in the thousands. A reasonably priced restaurant is also on the premises and features Indian foods.

If you can time your visit for a weekend you're especially lucky, for authentic Indian dances are performed. This colorful spectacle is enjoyed by visitors of all ages. Exact times for the dances are posted. Native arts and crafts are also demonstrated at regular intervals on weekends. *The*

Cultural Center, 2401 12th Street NW, is open daily from 9:00am until 5:30pm. It is closed only on New Year's Day, Thanksgiving and Christmas. Admission is $3, but students with identification and seniors pay only $2.

If shopping is on your mind, you're in luck. Perhaps the single best place to shop for Southwestern goods in Albuquerque is located next to the Indian Pueblo Cultural Center. The **Indoor Mercado**, *12th Street at I-40*, has more than 200 merchants selling arts and crafts, jewelry, clothing, paintings, ceramics and more in a colorful flea market atmosphere. There's also a food court that's a great place for a quick lunch. *The market is, unfortunately, only open on weekends (Friday from noon to 6:00pm and Saturday and Sunday from 10:00am to 6:00pm).* But that's okay, in a way, since that's also the best time to be at the Indian Pueblo Cultural Center. There's no admission charge.

Upon leaving the area of the Cultural Center, continue north on 12th Street for about a mile to Candelaria Road. Turn left and follow that street until it reaches its end at the **Rio Grande Nature Center State Park**, *Tel. 344-7240*. This interesting park has two main areas. First, an indoor visitor center with numerous displays on local flora and fauna as well as the various life zones of the nearby Sandia Mountains. You can get brochures at the visitor center that will enhance your enjoyment of the second part of your visit. Two nature trails, each approximately a mile in length, wind their way through the natural environment of the riverbank. While a number of small animals inhabit the park, you won't be very likely to see them during the daytime. However, there's a much better chance of spotting one or more of the hundreds of bird species that make the park their home for at least a portion of the year. *The State Park is open every day of the year except Thanksgiving and Christmas from 10:00am to 5:00pm. Admission is $1 for adults and 50 cents for children 17 and under.*

Not far from the park is the **Anderson Valley Vineyards**, *4920 Rio Grande Blvd., Tel. 344-7266*. Take Candelaria back about a mile to Rio Grande Boulevard. Turn left and you'll reach the Vineyards in just over another mile. Visitors are given a complete tour which describes the winemaking process and are offered tastes of five different wines. You can also visit a grape arbor. *The vineyards are open Tuesday through Sunday from 12:00 noon to 5:30pm. However, tours are given only on the hour from 1:00 until 4:00. Closed major holidays. Tours are free of charge but there is a $1 fee for tasting.*

The final stop on this tour is on the west bank of the Rio Grande. It's not far but is a little tricky to find. Continue north for a short distance on Rio Grande until the Paseo del Norte. A left turn will take you across a bridge spanning the river. Make the first left (North Coors Boulevard) and follow that road for about 2 1/2 miles, turning right on Montana Road. Then turn right again on Unser and proceed to the **Indian Petroglyphs**

National Monument, *Tel. 839-4429*. Here you'll find many examples of ancient Indian paintings on the rocks. Short trails, all involving at least some steps, lead from several parking areas past the rock drawings. A lot of them are in poor condition and require careful observation to see. Others, however, are still quite vivid and will get you in the mood for some amateur archaeology and anthropology as you try to figure out the meanings of the inscriptions. The area was subjected to a lot of vandalism prior to becoming a national monument and, unfortunately, some hooligans still think that their modern graffiti belongs in the same class as the petroglyphs. *The monument is open every day during daylight hours and is free of charge.*

Getting back to Albuquerque is a lot easier. Head back the other way on Unser Boulevard until it runs into Coors Blvd. The latter intersects I-40 and you can make your way back into town from there.

Tour 4: Eastern Albuquerque

Approximate duration including sightseeing is 5 hours. Begin at the National Atomic Museum at Kirtland Air Force Base.

My final in-city tour covers the biggest geographic portion of the city. The attractions, however, are in relative proximity to one another once you begin. The easiest way to get there is to take I-40 eastbound to Wyoming Boulevard (Exit 164B) and drive south to the entrance of Kirtland Air Force Base. You'll be greeted by a friendly guard who will issue you a special pass that allows you to drive on the base and be directed to the large building housing the **National Atomic Museum**, *Tel. 845-6670*. The facility documents the development of atomic weapons. Oh, I know, some of you are going to say "I don't want to see anything having to do with nuclear weapons or war." My simple answer is to get real. It's a part of history. You're sure to learn something at this very informative museum which doesn't, in any way, glorify nuclear weapons technology.

Among the many items on display are an original hydrogen bomb. An outside exhibition area displays several fighter aircraft and bombers. Other exhibits feature peaceful uses of atomic energy. If you have extra time (not included in the Tour 4 estimate), a 53-minute film entitled "Ten Seconds That Shook The World" is shown four times daily and is an excellent documentary on the Manhattan Project. *The museum is open daily from 9:00am until 5:00pm except for New Year's Day, Easter, Thanksgiving and Christmas. Admission is free. You must have proper identification to be admitted to Kirtland Air Force Base.*

After leaving the base, go back up Wyoming Boulevard and turn left on Zuni Road. This turns into Lead Avenue, which you should stay on until you get to Girard Blvd., a total distance of a little more than two miles. A left on Girard will soon bring you to the **Ernie Pyle Home**, *Tel. 256-2065*. Mr. Pyle was a noted World War II correspondent and his home is filled with hundreds of items from his career. Perhaps of most significance to veterans, the house makes an interesting, if brief, stop. Then retrace your route to Lead Avenue but turn left. In a few blocks you'll reach the next attraction on this tour.

The **Spanish History Museum**, *Tel. 268-9981,* is in close proximity to the University of New Mexico's campus, but is not affiliated with the many different museums located there. The museum is the creation of one man's lifetime devotion to collecting items that reflect the importance of Spain's contribution to New Mexico, the Southwest, and the entire United States. Mr. Elmer Martinez has done a fine job. Although the museum is not large, it contains a fascinating collection, including many Spanish contributions that most Americans are not aware of. For instance, did you know that our famous dollar sign was actually a symbol for the peso? Got'ya, huh? If you're of Spanish ancestry you can probably trace the roots and heraldic emblem of your ancestors. A popular exhibit depicts Columbus' arrival in the new world. *The museum's hours are generally from 1:00pm until 5:00pm every day except Thanksgiving and Christmas. However, as this is a small family operation they are subject to change. Admission is $1 but free for children age 12 and under.*

Now take a ride (or walk) several blocks to the north (one block north of Central Avenue) where you'll find the **University of New Mexico**. Parking lots are generally restricted to faculty or students so use the ample metered parking at the west end of the campus off of Redondo Drive. The largest institution of higher education in the state and one of Albuquerque's biggest employers, the 640 acre campus is very attractive, featuring a number of buildings done in the modern Pueblo style. A stroll around the campus provides a relaxing break from sightseeing. Information on various buildings is available at the visitor information office at Las Lomas Road in the northwestern corner of the campus. There's also metered parking available there.

A picturesque portion of the campus is the large duck pond. However, most visitors come to the University to see one or more of the many fine museums. The museums include the **Art Museum of New Mexico**, *Tel. 277-4001,* which features 19th and 20th century paintings, especially those with a Southwestern emphasis; the **Geology Museum**, *Tel. 277-4204,* in Northrup Hall has almost two dozen exhibits on various aspects of earth sciences (one of the best of its type in the country); and the **Jonson Gallery**, *Tel. 277-4967,* of modern painting. Two lesser known but interesting museums are the **Meteroric Institute**, *Tel. 277-2747,* and the **Museum of Southwestern Biology**, *Tel. 845-6670*. Besides the well-known

Art and Geology Museums, the best of the bunch is the **Maxwell Museum of Anthropology**, *Tel. 277-4404*. While cultural anthropology from around the world is to be found in the many exhibits, the museum highlights the Southwestern tradition, especially of the Anasazi and their descendants. The single most interesting feature is the "People of the Southwest" exhibit, which has been designed to look like a real archaeological dig site.

Museum hours are from Tuesday to Friday 9:00am to 4:00pm and Sundays from 1:00pm to 4:00pm. The Maxwell Museum is also open on Saturdays from 10:00am to 4:00pm. All museums are closed on holidays. Admission to most of the museums is free but donations are requested at the Geology and Maxwell Museums as well as at the Jonson Gallery and Meteoritic Institute.

You can use Lomas Boulevard on the north side of the campus to return to downtown Albuquerque or for access to the Interstates.

THE NEW MEXICO STATE FAIR

This is another Albuquerque mega-event. It takes place each year for two weeks in the middle of September at the ***State Fair Grounds****. It is one of the largest and most colorful state fairs in the United States, attracting about a million people each year.*

Beginning, as did most state fairs, as an agricultural and livestock trade show, you'll still find plenty of those types of exhibits. There are even livestock competitions that you can attend or you can see small farm animals with their little offspring. This being New Mexico, there is a strong Native American presence at the Fair which has especially good Indian arts and crafts exhibits. There's a major rodeo, a huge midway carnival featuring more than 100 concessionaires and rides ranging from tame to a wild roller coaster, and nightly concerts featuring country-western and other artists (many of which are nationally famous). Thoroughbred and quarterhorse racing is also a part of the Fair's agenda at the Albuquerque Downs.

It seems that a favorite activity for a lot of Fair visitors is just to eat. If that's what you're looking for you certainly won't be disappointed. Dozens of booths feature Southwestern cuisine and just about everything else. It's all very informal and finger-lickin' visitors can be seen strolling through the Fair Grounds.

The Fair Grounds can be reached by taking I-40 to Louisiana Boulevard (Exit 162). Go south about a half mile to the main parking gates located on Louisiana. Admission varies depending upon the day and time. Additional fees are charged for rides, some attractions, concerts and the rodeo. There's also a parking fee. Call ***265-1791*** *for schedules and information.*

NIGHTLIFE & ENTERTAINMENT

Performing Arts

- **Albuquerque Civic Light Opera Association**, *4201 Ellison NE. Tel. 345-6577.* Broadway musicals are presented during March, June, July, September, and December.
- **New Mexico Symphony Orchestra**, *3301 Menaul Boulevard SE. Tel. 881-8999.*
- **Popejoy Hall**, *University Fine Arts Center, Tel. 277-3824.* Features both national and local companies performing musical and dramatic works.

Out on the Town

As nightlife hot-spots in cities tend to change rather frequently, it's always a good idea to look at current visitor publications to see what's new. Almost all of the larger hotels have lounges with entertainment. However, among the local populace, the most popular places to burn the midnight oil in town are:

DAQZ BAR & GRILL, *406 Central Avenue SW. Tel. 244-9220.*

The large two-level bar features ten automatic daiquiri machines downstairs. Isn't that just what the world needed! There's also a live disc jockey. The upstairs room has pool tables and boasts more than 130 different beers to choose from.

LAFFS COMEDY CLUB, *3100-D Juan Tabo Boulevard NE. Tel. 296-JOKE.*

Revolving comedians, some of whom may be nationally known. Like all comedy clubs, how good a time you have depends on who is appearing. Some are really funny while others will bring out a good yawn. Full service restaurant on the premises.

MIDNIGHT RODEO, *4901 McLeod NE. Tel. 888-0100.*

The theme here is strictly country and western and is one of the most popular places in town for dancing. Midnight Rodeo even offers free lessons. Sorry, guys, you won't have the excuse that "I can't dance" to keep you away from this one. They also have a very low priced buffet, sometimes with real good roast beef.

THE ZONE NIGHTCLUB/Z-PUB, *120 Central Avenue SW. Tel. 343-7933.*

This large and very popular place consists of two adjacent entertainment centers. The larger and noisier Zone Nightclub is reminiscent of a New York disco. With four different bars, each located on a separate level, patrons can almost always easily find a musical format to their liking. It's kind of gaudy and attracts a generally young crowd, but might well be the liveliest spot in town.

The Z-Pub is a quieter and more sophisticated atmosphere centered around a horseshoe-shaped bar. The clientele consists more of business people. At the Z-Pub you can dine from a full menu, although the food is only so-so.

SPORTS & RECREATION

Amusement Parks

- **Beach Waterpark**, *1600 Desert Surf Loop, Tel. 345-6066*
- **Cliff's Amusement Park** (formerly Famtastic A-Maz-Ing Family Fun Center, *Osuna Road, Tel. 881-9373*
- **Planet Fun**, *2266 Wyoming Blvd., Tel. 294-1099*

Bicycling

If you bring your own bike with you and want to join with other riders, contact the **Albuquerque Wheelmen**, *Tel. 291-9835*. If not, try **Old Town Bicycles**, *2200 Old Town Road. Tel. 247-4926.*

Golf

- **Arroyo del Oso Golf Course**, *Osuna Road, Tel. 884-7505*
- **Championship Golf Course**, *at the University of New Mexico, University Blvd., Tel. 277-4546*
- **Ladera Golf Course**, *3401 Ladera Drive NW, Tel. 836-4449*
- **Paradise Hills Golf Club**, *10035 Country Club Lane NW, Tel. 898-7001*
- **Puerto del Sol Golf Course**, *1800 Girard SE, Tel. 265-5636*
- **Rio Rancho Country Club**, *500 Country Club Drive, Rio Rancho (just west of Albuquerque), Tel. 892-8440*
- **Tanoan Country Club**, *10801 Academy Road NE, Tel. 822-0433*

Horseback Riding

- **Sandia Trails Horse Rentals**, *10601 N. 4th Street. Tel. 898-6970.*
- **Turkey Track Stables**, *1306 US 66 East Tijeras. Tel. 281-1772.*

Horse Racing

- **The Downs At Albuquerque**, *New Mexico State Fairgrounds, Tel. 262-1188*. Seasons are January to April and September to October.

Hot Air Ballooning

- **Balloon Rides-Hot Alternatives**, *8400 Menaul NE. Tel. 1/800-322-2262.* Year-round.
- **Hot Air Extraord-in-air**, *3416B Constitution NE. Tel. 266-9744.* Year-round.
- **Rocky Mountain Tours**, *Tel. 1/800-231-7238.* Dawn departures all year

round; sunset departures October through April (weather conditions permitting)
- **World Balloon Corporation**, *4800 Eubank NE. Tel. 1/800-351-9588.* Year-round.

Skiing
- **Sandia Peak**, *Tel. 242-9133.* Season is mid-December to mid-March.

Spectator Sports

Not a "big league" town by any means, Albuquerque's most important spectator sports are provided by the full intercollegiate athletic program of the **University of New Mexico**. The "Lobos" football and basketball teams are part of the Western Athletic Conference and are only a small notch beneath the very highest quality in college sports. The football stadium and basketball arena (affectionately called "The Pit") are both on the UNM campus. *Schedules and other information is available for all UNM sports by calling Tel. 277-4569 or 277-2116. To purchase tickets by phone, call 851-5050.*

The **Dukes** of the Pacific Coast League provide high-level minor league baseball action. They're a farm club of the Los Angeles Dodgers and their field is located at the corner of Stadium and University. The season runs from early April through late September. *For information, call 243-1791.*

EXCURSIONS & DAY TRIPS

Several major attractions are located very close to the city and should be made part of any visit to Albuquerque itself. A car is nearly essential for most of them, although the Sandia Peak tram can be reached by Sun-Trans bus. Also, Gray Line has a number of Albuquerque tour options which include most of the attractions on these excursions. For information, inquire at your hotel or call **Gray Line of Albuquerque**, *Tel. 1/800-256-8991*. I have developed three separate excursions, with the first being the "must" for most visitors.

Sandia Peak & Coronado Monument

This excursion covers only about 40 miles round trip from downtown Albuquerque and can be done in a half a day, although longer can be taken if you plan to do a lot of walking or hiking on top of Sandia Peak. More about that later. Take I-25 north to Tramway Road (Exit 243), and follow the road to the right until you reach the base station. Visitors coming from the western part of Albuquerque can take I-40 to Tramway Boulevard (Exit 167) and proceed north.

The **Sandia Peak Tramway**, *Tel. 856-6419,* is 2.7 miles long and is one of the world's longest. Some say it is the longest – the experts can never agree on these things. In any event, the 18-minute ascent is a breathtaking experience as you climb in altitude over 3,800 feet from the base station to the summit terminal in one of two 55-passenger cars. You'll have a brilliant view of Albuquerque and its suburbs in the distance. More spectacular are the contrast between the flat valley and the towering peaks that surround it. At times it seems you can almost touch the clouds that frequently roll in at the top, but clear skies and sunshine are almost sure to be in order for a good portion of your adventure. Take note of the narrow and deep canyons and rock crevices as you travel up or down the mountain. You'll pass through several climatic zones and notice changes in the terrain's flora.

At the top there are miles of trails ranging from nearly flat and easy to very strenuous, both for hiking and biking. Winter visitors, besides the usual great views, get to see the snowcapped mountains in all their glory. There's also great skiing at Sandia and you can ride the ski-lift into a depression on the east side of the mountain. This is also open in the summer on weekends. Of course, there's a summit restaurant for those who want to dine on a higher level. Pardon my pun – on a more serious note, the view at night with the lights of Albuquerque and the stars both twinkling also makes for a memorable visit.

The tramway operates from 9:00am until 10:00pm from Memorial Day through Labor Day and on a more limited schedule at other times. If traveling at those times of the year call the Tramway for information. The round-trip fare (you can walk one way if you like) is $12.50 but there's a reduction in rate if you eat at the summit restaurant. For an additional $4 you can ride the chairlift. Parking is $1. Most major credit cards are accepted.

Upon returning to the lower world and taking a last glance at the new arrivals making their way towards the top of Sandia Peak, head back to I-25 and proceed north to the town of **Bernalillo** at Exit 242. An old town that predates the refounding of Albuquerque, Bernalillo is today still a farming community but is slowly being transformed into a bedroom community for Albuquerque. Two miles northwest of town via NM 44 is the **Coronado State Monument**, *Tel. 867-5351.* This is the site of the ruins of the Kuaua Pueblo. The name of the monument is derived from the fact that the Spanish explorer Coronado visited the area in 1540 when the pueblo was thriving.

There's an interesting visitor center that depicts pueblo life in the 16th century as well as documenting the Coronado expedition. Some original Spanish body armor is on display. Most of the pueblo is in ruins, making it less impressive than many other New Mexico pueblos, but interesting nonetheless. The kiva (the round ceremonial chamber) has been partially restored and you can explore the interior.

The Monument is open every day from 9:00am until 6:00pm, but opens and closes an hour earlier from the middle of September through April. It's closed on New Year's, Easter, Thanksgiving and Christmas. Admission is $2 for those aged 18 and above.

When you've completed your own expedition at Coronado State Monument, you can make the quick and easy return to Albuquerque by going back to I-25 and heading south.

San Agustin de Isleta

This short excursion can be done in a few hours. Located about 16 miles south of Albuquerque via I-25 (use Exit 209), the **Mission of San Agustin de Isleta**, *Tel. 869-3398,* is on the Isleta Pueblo. The original church was built in 1613 but was partially destroyed during the 1680 Pueblo Rebellion. It was rebuilt shortly after the reconquest in 1692 and has been in constant use as a church from then until the present day. It is still the centerpiece of the pueblo, whose market square and small adobe structures surround the high walls of the church. The interior of the church has several paintings of Catholic saints.

Church open daily from 9:00am until 6:00pm. There is no admission. The Isleta pueblo, except for the casino, restricts visitation. Inquire locally.

The Turquoise Trail

This is the longest of the Albuquerque excursions. It covers about 110 miles and about 25 more than that if you add the optional detour up to the **Sandia Crest**. You should allow at least a half day but a full day would be better, especially if you're going to be driving up to the Crest. This trip combines history and scenery and will take you into the "real" New Mexico, even though you're only a short drive from cosmopolitan Albuquerque.

Leave Albuquerque via I-40 eastbound. Use Exit 175 at the quaint little town of Tijeras. **NM 14** is known as the **Turquoise Trail** because it connects a number of small former mining towns where turquoise was found. One of them was once owned by the world famous Tiffany Jewelers. NM 14 is a scenic road on the eastern slope of the Sangre de Cristo mountains. It follows more or less the same route as I-25 and goes all the way to Santa Fe. (You could also make a Turquoise Trail excursion from Santa Fe instead of Albuquerque but it would be a little longer.)

Upon departing the Interstate, take NM 14 north for six miles to NM 536. Then head west for about a mile-and-a-half to the interesting **Tinkertown Museum**, *Tel. 281-5233.* You know this is an unusual place when you see the fence surrounding the museum – it's constructed of 46,000 glass bottles cemented together! The museum itself has a miniature western town. All of the items – the buildings, a circus, vehicles, and the town's people – are hand carved from wood.

The museum is open daily from April through October. The hours are 9:00am to 6:00pm. Adult admission is $2.50; senior citizens get in for $2 and children ages 4 through 16 for $1.

You now have the decision whether to go back to NM 14 and continue on the Turquoise Trail, or stay on NM 536 for an 11-mile section known as the **Sandia Crest Road Scenic Byway**. The road is paved and is open in all weather. It has some steep grades and sharp turns but isn't particularly difficult for anyone with some experience in driving on mountain roads. An observation deck at the crest provides a spectacular view that encompasses almost 15,000 square miles. The view from the top of the Sandia Peak Tramway has been measured at 11,000 square miles. If you're at all hesitant about the road, and especially if you've been up to Sandia Peak or are pressed for time, then you can opt to skip this portion.

Continuing on the Turquoise Trail, NM 14 passes through the tiny hillside town of San Antonito before arriving in **Golden**. Gold was discovered here in 1825. Silver, however, proved to be the most abundant ore, and the Cash and Carry Mine once employed 1,300 people. A church from the mining hey-day remains. Another 12 miles up the road comes the town of **Madrid**. During the late 19th century, Madrid was a major coal mining center. By the 1930s, the glory years were over and the town went into decline. By the 1970s, it was a virtual ghost town but its fortunes reversed when a lot of artists began moving here.

Today, many of the modest miners' shacks are either art studios or boutiques or gift shops for the many tourists who travel the Turquoise Trail. There's even a chamber music series on summer Sundays. Locals and visitors alike enjoy hanging out at the **Mine Shaft Tavern**.

A few miles further on is the town of **Cerillos**. It was in this area that most of the turquoise mining was done. The small and quiet village is like paying a visit back in time. There aren't any paved streets, but there are plenty of interesting shops featuring antiques and just about everything else. There's even an authentic old-fashioned general store.

Make your way back to Albuquerque in one of two ways. You can simply follow the reverse route or you can continue north on NM 14 from Cerillos to the intersection of I-25 and head south. The latter adds about 20 miles to your trip but will probably take about the same amount of time.

PRACTICAL INFORMATION

- **Tourist Office/Visitors Bureau**: *121 Tijeras Street, Tel. 243-3696 or 1/800-284-2282*
- **Airport**: *Tel. 842-7030*
- **Airport Transportation**: *Tel. 765-1234 or 751-1201*
- **Bus Depot**: *Tel. 242-4998.*
- **Train Station**: *Tel. 842-9650*
- **Municipal Transit Information**: *SunTran, Tel. 843-9200*
- **Taxi**: *Checker Cab, Tel. 243-7777; Yellow Cab, Tel. 247-8888*
- **Hotel Hot Line**: *Tel. 1/800-473-1000*
- **Hospital**: *University and eastern sections, Tel. 843-2111; Downtown/Old Town, Tel. 841-1234*
- **Police** (non-emergency): *Tel. 768-1986*

14. SANTA FE & LOS ALAMOS

When **Santa Fe** was founded in 1610, it was given a lengthy name. The Royal City of the Holy Faith of St. Francis of Assisi has, fortunately, become less of a mouthful to handle. In some ways it's one of the few things that has changed in almost 400 years. And that, as much as anything else, is what makes Santa Fe so special. New Mexico's premier visitor destination is a world-class tourism city despite having a small population.

Filled with history no matter what narrow and crooked street you wander down, New Mexico's capital is also the picture-perfect blend of the Native, Hispanic, and Anglo cultures of the Southwest. It's a haven for shoppers looking for Indian crafts or the art connoisseur looking for a masterpiece to grace his or her home. Even the architecture is special. Almost everything is in the pueblo style, whether it is a building from the city's earliest days or a new office building. There are a couple of reasons for that beyond the desire of residents to keep Santa Fe's visual harmony. First, pueblo construction has proved to be extremely durable. Very few of Santa Fe's oldest buildings "look their age." Second, despite all of the advances made in almost every aspect of technology, modern architecture has failed to produce a structure that is much more energy efficient than what was achieved by the Pueblos so many centuries ago.

The treasures to be found during a visit to Santa Fe are almost unlimited. But it doesn't stop within the town. Santa Fe, nestled in the magnificent **Sangre de Cristo Mountains**, is located in one of the most scenic areas of New Mexico. You're only minutes away from peaceful streams, dense forests, and vast panoramas of rugged mountains.

With so much to offer in such a small area, it's no wonder that Santa Fe has awarded itself the unusual nickname of the *City Different*. Its history, people, culture, and appearance are like no other city in America or, for that matter, the whole world. Some people don't think that City Different is an "enchanting" enough name for the capital of the Land of Enchantment. They like to use a more exotic sounding reference for Santa Fe, such as the Camelot of the Southwest or something like that. But no matter what you call it upon your arrival, by the end of your trip you'll end up calling it a most wonderful place to visit.

Los Alamos, even smaller than Santa Fe, is nestled in a similarly beautiful setting. The very rural area was almost unknown until the 1940s when Los Alamos was put on the map by the **Manhattan Project**, which was placed there largely because of its prior anonymity. It would actually be more correct to say that it was unknown to most of the outside world until the late 1950s when the "secret town" was declassified. The once quiet community is now a bustling town that, despite its economic dependence on high tech research and development, is still very much a part of the slower paced life-style that is so important in New Mexico.

The people of Los Alamos don't attach any stigma to atomic energy. They still fondly call their home *The Atomic City* and proudly sell T-shirts advertising that name. All of this is with good reason, since the **Los Alamos National Laboratory** is the major employer for the city of 20,000 and the surrounding communities. Both Santa Fe and Los Alamos can serve as a base for several fascinating excursions into the natural wonders of the region.

SANTA FE

ARRIVALS & DEPARTURES

If you're arriving by bus (either Greyhound or Amtrak shuttle bus from the nearest station in Lamy), the terminal is downtown just a few blocks from the central Plaza.

The airport, served by **Mesa Air**, *Tel. 1/800-MESA-AIR*, is a few miles southwest and you can catch a cab into town.

Most of you, however, are almost certain to arrive by car. I-25 doesn't enter the city itself but comes real close. Coming from Albuquerque it's only a 60-mile drive and will take about an hour. You can use Exit 278 (which is NM 14) for access into town. This highway becomes Cerrillos Road and ends in the heart of the city. Exit 282 (St. Francis Drive) can also be used to get into downtown. If you are arriving in Santa Fe from the north, take Exit 284 (Old Santa Fe Drive). The latter two exits are within a couple of minutes drive from downtown and even the Cerrillos Road route doesn't take much longer.

ORIENTATION

Because of the narrow streets and tourist congestion you should, whenever possible, leave your car at your hotel or motel and get around by foot. Most of Santa Fe's attractions are within a relatively small area, bounded by the Paseo de Peralta on the north and east, the Alameda (which runs along the Santa Fe River) on the south, and North Guadalupe Street on the west. Other important areas lie to the south of the river but are also easily managed on foot. I'll let you know when a car is needed to get to some of the more outlying attractions.

GETTING AROUND TOWN

If you must drive into downtown, leave your car in one of several public parking areas as you simply won't find on-street parking, especially during the summer. There are no fewer than ten large parking areas within several blocks of the Plaza. Rather then listing them it is easier just to follow the signs, because trying to negotiate the confusing maze of winding streets of Santa Fe in a car is another reason to use your legs.

If you tire of walking, Santa Fe does have a municipal bus system called **Santa Fe Trails**. One of six routes can get you within reasonable distance of any sight within the city. It doesn't operate on Sunday. Route and schedule information is available at visitor centers and libraries as well as on each bus. If you want bus information or a taxi, some helpful numbers are provided below in the *Practical Information* section for Santa Fe.

Friendly and helpful staff are available at two **visitor information centers** to assist you with questions and problems. One is located adjacent to the Sweeney Convention Center, four blocks northwest of the Plaza at Grant Avenue and West Marcy, *Tel. 984-6760*. The other is on the south side on the Old Santa Fe Trail near San Miguel Mission and the State Capitol.

WHERE TO STAY

WITHIN SANTA FE

Very Expensive

THE BISHOP'S LODGE, *Bishop's Lodge Road. Tel. 983-6377, Fax 989-8739. Rates: $205-255; Deluxe rooms and suites $295-355; MAP Available for about $75 additional per night. 106 Rooms. Major credit cards accepted. Toll-free reservations 1/800-732-2240. Located 3-1/2 miles north of the Plaza via Washington Avenue, which becomes Bishop's Lodge Road.*

So called because it occupies the former estate of frontier Archbishop Jean Baptiste Lamy, the site certainly befits the powerful Bishop. Covering more than a thousand acres at the 7,300-foot level of the beautiful Sangre de Cristos, it was acquired by the Thorpe family in 1918 and has remained under the same family's control since then. Some portions of the property are listed in the National Register of Historic Places (specifically the beautiful gardens and chapel). Built in the traditional adobe pueblo style and arranged in graceful tiers, the secluded valley location is almost worth a trip in itself.

A wide variety of guest rooms is available, ranging from standard to superior deluxe and beyond that to suites. All rooms are furnished in comfortable, colorful, and traditional Southwestern decor. The better rooms and all suites are huge and even have kiva-style fireplaces. Natural wood beam ceilings add to the wonderful warmth that the rooms exude. Many rooms have large private patios. Among the nice touches guests will find at The Bishop's Lodge are plush bathrobes, daily newspapers, in-room safes, and even nightly bed turndown service.

Informal Santa Fe style dining is available at the bright and delightful El Rincon restaurant. The Bishop's Lodge Restaurant is one of the best in New Mexico. Activities at Bishop's Lodge are many and varied. They include a complete spa facility (heated pool, Jacuzzi, saunas, and exercise room as well as massage by appointment only), tennis, skeet and trap shooting, fishing (there's a stocked trout pond on the premises), horseback riding and more. The Bishop's Lodge makes a great place to return to after a busy day of sightseeing and shopping, or as a vacation destination in itself.

Selected as one of my Best Places to Stay (see Chapter 12 for more details).

ELDORADO HOTEL, *309 W. San Francisco Street. Tel. 988-4455, Fax 995-4555. Rates: $209-339. 219 Rooms. Major credit cards accepted. Toll-free reservations 1/800-955-4455. Located 2 blocks west of the Plaza.*

Here's a hotel with an old-world style elegance plus all the modern amenities you could hope for, all located within a short walk of Santa Fe's greatest attractions. The luxury is apparent from the moment you walk through the front door. Constructed in the so-called Pueblo-Revival style of architecture, the Eldorado is generously decorated throughout with beautiful Southwestern works of art, all created by Santa Fe's artisans. Despite the atmosphere of elegance throughout, you won't be put off by any feeling of stuffiness – it's a bright and informal feeling despite the opulence.

The large guest rooms are beautifully decorated in Southwestern style. Plush chairs, flowers and a warm fireplace create a feeling of being home. Here, too, guests are treated to terry cloth robes and nightly turndown service. Personal service is the hallmark of the Eldorado, even in the lowest priced rooms. However, for the ultimate in living like the rich and famous, try one of the hotel's deluxe rooms or suites – they offer private butler service. Only too happy to oblige their guests's every wish, these butlers will press a shirt or run an errand for you. Every Eldorado guest is invited to take advantage of the expert concierge staff.

Among the many facilities of the Eldorado are a beautiful rooftop swimming pool and whirlpool. There's also a well equipped fitness center and sauna. Dining at the Eldorado is also an experience to remember. The Old House restaurant is an elegant gourmet dining establishment which claims to have the largest selection of wine by the glass in all of Santa Fe. For a less formal dining experience, try the relaxing Eldorado Court. The latter has a lively lounge while the former offers a large bar.

INN OF THE ANASAZI, *113 Washington Avenue. Tel. 988-3030, Fax 988-3277. Rates: $230-260. 59 Rooms. Major credit cards accepted. Toll-free reservations 1/800-688-8100. In the Plaza district.*

Ah, the delights of Santa Fe are in no greater evidence than at the centrally located Inn of the Anasazi. Here's a truly unique hotel that seems to have been built to honor the time honored traditions of New Mexico's native cultures while at the same time ensuring the comfort and needs of every guest. Within sight of the Plaza's shops, you see the dark adobe walls of the Inn, with large round wooden beams protruding from the front wall beckoning you to enter through the huge hand-carved front doors.

Inside the atmosphere is true Southwest. The traditional architecture and the Southwestern decor is authentic in every detail. It is like walking into the past, almost a museum collection but too livable to be called that. The interior decoration of public areas has been carefully selected to represent all three of New Mexico's cultural heritages, in the form of paintings, blankets, pottery, or baskets. The gentle sound of running water from a two-floor high indoor waterfall adds the final touch. No, not quite, for I think there's something even more interesting to be found at the Inn – a gorgeous library houses a fine collection of books on Southwestern art, history, and culture. Guests are invited to browse and read in this tranquil environment. You may never want to leave.

All of the guest rooms are furnished with gas-lit kiva-style fireplaces, giant four-poster beds, handwoven Indian rugs in traditional colorful geometric patterns, and fine works of art on the walls. The wood ceilings are also traditional Southwestern style. Even the bathroom toiletries are genuine – organically created from extract of native cedar trees. In fact, the Inn of the Anasazi is dedicated to protecting the environment and recognizes the ancient Indians' understanding of the relationship of man and nature. All rooms have honor bars, coffee makers, and safes.

An excellent dining room called the Anasazi Restaurant is on the premises. The interior resembles a kiva ceremonial chamber and the cuisine reflects both Southwestern and continental influences. Other facilities include an exercise center and cocktail lounge. The Inn's management arranges individualized tours of Santa Fe and sponsors fireside chats in the hotel's "living room" where guests can interact with artists, historians, and archaeologists – all experts in their own field of Southwestern culture.

Selected as one of my Best Places to Stay (see Chapter 12 for more details).

THE INN AT LORETTO, *211 Old Santa Fe Trail. Tel. 988-5531, Fax 984-7988. Rates: $145-175. 137 Rooms. Major credit cards accepted. Toll-free reservations 1/800-727-5531. Located 3 blocks from the Plaza, just north of the river between The Alameda and Water Street.*

Named for the famous Loretto Chapel that is only a few steps away, the Inn at Loretto has won numerous architectural awards for its brilliant and beautiful pueblo design. It's very modern but looks so much like the ancient pueblo of Taos that you would never know it's a hotel at all, save for the small sign outside. The warm reddish brown hue of the terraced structure has come to be a Santa Fe landmark and one that you should definitely see even if you don't stay here.

All of the guest rooms feature a private balcony where you can look out on the excitement of the streets of Santa Fe, in view of many of the best sights. The rooms are extremely attractive, also in the Southwest style, but with a more modern flair than in some of the other traditional hotels. Refrigerators and coffee makers are among the in-room amenities.

The hotel's dining room serves all three meals and features Southwestern cooking. There's also a popular drinking establishment known simply as The Lobby Bar. The hotel's knowledgeable concierge staff can help guests make arrangements for recreational activities and answer questions on Santa Fe's sights and shops.

INN OF THE GOVERNORS, *234 Don Gaspar. Tel. 982-4333, Fax 989-9149. Rates: $159-269, suites $289. 100 Rooms. Major credit cards accepted. Toll-free reservations 1/800-234-4534. From the Plaza, San Francisco Street to Don Gaspar, turn left and go 2 blocks to Alameda.*

Not far from the Palace of the Governors, the builders of this fine hotel took part of that name for their own. And why not – the Inn of the Governors is another great example of traditional Southwestern architecture in both style and substance. In a change from the commonly found adobe, however, this hotel chose the Territorial architectural style that was popular during the late Spanish and early Anglo periods. There's a truly wonderful walled inner courtyard that contains a huge kiva fireplace. I can think of no lovelier setting to sit on colorful patio furniture under umbrellas and shade trees on a warm summers' day. At other times of the year it might be a little chilly to gather round it, so you can partake of the one located inside the hotel's restaurant.

Room accommodations are excellent, consisting of deluxe rooms, some mini-suites, and smaller rooms. They're all bright and cheerful and feature many wonderful touches, such as wrought-iron wall lamps, hand-carved headboards, flower arrangements, woven baskets and hand-stenciled designs in beautiful colors. Larger rooms have wood burning kiva fireplaces and some have balconies. One side of the hotel faces the center of town while the other looks towards the nearby mountains. All rooms also have either a small refrigerator or mini-bar.

The Inn's Mañana Bar and Restaurant has excellent food in an informal atmosphere and the bar has nightly entertainment. Both American and Southwestern cuisine are on the menu and beer lovers can sample a micro-brew. Among the other features of the hotel are a heated outdoor pool, dining al fresco in the courtyard, and a helpful and gracious staff.

LA FONDA, *100 E. San Francisco Street. Tel. 982-5511, Fax 988-2952. Rates: $174-189, suites $200-250. 153 Rooms. Major credit cards accepted. Toll-free reservations 1/800-523-5002. Located on the Plaza.*

Known as the "Inn at the end of the Santa Fe Trail," La Fonda is one of the most remarkable hotels in a city of remarkable properties. A member of Historic Hotels of America, the graceful pueblo-style building evokes the atmosphere of an era that has long since passed in most places, but lives on in Santa Fe. La Fonda means "the inn" and there has been an inn on this sight since as early as 1610. The current La Fonda has a rich history that includes many famous guests dating back to Kit Carson.

There can be no better place to enjoy the area's rich heritage than at La Fonda. It's more than a hotel – it can well be a part of Santa Fe sightseeing. For instance, La Terraza, a casual restaurant on the third floor, has an outdoor patio with a great view of the Cathedral of St. Francis. It seems like you can almost reach out and touch it with your fork! The Bell Tower Bar on the fifth floor roof has outstanding views of the Sangre de Cristo mountains and is an immensely popular place to be for spectacular sunsets. (The bar, by the way, is located under a structure that architecturally would serve as a mission bell tower.) The award-winning restaurant should be seen as well – even if you don't eat there – just to see the beautiful sky-lit courtyard setting. Azure blue table clothes and napkins contrast with the dark wood chairs and generous greenery.

No two of La Fonda's rooms or suites are quite alike. However, they all feature rich hand-carved furniture and works of art by local Pueblo Indians. Many have balconies and/or fireplaces and some on the upper floors feature dramatic mountain vistas. Graceful arched doorways and luxurious bedspreads are among some of the other little things that will make you remember a stay at La Fonda.

Public areas and facilities include a variety of restaurants, lounges, art galleries, upscale retail shops and tour services. La Fonda's bars are famous for their margaritas. They even established a cooking school to teach guests how to make Southwestern cuisine the La Fonda way. In fact,

La Fonda wants to make sure that their guests have a complete vacation experience. Besides the helpful concierge staff, the hotel publishes *TrailBlazing*, a quarterly guide that gives visitors to Santa Fe a lot of useful tips. Be sure to pick up a copy. Another unusual feature: La Fonda's senior staff conducts "behind the scenes" tours of the hotel. Included on the tours are the kitchen and laundry. Offered two times a week, ask the concierge for further information.

Selected as one of my Best Places to Stay (see Chapter 12 for more details).

RANCHO ENCANTADO, *NM 592 in Tesuque. Tel. 982-3537, Fax 983-8269. Rates: $175 for rooms in main lodge. Cottages and suites from $210-375. 90 Rooms. Major credit cards accepted. Toll-free reservations 1/800-722-9339. Located north of Santa Fe via US 285. Take the South Tesuque Exit and follow that road for 2 1/2 miles to NM 592; turn right and proceed 2 miles.*

Only ten minutes from downtown, Rancho Encantado is in a world of its own. Like so many places in New Mexico, it has a fascinating history. An Ohio woman, Betty Egan, was so enthralled with the Santa Fe area during her visit that she returned in 1968 and founded the Rancho Encantado. It has since passed to the control of others who retain her love of the mountains of northern New Mexico and her dedication to the comfort of guests. Sitting on a 148-acre site in the Sangre de Cristo foothills, the attractive buildings of Rancho Encantado are a unique blend of both Indian and Spanish architecture. The lush green trees and the deep red earth are in lovely contrast to the golden yellow building exteriors.

A variety of accommodations are available and the choice is difficult. The Main Lodge contains traditional hotel rooms while separate cottages and *casitas* offer the ultimate privacy and luxury of suites. There are even one and two-bedroom villas in the highest price category. Regardless of the class of accommodations, they're all first-rate. The rooms are each unique – no cookie-cutter decoration here. Main Lodge rooms are spacious, with traditional Southwestern decor. Cottages and suites have living rooms with adobe kiva-style fireplaces and refrigerators.

The visitor's palate will find delight in the Rancho's fine Southwestern restaurant, which features great views of the Rio Grande Valley and Jemez Mountains, or you can just have some fun at the Mexican style cantina. Activities include swimming, horseback riding, walking on the grounds, or simply relaxing on the spacious and beautiful patio.

Expensive

HILTON HOTEL OF SANTA FE, *100 Sandoval. Tel. 988-2811, Fax 986-6439. Rates: $130-245. 158 Rooms. Major credit cards accepted. Toll-free reservations 1/800-336-3676. Located 3 blocks west of the Plaza.*

The Hilton organization wisely decided not to have its Santa Fe location look like just any other Hilton. It's a very modern structure but is built in the 19th century Territorial style and blends in nicely with the historic surroundings. Speaking of that, the hotel literally surrounds the historic Ortiz House, a 250-year old residence that now serves as the hotel's dining room. One of Santa Fe's larger hotels, the Hilton features three restaurants. I especially like the El Canon restaurant, with its informal atmosphere and hearty home-style cooking. A unique feature here is the wine tasting, which both connoisseurs and the average person can appreciate.

Guest room decor is in keeping with the Southwestern theme. Many rooms and *casitas* feature four-poster beds and kiva-style fireplaces. Colorful geometric patterns adorn bedspreads and throw rugs. In-room amenities include coffee makers, honor bar, and safes.

Besides the wide variety of dining places to choose from, the Hilton features all of the facilities and personal and business services you would expect from one of the finest names in lodging. These include a large heated pool, whirlpool, health club (massage is available), and a cocktail lounge.

INN ON THE PASEO, *630 Paseo de Peralta. Tel. 984-8200, Fax 989-3979. Rates: $100-155. 19 Rooms. Major credit cards accepted. Toll-free reservations 1/800-457-9045. Continental Breakfast included. Two-night minimum stay if a Friday or Saturday is included. Located northwest of the Plaza; take Guadalupe Street to the Paseo de Peralta and turn left. Inn on the left just before St. Francis Drive.*

The Inn is a large Bed & Breakfast style facility within easy walking distance of all of Santa Fe's biggest attractions. This lovely property consists of two historic residences at each end, joined by a newer building in the center. Innkeepers Nancy and Mick Arseneault have, in the five years that they have operated Inn on the Paseo, created a wonderful environment that complements a Santa Fe visit. The reading room or sun deck is a great place to discuss the day's events with other guests. The inn is completely smoke-free, both in guest rooms and public areas, so you can always count on the delicious mountain air aroma.

Each guest room is spacious and beautifully decorated in a contemporary, bright, and colorful Southwestern style. These charming rooms have beds that feature down comforters and handmade patch-quilts. In-room fireplaces and local works of art are some of the many other nice touches. For an even greater feeling of warmth try one of the cozy loft suites.

The generous continental breakfast is served during the warmer months on the Inn's pretty outdoor garden patio and sun deck. At other times of the year breakfast can be had indoors in the small but attractive dining room, warmed by the piñon fireplace. The patio is also the place for some afternoon refreshments and snacks.

LA POSADA DE SANTA FE, *330 E. Palace Avenue. Tel. 986-0000, Fax 982-6850. Rates: $110-295, Suites from $189-397. 119 Rooms. Major credit cards accepted. Toll-free reservations 1/800-727-5276. Located 2 blocks east of the Plaza and the Palace of the Governors.*

Only a few blocks from "everything," La Posada de Santa Fe is a tranquil oasis in the heart of a bustling environment. The adobe style inn features a "village" atmosphere – small buildings (or *casitas*) grouped around an impeccably landscaped courtyard covering about six acres. The site occupies the former estate of a wealthy Santa Fe mercantile family who were good friends of Archbishop Lamy. The gardens are criss-crossed by brick walkways that meander past colorful flowers, trees, and brick or wooden structures housing Southwestern pottery.

No two rooms are exactly alike, something quite unusual for a larger hotel. The rooms reflect the architectural history of Santa Fe and range from traditional adobe to Victorian. The majority of rooms (90 to be exact) have kiva fireplaces and most also feature wood beamed ceilings and private patios. Traditional Southwestern furniture, blankets, and works of art grace each room. Stunning wooden floors or tiled areas are accented with Indian rugs in a variety of geometric patterns.

The large pool, surrounded by mature aspen trees, is a great place to relax and take in the beauty of the nearby mountain scenery. The Staab House Restaurant (the Staab family was the original owner of the estate) features both Continental and New Mexican cuisine in an elegantly modern Southwestern atmosphere. I think the chandeliers, which have the simplicity of the old west combined with rich golden fixtures, add a special touch to the room. The restaurant also has a piano and small dance floor. Completely different, but also luxurious, is the Victorian-era bar that recreates the atmosphere of a private parlor with rich leather chairs, crystal chandeliers, and rich wall coverings. It's a great place to relax, but so is The Library, if you aren't in the mood for libations.

HOTEL ST. FRANCIS, *210 Don Gaspar Avenue. Tel. 983-5700, Fax 989-7690. Rates: $135-180. 83 Rooms. Major credit cards accepted. Toll-free reservations 1/800-529-5700. Located 1 block south of the Plaza.*

This is another historic Santa Fe location. The hotel was built in 1923 and was originally called the DeVargas Hotel. It was renamed upon a complete renovation that took place in 1986. However, the original charm has been retained and the structure is listed on the National Register of Historic Places. The entrance area, with its small outdoor cafe, is very reminiscent of a fine European hotel, but it is also distinctively Southwestern in nature. The clay tile floors and iron chandeliers are typically New Mexican. The historic flavor is also kept through the use of period furniture, which has been meticulously refurbished to its original luster. A popular Santa Fe tradition is the Afternoon Tea that is served daily in the St. Francis' lobby or outdoors on the lovely veranda, depending upon the weather.

All of the hotel's rooms are unique, combining the ambiance of yesteryear with all of the modern amenities you expect, such as a refrigerator and room safe. The rooms are bright and airy and have a feeling of "home" more than being away at a hotel. Rooms on the upper floors that face the front have views of the Plaza and the distant mountains. Those on the opposite side of the building face the river.

Besides the Afternoon Tea, the St. Francis is known for fine dining in its elegant restaurant and during the summer on the lovely garden patio. There's also a lounge called the Artist's Pub that features light meals and is a popular spot to get together day or evening. Patrons like to watch the people pass by on the street through the pub's large windows.

Moderate

ALEXANDER'S INN, *529 E. Palace Avenue. Tel. 986-1431, Fax 982-8572. Rates: $85-150. 7 Rooms. Master Card and Visa only. Breakfast included. Located 6 blocks east of the Plaza.*

This bungalow-style Bed & Breakfast inn is a Victorian masterpiece, built in 1903. The careful craftsmanship of that era shows both in the exterior construction and the interior, where beautifully stenciled art adorns the walls. The lobby and guest rooms are wonderful - filled with antiques. A lovely garden of roses and lilacs surrounds the Inn, creating a delight for the senses. Each room is uniquely furnished. The Alexander also prides itself on outstanding personal service to each guest, whether that means making sure you're comfortable or answering a question about Santa Fe.

Breakfast at Alexander's is a bountiful treat, all home made. While tea time here may not be as famous as at the St. Francis, it's a most pleasant experience and one that you should find the time to enjoy if you're staying here.

EL REY INN, *1862 Cerrillos Road. Tel. 982-1931, Fax 989-9249. Rates: $79-96; Suites and 2-bedroom units from $95-155. 56 Rooms. Major credit cards accepted. Continental Breakfast included. Located 2 1/2 miles southwest of the Plaza on the I-25 business loop (Cerrillos Road).*

Lodging bargains are extremely hard to come by in Santa Fe, but the El Rey certainly qualifies as one of the few. The bright whitewashed exterior reflects a modified pueblo style and the buildings are arranged so that all of the guest rooms open out onto a spacious garden. The garden is filled with patio areas, tiled walkways, fountains, and stately elm trees. The end result is a tranquil oasis not far from the action.

Every room is also unique at the El Rey and features a Southwestern decor appropriate to Santa Fe. These include Indian pueblo style, Spanish Colonial, or Victorian. Wood-beamed ceilings, brass, tile, and other accents add to the comfort. Ten deluxe rooms are decorated exclusively by local artisans and combine the Southwestern motif along with influences from the inns of France.

Continental breakfast is served in the bright and cheery Breakfast Room. Other features include a heated pool amid the gardens, hot tub and cabana and children's playground. There's also a self-service Laundromat on the premises. Many restaurants are located nearby on Cerillos Road, or you can head downtown for a better choice.

Budget

LUXURY INN, *3752 Cerrillos Road. Tel. 473-0567, Fax 471-9139. Rates: $55-90. 51 Rooms. Major credit cards accepted. Continental Breakfast included. Located near the Cerillos Road exit of I-25, about 10 minutes from the Plaza.*

There's nothing particularly special about the Luxury Inn. However, it's extremely difficult to find anything in the "budget" category during Santa Fe's high season. Part of a new small chain, this property's rooms feature queen or king-size beds. There's a swimming pool and whirlpool. Lots of lower priced restaurants are located nearby on Cerrillos – you'll have to venture back downtown for most of the better places.

NEARBY COMMUNITIES

Expensive

INN AT THE DELTA, *304 Paseo de Onate in Espanola. Tel. 753-9466, Fax 753-9446. Rates: $100-150, including Continental Breakfast. 10 Rooms. Most major credit cards accepted. Toll-free reservations 1/800-995-8599. Located one mile north of the town of Espanola on US 84/285 (Chama Highway).*

Espanola is conveniently located between Santa Fe and Taos. It's about 25 miles north of the former and approximately 50 miles south of the latter. You could easily stay here for activities in either of those cities. Making things even more convenient is the fact that Espanola is located in the middle of the Northern Pueblo country, a big sightseeing area as described later. However, I especially wanted to include Inn at the Delta because it's a very beautiful place worthy of your consideration.

This sparkling new lodging facility is constructed in traditional adobe style and fits in perfectly with its surroundings. hand-made Mexican tile floors fill the main building, made even more attractive by numerous graceful portals. The spacious lobby living room and other guest areas are filled with beautiful Indian rugs, pottery, flowers, and much more to please your senses, including the extensive private collection of Indian and Spanish art works of the proprietors – the Garcia family.

The ten oversized rooms are wonderfully decorated in the classic Spanish Colonial style and are accented with hand-carved furniture and original works of art by New Mexico residents. The amenities in every room include a deluxe whirlpool tub and kiva-style fireplace. The rooms are more like suites in that each has a sitting area separate from the sleeping area. Queen sized beds are standard with two units having two beds. Every room is named – they are the San Ysidro, Santiago, San Rafael, San Miguel, San Pedro, San Gabriel, San Francisco, San Judas, San Antonio and San Teresita.

A rather extensive continental breakfast is served daily in the main house. Dinner at the inn is also an unforgettable experience at the garden like Anthony's at the Delta restaurant. More about that under *Where to Eat*. The final touch for a memorable stay is provided by the friendly and warm Garcia's, who are more than happy to help guests with information on sightseeing and area recreation.

Budget

COMFORT INN, *247 South Riverside Drive in Espanola. Tel. 753-2419, Fax 753-5131. Rates: $63-70. 41 Rooms. Major credit cards accepted. Continental Breakfast included. Toll-free reservations 1/800-228-5150. Located on US 84 and 285 less than a half mile south of the junction of NM 68.*

Because of the often great difficulty in obtaining budget category rooms in or very close to Santa Fe during the summer months, it's sometimes necessary to expand your geographic horizons when trying to save some money. Espanola and this new, modern Comfort Inn help you to do that. The exterior design is done in a very lovely Pueblo style while the interior is modern Southwest. It's a very nice motel with a heated indoor pool and whirlpool. Restaurants are located close by.

CAMPING & RV SITES

The telephone number for the office of the **Santa Fe National Forest** is *988-6940*. Among the private campgrounds in and around Santa Fe are:

- **Chimayo**, *32 miles north of Santa Fe, near Espanola. Tel. 351-4566*
- **Los Campos**, *Tel. 473-1949*
- **Pinon RV Park**, *10 miles south in Los Pinos. Tel. 471-9288*
- **Rancheros de Santa Fe**, *Tel. 466-3482*
- **Santa Fe KOA**, *11 miles southeast. Tel. 466-1419*
- **Tesuque Pueblo RV Campground**, *10 miles north in Tesuque. Tel. 455-2661*

WHERE TO EAT

Very Expensive – $31 or more

COYOTE CAFE, *132 West Water Street. Tel. 983-1615. Major credit cards accepted. Lunch on Saturday and Sunday; dinner nightly. Reservations suggested.*

Celebrity chef Mark Miller has created an upscale Southwestern and American restaurant. This is the original location, although you can now find the Coyote both in Austin, Texas and in Las Vegas, Nevada. Somehow I always find the original to be the best. There is a prix fixe dinner menu featuring unique and innovative Southwestern dishes. Mr. Miller calls it modern Southwestern. By any name the food is delicious, if a bit overpriced. There's an extensive wine list. Lunch (and drinks at all times) are served on an attractive rooftop patio that overlooks downtown Santa Fe.

Expensive – $21-30

THE BISHOP'S LODGE RESTAURANT, *Bishop's Lodge Road. Tel. 983-6377. Major credit cards accepted. Lunch and dinner daily; Sunday brunch. Reservations suggested.*

Overlooking the Sangre de Cristo Mountains, the restaurant at The Bishop's Lodge befits this spectacular property and the even more wonderful beauty that surrounds it. The relaxed and casual atmosphere is authentic Southwestern both in the indoor dining room or outside on the patio called the Sunset Terrace, complete with fireplace. The lounge is located on the patio as well.

The cuisine is nouveau American and contemporary Southwestern. There are special menus for children and for seniors. You can't make a bad choice from any menu – everything is expertly cooked, delicately seasoned, and served with professionalism and class. Sunday brunch is simply spectacular, with dozens of items to choose from.

EL NIDO, *on US 285 in Tesuque, about 5 miles north of town. Tel. 988-4030. Major credit cards accepted. Dinner only. Closed on Monday. Reservations suggested.*

Housed in a delightful 70-year old adobe structure, El Nido has been serving visitors and locals alike for nearly 50 years. The cuisine is American with fresh seafood and choice aged beef always being staples on the menu. However, the daily specials often are the best choice if you're looking for something delicious and a bit more out of the ordinary. The dining room is warm and charming, truly Santa Fe in every detail. Sparkling white adobe walls contrast with dark decorative trim and crafts as well as the beautiful lilac tablecloths. A burning fireplace centrally located in the dining room adds to the wonderful ambiance. Full bar facilities are available.

LA CASA SENA, *416 Agua Fria. Tel. 988-9232. Major credit cards accepted. Lunch and dinner daily.*

Another great Santa Fe tradition, La Casa Sena is a beautiful restaurant nicely situated in a historic little plaza just steps east of the Governors Palace. There's a dining room as well as a cantina, each with its own special charm. The dining room features Southwestern cuisine cooked with a local Santa Fe flair, with a wine list numbering more than 800 selections. Even the toughest wine critic should be able to find something appropriate from that. The cantina is more than just a bar – you can dine on lighter fare for both lunch and dinner while enjoying the entertainment provided by the singing cantina staff.

LA PLAZUELA, *100 East San Francisco Street (in the La Fonda hotel). Tel. 982-5511. Major credit cards accepted. Reservations suggested.*

One of the most beautiful dining rooms in the state, La Plazuela is in a two-story high covered courtyard with a dramatic skylight. It's surrounded on all sides by stained glass windows and an upstairs balcony and has an unusual tile floor. It all creates the illusion of dining outdoors. Delicious New Mexican and American dishes are prepared to order by an award-winning chef and his first-rate culinary team. La Plazuela, like everything else at La Fonda, has a tradition of service and continuity. Several members of the staff have been with the restaurant for more than 30 years.

SANTACAFE, *231 Washington Avenue. Tel. 984-1788. MasterCard and VISA accepted. Lunch and dinner served daily. Reservations suggested.*

Let me say right up front that Santacafe has been included as one of the best restaurants in Santa Fe and in America by many different sources. While you are the ultimate judge, I don't hold it in such lofty esteem. Not that I have any complaints regarding what is one of many fine restaurants in Santa Fe. Located in a carefully restored home from the middle of the 19th century, the setting is certainly beautiful and the service is very fine. The menu consists primarily of American dishes but is liberally influenced by a variety of other cooking methods, not the least of which is Southwestern. There are many fine wines to select from and the staff is both knowledgeable and professional. Outdoor dining on the patio in summer makes a visit to Santacafe even more enjoyable.

Moderate – $11-20

ANTHONY'S AT THE DELTA, *228 Onate NW in Espanola. Tel. 753-4511. Major credit cards accepted. Dinner nightly; Sunday brunch.*

This is a very special dining experience. The outgrowth of a bar that opened in 1949, Anthony's has developed into one of the finest restaurants in New Mexico. An adobe style building with whitewashed interior walls and dark wood furnishings, the restaurant is extremely attractive and has a sort of casual elegance. Art work by New Mexicans is everywhere, including paintings, pottery, and weaving. Start out with cocktails amid the beautiful flower gardens and landscaped grounds. Fresh flowers adorn your dining room table underneath a tree-filled skylight. Or you can dine on the outdoor patio. The menu includes generous portions of a variety of seafood and steaks and some Southwestern items. Desserts are simply out of this world. After dinner keep the good times going by visiting the adjacent candy shop and fresh flower market.

ATALAYA, *320 South Guadalupe. Tel. 982-2709. Major credit cards accepted.*

A nice little place that specializes in baked goods. Regional entrees as well as American and international cuisine are on the menu (a little of each) and are nicely prepared. However, even though the food is good, Atalaya is one of those restaurants where people come because of the desserts. All of them are made right in Atalaya's own bakery. In fact, the baked goods are in so much demand that the bakery is open to the public for sales. Cakes, pies, pastries, and sourdough bread are all wonderful. The service in the restaurant is friendly and efficient.

THE BULL RING, A PRIME STEAKHOUSE, *150 Washington Avenue. Tel. 983-3328. Major credit cards accepted. Lunch on weekdays; dinner nightly.*

While great steaks are the star at The Bull Ring, it isn't only that by any means. The extensive menu includes expertly prepared fresh fish, ribs and prime ribs, lamb, veal and pork chops. The steaks are corn-fed prime Midwestern beef prepared sizzling to your exact specifications. The sight of one of these huge three-inch thick pieces of meat will set your mouth watering. And just wait till you taste it, as it almost literally melts in your mouth. A good variety of side dishes as well as a bar and excellent wine list add to the overall picture. Definitely the very finest steak house in Santa Fe (if not New Mexico), and that's quite a complement because there are several good ones.

CORN DANCE CAFE, *409 West Water Street. Tel. 986-1662. Most major credit cards accepted. Lunch and dinner daily.*

While almost every New Mexican or Southwestern dish is influenced at least in part by Native American cooking, there are relatively few American Indian restaurants. This is one of them. The food is similar in many ways to Mexican, featuring a lot of dishes made with flour and vegetables. It's quite tasty although not nearly as spicy as a lot of Southwestern cuisine. The friendly waiters will be glad to answer your questions about each dish so you can make an informed choice.

COWGIRL HALL OF FAME, *319 South Guadalupe. Tel. 982-2565. Most major credit cards accepted. Lunch and dinner daily. Reservations suggested.*

There are a lot of restaurants in Santa Fe that work on the theory that dining should be fun. And this is one that translates that theory into action. The menu is an interesting combination of Texas-style barbecue and Southwestern dishes, especially vegetarian items. You can get either one separately or choose a selection that has portions of both. You should try one of their great margaritas or sample one of several local micro-brews from the tap.

The fun part is the nightly entertainment in the dining room. Full-fledged theatrical productions are staged in the adjoining Opry Room. For children there is a play area. Diners who like their food under the stars aren't ignored either. The attractive patio is open during the summer for both lunch and dinner.

EL CANON, *308 West San Francisco in the Hilton of Santa Fe. Tel. 986-6417. Major credit cards accepted.*

This is, in terms of elegance, the "number two" restaurant at the Hilton. In some ways it's a super coffee shop, but I find it to be a great place to go for a really good meal when you're not overly hungry. The fare is on the lighter side (sandwiches for lunch and either Mexican or American for dinner). An ever changing selection of fine wines and one of the biggest choices of specialty beers in town add to the dining experience. A very popular feature of El Canon is their so-called "flights" – where guests get to sample several different wines.

MARIA'S NEW MEXICAN KITCHEN, *555 W. Cordova Road. Tel. 983-7929. Most major credit cards accepted. Lunch and dinner daily.*

A Santa Fe tradition for more than 40 years, Maria's is a colorful and fun-filled treat. It's hard to find a place that exemplifies the cuisine, atmosphere, and style of Santa Fe any better than at the New Mexican Kitchen. Perhaps the best tortillas in town are prepared by Native Americans as you watch. The menu includes a wide selection of South-western, Mexican, and Native American dishes. No restaurant has more varieties of margaritas than Maria's. Maria herself literally wrote the book on margaritas – *Maria's Real Margarita Book* is on sale at the restaurant. You can also pick from a huge selection of imported Mexican beers. The great food and wonderful atmosphere is topped off with nightly Mariachi performers.

OLD MEXICO GRILL, *2434 Cerrillos Road. Tel. 473-0338. Discover, MasterCard and VISA accepted. Lunch on weekdays, dinner nightly. Reservations suggested.*

This is an authentic Mexican restaurant in every detail. The food has not been influenced by New Mexican, Santa Fe, or Native American traditions. So if you want "real" Mexican, then this is definitely the place to go in Santa Fe. Of course, many Mexican dishes such as fajitas, chile rellenos, and others have been adopted by New Mexico, so the menu isn't entirely unique. But carne asada, mole poblano, and other dishes at the Old Mexico Grill are less easily found elsewhere. The dining room is attractive and the atmosphere is casual and relaxed.

PALACE RESTAURANT, *142 West Palace Avenue. Tel. 982-9891. Major credit cards accepted. Lunch and dinner daily. Reservations suggested.*

As delightful as Southwestern cuisine and decor are, after a couple of nights in Santa Fe you might have a taste for something else. That makes the Palace a good choice. The atmosphere here is Victorian, at least as the old American West saw that genre. The menu features both continental and Italian cuisine, nicely prepared. Both indoor and outdoor dining rooms are available in summer and there is nightly entertainment. Jackets for men are suggested although the casual look won't make you feel uncomfortable.

STEAKSMITH AT EL GANCHO, *Old Las Vegas Highway, south of town on the I-25 frontage road. Tel. 988-3333. Dinner only. Reservations suggested.*

Nearing its 25th anniversary in Santa Fe, the Steaksmith also offers excellent seafood and Southwestern dishes. But it is the great steaks that people come here for. It's only a small notch below The Bull Ring and that's not an insult – in fact, it's a complement. Besides the attractive dining room, the Steaksmith features a very lively lounge featuring a large variety of *tapas*, small appetizer-size dishes.

Budget – $10 or less

MUCHO GOURMET SANDWICH SHOPPE, *135 West Palace Avenue, 2nd floor. Tel. 988-2223. No credit cards. Breakfast and lunch daily.*

What more can you say than is already described by the name of the establishment? It's not a fancy place but it will likely be very crowded with tourists and locals. A wide selection of overstuffed sandwiches, both American and New Mexican, served on a choice of fresh breads.

NEW YORK BAGEL SHOP AND DELI, *720 St. Michael's Drive. Tel. 474-5200. Most major credit cards accepted.*

The selection here is somewhat smaller than at Mucho Gourmet but they also know how to make a great sandwich. The bagels aren't really like in New York (the fact is that the water is different out west than in New York, so the bagels have to come out different). However, they're very good and offer a change from the usual New Mexico sandwich. If you like your sandwich on bread, the deli has that too.

PLAZA CAFE, *54 Lincoln Avenue. Tel. 982-1664. Discover, MasterCard and VISA accepted.*

A casual place offering a good selection of Southwestern dishes as well as several American entrees. The atmosphere is that of a '60s diner. While the Plaza Cafe doesn't have the fine touches of many of Santa Fe's restaurants, it's a good bargain. It's difficult to find a place to have a decent dinner in the budget category. But if you want to do that without going to a cafeteria or a national family restaurant chain, then the Plaza Cafe is a wise choice.

SEEING THE SIGHTS

There are so many things to see and do in Santa Fe that it can seem, at first, to be a rather daunting challenge. However, I have divided things into three separate tours. Taken one at a time you can see everything that's important in Santa Fe with a minimum of logistical problems. The first two tours are most definitely walking tours. The third requires a car.

On both of the first tours you will encounter, in addition to many historical sights, dozens of lovely boutiques, gift shops, art galleries, and Native Americans (and others) selling their craft works in the street. I'll mostly ignore that aspect of your Santa Fe visit and let you know about all those goodies for sale in a special shopping section following the three tours.

Tour 1: The Plaza & Vicinity

Approximate duration including sightseeing is 7 hours. Begin at the Plaza, located in the center of the city bounded by Palace Avenue and San Francisco Street on the north and south, and by Lincoln and Washington on the west and east.

If you have only a single day to spend in Santa Fe, make the best of it by following this tour. For Tour 1 is the very essence of Santa Fe – its history and culture are embedded in practically every turn.

The **Plaza** is the heart of Santa Fe's history and current economic vitality. The large grassy area is graced by stately old trees, laced by paths and plenty of benches for you to relax or just take in the scene that surrounds you. That scene is quite remarkable. The architecture of Santa Fe and all of New Mexico is best exemplified by the buildings that surround the Plaza.

On the north side of the Plaza is perhaps the best known building in the Southwest, the **Palace of the Governors**, *Tel. 827-6483*. This single-story adobe structure was built in the year 1610. From behind its massive walls, New Mexico was ruled for exactly three centuries – starting with the Spaniards and then, successively, Native Americans, Mexican, and US territorial governments. The many rooms of the Palace are arranged around an open courtyard. Each room contains artifacts and exhibits that provide a chronological record of Santa Fe's history. There's also an excellent gift and book shop. Another feature of the Palace, and one of the most rewarding to visitors, takes place every day on the long porch in front of the building. Here you'll find dozens of Native Americans in traditional dress sitting on their blankets from one end of the palace to the other, awaiting potential customers to buy their hand-made jewelry, blankets, pottery, and many other items. There are always many willing buyers, but be prepared to bargain over price. It's one of the most famous and colorful scenes in Santa Fe. The Palace is part of the Museum of New Mexico. See the sidebar below for visitor information.

VISITING THE MUSEUM OF NEW MEXICO

Some of the state's most important historic places and museums are collectively part of what is called the ***Museum of New Mexico****. Within Santa Fe there are four different sites that belong to the Museum. Actually, there is a fifth but it is only open for scholarly research. That rules most of us out, but if you fall into that category you can get information from that unit, the Laboratory of Anthropology,* ***Tel. 827-6451****. The portions of the museum that are open to the general public are as follows:*

- ***Museum of Fine Arts***
- ***Museum of Indian Arts and Culture***
- ***Museum of International Folk Art***
- ***Palace of the Governors***

All units are open daily from 10:00am until 5:00pm. In January and February the museums are closed on Monday. They are also closed on New Year's, Easter, Thanksgiving and Christmas. A single admission ticket costing $4.20 grants access to all four buildings on one day. A three-day pass is $5.25. Children under 16 are admitted without charge.

Now you should re-cross the Plaza and turn right on San Francisco Street. You'll see the beautiful cathedral, which is two blocks away at the end of San Francisco. However, before you reach it you'll encounter the **Institute of American Indian Arts Museum** *at the corner of San Francisco Street and Cathedral Place, Tel. 988-6281*. This facility has an excellent collection of Indian art done by contemporary Native Americans. There are also extensive displays of more traditional Indian arts and crafts such as pottery and weaving. *The museum is open daily from 10:00am (except from noon on Sunday) until 5:00pm. It is closed Mondays during January and February. Admission is $4 for adults. Senior citizens pay $2 while students with identification and those under 17 are admitted free of charge.*

Now you can enter the **Cathedral of St. Francis of Assisi**, *Tel. 982-5619*. The stately church was the first one located in the western United States to be elevated to the status of cathedral. It was built in the 1870s to replace the original mission church which was destroyed during the 1680 Pueblo Revolt. It was designed by French architects, including the

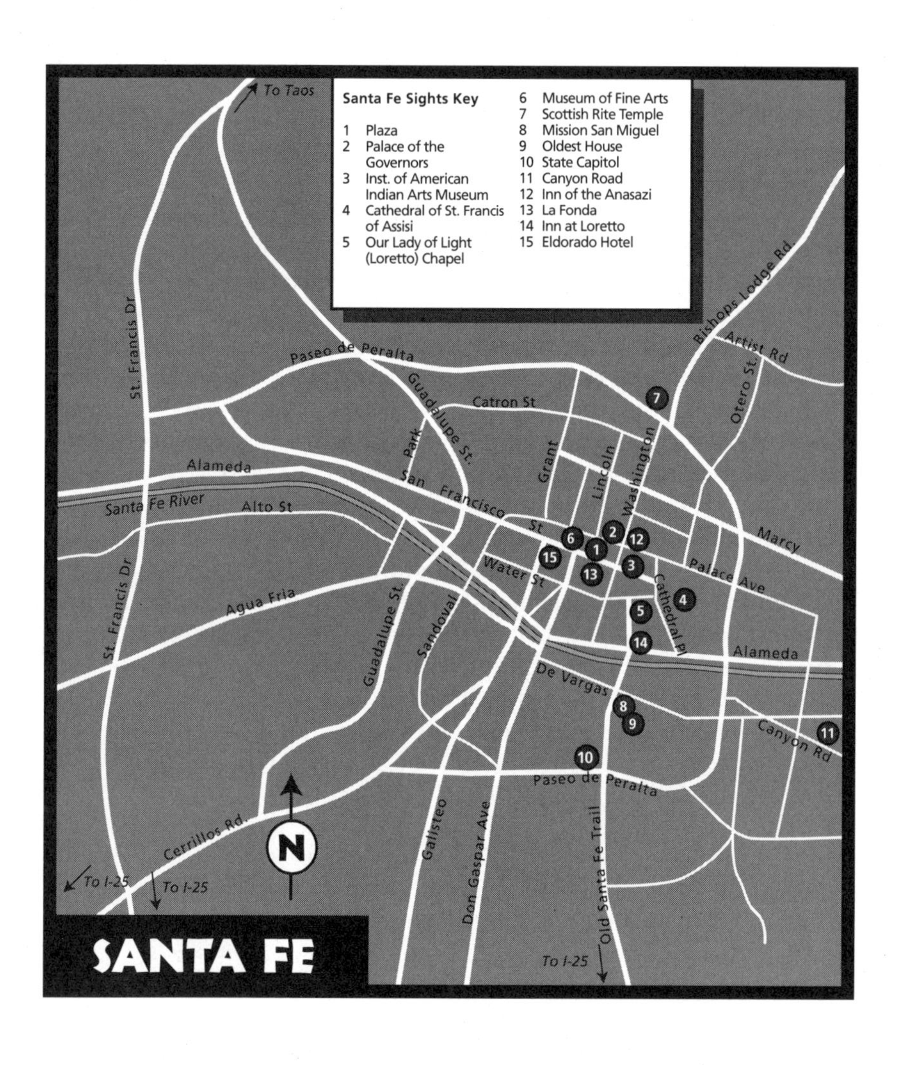
Santa Fe Sights Key
1 Plaza
2 Palace of the Governors
3 Inst. of American Indian Arts Museum
4 Cathedral of St. Francis of Assisi
5 Our Lady of Light (Loretto) Chapel
6 Museum of Fine Arts
7 Scottish Rite Temple
8 Mission San Miguel
9 Oldest House
10 State Capitol
11 Canyon Road
12 Inn of the Anasazi
13 La Fonda
14 Inn at Loretto
15 Eldorado Hotel
To Taos
St. Francis Dr
Paseo de Peralta
Guadalupe St.
Catron St
Bishops Lodge Rd.
Artist Rd
Otero St.
Park
Grant
Lincoln
Washington
Alameda
San Francisco St
Santa Fe River
Alto St
Marcy
Palace Ave
Water St
Cathedral Pl
Agua Fria
Sandoval
De Vargas
Canyon Rd
Cerrillos Rd.
Galisteo
Don Gaspar Ave
Old Santa Fe Trail
To I-25
N
SANTA FE

Archbishop Jean Baptiste Lamy, who is buried beneath the main altar along with a number of other important religious leaders. The Romanesque-style building is unique in Santa Fe which is so dominated by the Pueblo style. However, it seems to blend in rather nicely. Two bell towers gracefully flank the central section of the cathedral. *The Cathedral may be visited every day between 6:00am and 6:00pm. There is no admission but donations are appreciated. Proper decorum is essential, and visitors are requested to refrain from loud speaking if services are being conducted.*

Upon leaving the Cathedral, continue down Cathedral Place and turn right when you reach the Alameda, a lovely street that parallels the north shore of the narrow Santa Fe River. **Santa Fe State Park** runs along a stretch of the river and makes a nice place to stop for a brief rest. It's one of many good places for people watching, too. When you come to the first bridge you'll have reached the Old Santa Fe Trail. Stay on the north side of the river. Turn right and you'll soon bump into a fascinating attraction entitled **Footsteps Across New Mexico**. Here you'll see a 30-minute long presentation that takes you through New Mexico's long history. The multi-media exhibit makes use of a 70-square foot topographical map of New Mexico to put events and people into the larger perspective of the state's diverse cultural tapestry. *The multi-media performances are given continuously every day of the year except Christmas from 9:30am until 4:30pm. The admission is $3.50 for adults and $2.50 for children aged 6 through 16.*

Adjacent to the Footsteps theater is one of Santa Fe's prize attractions – the **Our Lady of Light Chapel**, *Tel. 984-7971*, more commonly referred to as the **Loretto Chapel**. The latter name comes from the Six Sisters of Loretto who were brought to Santa Fe by Archbishop Lamy of cathedral fame. The Chapel was built in 1878 and the interior is modeled after the Sainte Chapelle in Paris, France. Construction was halted before a staircase was built to the choir loft when the builder was killed by a jealous man who thought the builder was after his wife.

The spiral staircase was added soon after but has become the focal point of the entire chapel – the staircase was built without the use of nails and has no visible means of support. Well, it's been there for over a hundred years, so there's got to be something supporting it. Engineers and the religious faithful might differ a bit over just how it stays there. *The Church is open daily from 8:00am until 6:00pm , but from 9:00am to 5:00pm from mid-October through the middle of May. It is closed on Christmas. Admission is $1 for everyone age 7 and up.*

ORGANIZED WALKING TOURS OF SANTA FE

Despite the fact that guided tours offer interesting insights into things and places that you might not otherwise be aware of, I think that Santa Fe is the type of place that is most rewarding if you wander about and explore on your own. However, for those of you who think that a guided tour is the way to go (or who want to combine a little of both methods), there are several good walking tours of Santa Fe. ***Aboot About/Santa Fe Walks, Tel. 988-2774,*** *is probably the best known. This 2 1/2 hour walk departs from the El Dorado Hotel in downtown. Tours are given at 9:30am and 1:30pm. Only the morning tour is offered in January and February. The fee is $10 and $9 for seniors. Children under 12 can go along for free.*

Several other walking tours operate out of major hotels and offer similar tours. Two good ones depart from the Inn at Loretto. Or, you can have the experts design your very own personal guided walking tour. Contact the non-profit ***New Mexico Guides Association, Tel. 474-4263.*** *You can even take a bus tour on an open-air vehicle. The latter, however, doesn't provide the true flavor of Santa Fe, which can be experienced only by walking.*

Now turn left down Water Street and go a block to Washington. A right turn will soon bring you back to the Plaza area. Your next stop is the **Museum of Fine Arts**, *Tel. 827-4468,* on the east side of the Plaza. Built in 1917, the impressive adobe building houses one of the largest collections of Southwestern art in the world. Artists who reside in New Mexico are given priority attention. In addition to oil paintings there is a small collection of sculpture. Part of the collection deals with 19th and early 20th century works and is displayed on a permanent basis. Many works by contemporary artists are displayed on a rotating basis. *See the Museum of New Mexico sidebar for visiting information.*

To Sante Fe's already impressive list of museums will come another addition sometime during the summer of 1997. The **Georgia O'Keefe Museum**, *located near the Museum of Fine Arts,* will showcase the largest collection of works by the prolific artist. O'Keefe's work, which combines realistic and abstract features, are known for their large scale and most often display desert scenes, including regional flora and fauna. The artist came to New Mexico in 1949 and remained until her death in 1986 at the age of 99. The museum's operating hours and admission fees were not set at press time, but it will be included in the combination ticket for the Museum of New Mexico.

Your last stop on the Plaza area tour is located three blocks north of the Plaza on Washington Avenue. The **Scottish Rite Temple**, *Tel. 982-4414,* is architecturally interesting – portions of it are a miniature version of the Alhambra, Spain's Moorish masterpiece. Various art exhibits are open to the public. *The building is open weekdays (except holidays) from 9:30am until noon and again from 1:30pm to 4:00pm. Admission is free.*

Your first tour of Santa Fe will be complete after you take the short walk back to the Plaza via Washington Avenue. Before beginning the next tour, however, I should reiterate that several Santa Fe hotels can almost be considered as tourist attractions. This is even more the case if you aren't staying at a hotel that reflects the architectural essence of the city. The best "touring" hotels (all located within the geographic confines of Tour 1) are the Inn of the Anasazi, La Fonda, The Inn at Loretto, and the Eldorado.

Tour 2: South of the Santa Fe River

Approximate duration including sightseeing is 3 1/2 hours. Begin on the south side of the bridge over the Santa Fe River on the Old Santa Fe Trail.

One block south of the river is the **Mission San Miguel**, *Tel. 983-3974*. It is the oldest mission in the United States having originally been built at the time of Santa Fe's founding in 1610. Although the heavy adobe walls remained standing during the Pueblo Revolt, the interior buildings were severely damaged and mostly rebuilt in 1710. At that time the entire mission was strengthened with the addition of buttresses.

The interior houses many interesting examples of the type of religious art found in the early days of New Mexico. It includes paintings, many icons, and a 17th century statue of St. Michael. Another interesting relic is a church bell that was cast in Spain during the first half of the 14th century and was brought to this site almost 500 years later. You can gain additional insights into the mission's history by listening to a continuously offered 6-minute audio program. *The mission is open from May through October on a daily basis from 9:00am until 4:30pm except that opening time on Sunday is 1:30pm. During the remainder of the year its open from 10:00am to 4:00pm Monday through Saturday, and 1:30-4:30pm on Sunday. It is closed on New Year's, Easter, Thanksgiving and Christmas. Donations are requested.*

Right next door to the mission and worth a brief visit is the **Oldest House in Santa Fe**. Although it isn't certain that the house is actually *the* oldest, it certainly is the oldest one standing and might well be true to its claim. The small structure contains the remains of a Spanish soldier. According to local legend he was killed by witches who lived in the house. There have been no reports of similar attacks upon visitors for at least 375 years.

Continue down the Old Santa Fe Trail for another block until you reach the **State Capitol** building, *Tel. 986-4589*. The structure was completed in 1966 and is far different from the traditional neo-classical designs of most state houses. This one is round because it was built to resemble an Indian kiva. It also looks like the Zia sun symbol. The main central rotunda has a good collection of historical items as well as paintings in a separate gallery. *The capitol is open to visitors on weekdays from 8:00am to 5:00pm. Free guided tours can be taken at either 10:00am or 3:00pm.*

The south side of the Capitol faces a broad (for Santa Fe) street called the Paseo de Peralta. Head east (across the Old Santa Fe Trail) and follow the Paseo as it soon turns northward toward the river. Just before you reach the river, there will be a street angling in on the right side. This is **Canyon Road**, one of Santa Fe's most delightful areas. It was in this area that Santa Fe first became a prominent art colony in the early part of the century. Many artists settled along Canyon Road, which had been in use for centuries as an Indian footpath. Since the early days of the art colony, Canyon Road has become increasingly prosperous. Today it houses many of the city's finest art galleries. There are also very fashionable residences both old and new interspersed among the stores, shops, and fine restaurants.

While on Canyon Road, you'll also come upon the beautiful **Cristo Rey Church**, *Tel. 983-8528*. The church was built in 1940 to commemorate the 500th anniversary of Coronado's expedition. It is the largest adobe structure in the United States and contains one of the finest examples of Spanish Colonial art – a religious stone carving depicting God and several saints. The rock used for this was taken from an older portion of the Cathedral; fortunately, the adobe bricks used to build it weren't because there would be nothing left of the cathedral. About 200,000 bricks were used during the construction, all of which were made from the soil around the church site. *The church is open every day of the year from 7:00am until 7:00pm and there is no admission charge.*

Reverse your route on Canyon Road to complete this tour.

Tour 3: Around the "City Different"

Approximate duration including sightseeing is 5 hours. Begin by driving from the downtown area.

Make your way to the Old Santa Fe Trail by whatever route is most convenient or least congested. About two miles from the river crossing you'll reach the Camino Lejo. Turn to the right and you'll have arrived at a relatively new museum complex containing three attractions of interest. The site of these museums is extremely attractive, having been built on a hillside overlooking Santa Fe.

Two of the museums, the **Museum of Indian Arts and Culture**, *Tel. 827-6350*, and the **Museum of International Folk Art**, *Tel. 827-6350*, are parts of the Museum of New Mexico. The Indian Arts and Culture exhibits are housed in a huge modern building with a number of different galleries surrounding an impressive atrium. Within the galleries are artifacts from the museum's Laboratory of Anthropology that provide detailed insight into the art and culture of the Southwest's Native Americans. The two most dramatic areas are the "Rio Grande World," which documents the cultural history of the successive civilizations that have thrived along the river, and the "Living Traditions" area where Native American artisans demonstrate their crafts.

While the former museum devotes itself solely to Native American civilizations, the International Folk Art collection is the opposite – it is a journey around the world. The vast collection of more than 120,000 different pieces includes items from more than a hundred different nations covering Europe, Asia, Africa, and portions of the Western Hemisphere. Since this is folk art, you won't see famous paintings or sculpture. Rather, you'll find toys, puppets, good luck charms, little figurines and hundreds of other things that will delight you. This is the type of art museum that can be as much fun for children as for adults.

Visiting information on both of the above museums can be found in the Museum of New Mexico sidebar above.

The third museum in this area is the **Wheelwright Museum of the American Indian**, *Tel. 982-4636*. Although not part of the Museum of New Mexico, it would fit in nicely with that group in both quality and subject matter. It was built in 1937 as a means of preserving the ancient Navajo religion. In fact, the building is constructed in the style of a Navajo **hogan**. These are eight-sided structures with the entryway always facing east in order for the occupants to properly greet the rising sun each morning. The museum's collection has an extensive number of Navajo craft items. Woven products (rugs, baskets), pottery, and jewelry can be found along with Navajo religious artifacts and paintings. The museum also has one of the finest gift shops in the city. It sells only authentic Navajo goods. *The museum is open Monday through Saturday from 10:00am until 5:00pm and on Sunday from 1:00-5:00pm. It's closed only on New Year's, Thanksgivin,g and Christmas. Although there is no admission fee, donations are suggested.*

This final tour didn't require a car just to get to the museums located in close proximity to one another on the Camino Lejo. Convenient as it was to see these three great museums, you'll now have to do some driving to continue the tour. Return to the Old Santa Fe Trail and continue south for about a mile to Zia Road. Turn right and go to the Old Pecos Trail (about a half mile). A left on Old Pecos will soon bring you to I-25. Take the Interstate southbound until Exit 276 and then west for three miles to **El Rancho de las Golondrinas**, *Tel. 471-2261*. The name translates into English as "The Ranch of the Swallows." The location was once a major stopping place on the old Royal Road (Camino Real) that led all the way to Mexico City.

Today, the ranch is a living-history museum where visitors can get a good idea of what daily life was like during the Spanish colonial era. The site contains several restored buildings including the church, school, blacksmith shop, and other structures. Although some sites can be easily visited, be aware that some of the buildings are spread out on a trail that covers well over a mile. In addition, some portions are rather steep. While not overly difficult, physically challenged travelers may wish to omit visiting the ranch. *The ranch is open Wednesday through Sunday from 10:00am until 4:00pm during June through September. It is also open during April, May, and October, but only by prior appointment. Admission is $3.50 for adults but those over 62 and children ages 13 to 18 pay $2.50. For appointments and other informatio,n call 471-2261.*

Now you can drive back north on I-25, using the Cerrillos Road exit. Turn left when you reach Guadalupe Road and follow the latter street to the corner of Agua Fria, several blocks before the Santa Fe River. Here is the interesting **Santuario de Nuestra Señora de Guadalupe**, *Tel. 988-2027.* This is a small chapel built in the closing years of the 18th century and dedicated to the Our Lady of Guadalupe shrine. Besides the chapel there is a tranquil botanical garden. The site is used frequently for concerts, lectures, and various exhibits.

Time permitting, you can add one more stop to this tour. The **Santa Fe National Cemetery**, *Tel. 988-6400*, which can be reached by continuing on Guadalupe (eventually becoming US 285) for about two miles. The site was originally the cemetery for the military post of Santa Fe. It now houses the final resting place for soldiers from the Indian wars as well as several battles of the Civil War that were fought in New Mexico. *Open daily from 8:00am until 7:00pm (until 5:00pm from October through April). There is no admission charge.*

Come back via Guadalupe Street which provides easy access to the downtown area.

SHOPPING

With literally hundreds of shops, galleries, and more, it would simply be impossible to guide you to specific places. Not only would it be unfair to the businesses not mentioned (so many of which are truly high quality), but it would be unfair to you – because just wandering around and exploring the almost unlimited shopping opportunities is the biggest part of what makes shopping in Santa Fe so much fun.

Santa Fe is one of the largest **fine art** markets in the United States. It's also a great place for authentic silver jewelry, pottery, and finely woven textiles. Cowboy boots and other forms of western wear are also good choices. When buying Native American arts and crafts, make sure that there is a signature mark to ensure authenticity. New Mexico law prohibits street vendors in Santa Fe from selling non-Native American goods, but you can't be too careful. Impostors find their way into every place, even idyllic Santa Fe.

As mentioned briefly before, the two primary shopping areas are the finer stores and galleries along **Canyon Road** and the Native American market under the portico of the Palace of the Governors in the **Plaza**. Other good choices are in the **Guadalupe Railyard District** west of the Plaza, the boutiques of the larger **downtown hotels**, and the shops located in most branches of the **Museum of New Mexico**.

More traditional shopping opportunities are concentrated along **Cerrillos Road** west of downtown. There are even some small enclosed malls. But these lack the grace and charm of the true Santa Fe shopping experience, as do the outlet stores on the west side. However, many people insist that they can find good bargains at the latter. I have my doubts.

NIGHTLIFE & ENTERTAINMENT

There aren't many "hot" nightspots in Santa Fe (this is, after all, a small city). You can easily find music and dancing in the lounges of many of Santa Fe's hotels, as I mentioned in the *Where To Stay* section. However, a better way to enliven your nights in New Mexico's capital is by taking advantage of one or more of the many cultural performances that are available, especially during the summer months. In fact, the opportunities as well as the level of quality are out of all proportion to what would be expected for a city of this size. It's just another aspect of what makes Santa Fe the "city different."

Almost every type of performing art has found a home in Santa Fe. The casual music lover would have trouble deciding what to do given the many choices; the devotee of fine performing arts will find it almost impossible to decide. Some simple folks (like myself) may be thinking, "he wants us to go to one of those high-brow things like the opera." Not necessarily, since the entertainment runs the gamut from pop to sublime.

Among the most popular and well known Santa Fe music and theater events are the **Santa Fe Chamber Music Festival** held from July through August, *Tel. 983-2075*; the **Santa Fe Symphony and Chorus** held year round, *Tel. 983-1414*; and the **Santa Fe Music Hall**, *Tel. 1/800-409-3311*, a dinner theater presenting popular musical revivals on Guadalupe Street. A good way to see excellent free shows is by visiting **Summerscene**, *Tel. 438-8334 for information,* which are concerts given on the Plaza every Tuesday and Thursday from June through August.

The most respected of Santa Fe's performing arts venues is the world renowned **Santa Fe Opera**, *Tel. 986-5900 for information on schedules and* *ticket prices and the sidebar below for more details.* A completely different kind of classic entertainment and a most enjoyable evening that features a touch of Europe awaits you at the **Maria Benitez Teatro Flamenco**, *Tel. 982-1237*. Playing at the Radisson Picacho Hotel from June through September, this colorful and lively collection of Spanish music and dance has been delighting audiences for almost 30 years.

The six performances I've mentioned only begin to scratch the surface. If none of them tickle your fancy, just consult any of the weekly visitor guides that are available in almost every hotel. You're sure to find something that fits your tastes. One final note worth mentioning is that the vast majority of theaters and concert halls are small places seating only a couple of hundred people at most. (The Opera is one exception.) This means you can always count on a good seat and enjoy an intimate evening with the performers.

THE SANTA FE OPERA

Every year since 1957, the ***Santa Fe Opera*** *has been thrilling opera lovers and others from its magnificent outdoor amphitheater in the beautiful foothills of the Sangre de Cristo Mountains just a few miles north of downtown. Their prestige has grown to the point where Santa Fe Opera performances are world renowned and famous opera stars from all over come to perform here.*

Several different operas are offered each season. While most of the theaters and concert venues within town (whether they be inside or outside) are fairly small, the Santa Fe Opera is just the opposite. It seats 1,800. Even so, the acoustics are excellent from every seat, as is the view of the stage. Seats go surprisingly quick.

SPORTS & RECREATION

Bicycle Rentals

If you bring your own bicycle and are interested in joining with other riders, contact the **Roadrunner Cycling Club**, *Tel. 662-9790.*

Golf

• **Santa Fe Country Club**, *Tel. 471-0601*

Gyms & Health Clubs

• **Ten Thousand Waves Japanese Health Spa**, *Ski Basin Road, Tel. 988-1047*

Horseback Riding

- **Equus USA Horseback & Cowboy Vacations**, *Tel. 1/800-982-6861*
- **Lone Butte Riding Company**, *Tel. 471-8505*
- **Rocking S Ranch**, *Tel. 438-7333*

Horse Racing

- **The Downs At Santa Fe**, *Tel. 471-3311.* June through Labor Day

Hot Air Ballooning

- **Rocky Mountain Tours**, *217 W. Manhattan, Tel. 984-1684.* Trips at dawn (weather permitting) from July through September.

Rafting

- **Bandelier Rafting**, *Tel. 466-6226*
- **Known World Adventures**, *Tel. 983-7756*
- **Kokopelli Rafting Adventures**, *Tel. 983-3734 or 1/800-359-2627*
- **New Wave Rafting**, *Tel. 1/800-984-1144*
- **Rocky Mountain Tours**, *Tel. 984-1684 or 1/800-231-7238*
- **Santa Fe Rafting**, *Tel. 988-4914 or 1/800-467-RAFT*
- **Southwest Wilderness Adventures**, *Tel. 983-7267 or 1/800-869-7238*

Skiing

- **Santa Fe Ski Area**, *Tel. 242-9133.* Late November through early April.

PRACTICAL INFORMATION FOR SANTA FE

- **Tourist Office/Visitors Bureau**: *201 W. Marcy Street, Tel. 984-6760 or 1/800-777-CITY*
- **Airport Transportation to/from Albuquerque**: *Shuttlejack, Tel. 243-3244 (in Albuquerque call 764-9464); Twin Hearts Express & Transportation, Tel. 751-1201*
- **Bus Depot**: *Tel. 471-0008*
- **Bus Service to Lamy Train Station**: *Santa Fe Trails, 984-6730*
- **Municipal Transit Information**: *Santa Fe Trails, 984-6730*
- **Taxi**: *Capital City Taxi, Tel. 438-0000*
- **Hotel Hot Line**: *1/800-338-6877*
- **Hospital**: *Tel. 983-3361*
- **Police** (non-emergency): *Tel. 473-5000*

LOS ALAMOS & ENVIRONS

ARRIVALS & DEPARTURES

Los Alamos is located about 35 miles from Santa Fe. The ride goes through some very nice scenery and takes well under an hour. Head north from Santa Fe on US 285 until the junction of NM 502. Then follow that road west and you will soon find yourself in Los Alamos. The state highways that lead to and from Los Alamos become Trinity Drive within the city.

ORIENTATION

All of the in-town attractions and most visitor facilities are either on Trinity Drive or the other main business street, Central Avenue. The latter parallels Trinity and runs into it at either end of town.

WHERE TO STAY

Moderate

LOS ALAMOS INN, *2201 Trinity Drive. Tel. 662-7211 (also the Fax number). Rates: $71-76. 116 Rooms. Major credit cards accepted. Toll-free reservations 1/800-279-9279. Located in the center of town.*

There aren't many places to stay in Los Alamos in any price category, probably due to the wide choice available so close by in Santa Fe. However, if you want to stay in Los Alamos (even if it's only to avoid the higher prices of Santa Fe), then the Los Alamos Inn is probably the best choice. The largest hotel in town, it features large rooms with hot tubs, in-room refrigerators in some rooms, and coffee makers. There's a restaurant on the premises and several others within a short distance.

CAMPING & RV SITES

Both camping and RV hookups are available in the surrounding **Santa Fe National Forest**, *Tel. 988-6940*, and at nearby **Bandelier National Monument**.

WHERE TO EAT

Moderate – $11-20

DE COLORES, *820 Trinity Drive. Tel. 662-6285. MasterCard and VISA accepted. Lunch served weekdays; dinner nightly except Sunday. Reservations suggested.*

A very popular place with the locals for many years, De Colores serves authentic New Mexican cuisine in an attractive Southwestern atmosphere. Specialties include mesquite grilled chicken and steaks with a variety of chile dishes. All entrees include great salsa and tasty sopaipillas. Margaritas from the adjacent lounge are as well known in the area as the restaurant.

KATHERINE'S RESTAURANT, *121 Longview Drive in White Rock between Los Alamos and Bandelier. Tel. 672-9661. Most major credit cards accepted. Lunch served Tuesday through Friday and dinner Tuesday through Saturday. Reservations suggested.*

Serving a fine selection of continental cuisine in an atmosphere of casual elegance, Katherine's is known especially for its fresh seafood and veal dishes. Absolutely sinful desserts and a good wine list add up to a memorable dining experience at a very reasonable price.

SEEING THE SIGHTS

While there aren't that many attractions within Los Alamos (the Los Alamos National Laboratory would probably be the best but it isn't, unfortunately, open to the public), the town serves as an excellent gateway to some of New Mexico's most spectacular scenery and a wealth of other attractions within a short drive. While Santa Fe and even Albuquerque are also gateways to these areas, Los Alamos is definitely the closest. In fact, it's right in the middle of things.

However, because of the greater availability of accommodations in Santa Fe, not to mention its greater charm, Los Alamos isn't the base of operations for most visitors. We'll use it as such in describing the sights in this section, but keep in mind that it's the same as if you're coming from Santa Fe – just add on the distance from Santa Fe. Let's first take a look at the things in town.

The most famous attraction within Los Alamos is the **Bradbury Science Museum**, *Tel. 667-4444*. It's the next best thing to getting into the National Laboratory. Built in 1993, the large and modern glass building details the history of the Los Alamos National Laboratory, from the days of the Manhattan Project through the present day. Besides the excellent exhibits on the atomic bomb project, you'll be amazed at some of the things currently being done at the lab. So, you'll find exhibits on lasers, computers, defense projects, energy and natural resources, even health research. Almost all of the projects at Los Alamos today are geared towards peaceful purposes. *The museum is open Tuesday through Saturday from 9:00am to 5:00pm and Sundays and Mondays from 1:00pm to 5:00pm during June through September. During the remainder of the years the shorter hours are on Saturday and Sunday. It is closed on holidays. There is no admission charge.*

The nearby **Fuller Lodge Art Center**, *Tel. 662-9331*, features paintings and other works of art by residents of New Mexico. Exhibitions change several times a year. While some of the works are very good, many visitors may find themselves more interested in the large log structure which houses the collection. It originally served as a dining and recreation hall for the Los Alamos Ranch School for Boys. Then it was used by scientists working on the Manhattan Project. *The center is open daily from 10:00am until 4:00pm except on Sunday when it opens a 1:00pm. Donations are requested.*

The final attraction within town is the **Los Alamos County Historical Museum**, *Tel. 662-6272*, located adjacent to the Fuller Lodge. It was also once part of the Ranch School, serving as the infirmary. The museum is small but contains a number of interesting exhibits which document the history of the Los Alamos area from prehistoric times (represented by the remains of a 13th century Indian settlement), through the early days of the Anglos (a homesteader's cabin), and focusing on the Manhattan Project years. *The museum's hours are Monday to Saturday from 9:30am to 4:30pm and on Sunday from 11:00am to 5:00pm during May through September. Off season hours are 10:00am to 4:00pm except on Sunday when its open from 1:00-4:00pm. Closed on New Year's, Easter, Thanksgiving, and Christmas. Donations are requested.*

Bandelier National Monument

This loop excursion will take you back in time to the era of the Anasazi and give you the opportunity to experience some of the Southwest's most dramatic scenery. If you're going to be starting and returning from Los Alamos, you can easily do it in about a half a day, although it's also possible to make a full day of it.

Leave Los Alamos via NM 502 heading east back towards Santa Fe. In a few miles you'll reach the point where NM 4 begins. Follow that route. In a couple of hundred yards there will be a pull-off for the **Tsankawi Ruins**, administered by Bandelier National Monument but physically separate from it. It served as an outpost for a larger pueblo for almost 500 years beginning in the 12th century. Sounds interesting, and it is, but not for everyone. To reach the actual ruins you have to walk on a steep and sometimes difficult trail that covers three miles round-trip. To make matters worse, the trail is often at the edge of sharp drop-offs that require great care. There are also ladders to ascend and descend to get into the ruins. For the more adventurous souls, it's a worthwhile trip.

Most of you will just continue on NM 4, a winding road that climbs through the mountains and provides beautiful vistas. The best view requires that you leave the road a couple of miles south of Tsankawi following signs for the **White Rock Overlook**. There's a park here where you can look out on a magnificent vista that includes portions of the Santa

Fe National Forest, the deep river gorge of the Rio Grande, and colorful mountain peaks both near and distant.

Continuing on NM 4, the road climbs the Pajarito Plateau and, in the final approach to Bandelier, you'll have to negotiate a series of dramatic switchbacks where you'll be able to see the road above and below you. The road then suddenly straightens out and you'll soon reach the entrance station to **Bandelier National Monument**, *Tel. 672-3861*, a sure highlight of any trip to New Mexico.

Occupying a portion of the **Pajarito Plateau**, Bandelier (named for an anthropologist who did research in the area during the 1880s), contains large remnants of a sizable Anasazi community that lived in both pueblos and cliff dwellings about 800 years ago. The entrance road starts at the top of the plateau and descends into **Frijoles Canyon**, the narrow gorge in which the Anasazi built their city. The road ends at the Visitor Center where you can view a 10-minute long slide program and look at the exhibits, which document the habitation of Frijoles Canyon from about 1150.

Then you should take the 1 1/2 mile-long **Main Ruins Loop** trail which begins behind the Visitor Center and is entirely paved. Along the first portion of the trail you'll see the remains of a large kiva as well as the foundation of a moderately large pueblo built in a semi-circle around an open space. Then the trail climbs up to the cliff dwellings which were carved into the soft talus slopes of the canyon walls. The trail is a bit steep in spots but not overly difficult. However, if you want to actually go into some of the small cliff dwellings you have to climb some short ladders. It's not that difficult and children love it! Adults do too. The trail continues past dozens more cliff dwellings, including one known as the Long House. Depending upon how much time you have, you may want to turn around at this point.

Visitors with more time to spend can continue on the trail up to the **Ceremonial Cave**. This cave, however, is 140 feet above the canyon floor and requires ascending four ladders to reach it. Another option is to take a trail in the opposite direction from the Visitor Center to the Upper and Lower Falls of a small tributary of the Rio Grande called the **El Rito de los Frijoles**.

Regardless of how much time you spend in Bandelier, you'll come away in awe of the skill of the Anasazi who built this remarkable community and impressed by the beautiful natural setting in which it lies.

The monument is open during daylight hours every day of the year. However, the Visitor Center is open from 8:00am until 6:00pm from Memorial Day through Labor Day and until 4:30 the remainder of the year. It's closed New Year's and Christmas. Admission is $5 per vehicle including all inhabitants.

Upon leaving the Monument, continue along NM 4. In a few miles you'll reach the junction of NM 501, which will take you back into Los Alamos.

Jemez Mountain & Pueblo Trail

This excursion will take you through spectacular mountain scenery and a number of Native American sites of more than passing interest. You can do it as a separate entity from Los Alamos (or Santa Fe for that matter) or you can add it on to the excursion to Bandelier if you want to spend one long day.

Take NM 4 heading west (either from NM 501 from Los Alamos or simply by remaining on NM 4 after you leave Bandelier). The road gently climbs in altitude, providing great views of the colorful mountain peaks and lush greenery of the Santa Fe National Forest. Soon you will gaze out upon an area whose remoteness was just the thing that those in charge of the Manhattan Project were looking for. This is the **Valle Grande**, an immense 15-mile wide *caldera* (the term used to describe the collapsed summit of a volcano).

One of the largest calderas in the world, it covers 175 square miles and is about 500 feet deep. Access into it and the isolated narrow canyons of the Pajarito Plateau was virtually impossible until this century. NM 4 gracefully curves along an edge of the caldera and allows you to clearly see into the beautiful depression which looks like an enormous bowl. There is also a side road that leads to the **Pajarito Mountain Ski Area** that actually ascends an outer slope of the rim. That slope drops enthusiastic skiers almost 1,200 feet. But even the main road provides sufficient vistas, including an excellent view of 11,254-foot high **Redondo Peak**, just one of the many beautiful summits in the **Jemez Mountains**. These mountains are ruggedly beautiful but are tempered more than many other ranges of the Rockies by numerous green mountain meadows. There are also estimated to be as many as 7,000 Indian ruins scattered among the mountain's many gorges and cliffs. The road winds around for a few miles of more beautiful scenery before descending somewhat to the town of **Jemez Springs**.

In this area is the **Jemez State Monument**, *Tel. 829-3530*. These are the ruins of a partially excavated pueblo that the Jemez occupied at the time of the Spanish conquest. The Jemez were among the most resistant groups to colonization. They now live in a pueblo about 20 miles from the original site. Among the sites you can see here are the formidable remains of the **Jemez Mission**, built in 1622 with forced Indian labor, and the relatively small **Guisewa Pueblo ruins**. Also take a few moments to explore the visitor center explaining the history of the region and providing insights into Jemez culture and customs.

The monument is open daily from 9:30am until 6:00pm from May through mid-September and from 8:30 to 5:00pm the remainder of the year. It's closed on New Year's, Thanksgiving and Christmas. Admission is $2 for those age 16 and above.

Other things to see in the vicinity of Jemez Springs are the **Soda Dam**, an unusual natural dam created by the buildup of carbonate from the springs that reach the surface at this point. The 300-foot long dam is 50 feet high and equally wide at the base. It contains a number of small caves that you can climb into. More visitors seem to enjoy taking a break by taking their shoes off and putting their feet into the cold mountain spring. It's a refreshing sight even if you don't dip. The current **Jemez Pueblo** is only open to visitors on occasion, but the Indians are known to frequently sell a delicious bread and other goodies that they make in numerous roadside stands. Some of the stands are located in an area of vividly colored giant red rocks.

NM 4 ends soon beyond this area but you can, if you wish, continue on NM 44 to the **Zia Pueblo**. The Zia sun symbol graces the New Mexico flag and has become quite famous. The Zia are also known for their high quality pottery, much of which can be bought in the small towns along the road that run through the Zia reservation.

To get back to Los Alamos, you'll have to reverse the route, taking NM 4 back into NM 501. However, if you are going to be taking the Jemez Mountain and Pueblo Trail from Santa Fe, there's a quicker way to get back without using the same roads. Continue on NM 44 all the way to I-25 and then hop the Interstate north back toward Santa Fe. It is also possible for those making Albuquerque as their base to do this excursion. Upon completing the Coronado State Monument at Bernalillo, continue on NM 44 to NM 4.

The Northern Pueblos

The eight **Northern Pueblos** can be visited as an interesting day trip from either Santa Fe, Los Alamos, or Taos, as they form an almost continuous chain between the three cities. Or, if your itinerary is going to be taking you from the Santa Fe/Los Alamos area to Taos or other points north, then you can visit them along the way. I'll describe the route to take in a generally northerly fashion from Santa Fe, but it will be helpful to study the accompanying map on the next page to get a clearer picture of the positioning of the pueblos.

US 285 and NM 68 provide the fastest direct link between Santa Fe and Taos and allows you to visit several of the pueblos without going off the main route. However, several are located within a short ride off that route and can best be seen if you use the scenic high road to Taos, NM 76 and 75, rather than NM 68. Again, the map and your interests will help

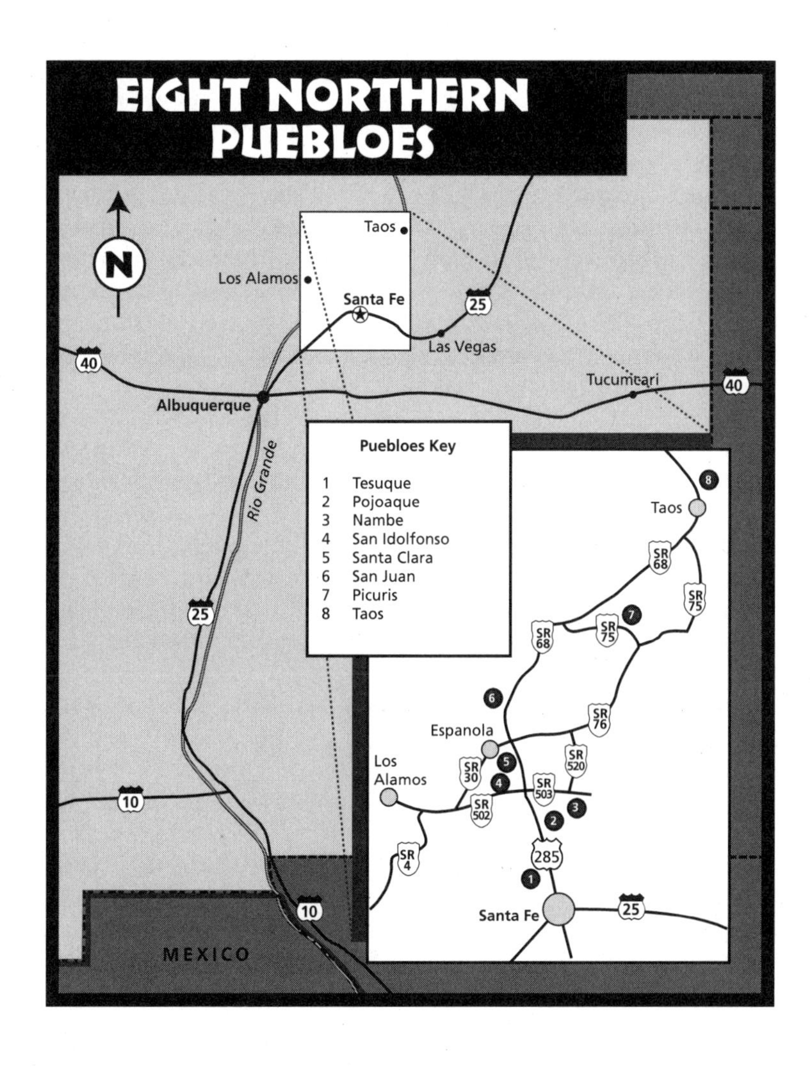
EIGHT NORTHERN PUEBLOES
N
Taos
Los Alamos
Santa Fe
25
Las Vegas
40
Albuquerque
Tucumcari
40
Rio Grande
25
10
10
MEXICO
Puebloes Key
1 Tesuque
2 Pojoaque
3 Nambe
4 San Idolfonso
5 Santa Clara
6 San Juan
7 Picuris
8 Taos
Taos
SR 68
SR 75
SR 68
SR 75
SR 76
Espanola
SR 520
Los Alamos
SR 30
SR 503
SR 502
SR 4
285
Santa Fe
25

you to decide. Access to all of the pueblos is easy and doesn't require traveling on any difficult roads. The pueblos generally welcome visitors during daylight hours. However, I'll let you know when the Pueblo's major feast days are held because these very colorful events make a great time to visit if you can work them into your schedule.

The first pueblo to be reached is the **Tesuque Pueblo** on US 285 about eight miles north of Santa Fe, *Tel. 983-2667*. The word means "place of cottonwood trees." There's a casino on the pueblo but not much else that the residents want visitors to see. However, their feast day (November 12th) is one on which they do encourage visitors. Just a few miles further north is the **Pojoaque Pueblo**, *Tel. 455-2036*. The Pojoaque run a visitor center that has displays on their history and culture and an excellent shop where you can buy some of the best Indian art works available anywhere. The **Poeh Cultural Center** promotes continuation of tribal customs and language. There's also a casino located here as well as some good restaurants featuring native food. Pojoaque, whose feast day is December 12th, means "a place to drink water."

Pojoaque is at the junction of two state routes: NM 502 and 503. A couple of miles east or west of the main US highway will bring you to another pueblo. East on NM 503 is the **Nambe Pueblo**, *Tel. 455-2036, same as Pojoaque Pueblo*. Nambe means "mound of earth in the corner." Continuously occupied for almost 700 years, the pueblo still contains quite a few structures from its inception. The pueblo encourages visitors to explore the area every day, not only on their feast day of October 4th. Visitors are allowed to take a short trail to the lovely **Nambe Falls**, located near the tribe's ceremonial grounds.

Now head back in the other direction, across US 285 onto NM 502 and you'll soon be at the **San Ildefonso Pueblo**. Before receiving its Spanish name, the pueblo's name in their native tongue meant "where the water cuts down through." The pueblo features a museum that is open to visitors and preserves the heritage of the tribe, which is traced from its Anasazi origins to the present day. The San Ildefonso have raised pottery, embroidery, and other crafts to a true art form and several of their best artisans have shops located in the Pueblo where you can make purchases. There's also a good visitor center and other shops in addition to the museum. The feast days for the San Ildefonso are January 22nd and 23rd.

Continue for a couple of miles on NM 502 until you reach the cutoff for NM 30. Take that north to the **Santa Clara Pueblo**, *Tel. 753-7326*. The name has been changed here, too. It originally was called Kha-P'o – "singing water." Fine pottery and other goods can also be purchased at a number of shops. The feast day is August 12th. The inhabitants of Santa Clara are direct descendants of an ancient tribe known as the Puye. Nearby, on a side road (NM 601), you can visit the remains of the Anasazi community now known as the **Puye Cliff Dwellings**. The dwellings extend along the underside of a huge cliff for nearly a mile. Although the tribe welcomes visitors to the cliff dwelling site, it is reached only by a rather difficult walk.

If you continue north on NM 30, it runs back to the junction of US 285 and NM 68. Go north on NM 68 and in a mile or so you'll come upon pueblo number six – the **San Juan Pueblo**, *Tel. 852-4400*. The pre-Anglo name translated as "we are the brothers" in the Tewa language, which is the native tongue of six of the current New Mexico pueblos. This is a very tourist-friendly pueblo. Aside from the modern casino, San Juan doesn't look that different than it would have 500 years ago. Visitors should be sure to see the two kivas that flank the Catholic Church. It is symbolic of the modern pueblo way of life – combining native and Catholic religious traditions. San Juan Pueblo also boasts an excellent Indian crafts shop and restaurants with Native American cuisine. The feast days are June 23rd and 24th.

Continue on NM 68 until the junction of NM 75. On NM 75 follow signs for the most isolated of the northern pueblos. This is **Picuris Pueblo**, *Tel. 587-2957*. The name is an adaptation of the native term for "those who paint." Although isolated and small (there are currently only a few hundred residents), Picuris welcomes visitors. The pueblo museum sells fine pottery, woven products, and beadwork. The **San Lorenzo de Picuris Church**, dating from the late 18th century, makes a very picturesque sight among the ancient structures of the pueblo. The feast day at Picuris is on August 10th.

From Picuris you can either return to NM 68 and head north towards Taos, or stay on scenic NM 75 for the end of the high road to Taos. The final pueblo is the most famous of all, Pueblo de Taos, which will be described in the next chapter as it's an integral part of contemporary Taos.

At most of the Northern Pueblos, visitors are free to wander around on their own so long as it isn't on a ceremonial day that is closed to outsiders. However, native guides are often available to show you around, sometimes on a regularly scheduled basis, but are more often available on request. For some visitors this is a more enjoyable and informative way to visit the pueblos. Some guided tours are available from Santa Fe. During the summer months, the **Nambe Pueblo Tours** conduct nightly excursions that include a traditional Pueblo meal, native dances, and storytelling. *Advance reservations are required and may be made by calling 1/800-94-NAMBE.* This organization also offers a variety of other Native American tours, all of which provide the visitor with a unique perspective on Native American culture and daily life

Before moving on, I would like to briefly reiterate the importance of proper behavior in the pueblo communities. That means following all of the rules and regulations set by the pueblo government. Remember that each one sets its own rules. Although there are many similarities, be aware of the differences. Rules are always posted in full view, so don't get caught having to make the excuse "I didn't know I wasn't allowed to do that."

SPORTS & RECREATION

Golf

- **Los Alamos Golf Course**, *4250 Diamond Drive, Tel. 662-8139*

PRACTICAL INFORMATION FOR LOS ALAMOS

- **Tourist Office/Visitors Bureau**: *Tel. 662-8105 or 1/800-444-0707*
- **Hospital**: *Tel. 662-4201*
- **Police** (non-emergency): *Tel. 662-8222*

15. TAOS & THE ENCHANTED CIRCLE

Taos is magic. Nicknamed the "soul of the Southwest," it is an impressive collection of cultural, artistic, and historic features. In that sense it is much like Santa Fe, but it is far smaller – a village atmosphere prevails, making it more personal. Cozy would be a good term to describe its feeling. Perhaps what really sets Taos apart from other places is the much talked about but difficult to describe presence of a "spiritual force."

This force has long been claimed to exist by the Native Americans who have inhabited this land for centuries. But it has been felt by the artists who turned Taos into a cultural mecca as well as by millions of visitors who swear that it exists. Perhaps it is the beautiful manner in which the various cultures blend. They live in harmony and as part of a whole, while each maintains a separate and distinct nature. Perhaps it is the beautiful and almost serene setting of Taos on a plateau bordered by the Rio Grande and the foothills of the Sangre de Cristo. Perhaps it is the very nature of the people. Whatever the reason, Taos is special and I wouldn't be at all surprised if you come away saying that you have felt the "spiritual force," the soul of the Southwest.

Taos dates back hundreds of years. The modern era began around the turn of the century when several artists who were visiting the area found inspiration for their work and never left. In 1912, a small number of them founded the **Taos Society of Artists**. The rest is history. The society was originally comprised of painters, but the Taos culture soon grew to encompass all fine arts and performing arts as well.

The paintings of Taos grabbed the attention of the world and travelers have been visiting Taos ever since. Despite a bit too much commercialism in the past few years, almost everyone who comes to Taos will still return home feeling that their lives have somehow been greatly enriched by the experience.

ARRIVALS & DEPARTURES

Taos is located 72 miles north of Santa Fe and can be reached in about 1 1/4 hours via NM 68. That road runs into US 64 upon reaching town. US 64 is a major east-west through route in northern New Mexico. There is bus service from Albuquerque as well as air transportation by FAA-certified **Edelweiss Air**. The bus depot, if you can call it that, is located at an auto service station at the junction of the US 64 bypass, while the airport is a couple of miles west of town off of US 64.

ORIENTATION

With a population of less than 5,000 people, Taos is not the kind of town that requires a very detailed map to get around. A lot of the streets are narrow and winding, but you have to keep little else in mind besides the main street – the **Paseo del Pueblo**. In the southern portion of town it has the suffix "South" or "Sur." After the Plaza area the suffix changes to "North" or "Norte."

When NM 68 ends, the Paseo del Pueblo continues as US 64 as it swings to the west and toward the Rio Grande. Almost all of the sights are located on, adjacent to, or very near the Paseo del Pueblo.

GETTING AROUND TOWN

Although you can walk to all of the sights within Taos, a car is an absolute must for exploring the vicinity, especially the Enchanted Circle. However, tours can be arranged through **Pride of Taos Tours/Shuttles**, *Tel. 1/800-273-8340*. **Gray Line** offers Taos tours originating from Santa Fe.

Parking is very tight everywhere in Taos. If you're going to be in the Plaza area it's best to leave your car at your hotel and walk. There are several parking lots scattered about. Just follow the signs but don't expect to always find a free parking space without some trouble. During the summer you can also count on a lot of congestion, especially on the main thoroughfare through town. Such are the drawbacks of success. Don't let them or some of the tacky souvenirs bother you.

If you find yourself in need of any additional information upon getting into town, the **Taos Visitor Center**, *Tel. 758-3573 or 1/800-732-8267 at the junction of NM 68 and US 64,* has an efficient and friendly staff who will be glad to provide assistance.

WHERE TO STAY

Very Expensive

FECHIN INN, *277 Paseo del Pueblo Norte. Tel. 751-1000, Fax 982-6638. Rates: $149-269. 85 Rooms. Major credit cards accepted. Continental breakfast* *is included. Toll-free reservations 1/800-811-2933. Located on the main street about half-way between the Plaza area and the Pueblo de Taos.*

The Fechin Inn is Taos' newest luxury hotel, having opened its doors for business in June 1996. Located on the grounds of the Fechin Institute (described in *Seeing the Sights* below), the traditional and beautiful low-rise pueblo design blends in with the surrounding green spaces in dramatic fashion. Throughout the hotel you'll find many works of the multi-talented Russian-born Taos artist for whom the Inn is named. Besides the attractive design, the Inn features a spacious courtyard and a library where guests can gather in serene surroundings to contemplate and discuss the unique nature of Taos.

There are three classes of accommodations; superior (with either two Queen beds or one King), King rooms with kiva-style fireplace, and suites with fireplace. Many rooms have either a balcony or private patio overlooking the lovely courtyard. All rooms are decorated in a highly distinctive Southwestern decor that also reflects the style of Nicolai Fechin. Rich woodworking on the furniture is especially prominent.

Although there isn't any restaurant, guests receive a lavish breakfast spread that belies the term Continental. However, with its close proximity to the Plaza you shouldn't have any trouble walking to an eating place of your choice. Facilities at the Fechin include a lounge for cocktails, a large fitness center with state-of-the-art equipment, and an open-air whirlpool.

Expensive

CASA BENAVIDES BED AND BREAKFAST INN, *137 Kit Carson Road. Tel. 758-1772; Fax 758-5738. Rates:$85-195. Includes full breakfast. 30 Rooms. Most major credit cards accepted. Located walking distance from the Plaza, one block east of US 64 (Paseo del Pueblo).*

Meaning the "House of Good Life," this large Bed & Breakfast is a true delight. Run by former schoolteachers Tom and Barbara McCarthy, Taos "natives" who used to pass by the home that is now the Casa Benavides on their way to school. In fact, the building was the home of a famous Taos artist, Tom Lewis, and is listed on the National Register of Historic Places. The McCarthys converted and enlarged the property in 1988.

Each of the 30 rooms is uniquely furnished and decorated – in fact, they are so unique that every one has its own name. The so-called main building, besides containing the dining room and offices, has six rooms, each with hand-made Mexican tiles, wooden *viga* ceilings, kiva fireplaces, and adobe construction. The small Artist's Studio has two rooms with similar features. Opening out onto a lovely patio are the six rooms of the Benavides Home. Another six rooms are in the Miramon House while eight rooms are in the Back Building. The Miramon rooms open onto wide porches facing the gardens. The split-level Back Building is also on the patio with covered portals that wrap around the sides of the building and offer great mountain views. Room sizes vary from small to huge (generally in line with the rates). Regardless of room size, you can count on exquisite Southwestern style and furnishings, including dramatic spreads and rugs in colorful patterns. Some rooms have kitchens. Not all rooms are air conditioned, but then again, summer evenings in Taos are generally quite comfortable.

The handsome breakfast room is where you'll be treated to a lavish gourmet breakfast – it's also the place for delightful afternoon tea. In the warmer months both take place outdoors on the patio. Either way, it's a breath of fresh air.

Selected as one of my Best Places to Stay (see Chapter 12 for more details).

CASA ENCANTADA, *416 Liebert Street. Tel. 758-7477. Rates: $75-155 including full breakfast. 10 Rooms. Most major credit cards accepted. Toll-free reservations 1/800-223-TAOS. Located a half mile east of the Plaza via Kit Carson Road to Liebert Street, then right.*

Much smaller than the Benavides, this B&B still has the same level of charm. Built in the Territorial architectural style, the hacienda-like structure is true Taos. All of the rooms in this walled property are arranged around small courtyards that offer the guest both privacy and serenity. The Southwestern decor of the spacious adobe rooms is as authentic as you can get. Most of the rooms feature kiva fireplaces. Coffee makers are standard in all rooms. A delicious and bountiful breakfast is served each morning in the bright and cheerful sunroom overlooking its own courtyard.

HISTORIC TAOS INN, *125 Paseo del Pueblo Norte. Tel. 758-2233, Fax 758-5776. Rates: $85-195. 37 Rooms. Major credit cards accepted. Toll-free reservations 1/800-TAOS-INN. Located on the main highway through town, two blocks north of the Plaza area.*

A collection of adobe buildings dating from the 19th century, the Historic Taos Inn (it's rare to see the name without the "historic" prefix, although you'll sometimes see it in listings as "Taos Inn, Historic") fits perfectly into the quaint surroundings of the Plaza vicinity. The main building's lobby is two floors high and is wonderfully decorated in the Southwestern style.

The rooms span a great variety in both size and decor. Many are on the small side (referred to as "cozy" in the trade), but some are very large. About half of the rooms have fireplaces. Most first floor rooms surround a small patio and courtyard. Some rooms have refrigerators. Regardless of the size of the room you'll have locally made handcrafted furniture and decorative accents that match the historic ambiance of the Inn.

The Taos Inn features many amenities and public facilities. These include a heated pool and Jacuzzi (the latter located in a unique greenhouse setting), cocktail lounge, and the locally famous Doc Martin's Restaurant, which has entertainment as well as fine dining.

HOLIDAY INN DON FERNANDO, *1005 Paseo del Pueblo Sur. Tel. 758-4444, Fax 758-0055. Rates: $94-149. 126 Rooms. Major credit cards accepted. Toll-free reservations 1/800-759-2736. Breakfast and package plans are available. Located just north of the intersection of US 64 and NM 68 at the southern end of town.*

Since I've tried to focus on "special" properties in choosing which hotels to select, you haven't seen many of the chain properties which, although nice and comfortable, tend to be all the same no matter where in the world you go. It's interesting to note that the Holiday Inn chain has two locations in New Mexico where they've caught the "Land of Enchantment" fever and created something different than the typical chain hotel. Like the Holiday Inn Pyramid in Albuquerque, the Holiday Inn Don Fernando de Taos has won several awards and consistently scores near the top of the chain's thousand-plus properties in their own rankings. The large property consists of several two-story adobe style structures set amidst immaculately landscaped grounds. The public areas are both spacious and very attractive.

Some rooms have fireplaces and refrigerators. The decor has the expected Southwestern motif, although there is something a bit too modern about it all. Nonetheless, every room is attractive and comfortable. The level of maintenance is exceedingly high and you'll have all of the amenities that are found in any Holiday Inn location. The hotel also has a large pool, whirlpool and a tennis court. There's a cocktail lounge and Don Fernando's Restaurant on the premises.

KACHINA LODGE DE TAOS, *413 Paseo del Pueblo Norte. Tel. 758-2275, Fax 758-9207. Rates: $95-125. 118 Rooms. Major credit cards accepted. Toll-free reservations 1/800-522-44632. Member of Best Western Hotels. Located on the main highway near the north end of town just before the road to Pueblo de Taos.*

Although the hotel is right on the busy main route through Taos, the spacious grounds allow it to be well set back from the road, almost as if it were in its own private park. The two-story hotel was completely renovated in 1993. All of the rooms surround a huge central courtyard providing a private oasis for guests.

The guest rooms are large and feature Southwestern decor. A small number of rooms have kitchen facilities. While the rooms don't quite have the authentic feel and atmosphere of many other Taos inns, the accommodations are very comfortable, well maintained, and represent a relatively good bargain.

The Kachina Lodge is one of Taos' larger establishments and has a wide variety of attractive public facilities. These include two restaurants, one of which is the excellent Hopi Dining Room, a cocktail lounge with nightly entertainment, swimming pool and whirlpool. The Lodge has also become quite popular as the locale for evening performances of Indian dances held nightly on the grounds from May through October.

QUAIL RIDGE INN RESORT, *Taos Ski Valley Road. Tel. 776-2211, Fax 776-2949. Rates: $60-295. 110 Rooms. Major credit cards accepted. Toll-free reservations 1/800-624-4448. Breakfast and package plans available. Some minimum stay restrictions during the height of the ski season. Located four miles northeast of town off of US 64 at the beginning of the Taos Ski Valley Road.*

There are a lot of nice (and mostly very expensive) lodges located in the Taos Ski Valley area. Since the majority of readers will probably be coming during the summer months, I've deliberately selected most accommodations to be in or closer to the town of Taos. The Quail Ridge Inn is between town and the ski area, so it is a pretty good location regardless of the time of year you're visiting.

The resort covers a large area in a very attractive natural setting at the entrance to the lovely Taos Ski Valley. Guest rooms and other facilities are located in several different buildings. The rooms, all of which have a warm fireplace, are large and attractive. Some rooms have coffee makers, microwaves, or refrigerators and many have full kitchens. There are also quite a few multi-room condominium units available to rent (these range in price from $170-$420) and can actually be a bargain when there are two or more couples traveling together.

As a resort, Quail Inn has extensive facilities for sports and recreation regardless of the season. If you're not going to take advantage of those facilities, however, you may find it more convenient to stay in town. Among the summer sports amenities are indoor and outdoor tennis, squash, racquetball, and a complete fitness center including swimming pool, whirlpool, and sauna. The Inn has a resident tennis pro who provides lessons. Child care facilities are also provided. There's a good restaurant called the Renegade Cafe which also has a cocktail lounge.

TAOS COUNTRY INN, *Upper Ranchitos & Karavas Road. Tel. 758-4900. Rates: $110-150, including breakfast. 9 Rooms. MasterCard and VISA accepted. Toll-free reservations 1/800-866-6548. Children under 12 are not permitted. Located approximately two miles east of the Plaza. From US 64 take Ranchitos Road for about 1-1/2 miles to Upper Ranchitos, turn left and proceed for a half mile to Karavas Road. Turn left again to hotel.*

Going by the full name of Taos Country Inn at Rio Rancho, this small but exquisite property is situated on 22 acres of lovely grounds alongside the tranquil Rio Pueblo. The one-story hacienda style adobe building was constructed in 1850 and has been carefully restored to appear as it did in those days – except that all of the customary modern amenities have been added. The grounds, once pasture land for a sizable ranch, are now covered with nicely cultivated gardens and graced by centuries-old willow and cottonwood trees.

Each of the nine suites are beautifully appointed with hand-carved furniture, original Southwestern works of art, leather sofas, and even real down comforters. Most provide sweeping vistas of the mountains and those that don't still have an excellent view – the river and colorful orchards. The DeVeaux and DesGeorges rooms feature separate sleeping and sitting areas separated by hand-carved double doors. These, as well as the Trujillo, Velarde, Riviera, Alyda, Alexsis and Adriana rooms are all on the first floor, while the Alejandro is the only upstairs room. All rooms have, as you might expect, kiva fireplaces. One room is more delightful than the next. The Taos Country Inn is a non-smoking facility.

Wonderful full breakfasts are served each morning in a small but lovely sun-drenched dining room. There is no restaurant for other meals but plenty of good eateries can be found within a five-to-ten minute drive. If you're looking for great accommodations without all of the extra services and facilities provided by larger hotels, then it simply doesn't get much better than this.

THE WILLOWS INN, *Kit Carson Road and Dolan Street. Tel. 758-2558, Fax 758-5445. Rates: $95-130, including breakfast. 5 Rooms. MasterCard and VISA accepted. Toll-free reservations 1/800-525-TAOS. Located about a half mile east of the Plaza via Kit Carson Road at the corner of Dolan Street.*

Another small B&B in the fine tradition set by places such as the Taos Country Inn, the Willows Inn was originally a walled-in estate that was the home and studio of Martin Hennings, a member of the Taos Society of Artists in the 1920s. The Inn is now listed on both the National and State Registers of Historic Places. Covering about an acre, the five rooms surround a beautiful garden and patio area. There is a pretty fountain which guests like to sit around, as well as two tremendous willow trees, among the largest in North America, for which the Inn is named.

The primary public area of the inn, besides the garden courtyard, is the Living Room, which contains a television and a library of recordings. There's also a game nook. Little extra touches add elegance to a stay at The Willows. For instance, guests are greeted upon arrival with freshly baked cookies and fruit or flowers in their rooms. Breakfasts usually include at least one item from the Inn's garden. Refreshments are served in the afternoon. You'll also probably be greeted by the owners' two dachshunds and cat. However, no other pets are permitted.

Each of the five rooms is unique and represents a different aspect of New Mexico's history and culture. These are reflected in the names of the accommodations – the Cowboy Room (featuring steer horns, cowhide rug, rustic log furniture and hand-made quilts); the Anasazi Room (hand-crafted Zuni items and pottery); the Conquistador Room (antique chest and Spanish chairs and other massive style furniture); the Santa Fe Room (bright colors, open viga beams, whitewashed walls and Southwestern art); and the Henning's Studio, the largest room with 12-foot ceilings and a bed with 7-foot high headboard. All rooms have kiva fireplaces.

Good restaurants are within walking distance but a better choice is available within a five minute ride. I recently said that it didn't get any better than at the Taos Country Inn – well, excuse me – this is just as good!

Moderate

SAGEBRUSH INN, *Paseo del Pueblo Sur. Tel. 758-2254, Fax 758-5077. Rates: $60-140. 100 Rooms. Full breakfast is included. Major credit cards accepted. Toll-free reservations 1/800-428-3626. Located just south of town along NM 68 north of the junction of NM 518 (about half-way between the San Francisco De Asis Church and the Taos Visitor Center).*

If you're looking for what I consider to be the best overall dollar value in Taos lodging, this is probably it. For prices that are considerably below many other places, you'll get a great deal at the Sagebrush Inn. Constructed in 1929 in the pueblo mission style, this attractive adobe inn has 24-inch thick walls and is authentic New Mexico in every way. Guests will immediately be taken in by the large collection of Southwestern art in the lobby and all public areas, including the restaurants. Not surrounded by other buildings, as is the case of many hotels in the center of town, the Sagebrush Inn offers spectacular views of the mountains. The nicely landscaped central courtyard is a good place to appreciate the wonderful architecture, with its extensive use of portals and patios.

The guest rooms are as charming as the public areas. Standard rooms, representing about a third of the total, are cheerfully furnished in the Southwestern style and feature authentic Navajo rugs. The next level of rooms, in the original building, have a variety of shapes and configurations but all have fireplaces. Then there are both small and large suites (all with fireplaces) and featuring refrigerators and/or microwaves. All rooms have coffee makers.

The Sagebrush is also one of Taos' best known places for dining and entertainment. Two great restaurants are located in the main building. One is a more casual country-western style place and the other is a beautiful adobe walled room featuring steaks and New Mexican cuisine. Other facilities include both an outdoor swimming pool, two indoor hot tubs, and tennis courts. Nightly entertainment is offered in the lively lounge that features country western dancing.

Selected as one of my Best Places to Stay (see Chapter 12 for more details).

SUN GOD LODGE, *919 Paseo del Pueblo Sur. Tel. 758-3162, Fax 758-1716. Rates: $45-95. 55 Rooms. Major credit cards accepted. Toll-free reservations 1/800-821-2437. Located on US 64 about 1-1/2 miles south of the Plaza area.*

A more modern facility, the Sun God Lodge is designed in the Southwestern style. This applies both to the exterior appearance of the building, the layout of the property around a tree-filled courtyard, and the room decor.

There's a wide variety of rooms and suites, including some with refrigerators or microwaves. All suites have fireplaces while every room features a coffee maker. The room interiors are bright and cheerful as well as spacious. Many restaurants are located within a short distance and guests also have privileges at a nearby health club.

Budget

TAOS MOTEL, *Paseo del Pueblo Norte in Rancho de Taos. Tel. 758-2524, Fax 758-1989. Rates: $34-52. 28 Rooms. Most major credit cards accepted. Toll-free reservations 1/800-323-6009. Located on US 64 about 1-1/2 miles north of the Plaza area adjacent to the Van Vechten Lineberry Museum.*

As was the case in Santa Fe, it's hard to find good accommodations at a low price in Taos at any time of the year. However, the Taos Motel meets the affordability test and provides decent size, nice looking, and well maintained rooms. You'll find only basic accommodations here with few amenities. If you're just looking for a nice place to catch a few z's between sightseeing and shopping, this fits the bill. There are plenty of good restaurants nearby, including a family-style restaurant located within a short walking distance.

CAMPING & RV SITES

Besides the many campgrounds in the **Carson National Forest**, the following commercial facilities can be found in and around Taos:

- **Enchanted Moon,** *11 miles east on US 64, Tel. 758-3338*
- **Roadrunner Campground,** *in Red River, Tel. 1/800-243-2286*
- **Taos RV Park,** *Tel. 758-1667*
- **Taos Valley RV Park,** *Tel. 758-4469 or 1/800-999-7571*
- **West Lake RV Park,** *in Angel Fire, Tel. 377-7275*

WHERE TO EAT

Very Expensive – $31 or more

VILLA FONTANA, *Highway 522, about five miles north of Taos. Tel. 758-5800. Major credit cards accepted. Lunch served only during the summer; dinner nightly. Reservations suggested.*

Owner and chef Carlo Gislimberti has created an exquisite masterpiece that may well be the best dining experience in all of Taos. The setting is a stately old adobe home consisting of several small and intimate dining rooms. Summertime lunch is served, however, in an attractive garden setting. In addition to the usual furnishings you would expect in a rich adobe residence, the walls are covered with the original oil paintings of the multi-talented Gislimberti.

The delicious northern Italian cuisine makes heavy use of local fresh ingredients, including the best wild mushrooms you ever tasted. Every dish is carefully prepared and served with expertise in the traditions of the finest European restaurants. There's a substantial wine list to choose from. If it sounds like Villa Fontana is the type of place for a stuffy dinner, it isn't. There's a children's menu and a number of entrees prepared especially for the health conscious diner. The prices are only marginally in the Very Expensive category, with several choices available in the next lower price range.

Expensive – $21-30

DOC MARTINS AT TAOS INN, *125 Pueblo del Paseo Norte in the Historic Taos Inn. Tel. 758-1977. Major credit cards accepted. Reservations suggested.*

One of Taos' most popular dining spots, Doc Martins is housed in a residence dating from the 1800s. The cheerful decor is well suited to the colorful Southwestern cuisine which takes both traditional and contemporary forms. Fresh seafood and local game dishes are always on the menu. Doc Martins also has what may well be the largest wine list of any restaurant in Taos. Diners may opt to eat outdoors on the pretty patio during the summer. There is a children's menu and, like many places in health conscious Taos, lighter fare that's good for you as well as tasty.

THE HOUSE OF TAOS FRENCH RESTAURANT, *1587 Paseo del Pueblo Norte. Tel. 758-3456. Major credit cards accepted. Dinner only, Tuesday through Saturday. May be closed either May or November. Reservations are required.*

This is a small and very intimate restaurant occupying a traditional adobe structure from the late 19th century. The menu features only Provencal French cuisine that is both prepared and personally served to you by the restaurant's owner-chefs. This avoids having a middle-man relay any of your complaints – which you're not likely to have at the House of Taos. The substantial four course dinners can be accompanied by either beer or imported French wines. The surroundings are casual – typical whitewashed adobe walls adorned with the work of local artists. However, the House of Taos has a dress code. Jackets are required for men.

Moderate – $11-20

APPLE TREE RESTAURANT, *123 Bent Street. Tel. 758-1900. Most major credit cards accepted. Lunch and dinner served daily.*

There must be something about old adobe homes that inspires chefs and diners alike because here's the fourth restaurant in a row to fit that description. Apple Tree features several different dining rooms, most of which also look like the local art gallery. Dining on the patio in summer is another popular Taos tradition which can be fulfilled at the Apple Tree. The extensive menu includes a variety of cuisines so that everybody should be able to find something to their liking. Included, besides delicious New Mexican dishes, are beef, fresh fish, and vegetarian entrees. There's an excellent selection of wines (beer is also available) and the youngsters can select from their own menu.

CASA CORDOVA, *on the Taos Valley Ski Road about 9 miles north of Taos Plaza. Tel. 776-2500. Most major credit cards accepted. Dinner only, served nightly except Sunday. Reservations are suggested.*

Make it five out of five. This fine continental restaurant is in a 150-year old adobe Spanish colonial style house. The chef proudly points out that all of the food at Casa Cordova is free of any harmful modern additives. Meats are chemical free, the fresh fish is all farm raised, and the vegetables are grown organically by local producers. The old fashioned style food from a rather long menu is matched by the atmosphere that speaks of a long lost era. Maybe that era isn't so lost in Taos. Casa Cordova has a full service bar and guests are entertained on the weekend with live piano music. A truly delightful place at a very reasonable price, you can't go wrong with Casa Cordova if you're looking for a restaurant that "is" Taos. Being a very casual person who doesn't like getting all dressed up, my only complaint is the dress code.

DON FERNANDO'S RESTAURANT, *1005 Paseo del Pueblo Sur in the Holiday Inn. Tel. 758-4444. Major credit cards accepted. Reservations suggested.*

Adobe house? No. Not this time. Located in the modern Holiday Inn, Don Fernando doesn't have the authentic surroundings, but it does have very nice Spanish decor and good food. That's apparently enough, because it's a very popular spot in Taos. The varied menu includes American, Continental, and New Mexican entrees all nicely prepared. I like the excellent salad bar and the attractive cocktail lounge for either before or after dinner drinks and talk. Special menus for children and seniors.

EL PATIO DE TAOS, *121 Teresina Lane in the north Plaza area. Tel. 758-2121. Major credit cards accepted. Lunch and dinner served daily; Sunday brunch.*

In the middle of old Taos, El Patio is an attractive, quaint restaurant with an authentic atmosphere. It consists of a small restaurant and an adjacent Mexican cantina. The menu is regional Mexican and is very good, as is the friendly service. Margaritas and other local drinks from the cantina are excellent. Located in the maze of small streets surrounding the Plaza, El Patio has the feel of being in a hide-away even though you're only steps from one of the state's most popular tourist destinations.

HOPI DINING ROOM, *413 Paseo del Pueblo Norte in the Kachina Lodge. Tel. 758-2275. Major credit cards accepted. Lunch and dinner daily.*

This is a very attractive and large restaurant decorated to reflect the artistic influences of the Native Americans. The cuisine is "Northern New Mexican" which means that the culinary style of those same Native Americans is an important ingredient. The food is quite good, the service better than average, and the surroundings pleasant. It all adds up to a good meal. Full-service bar and good wine list.

LA LUNA RISTORANTE, *Paseo del Pueblo Sur. Tel. 751-0023. Most major credit cards accepted. Dinner served nightly.*

Italian cuisine is the order of the day at La Luna. Veal, fish, and pasta are all on the menu as well as a variety of pizzas for those seeking something less formal. The latter is prepared in a wood-burning oven that does something inexplicably good for the taste. All of the pasta dishes are freshly made on the premises each day, as are both the excellent home-made bread and delicious pastries for dessert.

LAMBERT'S RESTAURANT, *309 Paseo del Pueblo Sur. Tel. 758-1009. Most major credit cards accepted. Lunch and dinner served nightly. Reservations suggested.*

This is a very interesting contemporary restaurant, something you don't find that much of in Taos. The surroundings are attractive, light, and spacious. And if you're looking for a break from Southwestern cuisine (i.e., you want mainstream American), than Lambert's may be the place. Although the large menu features a good variety of dishes, the emphasis is on seasonally fresh items expertly prepared by the owner-chef. Portions are large but there are several lighter choices if you're not a big eater, and there's also a children's menu. No cocktails are served, but there's beer and a good selection of wines available.

LOS VAQUEROS STEAK HOUSE, *Paseo del Pueblo Sur, 3 miles south of the Plaza in the Sagebrush Inn. Tel. 758-2200. Major credit cards accepted. Lunch and dinner only.*

Excellent food and service in beautiful surroundings quickly says it all. Featuring prime rib, rack of lamb, and fresh seafood, Los Vaqueros may be listed as a steak house but the menu is varied enough to please most diners. The very generous portions are expertly prepared to order and served by an efficient and most attentive staff. The contemporary Southwestern decor is bright and cheerful and features a large *kiva* fireplace as well as attractive arts and crafts. There's a full service bar and a good wine list. Some of the entrees make it well into the Expensive price category but the majority are moderate.

Budget – Less than $10

BENT STREET DELI AND CAFE, *Bent Street, in the Plaza area. Tel. 758-5787. No credit cards.*

At the Bent Street Deli you can get everything from a light sandwich to a full course dinner, all at extremely reasonable prices (although some dinner selections fall into the moderate range). The menu features both American and New Mexican style dishes. There's outdoor dining during a good part of the year as the patio is heated. The atmosphere is casual and friendly and the service is fast.

MICHAEL'S KITCHEN, *304 Paseo del Pueblo Norte. Tel. 758-4178. American Express, Discover, MasterCard and VISA accepted. Closed in November.*

If you're looking for the best value in town, Michael's is the answer. If you're also the type of person who likes informal dining, as I do, Michael's again fits the bill. Combining a number of adjacent storefronts, the combination cafeteria-coffee shop-sit down restaurant is one of the most eclectic places in town. The walls look like the remains of an old general store; the wooden tables with their red and white ersatz linen covers certainly aren't beautiful, but is most assuredly interesting.

But you don't come here for the atmosphere. You come for the food. And you'll have a large menu of Spanish, Mexican, and American entrees to choose from. The portions are large and the food is very tasty. Desserts, from the on-premises bakery, are varied and absolutely delicious. Service is fast and friendly, especially considering the crowds who usually pack the place in.

SEEING THE SIGHTS

What most visitors consider to be Taos is actually four distinct local jurisdictions. These are the **town** itself, **Ranchos de Taos** (immediately south of town), the **Pueblo de Taos** (just north of town), and **Taos Ski Valley**, which is about 15 miles away.

I'll divide Taos sightseeing into three tours. The first covers the Plaza and immediate vicinity. This is definitely a walking tour. Not only are the distances involved very short, but if you try to drive from one attraction to another, you'll wind up spending more time in traffic and looking for a place to park than it would take to walk. The second covers other parts of town and requires using a car. The third is devoted solely to the Pueblo de Taos. You can either drive or take a taxi to reach the Pueblo from town. The Taos Ski Valley is included in the separate section on the Enchanted Circle.

Tour 1: The Plaza & Vicinity

Approximate duration including sightseeing is 3 hours. Begin at the Plaza, located just west of the Paseo del Pueblo and Kit Carson Road.

The **Taos Plaza** isn't as large as the one in Santa Fe. The rectangular plaza is filled with trees, benches, and historic markers and is surrounded by typical adobe buildings housing restaurants, art galleries, and shops of all kinds. There aren't any broad avenues leading off of the Plaza; only narrow winding streets with more of the same charm as the Plaza itself. So feel free to wander.

From the Plaza head east two blocks on Ledoux Street to the **Ernest Blumenschein Home and Museum**, *Tel. 758-0505*. There's a lot of fascinating history connected with the man and the house. The home was originally constructed in the 1790s, but it was expanded when Mr. Blumenschein purchased it in 1919. He was an artist who had come into Taos while on an excursion from Santa Fe because he had to get a wagon wheel repaired. He never left and several years later was one of the co-founders of the Taos Society of Artists. The home contains the original furnishings of the Blumenschein family as well as many works by him and his wife and daughter, who were also artists. *The house is open daily from 9:00am until 5:00pm except New Year's, Thanksgiving and Christmas. Regular admission is $4 for adults but see the sidebar on combination tickets.*

Just a little further down the block on Ledoux Street is the **Harwood Foundation Museum**, *Tel. 758-9826*. The museum is housed in several adobe structures, some of which remain from the days of the Spanish colonial period. They're in remarkable shape and are museum pieces in themselves. However, the collection is of special interest, too. There are works of art from modern times dating back to the Native period. The collection is representative of all of the cultures which have contributed to Taos' art. The Museum also has many books by D.H. Lawrence and other famous residents of Taos. *The museum is open Monday through Friday from 10:00am till 5:00pm and on Saturdays from 10:00am-4:00pm. It is closed on Sundays and holidays. Admission is $2.*

Now return to the Paseo del Pueblo and turn left. In a couple of blocks you'll reach Kit Carson Road. Turn right and proceed about 25 yards to the entrance of the **Kit Carson Home and Museum**, *Tel. 758-4741*. The famous western figure lived in this house from 1843 through 1868. Several rooms are furnished as they were when Carson lived here, while some other rooms have been turned into a local history museum. The collection of guns, saddles, and Indian artifacts are especially interesting. There's a pretty courtyard that you must walk through before reaching the main house. Guided walking tours of Taos that last 1 1/2 hours are offered several times a day from the museum. *The museum is open daily from 8:00am through 6:00pm from June through October. Hours are reduced an hour*

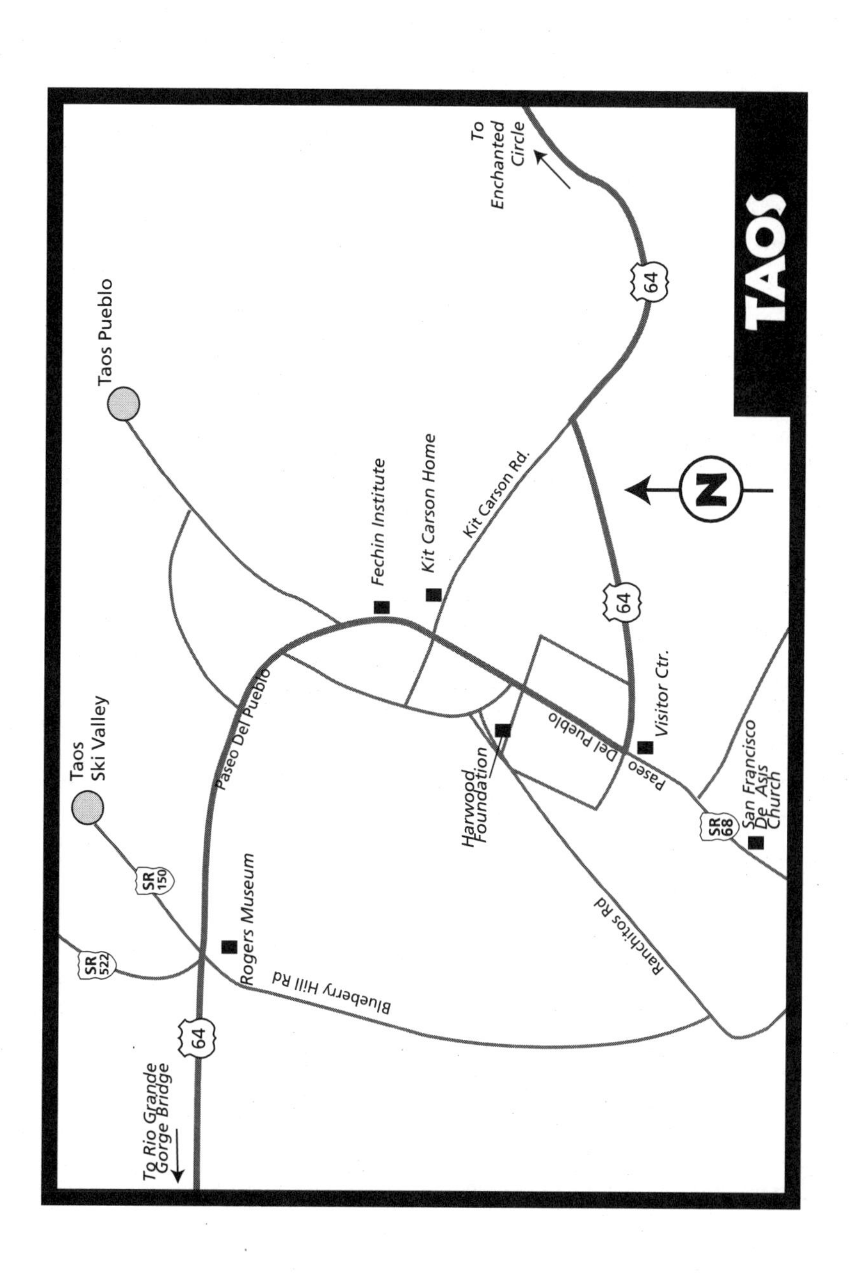
TAOS
N
Taos Pueblo
Taos Ski Valley
To Enchanted Circle
64
Kit Carson Rd.
Fechin Institute
Kit Carson Home
Paseo Del Pueblo
Visitor Ctr.
Harwood Foundation
San Francisco De Asis Church
SR 68
Ranchitos Rd
Blueberry Hill Rd
Rogers Museum
SR 150
SR 522
To Rio Grande Gorge Bridge

at both ends the rest of the year. Base admission is $4 but see the sidebar for combined admission reductions.

SAVING ON ADMISSIONS IN TAOS

Three of Taos' most important sights are administered by the same agency. These are the ***Blumenschein Home****, the* ***Kit Carson Home and Museum****, and the* ***Hacienda Martinez****. It usually costs $4 for each, but you can get a combination ticket good for either two or three of the properties. A ticket for two houses is $6 and for all three only $8, a substantial savings over the single ticket price. There are similar reductions available on senior citizen and children's rates. Another way to save money is by buying a family ticket. A $15 ticket will admit any number of members of the same family to one house. That's a good buy if you have a big group and may be cheaper than having everyone purchase their own combination ticket. Get your calculator out and figure which way is best.*

For visitors who will be spending more time in Taos and are planning on doing even more of the attractions, there's an even better buy. You can purchase a $20 combination ticket which offers admission not only to the above three museums, but also to the ***Fechin Institute, Harwood Museum, Millicent Rogers Museum****, and one place that I haven't even described elsewhere – the* ***Van Vechten-Lineberry Taos Art Museum****. The latter houses a collection that includes at least one work from each of the more than 50 members of the Taos Society of Artists.*

After seeing the Kit Carson House you can stroll back to the Paseo del Pueblo and hang a right for a couple of blocks to the **Kit Carson State Park**. This small municipal day-use park is a quiet oasis in the otherwise bustling activity of Taos. You can just sit for a while, but you might be interested in looking in on the park's cemetery where Kit Carson and other local notables are buried.

The last stop on the Plaza area tour is a short walk north of the park. The **Fechin Institute** is different than most of Taos' other "art" houses. It was the home and studio of Nicolai Fechin, a Russian artist who made wonderful wood carvings during his residence in Taos from 1928 through 1955. The interior of the house was itself intricately carved by Fechin. It houses many of his works, lots of which were in media other than wood, as well as the works of several other artists. Fechin often collected other works of art by trading his own works. Luckily he was prolific enough to trade and still have plenty of his own works to display. *The house and studio is open from Wednesday through Sunday. The hours are 1:00-5:30pm. It is only open from the Memorial Day weekend through early October. Admission is $3.*

Tour 2: Other Parts of Town

Approximate duration including sightseeing is 2 1/2 hours. Begin from the Plaza area.

Take the Paseo del Pueblo south out of Taos for about four miles. Directly on NM 68 is the **San Francisco de Asis Church**, *Tel. 758-2754*, definitely one of the most stunning religious structures in all of the American Southwest. Construction began in 1710 and it took over 40 years to complete the massive buttressed building. The central portion of the church is about 120 feet long, considerably larger than most Spanish Colonial period churches. The interior contains many valuable pieces of art, including images of important saints. One item of particular interest to people regardless of the extent of their faith is the Henri Ault painting located in the rectory. Entitled *The Shadow of the Cross*, Christ appears to be carrying a cross in certain types of light, while at other times it cannot be seen. No one has ever been able to offer a valid explanation of why this is so. *Visitors are welcome from Monday through Saturday between 9:00am and 4:00pm. However, the church is closed during the first two weeks of June. Donations are requested.*

Drive back north into Taos, but turn left on Ojitos Road just before reaching the Plaza. Ojitos will soon run into NM 240, called Ranchitos Road. In approximately two miles you'll see the entrance to the **Hacienda Martinez** on the right hand side of the road, *Tel. 758-1000*. This impressive villa was built in 1804 by Antonio Martinez. He was an important merchant in the early Taos community and also served as its *alcalde*, or mayor. The hacienda has been completely and magnificently restored to its original appearance and is one of only a very few in the entire country that is open to the public.

You'll first be struck by the massive adobe walls surrounding the complex. It was a frontier existence at that time and filled with many potential dangers, not least of which were the many personal enemies that Señor Martinez had made. The house itself contains 21 rooms, all of which are furnished in period, and which surround two *placitas*, which are large patio areas. *The hacienda is open daily from 9:00am until 5:00pm. It is closed on New Year's, Thanksgiving and Christmas. Admission for adults is $4 but see the sidebar on saving on admissions in Taos for combination ticket information.*

Now you should head back on NM 240. About a half mile from the Hacienda bear left onto Blueberry Hill Road until you reach the junction of US 64. Turn right and go one block to Millicent Rogers Road, which leads directly to the **Millicent Rogers Museum**, *Tel. 758-2462*. Mrs. Rogers was a wealthy woman (her family owned a huge stake in Standard Oil). Always a lover of art, she moved to Taos in 1947 and lived there for the final six years of her life. During that brief period she put together one of the world's largest private collections of Spanish Colonial and Native American art. Today, you can view her entire collection as well as many other works of art that have been donated by other patrons of Southwestern art. Many items in the pottery collection date from as far back as the 1300s. Also of interest is a life-sized diorama of a Navajo silversmith's workshop. *The museum is open daily from 9:00am to 5:00pm but is closed on New Year's, Easter, September 30th, Thanksgiving and Christmas. The admission fee is $4 for adults; $3 for seniors and students with proper ID; and $2 for children ages 6-16. There is also a family ticket available for $8.00.*

The last stop on Tour 2 is far different from what you've been seeing. It's time for a bit of scenery instead of art and history. Go back to US 64 and turn left (westbound). In a few miles you'll reach the remarkable **Suspension Bridge over the Rio Grande Gorge**. Carrying US 64 traffic across it, the bridge is one of the highest highway spans in the world. Stop at one of the parking areas located at either end of the bridge and use the pedestrian lane on either side of the roadway to cross into the center of the bridge. From there you'll have a dramatic view of the deep, dark, and forbidding gorge that shelters the Rio Grande on its southward journey. Most remarkable is the fact that you don't even know the gorge exists as you approach it by car. The plateau on either side is very flat – then suddenly, this wide crevice in the earth seems to open up before your eyes. It's quite a sight and should not be missed.

Take US 64 back into town to complete your Taos area tour.

Tour 3: Pueblo de Taos

Approximate duration including sightseeing is 1 1/2 hours. Begin from the Plaza vicinity.

Head north on the Paseo del Pueblo. A couple of blocks north of Kit Carson Road the road will fork. Bear to the right (there will be signs pointing you in the direction of the Taos Pueblo). This side road ends at the entrance to the **Pueblo**, which is located about 2 1/2 miles north of the Plaza, *Tel. 758-1028*. Leave your car in the large central parking area and prepare to wander around on foot in this journey to another time.

First take a look at the ruins of the **Mission San Geronimo de Taos**, which are right near the pueblo's entrance. Once a huge complex, all that remains of the original mission are some of the massive adobe walls and a small section of a bell tower. The mission was originally constructed around 1598 and was destroyed in the 1680 Pueblo Revolt. It was rebuilt 25 years later only to be destroyed by American forces during another revolt that occurred in 1847. A smaller mission of the same name is also located in this area and is still in use.

Taos is easily the most famous of all the New Mexico pueblos. It has been continuously occupied for more than 700 years. Well known for its two large terraced communal dwellings, each five stories high, you'll recognize it from pictures as soon as you enter. It is the tallest Pueblo still in use and, some say, the most picturesque. A small creek runs through the center of the Pueblo and is often the site of friendly but passionate foot races between the two major groups inhabiting Taos Pueblo. Visitors come to Taos all year, but the summer is always filled with gawking crowds. Winter time is much more quiet and, in some ways, even more beautiful when the snow gently covers the red adobe roofs with a thin blanket. Visible from the Pueblo is **Wheeler Peak**, the highest point in New Mexico and a sacred place to the Native Americans of Taos.

While a visit to Taos Pueblo is a fascinating experience at any time of the year, it is at its very best when one of the many time-honored ceremonies of the people is taking place. Many of the festivals are open to the public. However, no cameras are allowed on the Pueblo during feast days. Among the best ceremonies are the Turtle Dance on January 1st, the Feast of Santa Cruz on May 3rd, The Feasts of San Antonio and San Juan on June 13th and 24th, the Taos Pueblo Pow Wow on the second weekend of July, the Feast of San Geronimo on September 29th and 30th, and the Procession on Christmas Eve or the Deer Dance on Christmas Day.

Pueblo de Taos is open daily from 8:00am until 5:30pm. Although the Pueblo welcomes tourists, the inhabitants are very conservative and shun all modern amenities. You must abide by the posted rules and remember to respect the privacy of the residents – this is, after all, their home. There is a parking fee and additional fees for taking pictures, making sketches or using a video camera. These fees range from $5 to $10.

TAOS EDUCATIONAL FACILITIES

Taos is a major educational center for the arts. Despite its small size it has some of the best art schools in the world. Many other forms of cultural education are also available. While many people who come to learn and develop their art skills are very serious about their studies, an increasing number of "ordinary" people also have an interest in learning more about the Southwest or seeing if they have any artistic skills buried deep within themselves.

*Among the best known facilities are the **Taos Art School**, Tel. 758-0350, which offers weekly workshops on art as well as the culture and literature of the Southwest. The **Taos Institute of Arts**, Tel. 758-2793, offers week-long courses. Both of these schools are fully accredited and many of the courses and workshops provide college level credit. So, if you're an art or literature student on summer vacation, you can combine some fun and get credit for it too!*

NIGHTLIFE & ENTERTAINMENT

Like Santa Fe to the south, the performing arts and other forms of entertainment in Taos are available on a scale that is out of all proportion to the size of the community. On the cultural side the Taos area is best known for the summer music program in Angel Fire which runs for several weeks beginning in the latter part of August. Known as **Music From Angel Fire**, the series features classical chamber music in a marvelous setting. *Information can be obtained by calling 377-3233.*

Both local theater companies and national theater and dance touring groups perform at the **Taos Community Auditorium**, *Tel. 758-4677*. Schedules and information are available from the box office. Many other evening cultural events take place during the summer. Contact the visitors bureau or consult local publications for what's happening during the time you'll be in Taos.

The best known night spots, like in Santa Fe, are generally located in the larger resort hotels. A sampling follows.

THE ADOBE BAR, *in the Taos Inn at 125 Paseo del Pueblo Norte. Tel.. 758-2233.*

Step into what looks like a bit of Mexico and then continue the feeling with some of the best margaritas north of the border. Live music with both Mexican and American food adds to the ambience of this very popular watering hole.

THE CANTINA, *in the Sagebrush Inn, South Santa Fe Road. Tel. 758-2254.*

This spacious lounge off the lobby is also in keeping with the architectural style so popular in Taos. A variety of entertainment is offered but The Cantina is probably best known as *the* place in Taos for country and western dancing.

KACHINA CABARET, *Paseo del Pueblo Norte. Tel. 758-2275.*

Both music and comedy acts are featured at this lively night spot located just a little north of the Plaza area. There's nightly dancing to live bands between acts and a full service bar.

SHOPPING

The number of places to shop in Taos seems almost as plentiful as in larger Santa Fe. While there are dozens of specialty shops and places to buy souvenirs all over town, the majority are concentrated in the **Plaza area**, all along the **Paseo del Pueblo**, and on **Ledoux Street**.

Taos, above all else, is most famous for its **paintings**. There are no fewer than 60 art galleries in this tiny community. Most sell many other fine art items besides paintings. You'll find pottery, jewelry, and textiles that would make a fine addition to the most luxurious home or simple apartment. The **Taos Chamber of Commerce**, *Tel. 1/800-732-8267*, can provide you with a complete listing of the art galleries. You can also pick up a listing in person at the **Taos Visitors Center** south of town. Oddly enough, you won't find nearly as many street vendors in Taos as in Santa Fe.

SPORTS & RECREATION

All locations are within Taos unless specified otherwise.

Bicycle Rentals

- **Gearing Up Bicycle Shop**, *129 Paseo del Pueblo Sur, Tel. 751-0365*

Fishing

- **Eagle Nest Lake**, *between Angel Fire and Red River*. Kokanee salmon and trout.
- **Rio Grande Gorge National Recreation Area**. Trout.

Golf

- **Red Eagle Golf Course**, *in Eagle Nest, Tel. 754-2964*
- **Angel Fire Country Club**, *in Angel Fire,Tel. 377-3055*

Gyms & Health Clubs

- **Northside Health and Fitness Center**, *Tel. 751-1242*
- **Taos Spa and Tennis Club**, *Tel. 758-1980*

Horseback Riding

- **Llano Bonito**, *Tel. 587-2636*
- **Rio Grande Stables**, *Tel. 776-5913*
- **Taos Creek Stables**, *Tel. 758-7112*
- **Taos Indian Horse Ranch**, *Tel. 1/800-659-3210*
- **Road Runner Tours**, *in Angel Fire, Tel. 377-6416*
- **Bitter Creek Stables**, *in Red River, Tel. 754-2587*
- **Bobcat Pass Stables**, *in Red River, Tel. 754-2769*

Rafting

- **Big River Raft Trips**, *Tel. 758-9711 or 1/800-748-3760*
- **Far Flung Adventures**, *Tel. 758-2628 or 1/800-359-2627*
- **Los Rios River Runners**, *Tel. 776-8854 or 1/800-544-1181*
- **Native Sons Adventures**, *Tel. 758-9342 or 1/800-753-7559*
- **Rio Grande Rapid Transit**, *Tel. 758-9200 or 1/800-222-7238*

Skiing

- **Angel Fire Ski Area**, *in Angel Fire, Tel. 1/800-633-7463*. Mid-December through March.

- **Enchanted Forest**, *in Red River, Tel. 754-2374.* Cross-country skiing only from late November through early April.
- **Red River Ski Area**, *in Red River, Tel. 754-2223.* Late November through March.
- **Sipapu**, *south of Taos, Tel. 587-2240.* Mid-December through March.
- **Questa**, *north of Taos, Ski Rio, Tel. 1/800-227-5746.* Late November through early April.
- **Taos Ski Valley**, *Tel. 776-2291.* Late November through early April.

Swimming
- **Don Fernando Pool**, *120 Civic Plaza Drive*

PRACTICAL INFORMATION

All services are for Taos unless otherwise specified.

- **Tourist Office/Visitors Bureau**
  Taos: *Paseo del Pueblo Sur, Tel. 758-3573 or 1/800-732-8267*
  Angel Fire: *Tel. 377-6661 or 1/800-446-8117*
  Eagle Nest: *Tel. 377-2420 or 1/800-494-9117*
  Red River: *Tel. 754-2366 or 1/800-348-6444*
- **Bus Depot**: *Tel. 758-1144*
- **Hotel Hot Line**: *Taos Central Reservations, Tel. 1/800-821-2437*
- **Hospital**: *Tel. 758-8883*
- **Police** (non-emergency): *Tel. 758-2216*

THE ENCHANTED CIRCLE

Just about everyone who comes to Taos includes a drive on the **Enchanted Circle** as part of their visit. And why not? The scenery near Taos includes some of the best in the Southwest and is dotted with small, quaint towns and resort communities.

WHERE TO STAY

As the Enchanted Circle is primarily a day excursion from Taos, most visitors won't need to select lodging places along the route. However, should you choose to do so there is no shortage of great places to stay. In fact, because of the high prices in Taos, some visitors (especially in summer) may want to stay along the Enchanted Circle and drive into Taos to see the sights.

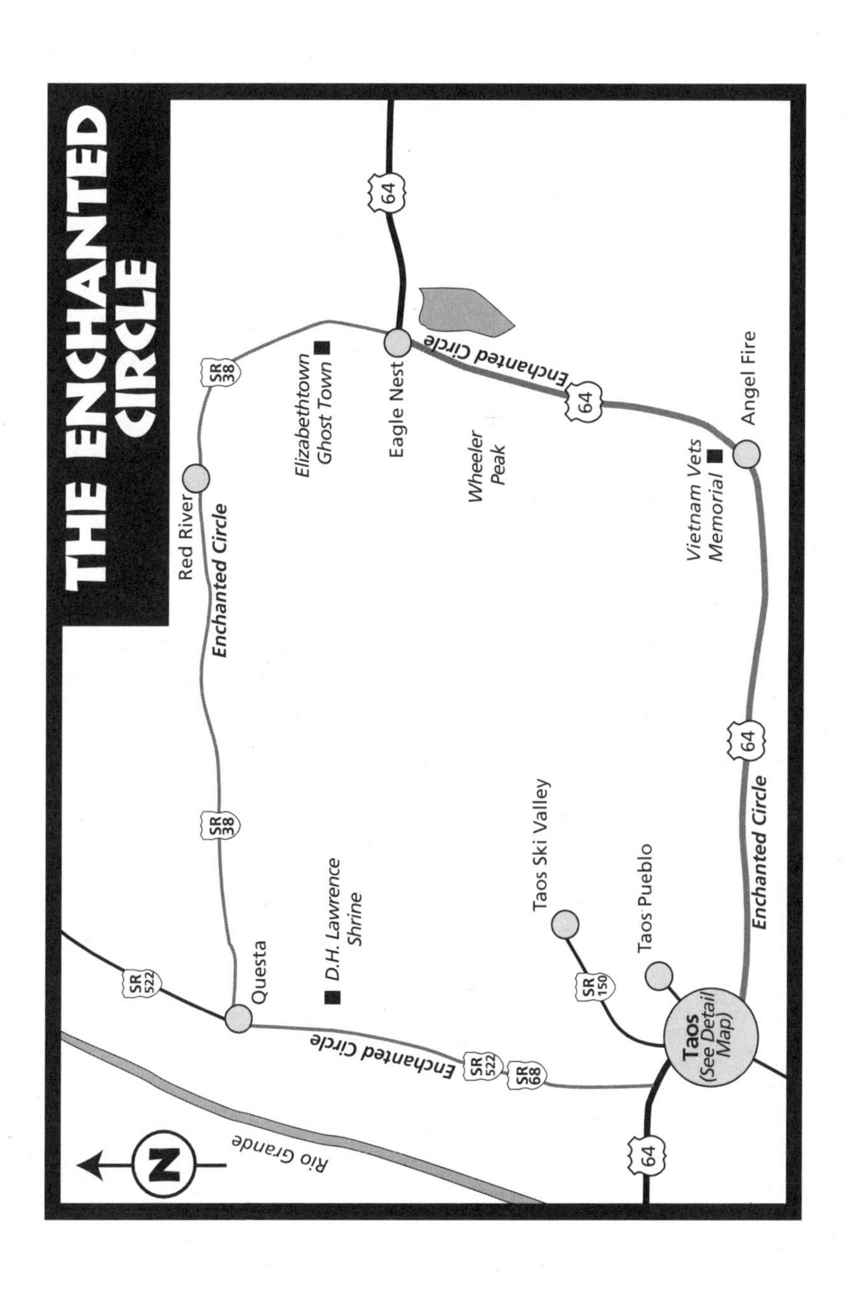
THE ENCHANTED CIRCLE
Red River
Enchanted Circle
SR 38
Elizabethtown Ghost Town
Eagle Nest
Enchanted Circle
64
Wheeler Peak
Angel Fire
Vietnam Vets Memorial
64
Enchanted Circle
SR 38
D.H. Lawrence Shrine
Taos Ski Valley
Taos Pueblo
SR 150
Taos (See Detail Map)
SR 522
Questa
Enchanted Circle
SR 522
SR 68
64
Rio Grande
N

Before you select this option, however, be aware that it's over 20 miles from Taos to Angel Fire and about double that to Red River. Those are the two Circle communities with most of the accommodations.

Moderate

ALPINE LODGE, *on NM 38 at Main and Pioneer Streets in Red River. Tel. 754-2952, Fax 754-6421. Rates: $49-64; multi-bedroom apartments from $78-134. 45 Rooms. Major credit cards accepted. Toll-free reservations 1/800-252-2333. Closed from the beginning of April through mid-May. Located in center of town.*

While primarily known as a ski resort, the Alpine Lodge makes a beautiful place to stay in any season. The hotel property fronts the Red River and the grounds are like a private park, complete with tables and grills for picnicking and a childrens' playground. There's also some fine fishing in the river. Some units face the park while others have panoramic mountain vistas. The three-story wooden structure is built in a modified European alpine style. Originally built in 1960, the lodge was completely renovated in 1992. The rooms are nicely furnished and very comfortable. Each one features either a balcony or porch. Many units have either limited or full kitchens.

There's a restaurant on the premises as well as a lounge with entertainment. A small wood-framed structure houses a nice whirlpool with a great view of the surrounding area. The lodge has a direct connection via pedestrian bridge to the chair lifts.

LEGENDS HOTEL, *North Angel Fire Road in Angel Fire. Tel. 377-6401, Fax 377-4200. Rates: $75-100; condominium units from $100-160. 128 Rooms. Major credit cards accepted. Toll-free reservations 1/800-633-7463. Closed during November. Located adjacent to the ski area.*

A modern lodge and conference center, the Legends is situated on acres of nicely manicured grounds at the foot of the beautiful Angel Fire ski area. All of the rooms, whether regular accommodations or condominium units, are spacious and are attractively decorated in a modern Southwestern style. Some have kitchens and/or fireplaces.

The Legends is a full-service resort with many activities and amenities. You'll find two restaurants as well as a deli for quick snacks and meals; an indoor pool with health spa; and six tennis courts. There's a year-round supervised children's program, a video arcade, and several attractive shops. Other recreational opportunities include lake trout fishing, wind surfing, and boating. You can even walk to a nearby golf course.

LIFTS WEST CONDOMINIUM RESORT HOTEL, *Main Street and Jumping Track Trail in Red River. Tel. 754-2778, Fax 754-6617. Rates: $49-108. 170 Rooms. Major credit cards accepted. Toll-free reservations 1/800-221-1859. Located in the center of town along NM 38.*

Here's a great-looking year-round resort at very reasonable rates. The large structure is relatively new but is built to remind you of yesteryear. Actually, it's sort of a combination of styles – half old west, and half alpine-style ski chalet. The end result, painted a bright yellow with natural wood trim, is a very pretty picture. While it may be on the main street, it simultaneously borders on nature – mountains and forest are a stone's throw away. To be more exact, the main ski lift for Red River is 250 feet away.

None of the rooms are the ordinary hotel type. Every unit is a suite, ranging from one to three bedrooms. Some of the larger units have two bathrooms. Most have fireplaces to go with fully equiped kitchens. In fact, you'll find just about all the comforts and conveniences of home at Lifts West.

Most of the public areas and facilities are located off an attractive and large atrium lobby that features a beautiful four-sided stone fireplace. Some of the other facilities you'll find include a heated pool with two Jacuzzis (indoor and outdoor) and a sauna; restaurant; lounge with nightly entertainment; and several retail shops. You can find a nice selection of ski wear year-round. The staff will gladly arrange for outdoor recreational activities in the area.

WHERE TO EAT

Moderate – $11-20

MORENO VALLEY COWBOY EVENING, *on NM 38 in Red River. Tel. 754-2769. Most major credit cards accepted. Dinner only, summer months. Reservations required.*

Here's an opportunity to spend a fun-filled evening. You'll begin by boarding a horse-drawn wagon for a leisurely paced ride to a working ranch nestled in beautiful mountain scenery. Upon arrival watch as the country chefs prepare your dinner – a choice of either steak or chicken. The food is simple but plentiful and very tasty. After dinner is completed guests sit around the campfire and partake of country and western entertainment before reboarding the wagon for the trip back into town. If you're looking for a good time and don't want anything fancy, this is surely a "different" kind of supper experience. Kids will really enjoy themselves.

SUNDANCE RESTAURANT, *on High Street in Red River. Tel. 754-2971. Most major credit cards accepted. Lunch and dinner only.*

A staple of the Red River scene for well over 20 years, the Sundance is an attractive facility specializing in New Mexican cuisine. The friendly staff will be glad to explain to diners unfamiliar with the local cooking what each dish is and how its prepared. Be sure to sample the delicious stuffed sopaipillas. For a main course I suggest the sizzling hot and aromatic fajitas. Chili Rellenos is a highlight of the menu and is a mild mannered dish, but Sundance also has chile that's so hot that it will knock your socks off.

Sundance also has a children's menu. Kids generally like chile, but if your little ones have never had hot New Mexican dishes before its advisable to start out on the mild side. There's a decent selection of wine and beer but many diners seem to settle on Sundance's well-known frozen wine margarita.

TEXAS REDS STEAKHOUSE AND SALOON, *on Main Street in Red River. Tel. 754-2922. Most major credit cards accepted. Dinner served nightly.*

The look and taste of the old west await you at the very popular Texas Reds. Now approaching nearly 30 years of service, the colorful front facade looks like something from a western movie. The atmosphere inside is more of the same. It's both lively and fun. The staff is very friendly and efficient. Big, juicy steaks are the main star of the menu, which also includes prime rib, ribs, and a variety of other dishes. The large full-service bar is popular with diners and with those just coming in for a drink and good conversation.

SEEING THE SIGHTS

The **Enchanted Circle** is a loop road beginning in Taos and winding through the surrounding mountains and forests. It's a pleasant and leisurely drive covering about 85 miles – a little longer if you take some of the several short side trips off of the main route. While you can run through the Circle in three to four hours, it is best to devote an entire day to give the Enchanted Circle its proper due.

I'll describe the route in a counter-clockwise direction from Taos and clearly delineate when you have to deviate from the circle to do the "side" attractions. The first portion of the Circle is via US 64 from Taos to Eagle Nest, then via NM 38 to Questa, where NM 68 takes you back into Taos. The roads are clearly marked and easy to drive, even for the individual who is not accustomed to mountain roads.

From Taos to Eagle Nest

Leave Taos via the Paseo del Canon (which is **US 64**) at the junction of the Paseo del Pueblo by the Visitor Center. You quickly leave town and the road climbs alongside a river through the Carson National Forest. Most of the mountains are blocked from view during this initial portion of the drive by the thick strands of trees. Nevertheless, the ride is scenic from the very beginning.

After a few miles you emerge from the forest above a broad, flat valley near the town of **Angel Fire**, located only 20 miles from Taos. Angel Fire is a year-round resort with skiing in the winter and golf in the summer. (See the *Sports & Recreation* section of this chapter for further information on Angel Fire and all the other resort communities encountered on the Enchanted Circle.) As part of the Enchanted Circle, however, it's best known as the site of the **DAV Vietnam Veterans National Memorial**, *Tel. 377-6900*. Visible from US 64 and reached by a very short spur road, the memorial was built by a family to honor the memory of their son who was killed in Vietnam. Completed in 1971 by Dr. Victor Westphall, the structure was proclaimed a national memorial by President Ronald Reagan in 1987.

Rising 50 feet from the hillside and commanding a panoramic view of the valley and the Sangre de Cristo Mountains, the Memorial is truly an inspiring structure. It's curvilinear design soars skyward. An adjacent visitor center, built right into the hillside itself, contains exhibits and displays. Obviously, the Vietnam War still provokes a lot of controversy in the American public and consciousness. Regardless of where you stand, you simply must stop here. You cannot help but be brought to the verge of tears upon seeing, and then entering, the memorial's simple but stirring interior. Pictures of Vietnam War participants who were killed in action are rotated on a monthly basis. *The Memorial never closes but the Visitor Center is open from 10:00am until 7:00pm every day except Monday. There is no admission charge but donations are appreciated.*

Upon returning to the main road and continuing in a northerly direction, you'll quickly descend into the **Moreno Valley**, with soaring mountain peaks surrounding you to the west and east. From here there is a good view of 13,161-foot high **Wheeler Peak** on your left. Wheeler Peak is the focal point of the scenic **Red River Mountains** that continue through much of the remainder of the Enchanted Circle. Just before the town of **Eagle Nest** is a lake of the same name. Its tranquil waters make for a picturesque stop even if you aren't going to be using the privately owned lake for fishing.

From Eagle Nest to Questa

At Eagle Nest, US 64 turns eastward, but you should continue on the Circle with **NM 38**, unless you are not going to be touring the northeast region. In that case, it's worth taking a ten mile detour on scenic US 64 as it winds along the Cimarron River to the **Cimarron Canyon State Park**. See Chapter 17, *The Northeast*, for more details..

About eight miles north of Eagle Nest, keep your eyes peeled on your left for the **Elizabethtown Ghost Town**. A booming mining town dating from 1865, its many buildings once included no less than six different saloons. There's not much left today, just some remains of walls dotting a brilliantly colored field of wildflowers that includes mariposa lily and Indian paintbrush. Then the road will begin a steep drop through the scenic **Red River Pass** engulfed by vistas of mountains and thick forests of ponderosa pine, aspen, Douglas fir, cottonwood and several types of spruce. You may not be able to pick out one type from another (I certainly can't) but the mosaic is beautiful even to those with little or no knowledge of flora.

The town of **Red River** has a permanent population of only about 500 hearty people. That doesn't stop it from being a major year-round resort destination with some of the best skiing in New Mexico. The chair lifts operate in summer for those wishing to get a different perspective of the Red River Valley below or who wish to hike in the mountains. Horseback riding and other forms of outdoor recreation bring visitors in the summer as well. Besides the activities listed under *Sports & Recreation* above you might be interested in taking one of the many popular four-wheel or jeep tours into the wild back country around Red River. Among the operators are **High Country Tours and Jeep Rental**, *Tel. 754-2441*, and **Jeep Trailways Rentals and Tours**, *Tel. 754-6443*. As you can tell, these services offer you a choice of renting a vehicle and exploring on your own (maps provided) or having someone who knows the area show you around. Both are located on Main Street.

Speaking of Main Street, the town itself runs only a couple of blocks and is a colorful reminder of the mining boomtown era. The building facades look almost like a scene from a western movie set. At an altitude of 8,750 feet, Red River's promoters like to point out that you're "more likely to see a herd of deer than a crowd of people."

To the west of town, NM 38 continues thrugh the Red River Canyon and reaches its end at the small farming community of **Questa**. The Enchanted Circle heads south at this point via NM 68, but you can take a detour on the **Wild River Byway** (see sidebar). On the way back to Taos you'll pass through the tiny town of **San Cristobal**, site of the **D. H. Lawrence Shrine**. Before you make definite plans to see this, be aware that it is reached by taking a six mile detour on a dirt road that winds its way up the side of **Lobo Mountain**. I would suggest that only those drivers with previous experience on this type of road attempt the trip. For those who do, the effort will be well rewarded.

Atop the mountain is **The Kiowa Ranch**, which was the residence of the famous author and his wife for a number of years. Although he died in France, at his request Lawrence's ashes were returned to this site and are enclosed in a small shrine located near the ranch house. Besides the simple but touching shrine, there are some wonderful panoramic views spanning the Taos Plateau and the Rio Grande Valley.

Back to Taos

Head south at Questa via **NM 68**, and you're now on the final leg of the Enchanted Circle as you near Taos. Before getting back into town, however, there's the opportunity for another detour. This one leads to the beautiful **Taos Ski Valley**, considered to be one of the foremost places for skiing anywhere in the world. While there isn't that much happening in the valley during the summer, it's still a beautiful place to just go and take a look.

What makes it so special is its location at the closed end of a small box canyon embedded within the magnificent Sangre de Cristo Mountains. The base is a very high 9,200 feet, while the peak soars to more than 11,800 feet.

WILD RIVER BYWAY

A portion of the ***Rio Grande*** *in northern New Mexico was officially designated as a Wild and Scenic River by a 1968 Act of Congress. The wild doesn't necessarily mean "wild" as in whitewater (although there are some sections that can get pretty rough) – it refers to the mostly pristine state of the river. By being granted such designation, it is hoped that with your cooperation it will remain pristine forever. The most beautiful and rugged section covers a little more than 50 miles and stretches from a few miles north of the Taos area all the way up to the Colorado state line. The sheer dark walls of the canyon are as high as a thousand feet in several places.*

From Questa, head north on ***NM 522*** *for about three miles and then take* ***NM 378*** *a short distance until it dead ends at the* ***Rio Grande Gorge National Recreation Area****. The rocky terrain of the gorge is similar to the view from the Suspension Bridge west of Taos, but here you can get up close to the river. In fact, you can hike to your heart's content on the moderate to difficult trails. There are also guided nature hikes during the summer. Trout fishing is a popular activity in the Recreation Area, but be forewarned that the fishing areas are only reached by those same trails leading from the canyon's rim. Adding this detour will only take a couple of hours, since the Wild River Byway is the shortest of New Mexico's designated back country routes.*

The area is managed by the Bureau of Land Management and you can get information by calling them at ***Tel. 758-8851****.*

16. THE NORTHWEST
- NATIVE AMERICAN COUNTRY -

The **northwestern** quarter of New Mexico is, except for the towns of Farmington and Gallup, a sparsely populated region of dramatic scenery. The land is not dominated by the towering peaks of the Rockies like it is around Santa Fe and Taos. Rather, the high plateaus and intervening valleys offer a harsher type of beauty – large areas devoid of the magnificent forests and gentle meadows. Instead you are confronted by vividly colored rock and numerous outcroppings of generally volcanic origin that have been sculpted by time into unusual and sometimes grotesque shapes. Some, like **Shiprock**, are famous while others, such as the **Bisti Badlands**, are scarcely known outside of New Mexico.

Culturally, too, the northwest is a wonderful place to visit. You may be wondering why I dubbed this region as Native American Country after just reading about the many pueblos scattered throughout the Taos to Albuquerque corridor. Well, there are some more pueblos here, including the wonderful **Acoma** and **Zuni pueblos**. But the Indian representation goes even farther because much of the land is occupied by major Indian reservations. These include the vast **Navajo Reservation** that extends into Arizona. The **Jicarilla Apache Reservation** and the **Laguna Reservation** are just two more of the many other important Indian lands.

The Native American presence is felt even beyond the Reservations. **Gallup**, the second largest community in the northwestern region, is not on a reservation but many of the inhabitants are Indians.

ARRIVALS & DEPARTURES

Public transportation is extremely limited. However, there are bus routes connecting Albuquerque and Santa Fe with Farmington, Gallup, and Grants. Gallup is also served by **Mesa Air**, *Tel. 1/800-MESA-AIR*, from Albuquerque and has an Amtrak station. Don't expect convenient schedules for any of these travel methods.

As a matter of convenience and logic, I'll follow a counter-clockwise route that picks up from the Santa Fe/Taos area. The major "stops" are in Chama, Aztec, Farmington, Gallup, the Zuni and Acoma Pueblos, and Grants before returning to Albuquerque.

ORIENTATION/GETTING AROUND

You can get a good idea of the area I refer to as the northwest if you consult the regional touring map in the beginning of the book and, more or less, visually overlay that onto a New Mexico road map. **I-40** traverses the region's southern area from west of Albuquerque to Gallup and beyond to the Arizona line, while **US 84** is roughly the eastern edge from Espanola (between Santa Fe and Taos) to Chama and the Colorado line. **US 64** runs west from Chama through the northern part of the region to Farmington, Shiprock, and the Four Corners area.

US 666 provides a north-south route in the western part of the region, connecting Shiprock and Gallup. There are few good roads in the interior, although **NM 44** does cut across a wide swath of the region from the Jemez Mountain area to near Farmington.

Other than these routes, most of the paved roads don't go very far or are designated as **Indian Routes**. They're generally not as well maintained as the state and US highways and I'll try and keep you on the main roads as much as possible. For the slightly more adventurous, or if you have a four-wheel drive vehicle, there are even more possibilities for seeing the country.

WHERE TO STAY

Now that we've finished with the "big three" of Albuquerque, Santa Fe, and Taos, the pickings for fine lodging become a bit more slim. Although tourism is important throughout the state, the great numbers of people who visit the aforementioned localities don't all find their way to the more rural portions of New Mexico. The result is a far less varied choice of places to stay.

Although there are some wonderful local, independent inns with a great deal of unique charm, I've found that most of the better places to stay are in some of the popular national chains. This applies not only to the towns in this chapter but in all of the regional touring chapters that follow. Don't fret, though, because you won't have any difficulty in finding a good place to spend the night. Listings are alphabetical by town.

CHAMA & ENVIRONS

Moderate

CASA DE MARTINEZ BED AND BREAKFAST, *Old Highway 84 in Los Ojos. Write to: PO Box 96; Los Ojos NM 87551. Tel. 588-7858. Rates: $55-*

95, including full breakfast. 6 Rooms. No credit cards. Shared baths. Located 9 miles from Chama just off US 64/84.

This historic family home was built over an almost 60-year period beginning in 1861. Providing views of the Sangre de Cristo and San Juan Mountains, the Casa de Martinez is for the traveler who really likes getting away from it all – you won't find in-room telephones, television, or air conditioning (none of which are needed in the tranquil environment of this region).

What you will find is a lovely family-type residence that is still operated by the same family as built the home more than a century ago. All of the rooms are furnished with original antiques. There are extensive public areas in the adobe structure, including a bright room where hearty breakfasts are served and a living room where guests mingle during quiet evenings.

BEST WESTERN JICARILLA INN, *US 64 & Hawks Drive in Dulce. Tel. 759-3663, Fax 759-3170. Rates: $68-80. 42 Rooms. Major credit cards accepted. Toll-free reservations 1/800-528-1234. Located approximately 27 miles west of Chama on US 64.*

The Inn is located in the middle of the Jicarilla Apache Indian Reservation, right across the road from the tribal headquarters and within walking distance of some small ruins. The setting, ranch country surrounded by towering mountains, is simply beautiful. Although it's about a half-hour drive from Chama, I include it because many people will need to stay in the Chama area after a late return from the Cumbres & Toltec train ride. There aren't many good places to stay in Chama itself and many readers may not want to stay at the B&B described above.

Rooms in the Jicarilla Inn are typical of a modern motel, both in design and amenities. The Inn itself has a nice, rustic appearance. Six of the units are efficiencies but no utensils are provided. There's an on-premise restaurant and cocktail lounge. Indian guide service is available for those who wish to hunt or fish on the Reservation. Indian gaming, in the form of bingo, is held at the hotel.

THE LODGE AT CHAMA, *Tel. 756-2133, Fax 756-2519. Rates: $200-375.*

This property, owned by the Jicarilla Apache Indian tribe and occupying a 32,000 acre ranch in the gorgeous San Juan Mountains, is described in a sidebar in Chapter 12, *The Best Places to Stay*. For several reasons (including the price and the fact that it is essentially a hunting lodge), the average visitor to New Mexico will not likely stay here. However, I would be remiss if I simply ignored an establishment of such high renown.

FARMINGTON

Moderate

BEST WESTERN FARMINGTON INN, *700 Scott Avenue. Tel. 327-5221, Fax 327-1565. Rates: $75-98. 194 Rooms. Major credit cards accepted. Toll-free reservations 1/800-528-1234. Located in the center of town at the intersection of US 64 (Bloomfield Boulevard) and Scott Avenue.*

This modern and attractive facility features large rooms with oversized king or queen beds. Some rooms have refrigerators and coffee makers. Mini-suites ($84-114) contain kitchenettes. A big atrium area contains a heated pool, sauna, and Jacuzzi. There's also a complete fitness center. The Inn also has a good restaurant, coffee shop, and cocktail lounge with entertainment.

HOLIDAY INN, *600 East Broadway. Tel. 327-9811, Fax 325-2288. Rates: $70. 150 Rooms. Major credit cards accepted. Toll-free reservations 1/800-HOLIDAY. Located on US 64 (Bloomfield Boulevard) near the intersection of Scott Avenue in downtown.*

Recently renovated, the hotel is typical of the two-story motor inns put up by the hundreds in the early 1970s. Certainly nothing special, but a convenient place to stay that provides what travel agents would refer to as "moderate first class" accommodations. All rooms feature coffee makers and some have refrigerators. Like all Holiday Inns, you'll also find a decent if somewhat overpriced restaurant, a cocktail lounge providing entertainment, and a pool. There's also a sauna and fitness center.

GALLUP

Moderate

RED ROCK INN, *3010 East Highway 66. Tel. 722-7600, Fax 722-9770. Rates: $62-125, including Continental Breakfast. 78 Rooms. Major credit cards accepted. Member of Best Western Hotels. Toll-free reservations 1/800-528-1234. Located on the east side of town, one mile west of I-40, Exit 26 on US 66.*

Be sure you check in at the right place – there are two other Best Westerns in town! This is an attractive, adobe-style building with large, comfortable rooms. Some rooms and small suites have refrigerators, kitchenettes, hair dryers, and video players so you can immediately view your camcorder travel epic. Many rooms have balconies with nice views of the surrounding red rock mesas from which the inn takes its name. Recreational facilities include swimming pool, whirlpool, and exercise room. Several restaurants are within walking distance and many more are just a short ride away.

HOLIDAY INN HOLIDOME, *2915 West Highway 66. Tel. 722-2201, Fax 722-9616. Rates: $65. 212 Rooms. Major credit cards accepted. Toll-free reservations 1/800-432-2211. Located on the west side of town, on US 66 near I-40, Exit 16.*

For a Holiday Inn this represents a surprisingly good value. It's over 30 years old but was refurbished less than ten years ago and converted into a "Holidome" – that is, a fairly standard Holiday Inn with a large enclosed courtyard containing swimming pool, sauna, whirlpool, and exercise room. The rooms are also standard fare, but clean and comfortable. There are two restaurants on the premises as well as a cocktail lounge providing nightly entertainment.

GRANTS

Moderate

HOLIDAY INN EXPRESS, *1496 East Santa Fe Avenue. Tel. 285-4676, Fax 285-6998. Rates: $79-89, including Continental Breakfast. 58 Rooms. Major credit cards accepted. Toll-free reservations 1/800-HOLIDAY. Located less than a half mile north of the Exit 85 interchange of I-40 along the main street into town.*

This is a spanking new facility that features oversized, nicely furnished rooms decorated in light pastel colors. In case you're wondering about the "Express" surname, that refers to smaller, generally less expensive Holiday Inns with fewer facilities. For example, there's no restaurant. However, there is a small heated indoor pool and hot tub. The bright lobby breakfast room is cheerful. Several restaurants are located nearby, including a couple within walking distance.

Budget

LEISURE LODGE, *1204 East Santa Fe Avenue. Tel. 287-2991. Rates: $30-38. 32 Rooms. Most major credit cards accepted. Located about a mile north of I-40, Exit 85 on the road into town.*

It isn't very often that you can find nice rooms at such reasonable prices these days along any major Interstate highway. I'm also happy to get away from the "Best Western/Holiday Inn" or other chain-only towns. The accommodations are fairly basic but clean and very comfortable. Many of the rooms are quite large. The motel has a heated swimming pool. Complimentary coffee is offered in the lobby. Many restaurants are located within a short distance.

CAMPING & RV SITES

- **Aztec Ruins Road RV Park**, *Aztec. Tel. 334-3160*
- **Cibola Sands RV Park**, *Grants. Tel. 287-4376*
- **The Downs RV Park**, *Farmington. Tel. 325-7094*
- **KOA Campground**, *Farmington. Tel. 632-8339*
- **Lavaland RV Park**, *Grants. Tel. 287-8665*
- **L & L Ranch Resort**, *Chama. Tel. 588-7173*

WHERE TO EAT

CHAMA & ENVIRONS

Moderate – $11-20

BRANDING IRON INN, *1551 West Main Street. 756-2808. Major credit cards accepted. Lunch and dinner daily.*

An attractive restaurant featuring a look that combines Southwestern and Old West themes. The food is of the same format, with both Southwestern dishes as well as steak and beef dishes. Outdoor dining on the patio during summer. Cocktails are served. A nice friendly place good for a quiet meal or for the whole family.

HIGH COUNTRY RESTAURANT, *on NM 17 just north of the junction with US Highways 64/84. Tel. 756-2191. American Express, Discover, MasterCard and VISA accepted.*

This part of New Mexico is steak country, so it's not surprising that the two best restaurants in town both feature thick juicy beef. High Country also has a decent selection of seafood as well as a few Mexican entrees. The restaurant has a good salad bar, efficient service, and a children's menu. Next to the dining room is an old-time saloon recreating the decor and atmosphere of the turn of the century west.

FARMINGTON

Moderate – $11-20

THE TROUGH, *on Main Street (US 550) approximately 8 miles east of town. Tel. 334-6176. American Express, Discover, MasterCard and VISA accepted. Dinner only, nightly except Sunday.*

I've mentioned a few times that rural New Mexico isn't a mecca of fine dining, but at The Trough you will find a high degree of big city sophistication and elegance than is usually the case in these parts. It does remain, however, a casual place. The large dining room has a rustic, old west decor with dim lighting adding to the atmosphere. Steak and seafood are the two big items on the menu, although fresh wild game is also available, the type depending upon the season. A full service cocktail lounge is on the premises. Service at The Trough is very good and the quality of food and portion size are both above average.

CLANCY'S PUB, *Hutton and 20th Streets. Tel. 325-8176. Most major credit cards accepted. Lunch and dinner served nightly.*

Clancy's bills themselves as an "Irish cantina." Now if that sounds like quite an unusual combination, it is. Serving a nice variety of homemade dishes, the menu includes both Southwestern and Irish specialties. The full-service bar also offers many Irish beers and stout ales in addition to the libations more commonly found in this part of the country. The pleasant atmosphere and a friendly staff combine with the good food to make dining at Clancy's a most enjoyable experience.

Budget – $10 or less

FURR'S CAFETERIA, *3030 East Main Street (US 550). Tel. 327-6011. American Express, Discover, MasterCard and VISA accepted. Lunch and dinner served daily.*

This is one of what seems to be hundreds of this national cafeteria chain. I don't usually include them in my recommendations. This isn't because they're not suitable, but rather because I think many travelers want something a little more "exotic" when on vacation. However, good budget restaurants are few and far between in the isolated northwest of New Mexico. In fact, if you're not looking for steak or New Mexican type cuisine, finding eateries in any price category can sometimes be a problem.

Furr's offers a wide selection of main dishes, sides of vegetables, and desserts all at very reasonable prices. You pay for everything you take, including a slice of bread or a pat of butter, after making your selections and placing them on your tray. It's fast and convenient. No frills, but you can eat as much or as little as you like. Most important, the food is decent. What goes for this Furr's applies, of course, to any of the many others you encounter during your travels.

GALLUP

Moderate – $11-20

THE RANCH KITCHEN, *3001 West US Highway 66. Tel. 722-4349. Most major credit cards accepted.*

This is an attractive facility that has been a fixture in northwestern New Mexico's dining scene for more than 40 years. The large menu has Southwestern, Mexican, and American entrees to choose from, all nicely prepared and efficiently served by a friendly staff. There's a good salad bar. No cocktails are served but beer and wine are available.

SIRLOIN STOCKADE, *2824 East US Highway 66. Tel. 863-5508. Most major credit cards accepted. Lunch and dinner only.*

Good food at reasonable prices are the order of the day. The menu is limited mostly to steaks although a couple of Mexican and Southwestern dishes are usually available. The dining room has an old west theme and is comfortable.

Budget – $10 or less

EARL'S RESTAURANT, *1400 East US Highway 66. Tel. 863-4201. American Express, Discover, MasterCard and VISA accepted.*

A good family restaurant that will be celebrating its 50th anniversary, Earl's primarily serves Mexican food with a smattering of both Southwestern and general American fare. There's nothing fancy about either the food or atmosphere, but dinner entrees are generous portions and quite tasty, especially considering the prices. I also think that the salad bar is one of the better ones in the region. The surroundings are simple but comfortable. A children's menu is available.

GRANTS

Moderate - $11-20

JARAMILLO'S, *213 North Third Street. Tel. 287-9308. Most major credit cards accepted. Lunch and dinner served Monday through Friday.*

A small and casual restaurant with friendly and efficient service, Jaramillo's is a good place to go if you're looking for authentic Mexican and Southwestern cuisine prepared in a simple, unpretentious style.

LA VENTANA STEAK HOUSE, *110 1/2 Geis Street. Tel. 287-9393. Most major credit cards accepted. Lunch and dinner served daily except Sunday.*

Thick, juicy steaks and prime rib as well as a few Southwestern items are featured in this attractive restaurant in the heart of town. La Ventana is more popular with locals because it's not located right off of the Interstate. That should immediately tell you something about the quality of the food. Cocktails are served.

Budget - $10 or less

FOUR B's RESTAURANT, *at the Exit 85 interchange of I-40. Tel. 285-6697. Most major credit cards accepted.*

Some budget entrees but borders on the moderate price category. Part of a chain that's spread throughout the Rocky Mountain states, Four B's features contemporary decor, much like many of the so-called family restaurants, that is bright and cheerful. The menu is primarily American cuisine but a number of Southwestern meals are also available. There's a good salad bar and complete dinners represent an extremely good value. Special menus for both children and seniors are available. Good selection of desserts. No alcoholic beverages are served.

GRANTS STATION, *932 East Santa Fe Avenue. Tel. 287-2334. American Express, Discover, MasterCard and VISA accepted. Sunday brunch.*

Very similar in just about every way to Four B's except that the menu is a bit heavier on its Southwestern emphasis, including some Mexican fare. There's also a salad bar, menus for children and senior citizens, and fast service. You can't go wrong for the price.

SEEING THE SIGHTS

Chama

The mountain town of **Chama**, with a population of a thousand people, sits only a few miles from the Colorado border. It is 106 miles north of Santa Fe via US 285/84 to Espanola, and then US 84 after the two roads split. If you're coming from Taos, the distance is 93 miles. Follow US 64 all the way to Chama. The town is on NM 17 just off of US 64. The last 13 miles between the town of Tierra Amarilla and Chama carry both US 64 and 84. Neither route has much traffic and the roads are good, so you can make the trip in about two hours from Santa Fe and in 90 minutes from Taos. Both routes traverse high plateaus interspersed with forested areas and are within view of high mountain peaks, so the ride is a pleasant one.

If you're coming from Santa Fe, plan on making a stop at the **Ghost Ranch Living Museum**, *Tel. 685-4312*, located 14 miles north of the town of Abiquiu, which is around the half-way point to Chama. The museum is run by the US Forest Service and is dedicated to promoting conservation education. It has features of both a zoo and a natural history museum in its exhibit areas and nature trails. It's presented in a manner that is entertaining to both adults and children. The animals, which include beavers, raccoons, mountain lions, badgers, elk, owls, eagles and bears, are all given cute names that your little ones can identify with. *The museum is open Tuesday through Sunday from 8:00am until 4:00pm. There is no set admission charge but donations are required and $2 is suggested for adults and $1 for children.*

Chama's origins are rooted in the mining era of the late 19th century. At that time a railroad was built that was but a small part of a vast network of mining rail lines that spread throughout the Southwest. Few remain today, but one that does has kept Chama on the map. The **Cumbres and Toltec Scenic Railroad** is right in the "heart" of town on NM 17. Jointly owned by the states of New Mexico and Colorado, the trip covers 64 miles through the mountainous country that straddles the state border. In fact, you will keep crossing from one state into the other at many points during the journey. Billed as "America's longest and highest narrow gauge steam railway," the C & T passes through some lovely scenery. Pulled by vintage coal-burning steam engines, passengers have the option of riding in closed or open air cars as you cross valleys and meadows and wind your way through the mountains. A long mountain tunnel and several trestles high above narrow gorges add a little excitement to the ride.

There are two basic trip options. The first way travels to the mid-point at **Osier** on the state border where the train turns around and heads back to Chama. Or, you can change trains at Osier and continue on to the other end of the line at Antonito, Colorado. Those making the full journey return to Chama by bus, which takes but a fraction of the time the train does. Either way you have to account for lunch. You can either bring your own lunch or add on a fee for a chuck-wagon type lunch at Osier while the trains wait for you. Actually, the staff is refilling the trains' massive steam engines with water. After all, the trains have to eat too!

Some people even decide that they want to turn their railroading adventure into an overnight trip. For those visitors who are staying in Taos and will not be continuing on with the northwestern portion of New Mexico, you can save some mileage by driving to the Antonito terminal via US 64 and US 285. This is 30 miles closer to Taos and saves an hour on a round-trip.

The rail trip isn't inexpensive and since it requires a full day with either option, many readers may wonder if it's worth the time. That depends. If you're not thrilled by scenery it can be a long day. Also, although there's nothing wrong with the view, it's not as spectacular as the scenery encountered along the Durango and Silverton Narrow Gauge Railroad in Colorado. If you've done that trip you may find yourself a bit disappointed by the C & T. For most visitors, however, I think this trip is an excellent way to see the countryside and you should seriously consider it unless you are really pressed for time.

The train leaves daily at 10:30am from Chama between Memorial Day and mid-October and returns at about 4:30pm. For those driving to Antonito, the departure and return times are 10:00am and 5:00pm. The cost is $32 if you're taking the train to Osier and back, and $50 for the complete through trip with return by bus. Reservations are highly recommended. Call 756-2151 for Chama departures and (719) 376-5483 for Antonito departures. Tickets are also available at AAA offices in Colorado and New Mexico.

The journey from Chama continues westward on US 64. Be sure to stay on 64 where it splits with US 84 about 13 miles west of Chama. Just before that split you'll pass the Continental Divide. Shortly after, at the town of **Dulce**, you'll enter the **Jicarilla Apache Indian Reservation**. The name, which sounds Italian, isn't – in the Apache tongue it means "little baskets," a reference to the high quality woven baskets and other goods produced by the Jicarilla. There's a small museum on the reservation where you can observe artisans at work and make purchases.

The next hour or so of driving will take you through the heavily forested Reservation and a portion of the Carson National Forest before reaching more open country as you approach the slightly more populated area in a triangle formed by the communities of Bloomfield, Aztec, and Farmington.

Farmington & Environs

There's quite a bit to see and do in this most northwestern corner of the state. Shortly before you get to Bloomfield, a side road, NM 539, leads to **Navajo Lake State Park**. The lake, created by the building of a dam on the San Juan River, is one of the state's largest and is a major haven for outdoor recreation. It's also very picturesque and worth the short detour of about six miles in each direction if you have some extra time.

The town of **Bloomfield**, with a population of a little over 5,000, was a true example of the wild, wild west days in the latter 1870s. A notorious local gang was actually headed by a former Bloomfield sheriff. Now it's an agricultural town with not much to see for the visitor. I'll have you come back this way in a little while, but for now head north for eight miles on NM 544 to the town of **Aztec**. A neat little community, Aztec's name is very wrong. Early settlers in the area thought that the nearby Anasazi ruins were built by the ancient Aztec civilization. Although they were far off base, the name has held ever since and is still used to identify both the town and the national monument located on the north edge of town.

Anyhow, the state highway becomes Main Street and is the location of the **Aztec Museum and Pioneer Village**, *Tel. 334-9829*. It chronicles the history of the region with its collection of artifacts from the Anasazi days through the turn of the century. There are both indoor and outdoor exhibit areas. The latter has a small number of buildings from the town's early days as well as equipment from the oil and gas industry, which was important here at one time. *The museum is open Monday through Saturday from 9:00am to 5:00pm from May through August. It closes an hour earlier during the rest of the year as well as on holidays. Admission is $1 but is free for senior citizens and those under age 15.*

The **Aztec Ruins National Monument** is reached by taking US 550 on the north edge of town to Ruins Road, *Tel. 334-6174*. Perhaps because of its location, the Aztec Ruins aren't that well known to the traveling public. But they should be, because they are among the biggest and best preserved of any Anasazi settlement. Located between Colorado's Mesa Verde to the north and Chaco Canyon to the south, Aztec is part of an important archaeological chain that has been used to study the Anasazi culture.

First built in the 11th century, the site was occupied by the Anasazi and their descendants until the middle of the 19th century. Several large pueblo structures were built and the largest, now referred to as the **West Ruin**, contained as many as 500 rooms. Parts of the structure are still largely intact and visitors can enter the interior, stooping down to pass through the low doorways that connected the maze-like room arrangement. The village also had a large ceremonial building dubbed the **Great Kiva**. This is the only such kiva that has been fully reconstructed and is a must-see. The original inhabitants had to climb down narrow ladders to enter the kiva, but today's visitor simply walks down a short wooden stairway.

Probably nowhere else will you get a better first-hand picture of what life must have been like for the Anasazi a millennium ago. Archaeological evidence found at this site has provided enough information for the kiva to be painted in what are believed to be its original colors. Aztec Ruins also has a fine visitor center where exhibits tell the story of the Anasazi as scientists and archaeologists have pieced it together. *The monument is open daily from 8:00am until 6:00pm from Memorial Day weekend through Labor Day and until 5:00pm the rest of the year. It is closed only on New Year's and Christmas. Admission is $2 for adults.*

NATIONAL PARK SERVICE PASSPORTS ARE GREAT!

While high admission prices at many tourist attractions have always been a source of annoyance to me, I've never felt overcharged at any area administered by the **National Park Service**. *Prices are always low, especially when you consider that some of the greatest attractions in the world await you past the entrance gate. But you can reduce or eliminate even these costs by taking advantage of one of the three National Park Service "passport" programs.*

The first is the **Golden Age Passport**, *available to any United States resident age 62 or over. There is a one-time cost of $10. For that small fee you and anyone traveling with you is entitled to free admission to any fee area administered by the NPS. Individuals who are deemed to be permanently disabled are entitled to a free* **Golden Access Passport** *which has the same privileges as the Golden Age.*

The third type of passport is available to anyone for an annual cost of $25. This **Golden Eagle Passport** *also enables the holder and everyone he or she is traveling with to get into NPS fee areas without additional charge. The Golden Eagle Passport can be purchased at any National Park fee area as well as at regional offices of the Park Service or US Forest Service. The other passports are available at most fee areas.*

None of the passports cover anything other than admission fees. Facilities within National Parks that are operated by private concessionaires (such as food, lodging, and many recreational activities) are not part of the passport program. However, passport holders may sometimes be entitled to discounts. Make individual inquiry where applicable, but don't be surprised if you have to pay full price. Regardless, the passports are truly the greatest travel bargain around.

After visiting the Aztec Ruins you have two options. If you've had enough ruins for now, you can head straight into Farmington via US 550, a distance of about 15 miles from the national monument. Or you can return by NM 544 to Bloomfield and then go west on US 64 to the **Salmon Ruins**, located about half-way between Bloomfield and Farmington, *Tel. 632-2013*. Constructed in the closing years of the 11th century, these ruins were once an outlying settlement of the larger Chaco Culture to the south. The pueblo was originally two stories high and extended for more than 400 feet in a "C" configuration.

Today you can visit the ruins, which are named for George Salmon, an early area settler. Not nearly as much remains as at Aztec, but you can get a good idea with a little imagination. Also open to visitors are remains of Salmon's home and other buildings of his farm, reconstructions of small surface and pit Indian dwellings, and a museum that contains many artifacts that were recovered from the site. The latter are housed in a section called **Heritage Park**. Then continue west on US 64 until you reach Farmington. *The ruins are open daily from 9:00am until 5:00pm except on New Year's, Thanksgiving, and Christmas. Admission, including Heritage Park, is $2 for adults. Persons over 65 pay $1.50 and children 6 through 16 get in for $1.*

One other option is available from Bloomfield, especially if you are not going to be visiting the Bisti Badlands (described in the next section). Fifteen miles south of Bloomfield via NM 44 is the beautiful **Angel Peak**. Part of the surrounding badlands, the mountain is an unusually shaped multi-colored mass of rock. Red, yellow, brown, tan and other shades occupy successive layers and are capped by a dark sandstone peak. A road with several overlooks winds its way to the summit.

The city of **Farmington**, with a population of 35,000, is the largest community in the northwest. It is a major center of trade for the **Navajo Indian Reservation** that begins to the immediate west of town. Farming and coal mining are the primary industries. The town is often referred to by Native Americans as "Three Rivers" given its location at the confluence of three waterways, including the **San Juan River**. While there isn't a whole lot of interest to the visitor within town, Farmington's location makes it a good place to stop on your journey through the northwest region of New Mexico. For those who are interested in a more detailed exploration of this corner of the state, Farmington can be a good base from which to operate.

The **Farmington Museum**, on Orchard Avenue off of US 64, *Tel. 599-1174*, provides a history of the town and the San Juan Basin. Both Native and Anglo cultures are documented and a portion of the museum is devoted to children's exhibits. *The museum is open Tuesday through Friday from noon until 5:00pm and on Saturday from 10:00am to 5:00pm. There is no admission charge.*

There are several annual events in Farmington that draw quite a few visitors. One of the biggest is the **Apple Blossom Festival** held in April. Dances, parades, and a rodeo highlight this event. There's a major **hot air balloon rally** in May and the annual **Trade Days** in June. However, the most unique event is held on Tuesday through Saturday evenings between the middle of June and mid-August. This is a historical musical pageant called *Anasazi: The Ancient Ones*. (Although other productions are also offered, this one is the best.) Performances are given outdoors in a natural amphitheater located in the Lion's Wilderness Park north of town and reached by US 550 to College Boulevard. A Southwestern dinner is offered prior to each performance, although tickets for just the show can also be purchased. Complete performance information can be obtained from the Farmington Convention and Visitors Bureau (see *Practical Information* at the end of this chapter).

These next two trips are not for everybody, but I know you'll really enjoy them if you have any spirit of adventure. Everyone else can continue west from Farmington on US 64 for the nearly 30 mile ride to the town of Shiprock. The ride is entirely within or on the edge of the Navajo Reservation.

Off the Main Path – The Bisti Badlands & Chaco Canyon

These trips offer an opportunity to see some of New Mexico's most unusual scenery and visit what may well be the single best example of Native ruins in all of North America. Unfortunately, neither are in what you would call easily accessible locations. Both are off of the main roads, and Chaco requires quite a bit of driving on unpaved roads. But let's push on.

The **Bisti Badlands** comprise a large area of eroded rock spires called **hoodoos** as well as a number of other bizarre formations. Many hoodoos look like giant mushroom caps. The landscape has been said to resemble that of the moon and is rather eerie. It is, in an unusual sort of way, quite beautiful. It's also a wild area with no visitor center like in a national park. It's simply you and nature at its weirdest. The area was a tropical paradise some 70 million years ago and is today rich in natural resources. Fortunately, a large tract of the badlands was given protection in 1984 under the San Juan Basin Wilderness Preservation Act. It is formally known under the name of the Nacimiento Badlands. I don't think you'll see much tourist development either and that's probably for the better as well.

To reach the Bisti Badlands, head south from Farmington on NM 371. The badlands are about 40 miles away. Watch for signs pointing to short side "roads" that provide access to portions of the wilderness badlands. The single greatest concentration of interesting formations in the Bisti Badlands is located via a two mile hike from a parking area, which is itself reached by way of a four mile gravel road, 37 miles from Farmington. Also visible from this route is beautiful Angel Peak. You should allow about two hours travel time to get to and from Farmington plus some time to look around.

Much of **Chaco Canyon** has been designated as the **Chaco Culture National Historical Park**. From around 750AD until about 1300, one of the largest and most important of all the Anasazi settlements was located here. They built a large pueblo and a number of smaller settlements scattered over several miles throughout the canyon. The largest pueblo was four stories high and had more than 600 rooms. The Anasazi also built canals and irrigation systems to bring water from summer storms into their fields. A system of arrow-straight roads measuring 20 to 30 feet in width connected the outlying communities with the main pueblo in the seven-mile long canyon. The Chaco Anasazi (the branch of the Anasazi who developed the canyon settlement) also used an isolated butte near this site as an observatory to time the arrival of spring and fall, which was critical to the planting of their crops. It should be mentioned that the Anasazi accomplished all of this without knowledge of the wheel and without beasts of burden to help in their building and irrigation projects.

Begin your visit at the excellent visitor center near the southern entrance to the park. Many artifacts are on display, not only from the Anasazi, but also from the Navajo. Interesting films are shown throughout the day. A one-way loop road connects the major pueblo sights (the road within the park is paved.) Most of the pueblos are located very close to the parking areas along the loop, although a couple require a good hike to get to. Fortunately, **Pueblo Bonito** is easily reached – it is the largest and most impressive of all the pueblos in the canyon.

You must allow at least a half day for this excursion from Farmington. It covers 140 miles, of which a minimum (depending on your route) of 29 miles are on unpaved roads. From Bloomfield, east of Farmington, take NM 44 to the Blanco Trading Post. There will be a cutoff for NM 57 (where the unpaved road begins) that leads into Chaco Canyon. There are no food or automobile services in the area. You might consider having a huge breakfast or packing a lunch. Make sure you leave with a full tank of gas whether you're traveling through or returning to Farmington.

The park is open every day of the year from 8:00am until 6:00pm (until 5:00pm from after Labor Day to before Memorial Day). Admission is $4 per vehicle to those not holding a National Park Service passport. A four-wheel drive vehicle is highly recommended. Bad weather can often close the roads leading into Chaco from both north and south, so it makes sense to call the park headquarters at Tel. 786-7014 before beginning your trip. If the roads are open but it has recently rained, then four-wheel drive is an absolute must.

If you're really adventurous and want to see both the Bisti Badlands and the Chaco Culture National Historic Park, it can be done in one long day that covers about 175 miles. Begin by following the route I described to the Bisti Badlands. However, don't head back after your visit there. Continue south on NM 371 to Indian Route 9. If you reach the town of Crownpoint you went too far – go back about a mile or so. Take the Indian Route east for 19 miles to an unpaved road marked with a sign directing you to Chaco Culture NHP. Once you reach and finish touring the park you should exit from the north side of the park and follow the route back to Farmington via NM 57 and 44 and US 64.

As an alternative, if you're not going back to Farmington (i.e., you don't want to see Shiprock), at the point where NM 371 and Indian Route 9 meet, you're only 24 miles from I-40 at the town of Thoreau. Just stay on 371 south. When you reach the interstate you can head west (to Gallup) or east to Grants.

Shiprock & Four Corners Country

The town of **Shiprock** is the headquarters for the **Northern Navajo Indian Agency**. There are many places in and around town where you can look for Indian arts and crafts. Before going on to the famous Shiprock formation, you may want to go to the **Four Corners Monument**, the only place in the United States where four states come together. There isn't really that much to see there – a large stone slab exactly at the confluence of the four borders with the name and seal of each state.

It's not very impressive, but it seems that many visitors simply cannot resist the urge to go there and manipulate their bodies in one way or another so that a picture of them occupying a portion of all four states at the same time can be taken. It's also a good place for shopping. Dozens of Indians from the Four Corners Region set up their wares every day in booths surrounding the monument. You can buy just about anything that the Indians can produce. *Four Corners Monument is open every day of the year from 7:00am until 8:00pm and costs $1 per vehicle. To reach it from the town of Shiprock, head west on US 64 for 27 miles (into Arizona) and then north for a few miles on US 160.*

The **Shiprock formation** is reached by taking US 666 south for seven miles and then eight miles west on Indian Route 33 (the highly scenic Red Rock Road), from where it is best viewed. If you're just traveling through and don't want to take that 16-mile detour, Shiprock can also be viewed directly from US 666. Shiprock is described by geologists as a "volcanic plug." That doesn't do it justice. This very impressive rock rises more than 1,700 feet from the flat desert floor around it. The Navajos called it "Winged Rock," which I think is a much better description than Shiprock. Anglos gave it the latter name because in certain light (namely, sunset) it appears to actually shimmer and float above the valley. Regardless of what time you see it, though, Shiprock is quite beautiful. Be advised that the Navajo have always considered *Tse Bida'hi* (the Navajo name) a sacred place. Therefore, you are not allowed to climb on it. Don't even think about it unless you want to get the Navajo very upset. It would be like someone trying to scale the Statue of Liberty.

Upon returning to US 666 you should head south once again. You'll pass through a half dozen or so small communities, all still on the Navajo

Indian Reservation. If you haven't yet picked up a Navajo gift or souvenir you can do so in any of these towns.

Gallup & The Zuni/El Moro Loop

Once you finally leave the reservation, you'll only be seven miles from **Gallup**. With almost 20,000 people and an Interstate location, Gallup is one of the most important communities in northwestern New Mexico. Although not on the reservation, it is the heart of "Indian country" and the main trading center for most of the Navajos.

Many Hollywood producers have chosen the area around Gallup as a site to make Western flicks. Home to almost countless trading posts, Gallup is a great source of Native American art, jewelry, rugs, baskets and pottery – from the tackiest souvenir to the sublime.

INDIAN MANDELAS

Looking for an attractive and unusual gift for someone or that special piece to grace the wall of your home? Then go no further than the Indian **mandela** *– surely an odd item in most of the country but very commonly found in the Southwest. I have one hanging on my bedroom wall.*

Mandelas were not a part of pueblo culture but were the creation of the Plains Indians. Their exact origins are lost somewhere in history. They were once an important part of Indian ritual but in more recent times have simply come to be symbols of good luck. The top portion is a ring with feathers hanging down each side. In the center of the ring can be a number of designs. Sometimes there are pictures of Indians or Southwestern scenes. These are not as authentic but many tourists like them. True mandelas have an animal skin stretched across it. Many of today's "skins" are artificial, except in the case of some of the most expensive specimens. Below the ring portion are several long feathered braids. Mandela feathers and other fabrics come in a great variety of colors, although Southwestern earth tones are most popular.

Prices vary considerably, from about $20 to triple digits, depending upon the size, quality, and authenticity. Since you can find them just about anywhere don't buy the first one you see. Shop around until you find one that just suit's your taste and pocketbook.

Gallup is a town of motels and tourist shops. The main point of interest is several miles east on I-40: **Red Rock State Park**, a beautiful area of towering red sandstone cliffs. Eons of erosion have sculpted and curved the soft rock. The park also contains a small museum that traces several different Southwestern cultures. Two nature trails provide a good way of taking in the scenery. One of the trails is handicapped accessible.

Within the park is a large natural amphitheater seating 6,800 that is the scene of Gallup's major events, like the **tribal dances** that are held every night at 7:30pm from Memorial Day through Labor Day. The colorful dances, with names such as the Eagle Dance and Buffalo Dance, are very popular with visitors. They have no religious connotation, as such dances cannot be performed in the presence of "outsiders." **Western Jubilee Week** in June is highlighted by one of the state's largest rodeos.

The biggest event at Red Rock is the **Inter-Tribal Ceremonial**. Native American participants from all across North America come to Gallup for this spectacular four day event during the second week of August. If you can time your visit for this period, by all means go for it.

The park is open daily from 8:00am to 9:00pm except between Labor Day and Memorial Day when it closes at 4:30pm. Admission to the park is free but donations are requested for the museum.

Head south from Gallup on NM 602 for 26 miles onto the **Zuni Indian Reservation**. At the junction of NM 53 turn left and take that road west for approximately ten miles to the **Zuni Pueblo**. This is among the largest of the existing pueblos. It was built upon the ruins of an earlier pueblo that was one of the so-called **Seven Golden Cities of Cibola** that were being sought by the Spanish explorer Coronado. The Zunis were not responsive to Christianity then and even today continue to retain much of their ancient traditions. The Zuni Pueblo is the only one that allows visitors to view the religious masked dances. Quiet observance is expected for this singular privilege and no photography of any kind is permitted. Also on the pueblo are a restored mission church, plus a newer church and several shops where you can buy native crafts. The Zuni are excellent carvers and jewelers. *Visitors are welcome at the pueblo from dawn to dusk.*

After visiting the Pueblo, drive back east on NM 53 for about 30 miles to the **El Moro National Monument**, *Tel. 783-4226*, which is surrounded on all sides by the **Ramah Navajo Indian Reservation**. El Moro, also known as Inscription Rock, is a large sandstone bluff rising from the valley. Because of a water hole at the base, the site has been occupied for centuries. The Anasazi built two villages on top of the bluff and made drawings on the base of the rock. Western pioneers and others (prior to protection of the bluff by the Park Service) added their own carvings to the ancient petroglyphs.

There's a visitor center with a museum covering 700 years of civilization at El Moro. Two self-guiding trails are available. The first is an easy paved half-mile trail that leads from the Visitor Center to Inscription Rock where you can view the petroglyphs. The other trail covers two miles and leads to the ruins at the top. It's fairly strenuous since it involves a 200-foot climb on mostly uneven surfaces. *The monument is open every day 9:00am to 7:00pm from Memorial Day through Labor Day and until 5:00pm* *during the rest of the year. It's closed only on New Year's and Christmas. Admission is $2 per person (up to a maximum of $4) for car unless you have one of the NPS passports.*

Grants & Acoma Pueblo – Sky City

Continuing eastbound on NM 53 after El Moro, you'll soon reach a privately owned natural site called the **Bandera Volcanic Crater and Ice Caves**, *Tel. 783-4303*. Located at the edge of a vast region of former volcanic activity, the cave maintains a constant temperature of 31 degrees, making it a good place to get out of the summer sun for a while. The cave is reached by a short trail over an ancient lava flow. Then you descend 75 steps (definitely not for the physically challenged) into the small cave that measures about a thousand square feet. The refreshing cool air is nice, and the perpetual ice is unusual because it's green – the result of algae growing on it. There's another trail leading to the top of 450-foot high **Bandera Volcano**, but there are better views coming up soon elsewhere so you are just as well off skipping this more difficult trail. *Open daily from 8:00am until 7:00pm from June through September and till 4:00pm the remainder of the year. The admission is $6.00 for adults and $3 for children.*

At this point NM 53 swings to the north as it heads back towards the Interstate. On your right is the edge of the **El Malpais National Monument and Conservation Are**a, *Tel. 285-5406*. Meaning "bad country" or badlands, you'll understand the name as soon as you get out and try to walk on the rocky lava flows. They may have cooled off over the years, but it's still very tough under foot. Wear sturdy shoes because the rock can be sharp in places. Hold onto your children at all times. The sight of the lava beds and other volcanic formations such as lava tubes and spatter cones is wild. You'll definitely think you're on another planet.

Some of the best sights, however, are on the eastern side of the Monument and I'll get to that in a jiffy. But first you reach the town of **Grants**. The town prospered in the 1950s with the discovery of uranium in the area, and that era lasted until depletion of the mines in the early 1980s. Since that time, Grants has enjoyed a more quiet type of prosperity, largely based on its gateway location to history and unusual scenery in the surrounding areas.

Use Exit 85 of I-40 and go a mile west to the town's big attraction – the **New Mexico Museum of Mining**, *Tel. 287-4802*. The museum covers the full story of Grants' uranium mining era. The highlight is a full-scale replica of a uranium mine located beneath the museum. The surprisingly large modern museum building is a bright and spacious gallery and the mine tour is very realistic. Not that I've ever been in a real uranium mine, but I can't imagine it being very different from what you'll see here. *The museum is open Monday to Saturday from 9:00am to 6:00pm and on Sundays* *from noon to 6:00pm. It is closed on Thanksgiving and Christmas. Admission is $2.*

With not much else to do in town, you can continue at your leisure with the rest of the El Malpais. Go east on I-40 to Exit 89 and then south on NM 117. This road stretches along the eastern edge of the Conservation area. After the ranger station there's a short road leading to the Sandstone Bluffs, an overlook with the best view. From this point you can see for miles over an area encompassing much of the El Malpais. Then continue seven miles south to the **La Ventana Natural Arch**. Located near the road, it is the largest such natural arch in New Mexico that is easily reached. In this case a short trail takes you to it. The brilliant color of the canyon walls are framed by the arch.

After you have seen the arch, head back to the Interstate, again picking it up in an easterly direction. This time you should get off at Exit 102, known as Acomita. A short ride south on Indian Route 38 will bring you to the **Acoma Pueblo**, *Tel. 470-4966*, also known as **Sky City**. Okay, another pueblo, you say. Had your fill of pueblos? I can understand that, because you can only take so much of a good thing. However, Acoma is a *must*. It is one of the most beautiful and fascinating of all the pueblos, so if you don't want to see them all at least make room for Acoma. You won't regret it.

Settled in the middle of the 12th century, Acoma is reputedly the oldest continuously inhabited site in the United States. Located on a flat mesa rising almost 360 feet above the surrounding terrain, the site provided adequate protection for the residents for centuries – although the more advanced weapons of the Spaniards finally proved to be more powerful than their defensive position. In reality, little has changed since the arrival of the Spanish.

Acoma gladly welcomes visitors, but you can't wander around on your own. There's a visitor center at the base of the mesa where you sign up for tours. Groups are taken to the top in small vans. A guided walking tour through the "streets" of Acoma lasts about an hour and includes a stop at the imposing **San Estevan del Rey Mission**, which was constructed in 1629 and is still in use. There are great views from the mesa top looking out over the surrounding valley and fields where the inhabitants of Acoma grow their crops.

You'll also see **Enchanted Mesa**, higher than Sky City at 430 feet and clearly visible three miles away. The Enchanted Mesa is the legendary ancestral home of the inhabitants of Acoma and is off limits to visitors. But it is beautiful to see. At the conclusion of the tour you can go back down in the van or opt to walk down. The walk is a little difficult, but is a good way to get an idea of what residents of Sky City had to do in the old days every time that they needed to go down to the fields.

Acoma is open daily from 8:00am until 7:00pm April to September and until 4:00pm the remainder of the year. It is closed from July 10th to 13th and on one weekend in October. It is subject to unannounced brief closures at other times. The $6 admission fee includes transportation to the mesa top and guided tour. Senior citizens pay $5 and children ages 6 through 17 are charged $4. There is also a $5 camera use charge.

Return to I-40 the opposite way if you're going back to Grants or via NM 23 if heading back to Albuquerque. Once you reach the Interstate, it's only 50 miles to Albuquerque, most of the trip on the **Laguna Indian Reservation**. They also welcome visitors and there are many craft shops. Once in Albuquerque, you have easy access to routes going to all of the other regional tours that follow in later chapters of this book.

NIGHTLIFE & ENTERTAINMENT

Besides the Anasazi historical pageant and other local festivals, you shouldn't expect to find anything remotely resembling big city nightlife in this region. Local clubs tend to be those in towns adjacent to Indian reservations. They aren't necessarily dangerous or "tough," but tourists aren't exactly welcomed with open arms either. You probably wouldn't feel comfortable enough to have a good time.

If you must find a place to drink or listen to some music during the evening, confine yourself to the larger lodging establishments that have lounges in either Farmington, Gallup, or Grants. One establishment that might be of interest is the **Rookies Sports Bar** in Farmington, *700 Scott Avenue*. It's located in the Best Western Inn and Suites and is one of the more lively places in town, frequented by both locals and visitors.

SPORTS & RECREATION

Golf

- **Civitan Municipal Golf Course**, *2200 N. Dustin, Farmington. Tel. 599-1194*
- **Pinon Hills**, *2101 Sunrise Parkway, Farmington. Tel. 326-6066*. Considered to be one of the best public courses in the United States.
- **Gallup Municipal Golf Course**, *Susan Street, Gallup. Tel. 863-9224*

Horseback Riding

- **Western Outdoor Adventures**, *Chama. Tel. 1/800-288-1386*

Swimming

- **Abiqiui Lake**, *Abiquiu.*
- **Farmington Aquatic Center**, *1151 N. Sullivan, Farmington. Tel. 599-1167*. Several pools, diving boards and water slides.

PRACTICAL INFORMATION

- **Tourist Office/Visitors Bureau**
  - **Aztec**: *Tel. 334-9551*
  - **Chama**: *Tel. 756-2306 or 1/800-477-0149*
  - **Farmington**: *203 W. Main Street, Tel. 326-7602 or 1/800-448-1240*
  - **Gallup**: *Tel. 863-3841 or 1/800-242-4282*
  - **Grants**: *Tel. 287-4802 or 1/800-748-2142*
- **Bus Station**
  - **Farmington**: *Tel. 325-1009*
  - **Gallup**: *Tel. 863-3761*
  - **Grants**: *Tel. 285-6268*
- **Train Station**, *Gallup: Tel. 863-3244*
- **Hospital**
  - **Farmington**: *Tel. 325-5011*
  - **Gallup**: *Tel. 863-6832*
  - **Grants**: *Tel. 287-4446*
- **Police** (non-emergency)
  - **Farmington**: *Tel. 327-0222*
  - **Gallup**: *Tel. 722-2231*
  - **Grants**: *Tel. 287-4404*

17. THE NORTHEAST

- CROSSROADS OF CULTURES -

Geographically dominated by an extension of the Great Plains, the **northeastern** quarter of New Mexico was once a great buffalo hunting area. Spaniards and Anglos soon discovered the importance of the area, both in terms of agriculture and as a gateway to points west. From a historical standpoint, this is the land of the **Santa Fe Trail**. A string of historic sights where once stood forts and trading posts line many of today's modern highways. A number of historic towns with stately homes attract tourists, including those in **Las Vegas** and **Cimarron**.

The visitor will also find a good amount of scenery, for the Plains is only a portion of the region. Views from **Capulin Mountain** are simply great. Recreational opportunities abound as some of the state's largest lakes and fishing rivers are located here.

ARRIVALS & DEPARTURES

To begin from Albuquerque, you just have to hop onto I-40 in an easterly direction. From Santa Fe head north on I-25, while those coming from Taos can take NM 518 through the Carson and Santa Fe National Forests and the Sangre de Cristo to Las Vegas.

The only city in the northeast with air service from Albuquerque is Clovis, which is served by **Mesa Air**, *Tel. 1/800-MESA-AIR.*

ORIENTATION/GETTING AROUND

The region which I refer to as the northeast is comprised mostly of a boot-shaped area within the confines of I-25 on the west and I-40 on the south, although some of the towns and sights do stretch a bit beyond those lines, as in the case of Fort Summer and Clovis. If you're going to be touring this region, the most logical place to begin is after your visit to the Albuquerque area. I'll use that method as we work our way through the northeast, beginning at Moriarty and going clockwise through Santa Rosa, Fort Sumner, Clovis, Tucumcari, Clayton, Raton, Cimarron and

Las Vegas. You could easily use either Santa Fe or Taos as the starting point for a northeastern loop by simply reversing the order.

Unlike the northwest, virtually all of the roads you'll travel on here are first class. Many miles will be on highways. It's unlikely that you will encounter anything resembling heavy traffic. There aren't any major population centers and although plenty of visitors come to this part of the state, they don't do so in nearly the great numbers as the cities and areas we've visited to this point.

Again, public transportation is limited and not a good way to get around. Greyhound bus service is available in Santa Rosa, Clovis, Tucumcari, Raton, and Las Vegas. Amtrak stations are in Raton and Las Vegas. Even if you make your way around by bus or train to a couple of places, there is the problem of how to get around the region conveniently. Car rentals are available in some places, but if you are ultimately going to be renting a vehicle it makes sense to do so from Albuquerque.

WHERE TO STAY

CLAYTON

Moderate

KOKOPELLI LODGE, *702 South 1st Street. Tel. 374-2589, Fax 374-8719. Rates: $60-78. 47 Rooms. Major credit cards accepted. Located on US 87, about a half mile from the town's main intersection with US 56/64.*

I can't find anything to rave about any of the accommodations in Clayton. However, since it's a major town along the main route it's probable that at least some of you will find it convenient to stay in Clayton overnight. The Kokopelli Lodge offers decent tourist class rooms in a two-story motor inn. Complimentary coffee and rolls are offered in the lobby but I wouldn't consider that as being a continental breakfast. A couple of restaurants are located within a short distance.

CLOVIS

Budget

BEST WESTERN LA VISTA INN, *1516 Mabry Drive. Tel. 762-3808, Fax 762-1422. Rates: $36-48, including Continental Breakfast. 47 Rooms. Major credit cards accepted. Toll-free reservations 1/800-528-1234. Located a mile east of the center of town on the main street, which is US highways 60, 70, and 84.*

The style of this one-story roadside motel is typical of many that were built during the 1950s when Americans first really started taking to the highway. It's not old and run down, however, having been renovated extensively in 1991. The rooms are fairly large and comfortable. Some rooms have small refrigerators. There's an outdoor heated pool, a game room, and self-service laundry room. Restaurants are located close by.

HOLIDAY INN, *2700 Mabry Drive. Tel. 762-4491, Fax 769-0564. Rates: $50. 119 Rooms. Major credit cards accepted. Toll-free reservations 1/800-HOLIDAY. Located 1 1/2 miles east of downtown on US highways 60, 70, and 84.*

A two-story motel. You know the type – walk up to the second floor's outside corridor, ice machine at the end of the building, etc., etc. Sorry, but that's what we're dealing with in a lot of these towns. It's not the kind of place you're going to remember for long either because its exceptionally good or bad. You will, however, find a restaurant on the premises, a cocktail lounge, swimming pool with sauna and whirlpool, and even a small fitness center.

LAS VEGAS

Budget

COMFORT INN, *2500 North Grand Avenue. Tel. 425-1100, Fax 454-8404. Rates: $54-59, including Continental Breakfast. 101 Rooms. Major credit cards accepted. Toll-free reservations 1/800-221-2222. Located on the main business street, which is US 95 and the I-25 Business Loop. Use Exit 347 from I-25.*

This is quite an attractive, modern hotel located close to the historic old town. Many rooms have good views of the nearby mountains. The pretty lobby and breakfast room features comfortable furnishings with a central fireplace. The rooms are spacious and well maintained. There's an indoor swimming pool with whirlpool. You'll find a full service restaurant immediately adjacent to the inn and more restaurants to choose from located within a few minutes.

INN ON THE SANTA FE TRAIL, *1133 North Grand Avenue. Tel. 425-6791, Fax 425-0417. Rates: $56-71, including Continental Breakfast. 42 Rooms. Major credit cards accepted. Take Exit 345 off of I-25 and proceed north on US 85 for a half mile and then west on Grand Avenue to the inn.*

Built in an attractive hacienda-style architecture in 1937, the Inn almost qualifies for historic consideration. The nicely kept property offers expansive landscaped grounds and beautiful guest rooms filled with handcrafted Southwestern style furniture (all made by New Mexican artisans). Some rooms have microwave ovens and/or refrigerators. There's a heated outdoor pool and spa for you to relax in. The inn doesn't have a restaurant but several are conveniently located.

THE PLAZA HOTEL, *230 Old Town Plaza. Tel. 425-3591, Fax 425-9659. Rates: $54-91. 38 Rooms. Major credit cards accepted. Member of Travelodge hotel chain. Toll-free reservations 1/800-328-1882 or 1/800-626-4886. Located in the center of town. Take Exit 345 of I-25 and proceed west to the Old Town Plaza.*

Built in 1882 in magnificent Victorian splendor, the Plaza has been carefully preserved. You'll go back in time as soon as you go through the front doors and feel a part of its long history, which has included visits by many famous (and some infamous) people in all walks of life. Although all of the large guest rooms have been modernized to include the amenities that today's travelers expect, you'll appreciate the Victorian furnishings and private dressing rooms. All rooms also feature coffee makers.

The Landmark Grill is probably Las Vegas' best restaurant (more details below in *Where to Eat*). There's also a good lounge (they call it a saloon in keeping with the hotel's traditions) with lively entertainment. Summer visitors can partake in additional entertainment by viewing the music performances given at the gazebo in the Old Town Plaza park directly across the street from the hotel.

RATON

Moderate

BEST WESTERN SANDS MANOR MOTEL, *300 Clayton Road. Tel. 445-2737, Fax 445-4053. Rates: $71-87. 50 Rooms. Major credit cards accepted. Toll-free reservations 1/800-528-1234. Located on US 64/87, two blocks west of I-25, Exit 451.*

A single-story roadside motel with parking at your door, the Sands Manor is a well-maintained property with very large and comfortable rooms, some of which have refrigerators. Facilities include a heated outdoor pool, play area for children, and a small gift shop. There's a moderately priced family restaurant on the premises that will do nicely if you're not looking for something fancy.

THE RED VIOLET INN, *344 North 2nd Street. Tel. 445-2355. Rates: $60-75, 5 Rooms. American Express, MasterCard and VISA accepted. Shared bathrooms. Located on the I-25 Business Loop. Use either Exit 454 (southbound) or 450 (northbound) and follow US 64.*

This small historic Bed and Breakfast inn is strictly for those who like simplicity. You won't find any telephones, televisions, or much else in the way of amenities. What you will get are large and beautifully furnished rooms in a quiet, relaxed setting. The refined atmosphere includes a social hour in the living room, complete with classical music. Delicious home-cooked meals are available with advance reservations (and at additional cost), or you can dine at one of several nearby restaurants.

Budget

HOLIDAY CLASSIC MOTEL, *Clayton Road. Tel. 445-5555, Fax 445-2981. Rates: $63. 87 Rooms. Major credit cards accepted. Toll-free reservations 1/800-255-8879. Located at the junction of I-25 and US 64/87 (Exit 451).*

The Holiday Classic provides good lodging and quite a few public facilities. Rooms are large, some with coffee makers, and are comfortably furnished. There's a restaurant and coffee shop as well as a lounge with live entertainment. For recreation you'll find an indoor swimming pool and game room.

SANTA ROSA

Budget

BEST WESTERN SANTA ROSA INN, *3022 Will Rogers Drive. Tel. 472-5877, Fax 472-5759. Rates: $48-58. 44 Rooms. Major credit cards accepted. Toll-free reservations 1/800-528-1234. Located a half-mile west of I-40, Exit 277. Will Rogers Drive is US 66.*

A simple one-story motel with drive-up parking convenience and limited special facilities. However, the large rooms all feature two queen-sized beds so you can really spread out. There's also an unusually big outdoor swimming pool for a motel of this size. For breakfast and in case you're starving, a Denny's restaurant is next door. For real food, you'll have to go further into town.

HOLIDAY INN EXPRESS, *3300 Will Rogers Drive. Tel. 472-5411, Fax 472-3537. Rates: $47-56, including Continental Breakfast. 100 Rooms. Major credit cards accepted. Toll-free reservations 1/800-HOLIDAY. Located just west of I-40, Exit 277.*

You should realize from the prices for a Holiday Inn that this is not a big overnight stopping place for hordes of tourists. On the other hand, if it's along your route, why not take advantage of a bargain when you come across one? Like all of the "Express" versions of Holiday Inn, you'll get a clean, large, and comfortable room with either king or queen beds, a heated pool, and an adequate sized breakfast to get you going in the morning. Several restaurants are located within a short distance.

TUCUMCARI

Budget

BEST WESTERN DISCOVERY MOTOR INN, *200 East Estrella Avenue. Tel. 461-4884, Fax 461-2463. Rates: $54-60, including Continental Breakfast. 107 Rooms. Major credit cards accepted. Toll-free reservations 1/800-528-1234. Located a block north of I-40, Exit 332 at the intersection of 1st Street and Estrella.*

While there's a pretty big quality range within the Best Western chain, most are quite good and the Discovery is among the better ones. The attractive contemporary style architecture houses very large rooms some with microwave, refrigerator, or wet bar. It also has a large outdoor swimming pool and an indoor spa and fitness center. Located on nicely landscaped grounds, the Inn also features a good restaurant.

COMFORT INN, *2800 East Tucumcari Boulevard. Tel. 461-4094, Fax 461-4099. Rates; $55-59, including Continental Breakfast. 59 Rooms. Major credit cards accepted. Toll-free reservations 1/800-221-2222. Located a half mile west of I-40, Exit 335 on the west side of town.*

This modern two-story motor inn doesn't have anything fancy, but you'll get a clean and comfortably furnished room. There's a small swimming pool to cool off in after a busy day on the road. A variety of restaurants can be found within a five minute ride.

RODEWAY INN WEST, *1302 West Tucumcari Boulevard. Tel. 461-3140, Fax 461-4237. Rates: $48-55. 61 Rooms. Major credit cards accepted. Toll-free reservations 1/800-424-4777. Located a mile east of I-40, Exit 331. Be sure you're on West Tucumcari Boulevard as there is another Rodeway on the east side of town.*

The decent size rooms are modern and attractive. A Continental Breakfast plan is available. Some rooms have coffee makers. There's also a small heated pool and the Inn has a restaurant on the premises. Cocktails are served. While it's a notch below the other motels, I've recommended for Tucumcari, it does cost less and still represents a good value.

CAMPING & RV SITES

- **Las Vegas KOA**, *in Las Vegas, Tel. 454-0180*
- **Pecos River RV Camp**, *in San Jose near Las Vegas, Tel. 421-2211*
- **Vegas RV & Storage**, *Las Vegas, Tel. 425-5640*

WHERE TO EAT

CLAYTON

Moderate – $11-20

THE EKLUND DINING ROOM AND SALOON, *15 Main Street, in the center of town. Tel. 374-2551. MasterCard and VISA accepted. Lunch and dinner served daily.*

Located in a beautifully restored dining room that's part of a hotel built in 1892, you'll feel the elegance of the rich Victorian decor. The attached saloon is "original equipment" and is filled with items tracing more than a century of service. Despite the elegance of the surroundings, the atmosphere is very casual and enjoyable.

Highlighting the menu are a number of entrees featuring delicious beef that is raised not very far from where you'll be sitting. There are also a few Mexican and Southwestern style dishes. The food is excellent and the service professional. Children's menu is available.

CLOVIS

Moderate – $11-20

POOR BOY'S STEAK HOUSE, *2115 North Prince Street, about 1 1/2 miles north of town on NM 209. Tel. 763-5222. American Express, Discover, MasterCard and VISA accepted. Lunch and dinner served daily.*

A good restaurant featuring, in addition to steak, seafood, and chicken entrees. Meals are enhanced by trips to a very nice salad bar. Children's menu is available. No alcoholic beverages are served.

Budget – $10 or less

GUADALAJARA, *916 West 1st Street. Tel. 769-9965. No credit cards accepted. Lunch and dinner served daily except Sunday.*

Authentic Mexican fare in at atmosphere reminiscent of a small Mexican cantina (although there's no bar). Try the enchilladas or burritos. Especially good for lunch.

LEAL'S RESTAURANT, *3100 East Mabry. Tel. 763-4075. American Express, Discover, MasterCard and VISA accepted. Lunch and dinner served daily.*

Popular with the locals, Leal's offers a very good selection of both Mexican and American dishes that are nicely prepared. Good quality and portion sizes, especially considering the low prices.

LAS VEGAS

Moderate – $11-20

ADOBE GRILL, *1814 7th Street. Tel. 425-0445. Most major credit cards accepted. Lunch and dinner served daily.*

An attractive hacienda-style building houses this very good restaurant that features a wide variety of cuisine. Choose from first class steaks, fresh seafood, or Southwestern dishes. They even have decent pizza if you're looking for lunch or something on the lighter side. Adobe also has a full service bar. The indoor Southwestern decor dining room is supplemented in the summer by an outdoor covered deck or an attractive tiled patio with gazebo and fountain. This is my choice for the nicest place in town.

EL RIALTO, *141 Bridge Street, in the Old Town near the Plaza. Tel. 454-0037. American Express, Discover, MasterCard and VISA accepted. Lunch and dinner served daily except Sunday.*

Housed in an historic structure dating from the 1890s, El Rialto is filled with interesting antiques and has a warm, comfortable atmosphere. Delicious Mexican food is the specialty of the house but you can also choose from a number of good American dishes. There's a salad bar and children's menu.

HILLCREST RESTAURANT, *1106 Grand Avenue. Tel. 425-7211. MasterCard and VISA accepted.*

The central portion of Grand Avenue is sort of Restaurant Row in Las Vegas, but most of them aren't worth any special mention. Hillcrest, on the other hand, is a very good family restaurant featuring a good selection of home-cooked American-style meals. They also have a smattering of Mexican and Southwestern.

There are two separate dining rooms. The first is a very casual coffee-shop style setting and the other is the slightly more formal Flamingo Dining Room. There's also a cocktail lounge. Hillcrest has been in business since the 1940s.

THE LANDMARK GRILL, *230 Old Town Plaza, in the Plaza Hotel. Tel. 425-3591. Most major credit cards accepted. Reservations suggested.*

It seems that the best restaurants in Las Vegas are all historic properties. The famous and stately Plaza Hotel is a fitting locale for this small but elegant looking dining room. The menu is surprisingly varied, featuring American and New Mexican dishes as well as several Italian entrees.

The atmosphere is casual but the service is first class. Children can select dinner from their own menu. Full-service cocktail lounge called Byron T's Saloon is adjacent.

RATON

Moderate – $11-20

COLT RESTAURANT, *at the junction of US 85 and US 64. Tel. 445-5991. No credit cards accepted.*

Several entrees are in the budget price category. Features both American and Mexican cuisine. The food and service are both decent but neither is remarkable. It's in a convenient location in the center of town and represents a good dollar value.

PAPPAS SWEET SHOP RESTAURANT, *1201 South Second Street. Tel. 445-9811. Most major credit cards accepted. Reservations suggested.*

Nearing 75 years of operation by the same family, Pappas is one of Raton's most historic institutions and its popularity is justified. The "Sweet Shop" in the restaurant name comes from the fact that the business started out as a candy and ice cream manufacturing company. In fact, the very interesting dining room is filled with antiques and memorabilia that documents the history of the Pappas' family business. It's a lot of fun and adds to the enjoyment of having a meal which, by the way, happens to be very good indeed. The menu is largely American fare, and there's a children's menu as well. Cocktails are served.

SANTA ROSA

Budget – $10 or less

CLUB CAFE, *561 Parker Avenue. Tel. 472-3631. No credit cards accepted.*

In business since 1935, the Club Cafe has enjoyed somewhat of a renaissance that coincides with the nostalgia boom surrounding the old Route 66. In fact, the restaurant's gift shop sells Route 66 memorabilia and does quite a business. As far as the food is concerned, it's average Mexican and American but is very low priced and represents a decent value for the money.

TUCUMCARI

Moderate – $11-20

GOLDEN CORRAL, *1234 West Tucumcari Boulevard. Tel. 461-0299. Most major credit cards accepted.*

With nearly 7,000 people, Tucumcari is almost "large" by New Mexico standards. Unfortunately, there aren't a great many good restaurants to select from. The Golden Corral is part of a western chain that offers standard American and Southwestern fare. The best part of eating here is the excellent salad bar, which you could make a meal in itself from. Come to think of it, that's not a bad idea.

Budget – $10 or less

EL TORO CAFE, *107 South 1st Street. Tel. 461-3328. MasterCard and VISA accepted. Lunch and dinner served Monday through Friday only.*

A small, family run business, the El Toro Cafe features very good Mexican dishes and quite a few American entrees. Very casual and friendly service make it an enjoyable experience. The prices are remarkably low.

SEEING THE SIGHTS

Along I-40 from Moriarty to Santa Rosa

Moriarty is located about 35 miles east of downtown Albuquerque via I-40. After Cedar Crest the elevation starts to drop rather rapidly. In fact, the 80-mile stretch between Moriarty and Santa Rosa is one of the flattest in New Mexico. It's one of the few long distances where the scenery can be said to be boring. Well, every mile can't be a gem. At least it's on the Interstate where the going is easy and the miles pile up quickly.

You can shoot right through Moriarty or, if you want to break up the ride for a while, make a brief stop at the **Moriarty Historical Museum**. Take Exit 194 which becomes Central Avenue in town and the locale for the museum. Afterwards, continue on Central until it rejoins I-94 a couple of miles on the east side of town. The museum has artifacts from the early days of the town with the emphasis on farming implements. Moriarty is still an agricultural community. *The museum is open May through December, Monday through Friday from 10:00am to 5:00pm but closes for lunch between noon and 1:00pm. From January through April it only opens on Tuesday, Friday and Saturday from 1:00-4:00pm. There is no admission charge but donations are accepted.*

THE SALINAS PUEBLO MISSIONS

Even before you begin the suggested northeast routing, you'll have to make a decision on a detour. The ***Salinas Pueblo Missions National Monument*** *are housed in three separate units spread out many miles apart. You can reach them from the Tijeras Exit of I-40 (exit number 175) and then proceeding south on NM 337, a very scenic route passing through the Manzano Mountains. The three sections, listed in the order you'll reach them, are* ***Quarai****, located eight miles north of Mountainair off of NM 55;* ***Abo****, located about nine miles west of Mountainair off of US 60; and* ***Gran Quivia****, 26 miles south of Mountainair on NM 55. There's also a visitor center right on US 60 in the town of Mountainair. A series of missions were constructed at each of these sites in the mid-17th century to serve the surrounding pueblos. Each was abandoned after less than a century which has left them all mostly intact. Besides the missions there are many small pueblo structures which can be explored.*

I include these missions because they are historically important and are fine examples of mission and pueblo architecture. But they are definitely out of the way for many visitors. Therefore, I suggest them only for those who are really "into" this type of historic attraction.

If you do visit the Salinas Pueblo Missions, you can avoid back-tracking all the way to the Moriarty area. After visiting Gran Quivia, return only as far north as US 60. Then go east to the town of Vaughn (about 66 miles from Mountainair) and then east on US 54. The latter will bring you to Santa Rosa. One advantage of this route is that you do avoid the barren stretch of I-40 that I described earlier.

All sites of the Salinas Pueblo Missions are open daily 9:00am to 6:00pm from Memorial Day weekend through Labor Day and to 5:00pm the remainder of the year. The visitor center is open from 8:00am to 5:00pm. This is not a federal fee area; all sites are free of charge. For more information, call ***847-2585****.*

Santa Rosa is an old community where a lot of the inhabitants can actually trace their family ancestry back to members of the Coronado expedition of 1540. The town is located in a semi-arid region where one expects water would be scarce. However, a number of artesian springs surface in and around Santa Rosa, giving rise to some of the largest natural lakes in New Mexico. While its not quite accurate to call Santa Rosa an oasis in the desert, the vividly blue lakes are somewhat surprising.

The **Blue Hole** is the most famous of Santa Rosa's spring lakes. It's 87 feet deep, 60 feet in diameter, and has a temperature of about 65 degrees. Because of the extremely clear water it attracts scuba divers from throughout the southwest and midwest. A permit is required from the local police department. Blue Hole is filled with goldfish, catfish, snails and other marine animals. To reach it from I-40, take Exit 275 and then Will Rogers Drive into Lake Drive and onto Blue Hole Road.

Nearby is another attractive body of water called **Park Lake**. **Santa Rosa Lake State Park**, located a few miles north of town. Remember that details on activities at these lakes and other such areas can be found under the *Sports & Recreation* heading below.

Fort Sumner, Clovis, & Tucumcari

Leave Santa Rosa via I-40 east but get off in a couple of miles at Exit 277. Then follow US 84 in an easterly direction for 42 miles to the town of **Fort Sumner**. Shortly before arriving in Fort Summer you'll pass a short cutoff leading to **Sumner Lake State Park**, a very popular recreation spot.

The early history of Fort Sumner had a couple of rather unpleasant distinctions. First, in the 1860s the United States government rounded up 3,000 Navajos and force-marched them over 300 miles into an area they didn't want to be in – namely, Fort Sumner. Second, the town is connected with the notorious outlaw Billy The Kid. Billy's legacy, at least, is good for tourism. The town's main street houses the **Billy The Kid Museum**, *Tel. 355-2380*, whose life and exploits are documented. You may be disappointed in the museum, even though it contains the jail cell where Billy was allegedly incarcerated, because most of the museum has nothing to do with the Kid. It's a mish-mash of artifacts somewhat related to Fort Sumner's history. *The museum is open daily from 9:00am to 5:00pm and charges $3 admission.*

The town's other attractions are located a short distance from the center and are in immediate proximity to one another. Take US 60/64 three miles east and then south for three more miles on Billy The Kid Road to the **Fort Sumner State Monument**, *Tel. 355-2942*. This is the site of the fort that was built to watch over the Navajos, but little is left except some markers.

However, a quarter mile east of the monument is the much more interesting **Old Fort Sumner Museum**, *Tel. 355-2942, same as Fort Sumner State Monument,* which has artifacts and exhibits dealing with the operations of the fort. There are also paintings telling the life story of Billy The Kid and a number of exhibits on Navajo culture. Behind the museum is

Billy The Kid's Grave, a rather simple resting place for Billy and a couple of his accomplices. There's a fence around the graves because the headstone has been stolen on several occasions by pranksters. *The museum, monument, and grave site can all be visited daily 9:30am to 5:30pm, except that the museum closes at 4:30 from mid-September through the end of April. It's also closed on holidays during that period of the year. Combined admission is $3 for adults and $2 for children ages 6 to 12.*

Once you return to US 60/64, continue east for 57 dull miles past a number of small towns until you reach **Clovis**. The town is fairly large for New Mexico, being home to almost 35,000 people. It's located less than ten miles from the Texas line on New Mexico's eastern edge. The building of the railroad spurred its growth, especially after the turn of the century. It's a major livestock center, although its major claim to fame in American pop culture is the fact that Buddy Holly recorded his first album here in 1958. There isn't much to see in town, although if you're traveling with children you might entertain them for a short while by paying a brief visit to the small **zoo** located downtown in Hillcrest Park. How can you go wrong for a buck?

There's a bit more of interest 19 miles southwest of Clovis via US 70 in the town of **Portales**. However, Clovis has a better choice of places to stay and eat, primarily because it is three times the size. If you just want to relax for a couple of hours, the **Oasis State Park** on NM 467 six miles north of town is a popular spot for outdoor fun. Portales also has two museums that might strike your fancy. First is the **Blackwater Draw Archaeological Site and Museum**, *Tel. 562-2202*. It is located off of US 70 about five miles before reaching Portales and is operated by Eastern New Mexico University (whose campus lies on the western side of Portales). This fascinating site was discovered in 1932 and opened to the public only in 1969. The site displays evidence of human occupation that goes back well before the Anasazi culture, as much as 11,000 years ago. Earlier life forms, such as mammoths, bison, saber tooth tigers, and even camels have also been found. Besides being able to go out onto the site and getting the same "feel" as working archaeologists do, Blackwater Draw has a museum displaying some of the significant finds and what it all means.

Both the site and museum's summer hours (Memorial Day to Labor Day) are 10:00am to 5:00pm Monday to Saturday and on Sunday from 12 noon to 5:00pm. During the rest of the year the museum operates 10:00am to 5:00pm Tuesday to Saturday and 12:00 to 5:00pm on Sunday. The site has the same hours during the winter except that it is closed to the public during November through February. The admission charge is $2 for adults and only $1 for children and senior citizens.

Now you should return to Clovis. Continue your journey by traveling north from Clovis on NM 209. This road will bring you to **Tucumcari** in less than two hours. It also prospered as a railroad town at the turn of the century and later as a stop on Route 66. Its location right off of I-40 still makes it a fairly busy place.

Tucumcari is home to about 7,000 people. The origin of the town's name depends on who you talk to. There are two theories. The one that's probably true comes from the Comanche word *tucumcari* which means lookout point. You see, there's a 5,000-foot high mountain peak right near town (called **Tucumcari Mountain**) that most likely served that very purpose. The other story is a lot more fun and is also the one that most people want to believe. It seems that there were two Indian lovers named Tocom and Kari. Unfortunately, Tocom was killed in a fight for the lovely Kari, who was the daughter of an Apache chief. Kari, however, loved only Tocom and killed the victor before taking her own life. Her father witnessed the whole thing and took his own life, but not before he cried "Tocom. Kari." Sounds like a good plot for a tear-jerking movie classic.

Anyhow, there aren't any monuments to either Tocom or Kari. You can, however, visit the **Tucumcari Historical Museum** on South Adams Street in the heart of downtown, *Tel. 461-4201*. It's no better or worse than most local museums of its genre. You'll probably find a few items that will catch your interest. *The museum is open daily from 9:00am to 6:00pm except on Sunday when it opens at 1:00pm. After Labor Day and until June 1st its closed on Monday and closes other days an hour earlier. It's also closed on all major holidays. Admission is $2 for adults.*

For something completely different you can visit a 770-acre municipal wildlife refuge. The **Ladd S. Gordon Wildlife Area** is located off of Tucumcari Blvd. at the east end of town. The marshlands is a stopping place for migrating ducks, geese, and even some eagles. *It's open during daylight hours.*

Now comes one of the longest rides in any of the regional tours in this book without something specific to stop and see. Take US 54 east from Tucumcari. In about 23 miles you'll pass **Ute Lake State Park**, which you won't stop at unless you want to partake of the recreational opportunities. However, you can glance at the Ute Dam which bottles up the Canadian River. Built in the early 1960s, the dam is almost a half-mile long and 120 feet high. Just before the Texas border at Nara Visa, leave US 54 and take NM 402 north, passing a number of towns on the 60 mile trek into Clayton.

Clayton & Capulin Volcano National Monument

I know it's been a while since you had a really major attraction. You won't get it in Clayton, but it is coming up very soon now. In fact, the rest of this northeastern jaunt will have lots of action. Patience will be rewarded.

Clayton is said by area supporters to be the "heart of dinosaur country." That's stretching it a bit, even though the area has produced a number of significant finds of dinosaur footprints. You can even see some in front of the chamber of commerce! Kids will more likely be impressed by the life-size dinosaurs located in downtown's **Clayton Historical Park**. Downtown is also home to the **Union County Historical Museum**. The building was constructed in 1919 and once was the historic First Methodist Church. It contains a number of interesting artifacts that chronicle Clayton's history. *The hours can be rather strange, so you may want to call 374-9508 to make sure it's open.*

As you leave town via US 64 West/US 87 North, take notice of two unusual volcanic peaks to the north called **Rabbit Ears Mountains**. The odd formation was an important landmark to travelers in the 19th century because it marked the location where a trail called the Cimarron Cut-off left the main Santa Fe Trail. Many Indian attacks also occurred in this area. A few miles out of Clayton the road actually crosses the Santa Fe Trail's Cimarron Cut-off. Some people like to stop and see if they can find wagon wheel ruts. You can if you look hard enough, but there are better places to see them that I'll tell you about later.

At the small town of Capulin, turn north on NM 325 and proceed three miles to the most dominating physical sight in northeast New Mexico – **Capulin Volcano National Monument**, *Tel. 278-2201,* standing guard a thousand feet above you. Surrounded by flatlands, the steeply rising slopes of the green mountain provide quite a sight as you approach it. Capulin was created by an eruption that occurred about 10,000 years ago and the subsequent flow of lava from a large vent at the base. The almost perfectly symmetrical cinder cone is one of the best examples of such a volcanic formation in the entire world.

Start your visit at the informative Visitor Center located at the base. There are exhibits on the story of Capulin as well as a film about volcanos in general with some beautiful scenes of one of nature's most violent forces. Then you can take the paved road that circles the mountain and winds its way up to near the summit, which is at an elevation of 8,182 feet. It's kind of narrow but not a very difficult road to drive, so don't let the "scary" looking trip put you off. At the rim there are two trails. The first one is about a mile long and reaches the summit and goes along the edge of the crater. From there you can see into Colorado, Kansas, and Oklahoma on a clear day. There's also a quarter mile trail that goes down into the crater. You really won't see much more on the latter, although the feeling of being at the bottom of the crater and looking up is kind of strange. A lot of visitors just want to be able to say they went into the crater.

Capulin's visitor center is open daily 7:30am to 5:00pm Memorial Day weekend to Labor Day and a half-hour less at each end the rest of the year. The *crater rim road is open daily from 8:00am until dusk. The park is closed only on New Year's and Christmas. Admission is $4 per vehicle for those not holding an NPS passport.*

Raton to Cimarron & The Santa Fe Trail

Now you are approaching the historic heart of the region where the modern roadway more or less parallels the old Santa Fe Trail. It will begin 27 miles east of Capulin via US 64/87 when you reach the town of **Raton**, located just a few miles south of the Colorado line at Raton Pass.

Raton has quite an interesting origin. In 1866, an industrious rancher blasted through a section of mountain to create a 27-mile wagon road through the Raton Pass. He charged a toll to use it but most people were only too happy to pay it since it saved a hundred miles over the original route of the Santa Fe Trail. He became rich and a town grew up nearby to serve travelers on the Trail as well as the railroad when that came through a number of years later.

Raton looks different than most New Mexico communities because of the large number of 19th century homes that were built in Victorian style and that are still standing. Most of these are along First Street. The Chamber of Commerce on Second Street can give you a map that describes a route passing about 30 Victorian treasures on a **Raton Historical Walking Tour**. Among the most elegant of the structures is the **Palace Hotel**. The **Yucca Hotel** is decorated with many Indian good luck symbols and is also of interest. (It was originally called the Swastika Hotel – a swastika was originally an ancient Indian hooked symbol – but that was changed during World War II and, of course, never reverted to its old name.).

Also located on First Street is the **Raton Museum** in the old Coors Building, *Tel. 445-8979*. Exhibits, artifacts, and photographs are used to give the visitor a feel of what Raton was like in the 19th century. Downtown's **Santa Fe Depot** is still used by Amtrak, although more people pass through the Spanish colonial structure as tourists than travelers. *The museum is open Tuesday through Saturday from 9:00am until 4:00pm during June through September and Friday to Sunday from 2:00-5:00pm the rest of the year. It is closed on holidays and has no admission fee.*

Two good attractions are located outside of town. First is **Sugarite Canyon State Park**, located about eight miles northeast of town via NM 72. (Take First Street north to Sugarite Avenue and follow NM 72 markers.) While the park contains recreational facilities for both summer and winter fun (skiing and camping, for example), it's worth seeing because of its beauty. The approach road is thickly lined with several types of trees as it winds its way into the canyon. Within the park itself are several gorgeous meadows where summer wildflowers are in abundance, setting a majestic foreground for the high rocky cliffs that surround the canyon.

The **National Rifle Association Whittington Center** is approximately ten miles south of Raton on US 64 West, *Tel. 445-3615*. Take I-25 four miles south from Raton to Exit 446. Now this is not the proper place for debating the pros and cons of the views of the NRA and I won't be tempted to get into that argument. Suffice to say that if you're interested in learning about how to shoot, marksmanship, or competition and wish to do it in a supervised and safe environment, this is the place. The 33,000 acre site covers some pretty countryside and contains an original stretch of the Santa Fe Trail, including wagon-wheel ruts.

Regardless of whether you go to Whittington Center, you'll still have to take US 64 to reach the next destination, which is the picturesque town of **Cimarron**. US 64 follows the exact path of the Santa Fe Trail's Cimarron Cut-off for a distance of 27 miles. The name means "wild" and can be used to describe Cimarron's early history of notorious outlaws and life style or the country surrounding it. Situated on the western edge of the Carson National Forest and the Sangre de Cristo Mountains, Cimarron presents breathtaking vistas to those who stop in this tiny community of less than a thousand people.

Like many small New Mexico towns, most of the better sights are located a few miles away. However, you should visit downtown's **St. James Hotel**. Recently renovated and fortunately spared damage during a rare tornado in the summer of 1996, the public areas still show a lot of history. It was built in 1873 and among the famous people who stayed there over the years were Buffalo Bill, Wyatt Earp, and Jessie James. Good-guys, bad-guys and everyone in between. The **Old Aztec Mill Museum** is south of town on NM 21 in a mid-19th century four story mill building, *Tel. 376-2913*. It's really two museums in one, because in addition to being able to see the still functioning mill equipment, there are several floors of exhibits on Native American crafts and history. *You can visit the museum daily from 9:00am to 5:00pm (except from 1:00pm on Sunday) during June through August and during the same hours on Saturday and Sunday only during May and September. The admission is $2 for adults and $1 for seniors and children.*

Continuing west from town on US 64, the road follows the course of the **Cimarron River**. After about 14 very scenic miles (just past the small town of Ute Park) you'll reach **Cimarron Canyon State Park**, one of the most beautiful in the state park system. Deeply notched granite cliffs, often referred to as the Cimarron Palisades, soar about 400 feet above the canyon floor in a magnificent vista of color and form. The park is also very popular with anglers and for viewing wildlife. Elk are especially common. After visiting the canyon, head back towards Cimarron. (If you're taking bits and pieces of each region, this is a good place to link up with Taos.

Another ten miles west of Cimarron Canyon, US 64 reaches Eagles Nest on the Enchanted Circle.)

Equally beautiful scenery and abundant wildlife can be found just north of Cimarron for those who are inclined toward the adventurous. The **Valle Vidal** (part of the Carson National Forest and not to be confused with Los Alamos' Valle Grande) is an immense valley ringed in on all sides by mountains. Reached by NM 204 from off of US 64 to the east of town, the area is known for the herds of elk and other wildlife. The state managed **Barker Wild Life Area**, providing similar activities, is reached by Forest Route 1950. This is also off of US 64 to the east of Cimarron. Various portions of each area are closed during different times of the year to allow the herds to calve their young. However, the majority of the region is open at any given time. If driving, a high-clearance vehicle is strongly recommended, although you can get away without four-wheel drive. Many visitors like to enter this primitive area on horseback, just as was done in eras past. Rentals and tours can be arranged in Cimarron.

Five miles southwest of town on NM 21 is the huge (nearly 140,000 acres) **Philmont Scout Ranch**., *Tel. 376-2281 for the ranch, Villa Philmonte, Seton Memorial Library, and the Kit Carson Museum.* The national camping center is visited by nearly 20,000 scouts each summer. However, you don't have to be a scout to enjoy some of the historic facilities that are open to the general public. These include **Villa Philmonte**, the fabulous ranch home built by oil baron Waite Phillips and modeled after a number of famous homes he had seen in various parts of Europe; the **Seton Memorial Library**, containing art works and the library of the naturalist and first chief scout of the Boy Scouts of America; and the **Kit Carson Museum**, which is not about Kit Carson at all but rather is a living history museum about life on a 19th century ranch complex. *The library and museum are open daily from 8:00am to 5:00pm during June through August. They have no set admission fee but do request donations. Tours of Villa Philmonte are generally given every half hour, but call 376-2281 for up-to-date information.*

Fort Union National Monument & Las Vegas

From Cimarron, you can head for your next stop in one of two ways. If in town, pick up NM 58 in an easterly direction and take it 19 miles to I-25. Go south for five miles (Exit 414) and the town of **Springer**. Or, if you were visiting the sights along NM 21, stay on that road as it winds its way directly into Springer. Of some interest here is **The Santa Fe Trail Museum**, *Tel. 483-2341*, again something of a misnomer. It has little to do with the Trail, except that it was important in the development of the town, whose history is portrayed here. The most interesting features are the only electric chair ever used in the state's history, (you can also climb a tower where the gallows were used prior to more modern methods), and an authentic covered wagon. *The museum is open during the summer months from 9:00am to 5:00pm except from 1:00pm on Sunday and the admission fee is $2 for adults and $1 for children.*

Now head south once again on I-25, passing by such interestlingly named towns as Wagon Mound before getting off at Exit 366. Take NM 161 eight miles following the sign for **Fort Union National Monument**, *Tel. 425-8025*. During most of the second half of the 19th century, Fort Union was the largest military establishment in the Southwest. It was the primary quartermaster depot for more than 50 forts whose purposes included protecting traffic on the Santa Fe Trail. It was located here because two branches of the Trail converged nearby. There have actually been three forts here, the first being a log structure, the second being more formidable because of the outbreak of the Civil War, and the third and largest which was built in the late 1860s.

Your visit to Fort Union consists of three parts. First, take a look at the visitor center which houses an excellent museum on the fort's lengthy history. It includes many original artifacts found throughout the ruins. The second portion involves a 1 1/4 mile long trail covering over a hundred acres. You'll see the remains of the red adobe outer walls as well as portions of dozens of buildings. Think back to all those old western movies and you'll be able to picture life on the frontier. It's even easier with the demonstrations that take place by costumed guides during the summer, the third and final aspect of touring Fort Union. *The monument is open daily 8:00am until 6:00pm from Memorial day through Labor Day and to 5:00pm the remainder of the year. It is closed only on New Year's and Christmas. Admission for those not holding one of the NPS passports is $4 per vehicle.*

After visiting the Fort, make your way back to I-25 and continue south for another 21 miles to Exit 345. That will bring you into **Las Vegas**. With a population of nearly 15,000, this quiet community certainly won't be confused with Las Vegas, Nevada. On the other hand, there are a number of very interesting attractions in the area. It, too, lies along the Santa Fe Trail and you can still see faint wagon wheel ruts right outside of town. Architecture represents the two main periods of development in the 19th century. Adobe structures in the heart of town date from Las Vegas' founding in the 1820s when it was primarily a Spanish community. Victorian architecture was added about 70 years later. Hundreds of Las Vegas' buildings are listed in the National Register of Historic Places.

The most logical place to begin touring Las Vegas is at the local **Chamber of Commerce**, *727 Grand Avenue*, because they'll provide you with brochures on self-guided walks through the historic districts. (Grand Avenue parallels I-25 and there is access to the highway at either end of town.) Right next door to the chamber of commerce is the **Rough Riders**

Memorial and City Museum, *Tel. 425-8726*. An interesting collection of pictures and artifacts traces the origins and exploits of Teddy Roosevelt's Rough Rider Brigade in the Spanish-American War. You're probably wondering, no doubt, how that wound up in Las Vegas, New Mexico. Well, for whatever reason, almost half of the Rough Riders were from New Mexico, including quite a few from Las Vegas. So, what better place to put a memorial? The museum also documents the history of Las Vegas. *The museum is open Monday through Saturday from 9:00am to 4:00pm. It's closed on all major holidays and accepts donations in lieu of a standardized admission fee.*

The area around the museum is the "new" downtown (i.e., from the turn of the century), with its Victorian architecture. Walk west on Bridge Street. It's a transition to the old town area and the buildings lining both sides of the street are reminiscent of a western boomtown. At the far end of Bridge Street is the old town **plaza**, complete with Victorian style gazebo. The surrounding buildings are mostly adobe style. The most interesting building on the plaza is **The Plaza Hotel**. It, too, brings back memories of yesteryear (see also the *Where to Stay* section) in its elegant public areas. Many famous and infamous people also have signed their names in the hotel's guest register over the years, including Billy The Kid and Doc Holliday.

Getting out of town now, the first place worth visiting is the **Las Vegas National Wildlife Refuge**, about six miles southeast via NM 104 and NM 281. The 8,700 acres are home to over 300 different species, about two-thirds of which are birds. Birds of prey, commonly referred to these days as raptors, are in great number. Several species of eagles and hawks can be seen on the seven mile driving tour. You can also get permits to go out on the somewhat difficult trails. *The refuge is open during daylight hours and there is no charge for admission. However, if you wish to get trail permits, the office that issues them is open only Monday through Friday from 8:00am to 4:30pm.*

If you have a couple of hours to spare, you can make a nice excursion to the northwest of town via NM 65. This begins as Hot Springs Boulevard at the northwest corner of the old town plaza. Five miles north is the **Montezuma Hot Springs**. The supposedly curative waters have been used since ancient times. The name comes from the alleged fact that the great Aztec emperor, Montezuma II, visited the springs to take to the waters. Most historians doubt that he ever traveled this far north. Regardless, today's visitors can come either to look at the series of natural pools or to soak in them free of charge. It is a good way to relax after a hard day of touring, even if it doesn't really cure anything.

Across from the Springs is a strange looking 77-room building known as **Montezuma Castle**, *Tel. 454-4277*. Montezuma definitely didn't sleep there, it isn't nearly that old. It has, however, served as a hotel and as a monastery for Mexican priests. Currently, it carries the long name of Armand Hammer United World College of the American West. An excellent prepatory school for gifted teens, the man of baking soda fame was also a noted philanthropist. The school attracts students from around the world and as close as the pueblos of New Mexico. Finally, before taking NM 65 back to Las Vegas, continue another six miles or so into scenic **Gallinas Canyon**. Besides recreational facilities, the main attraction is the heavily forested canyon and the road that hugs the cliffside along the river. It's very pretty.

Before completing your northeast regional tour and heading back to either Santa Fe or Albuquerque via I-25, you should pay a visit to the **Pecos National Historic Park**, a few miles north of I-25's Exit 307 on NM 63, *Tel. 757-6414*. It's about a 45-minute drive from Las Vegas. The park contains the ruins of a large pueblo and two missions from the 17th and 18th centuries. A variety of factors caused the pueblo to be abandoned. Descendants of the pueblo still reside in Jemez Pueblo.

A visitor center contains artifacts from the pueblo as well as a good film on pueblo life. Then you can go out on the relatively easy 1 1/4 mile trail that winds through the ruins. *The park is open daily from 8:00am through 6:00pm. After Labor Day and until Memorial Day weekend it closes an hour earlier. The admission fee, for those who don't have NPS passports, is $4 per vehicle.*

NIGHTLIFE & ENTERTAINMENT

The pickings here are about as slim as in the northwest region. Again, the major lodging establishments in Las Vegas, Raton, and Tucumcari are the most likely choices. Of all these places, the saloon in The Plaza Hotel in Las Vegas is the most lively and conducive to visitors.

SPORTS & RECREATION

Fishing

- **Janes-Wallace Memorial Park**, *Santa Rosa*. Bass, catfish, trout.
- **Santa Rosa Lake State Park**, *Santa Rosa*. Bass, catfish, crappie, walleye.
- **Oasis State Park**, *Portales*. Catfish, trout.

Golf

- **New Mexico Highlands University Golf Course**, *2118 8th Street, Las Vegas. Tel. 425-7711*
- **Raton Municipal Golf Course**, *Raton. Tel. 445-8113*
- **Santa Rosa Golf Course**, *121 N. 4th, Santa Rosa. Tel. 472-3949*
- **Tucumcari Municipal Golf Course**, *Tucumcari. Tel. 461-1849*

Horseback Riding

- **Pendaries Lodge and Country Club**, *Las Vegas. Tel. 425-6076*

Swimming

- **Blue Hole**, *Santa Rosa*
- **Clayton Lake State Park**, *Clayton*
- **Sumner Lake State Park**, *Fort Sumner*

PRACTICAL INFORMATION

- **Tourist Office/Visitors Bureau**
  - **Cimarron**: *Tel. 376-2417 or 1/800-700-4298*
  - **Clovis**: *Tel. 763-3435*
  - **Las Vegas**: *Tel. 425-8631 or 1/800-832-5947*
  - **Raton**: *Tel. 445-3689 or 1/800-638-6161*
  - **Santa Rosa**: *Tel. 472-3763*
- **Bus Depot**
  - **Clovis**: *Tel. 762-4584*
  - **Las Vegas**: *Tel. 425-8009*
  - **Santa Rosa**: *Tel. 472-5263*
- **Hospital**
  - **Clovis**: *Tel. 769-2141*
  - **Las Vegas**: *Tel. 425-6751*
  - **Raton**: *Tel. 445-3661*
  - **Santa Rosa**: *Tel. 472-3417*
- **Police** (non-emergency):
  - **Clovis**: *Tel. 769-1921*
  - **Las Vegas**: *Tel. 425-7504*
  - **Raton**: *Tel. 445-22704*
  - **Santa Rosa**: *Tel. 472-3338*

18. ALAMOGORDO

With a population of nearly 30,000, **Alamogordo** certainly doesn't qualify as a big city. However, it's a very important community to New Mexico. The nearby air force base is a major employer and pumps a lot of money into the economy. For the visitor to New Mexico, it's also important. Besides some interesting things to see in town, Alamogordo is the gateway to the fantastic natural sights of the **White Sands National Monument**. It's also only a short ride to the mountain and forest scenery around **Cloudcroft**, a major recreation area. Finally, Alamogordo makes a great starting point for touring the southeastern region of New Mexico (see Chapter 19, *The Southeast: Desert Landscapes & Natural Wonders* for more details).

Alamogordo and the surrounding areas were inhabited in prehistoric times, and also had some pueblos during the Anasazi era in the mountain-rimmed valley known as the **Tularosa Basin**. Upon abandonment of these pueblos (just about the time of the arrival of the Spaniards), the **Apache** settled the area. The name of the town derives from the 19th-century **Alamo Ranch**, which was bought by a man named Charles Eddy. He subdivided the ranch into 960 lots and attracted several thousand residents at the turn of the century.

Real growth began during World War II when the army began building an airfield. Alamogordo ushered in the nuclear age with the detonation of the first atomic bomb at the **Trinity Site**, a barren desert area some 60 miles to the northwest.

ARRIVALS & DEPARTURES

Alamogordo is located in south-central New Mexico, about 215 miles from Albuquerque. The easiest way to reach it from the latter is to take I-25 south to San Antonio (Exit 139) and then east on US 380 to US 54 at Carrizozo. US 54 meets up with US 70 and the two concurrently run into Alamogordo. Or, you can take I-25 to Las Cruces (Exit 6) and then I-70 east to Alamogordo. That way is longer but has a bigger percentage of the route on the Interstate. It's also a good way to get to Alamogordo if you're coming from the southwestern part of the state or from El Paso.

You can get to Alamogordo by air from Albuquerque via **Mesa Airlines**, *Tel. 1/800-MESA-AIR*. There's also bus service from major New Mexico cities. If you intend to visit only the southern portion of the state, you have the option of flying into El Paso International Airport (only about 85 miles away) and either renting a car there or taking the Alamo/ El Paso Shuttle, which has five round trips a day. It also stops at Holloman Air Force Base, because military personnel are the main user. Car rentals are available in Alamogordo so long as you intend to return it to the same location.

ORIENTATION/GETTING AROUND

Getting around Alamogordo is easy. There's only one main street – **White Sands Boulevard** – which is also US 54/70/82. At the north end of the town, US 54/70 heads to the northwest while US 82 goes east to Cloudcroft and beyond. South of town, after White Sands Boulevard turns towards the west, US 70/82 head southwest to Holloman Air Force Base and the White Sands National Monument, while US 54 goes to El Paso. Most of Alamogordo's lodging establishments and restaurants are located right on White Sands Boulevard.

WHERE TO STAY

ALAMOGORDO

Moderate

HOLIDAY INN, *1401 South White Sands Boulevard. Tel. 437-7100, Fax 437-7100, Extension 299. Rates: $70. 106 Rooms. Major credit cards accepted. Toll-free reservations 1/800-HOLIDAY. Located about two miles south of the center of town on the main thoroughfare. (White Sands Boulevard is the same as US 54/70/82.)*

A modern and attractive low-rise motor inn, this Holiday Inn features large, comfortable rooms with coffee makers. Some rooms have refrigerators and microwaves. There's a big heated swimming pool as well as a wading pool for small children. Yesterday's Restaurant serves good food and also has a cocktail lounge. Among other facilities are a beauty salon and a gift shop.

Budget

DAYS INN, *907 South White Sands Boulevard. Tel. 437-5090, Fax 434-5667. Rates: $55-60. 40 Rooms. Major credit cards accepted. Toll-free reservations 1/800-325-2525. Located on the main thoroughfare (US 54/70/82), about 1 1/2 miles south of the town center.*

In case you haven't stayed at a Days Inn a long time, you may be surprised to find that the chain has substantially upgraded its facilities since the time they first broke into the market big time in the southeastern United States. This small inn is typical of the new Days – nothing really fancy but very nice accommodations at a reasonable price. Executive class rooms have refrigerators and microwaves. There's a Denny's Restaurant across the street, or you can find numerous better dining spots within a short distance.

DESERT AIRE MOTOR INN, *1021 South White Sands Boulevard. Tel. 437-2110, Fax 437-1898. Rates: $44-58, including Continental Breakfast. Member of Best Western chain. 100 Rooms. Major credit cards accepted. Toll-free reservations 1/800-528-1234. Located on the main thoroughfare (US 54/70/82), about 1 3/4 miles south of the town center.*

An older motel than the other Alamogordo selections, this Best Western still has a lot to offer. All rooms (which have been extensively renovated) are large and nicely furnished. There's a big variety of room types including several with kitchens. Spa rooms (up to $99) have an in-room Jacuzzi. Other facilities include a heated swimming pool and whirlpool for the folks who don't have one in their room and a nice breakfast room where a good sized Continental breakfast is served daily. There isn't any restaurant on the premises but several are located within close proximity.

CLOUDCROFT

Expensive

THE LODGE AT CLOUDCROFT, *One Corona Place. Tel. 682-2566, Fax 682-2715. Rates: $75-125. 60 Rooms. Major credit cards accepted. Toll-free reservations 1/800-395-6343. Located just off US 82 (Cloudcroft's main street). From Alamogordo proceed north on White Sands Boulevard for three miles to US 82 and then east for about 16 miles.*

This beautiful and historic wooden structure was built in 1909 to replace a lodge from ten years earlier that had burned down. It was put up as a retreat for railroad workers who brought timber from the surrounding forest into Alamogordo. The Victorian style structure, with large areas of glass and a tall tower, has an almost fairy tale appearance. This is especially true at night. The grounds are extensive and attractive and you can, with a small walk, get some great views of the surrounding countryside.

All of the 47 rooms in the main lodge are large and charmingly furnished with turn of the century furniture and antique fixtures. The better rooms have coffee makers, microwave, and refrigerator. Several more rustic rooms, some with fireplaces, are located in an adjacent building called the Lodge Pavilion, which is a Bed & Breakfast facility.

Breakfast and various package plans are also available in the main building. There's also a separate four bedroom home called the Retreat. Guests in both the Pavilion and Retreat may make use of all the Lodge's facilities. The three-story main building has no elevator so if you have any physical disability you want to make sure that your room is located on a lower floor.

Facilities at The Lodge are extensive. They include an attractive heated outdoor swimming pool, Jacuzzi, sauna, and a nine-hole golf course. Skiing and ice skating is available during the winter months. Rebecca's, an award-winning restaurant is known for fine Continental cuisine. There's also a cocktail lounge but The Lodge isn't known as a place to look for action. It's a refined atmosphere, one where you can relax in style while taking in the brilliant sunsets and listening to music on the Grand piano.

Selected as one of my Best Places to Stay (see Chapter 12 for more details).

Budget

SPRUCE CABINS, *off of US 82 following signs from town. Tel. 682-2381. Rates: $37-60. 30 Rooms. Discover, VISA, and MasterCard accepted. Located 20 miles from Alamogordo via White Sands Boulevard to US 82 East.*

Set onto a hillside of the Sacramento Mountains just above Cloudcroft, Spruce Cabins provides the poor mans' alternative to The Lodge for those who wish to stay in Cloudcroft. Not that The Lodge is so high priced, but it doesn't fit for those on a tight budget. This does. There is a variety of cabins, some accommodating up to eight people. They're generally furnished in a plain, rustic manner, but there's plenty of room and you'll find them quite comfortable. Some have a kitchen and fireplace (wood provided).

Recreational opportunities include two tennis courts, two nine-hole golf courses, and picnic facilities. There isn't any restaurant but you can go into town or over to The Lodge to eat – either is just minutes away.

CAMPING & RV SITES

Contact the supervisor of the **Lincoln National Forest**, *Tel. 434-7200.*

WHERE TO EAT

ALAMOGORDO

Moderate – $11-20

EL CAMINO RESTAURANT, *White Sands Boulevard and 10th Street. Tel. 437-8809. Most major credit cards accepted. Lunch and dinner served daily.*

This restaurant serves authentic Mexican cuisine as well as American fare. Lighter meals are also available for lunch or simple dinner. It's nothing really special but Alamogordo, considering its status as the metropolis of the south-central portion of the state, has rather slim pickings. If you're not in the mood for the mostly Mexican menu than you may want to try Yesterday's Restaurant at the Holiday Inn, or even take a ride out to Cloudcroft for Rebecca's.

CLOUDCROFT

Moderate - $11-20

REBECCA'S, *located in The Lodge at Cloudcroft. Tel. 682-2566. Major credit cards accepted. Sunday Brunch.*

Like the Lodge at which it's located, Rebecca's features a very attractive turn-of-the-century decor and atmosphere of a conservatory. Large picture windows look out on the spacious grounds. The name (and the portrait in the lounge) is supposedly of a Lodge maid of many years ago who disappeared after being found with another man by her lover. The service is excellent without being overbearing. The menu specializes in continental cuisine, all carefully prepared. For dessert try one of the baker's delicious pastries. Rebecca's also features a children's menu and a full-service cocktail lounge. The live entertainment consists of mellow selections on a Grand piano.

SEEING THE SIGHTS

The sights in this chapter don't cover that big of a geographic area. However, it's always easier to cut things into more manageable bite-size pieces, so I'll do that here, too. The pieces are **Alamogordo** itself, the **White Sands National Monument**, and the **Cloudcroft** area.

Alamogordo

While you definitely won't come away from Alamogordo declaring it to be New Mexico's prettiest community, it does have a number of attractions both in town and nearby that still make it a good place to visit.

Several downtown attractions are conveniently located within close proximity to one another on White Sands Boulevard. All can be enjoyed by children as much as adults. The **Toy Train Depot**, *1991 N. White Sands Boulevard, Tel. 437-2855*, contains several hundred model and toy trains. The building was, fitting enough, a one-time train depot. *The train exhibit is open Wednesday through Monday from noon until 5:00pm. It's closed on New Year's, Easter, Thanksgiving and Christmas. Admission is $1.50 for adults and $1 for children. Train rides cost an additional $2 for adults and $1 for kids.*

Visitors can, in addition to viewing the models, take a train ride that goes through the adjacent **Alameda Park and Zoo**. The zoo is fairly large for a town of Alamogordo's size and contains more than 300 animals, mostly from the Americas but including some exotic species from around the world. The park has some lovely shade trees to relax under. While you're at it you may also wish to pay a brief visit to the **Tularosa Basin Historical Museum**, *1301 N. White Sands Boulevard*, which has exhibits featuring local history and Indian artifacts. *The park and zoo is open daily from 9:00am until 5:00pm and costs only a dollar for grown-ups and 50 cents for children. The Historical Museum is open daily (except for major holidays) from 10:00am till 5:00pm and is free of charge.*

Alamogordo's most famous attraction is the **Space Center**, *on Scenic Drive, Tel. 437-2840 or 1/800-545-4021*, atop a hillside overlooking Alamogordo and the Tularosa Basin. You can even see the white sand dunes on a clear day from this spot. The Space Center is one of New Mexico's best museums and is also one of the world's premier museums devoted to space science. Take White Sands Boulevard to Indian Wells Road. It's not difficult to find – just follow the signs. The first thing to strike you about the Space Center will happen even before you get there – the four story gold reflective glass building (known affectionately as "The Cube") is a wonderful piece of modern award-winning architecture. Visitors take an elevator to the top floor and then work their way down four levels of ramps through the International Space Hall of Fame.

The work of the United States and Russia is most in evidence, but every nation that has a space effort is included in the imaginative displays. Other areas of the center include the Air and Space Park, an outdoor display area of launch vehicles and spacecraft, the Astronauts Memorial Garden, Shuttle Camp for children and a simulated walk on the planet Mars. The Clyde Tombaugh Space Theater shows 70mm films and laser light shows on a 40-foot high wrap-around screen. You could easily spend several hours here, and that's without even seeing the films.

The center is open daily from 9:00am to 6:00pm June through August and until 5:00pm the remainder of the year. Admission for the center only is $2.25 for adults and $1.75 for seniors and children. There's a family rate of $7. Films are shown at 10, 11, 12, 2 and 4, while the laser light shows are at 7:00pm. A laser show set to rock music is given on Saturdays at 8:45pm. Theater admission is $3.75 for adults and $2.50 for children and seniors with a family rate of $11. Laser shows are $3.50. Combined Space Center and Theater admissions cost $5.25 for adults, $3.50 for seniors and children, or $15.50 for a family.

To the south of town (via US 54 for about 10 miles) is the **Oliver Lee Memorial State Park**. Located at the entrance to Dog Canyon in the Sacramento Mountains, the park contains unusual desert flora and historical exhibits relating to the early ranchers who owned property in the canyon and controlled the water supply in the canyon, which was important to other ranchers in the surrounding area. *The park is open during daylight hours and there is a $3 per vehicle admission fee.*

TRINITY SITE: VISITING 20TH CENTURY HISTORY

On July 16, 1945, an event occurred in the remote desert north of Alamogordo that was to change the course of history. Several years of tedious research and development taking place far to the north in Los Alamos culminated in the detonation of the first atomic bomb. The ground shook as a fiery explosion raised a mushroom-shaped cloud 40,000 feet into the sky. Aside from a huge crater, there was little damage done because ***Trinity Site*** *was about as desolate a place as could have been picked for the test.*

More than 50 years have passed, but little has changed in the small desert valley of the ***Jornada del Muerto*** *that is surrounded by mountains and lava beds. Trinity Site remains closed to the public and the curious and will likely remain so for the foreseeable future. There are only two exceptions. On the first Saturday in April and again on the first Saturday in October, the public is allowed to visit the Trinity Site, escorted by military police. There isn't a great deal to see, although the overall scenery of the surrounding area is mildly attractive in a strange sort of way. I guess the reason so many people want to go to Trinity Site is because the power that was unleashed that day has affected all of us in one way or another. I can understand the urge to be surrounded by that history.*

The passage of years has cleansed the local environment. The government measures the current radiation levels around Ground Zero to be approximately ten times as great as in areas further away. Don't let that scare you away, though, if you happen to be in Alamogordo at the proper time of the year. That doesn't represent any health hazard, especially for the amount of time you'll be there.

If you wish to sign up for the tours, call ***678-1134****.*

White Sands National Monument

As good as the Space Museum is, the real star of the Alamogordo area is located 16 miles southwest of town via US 70. The **White Sands National Monument**, *Tel. 479-6124,* is the world's largest gypsum sand dune field, covering almost 300 square miles of the Tularosa Basin. That doesn't begin to tell the fascinating story. This great natural wonder of the world features sand dunes whose brilliant white is brighter than snow. Many of the dunes rise to a height of 60 feet. Large tracts are filled only with the fine sand but some areas have a surprising amount of vegetation.

Gypsum was deposited more than 250 million years ago at the bottom of a shallow sea. Some 70 million years ago the gypsum had turned to rock along with the remains of small marine creatures in a large dome that was part of the uplifting of the Rocky Mountains. This dome collapsed about 10 million years ago and created the **Tularosa Basin**. So much for your earth science lesson. I still don't really understand it that well. But I'm better at understanding how the dunes still grow and move. Winds blowing across the basin pick up small particles of gypsum and carry them downwind, where they drop and slowly accumulate into a dune as the particles literally bounce up the gentle slope. But the leading edge of the dune is steep and eventually gravity pulls it down, which moves the whole dune forward and the process begins anew. Don't expect to see that process – it occurs very slowly. You will see the dramatic cumulative effect of that process over the years.

There's quite a bit of wildlife in the monument including rabbits, foxes, and coyotes. These larger animals usually only come out at night (you can sometimes see their prints in the sand if you come early in the morning). The only living creatures you'll likely to see (besides the very common species *touristus humanus*) are some lizards, insects, and even mice. Amazingly, some of these creatures have, over hundreds or even thousands of years, adapted to the environment by turning nearly as white as the sand. If you are to see animals, they'll mainly be on the Big Dune Nature Trail, where the soap yucca, cottonwood, and a few other hearty plants and trees have somehow managed to take hold in the sand and avoid being buried.

Now about your visit. Begin at the small but excellent Visitor Center just beyond the entrance gate where exhibits tell the complete story of the White Sands. You'll learn to differentiate between the four types of dunes at White Sands – something I'm sure will enrich your intellectual life, as well as how wildlife and plants adapt to the environment. Then you can begin the eight-mile long **Dunes Drive** (you must come back the same way) which leads into the heart of the dunes. There are several pullouts where you can read markers explaining the scientific side of what you're seeing.

There are many places where you can leave your car and climb up on the dunes, making your own trail and finding your way back by the footprints you left. The **Big Dunes Nature Trail** is one mile long and is relatively easy, but you should plan on doing it during the cooler morning hours – it get's real hot in the White Sands. Park Rangers offer guided activities during the summer. Schedules of activities are posted at the Visitor Center. Summers can be extremely hot, so it's a good idea to try and visit early in the day. Another advantage of a morning tour is that the lighting is more dramatic. Shortly after sunrise is when the rippling effect in the sand is most clearly visible.

The monument's drive and trail is open daily from 7:00am until 9:00pm Memorial Day to Labor Day and until 30 minutes after dusk during the rest of the year. The visitor center opens at 8:30 and closes at 5:00pm. The admission fee is $4 per vehicle unless you have a NPS passport. Please note that the White

Sands National Monument is completely surrounded by the White Sands Missile Range. There are usually one or two times a week when tests are being conducted resulting in the closure of US 70 to all traffic for periods of up to two hours. You probably won't run into this problem, but if you do, be patient – it's for your safety.

Cloudcroft

The attractive mountain resort and recreation center of **Cloudcroft** is located atop an 8,650 foot high peak of the Sacramento Mountains is 19 miles from Alamogordo via US 82 east. Cloudcroft is within the confines of the **Lincoln National Forest**. The town is home to only about 700 people, and there are only a few streets, one of which is US 82 running through the center. Among other things, Cloudcroft is known for having one of the highest golf courses in America.

The origin of Cloudcroft is different than most other places in this part of the state. A railroad company built a spur line leading into the mountains to enable it to bring timber to the valley. They built a lodge in 1899 to provide a nice place for their workers to get some recreation. The railroad and timber operations are gone, as is the original lodge which burned down in 1909, but the recreational purposes of Cloudcroft remain as they were a hundred years ago.

The ride to and from Alamogordo to Cloudcroft takes only about a half hour and is alone worth making the trip. Rising in dramatic fashion from the flat Tularosa Basin, the road goes through a mountain tunnel (the only highway tunnel of its kind in New Mexico) and continues to rise through the forest. Views of surrounding peaks and of the Basin are simply beautiful, especially on the way down. Just west of Cloudcroft are the remains of part of the old **Cloudcroft Climbing Railway** that rose more than 4,700 feet in the 30-mile trip from the Tularosa Basin. You can still see the graceful curve of the majestic high wooden **Mexican Canyon Trestle** (1899) silhouetted against the thick forest.

Once at Cloudcroft you can spend some time wandering about the cute and tiny town. Take a few minutes to visit the **Sacramento Mountains History Museum**, *Tel. 682-2932* which features exhibits on local history as well as a huge collection of arrowheads. Don't laugh – it's more interesting than you might think. There's also a small pioneer village with historic buildings and equipment. *Museum hours are daily from 1:00-4:00pm. During the winter skiing season the museum opens at 10:00am on Saturday. Donations are accepted.*

You can also visit **The Lodge** (see the *Where to Stay* section), built in 1911 to replace the original structure. The elegant wooden structure has played host to many famous visitors.

Finally, if you're interested in bird watching, the **Bluff Springs** is an attractive wildlife area located just a few miles south of Cloudcroft off of local route 6563. Follow the signs. Dozens of bird species inhabit the area. Perhaps the most interesting for visitors are the largest and the smallest – turkeys, on the one hand, and colorful and fascinating hummingbirds on the other.

THE SUNSPOT BYWAY

The second shortest of New Mexico's scenic byways begins at Cox Canyon Road at the western edge of Cloudcroft and dead-ends about 20 miles later at a place called Sunspot. It's near the edge of the Sacramento Mountains and thus provides one of the best views of the Tularosa Basin. But most visitors take the drive to visit the ***Sacramento Peak Observatory****, Tel. 434-7000. Originally an air force station, the observatory now is run by the National Science Foundation and conducts solar research. Some of the world's most advanced telescopic equipment is located here. The main telescope is so huge that it begins 200 feet below ground and rises to more than 13 stories high!*

Self-guided tours of the observatory can be taken most days. Call ***434-1390*** *to make sure that the facility will be open to visitors. Guided tours are usually offered on Saturday at 2:00pm from May through October. Again, it is best to call to make sure that it will be given. There is no charge for either method of visiting.*

NIGHTLIFE & ENTERTAINMENT

Basically limited to two places, one each in Alamogordo and Cloudcroft. The **Holiday Inn** in Alamogordo has a decent lounge with live entertainment, while for refined after-dinner drinks and entertainment you can visit the lounge at **The Lodge** in Cloudcroft.

There are quite a few bars scattered throughout Alamogordo, many of which are frequented by airmen from Holloman Air Force Base, which may not be the type of place you're looking for. On the other hand, some of you will likely enjoy that type of environment.

SPORTS & RECREATION

All locations are within Alamogordo unless indicated otherwise.

Golf

- **Apache Mesa Golf Course**, *on Holloman Air Force Base, Tel. 479-3574*
- **Desert Lakes Golf Course**, *2351 Hamilton Road, Tel. 437-0290*
- **The Lodge Golf Course**, *Cloudcroft. Tel. 682-2098*

Horseback Riding

- **Chippeway Stables**, *Cloudcroft. Tel. 682-2565*
- **Mike Pittman Stables**, *Tel. 437-1111*

Skiing

- **Cloudcroft: Snow Canyon**, *Tel. 1/800-333-7542*. Mid-December through March.

PRACTICAL INFORMATION

All information is for Alamogordo unless specified otherwise.

- **Tourist Office/Visitors Bureau**
  Alamogordo: *Tel. 437-6120 or 1/800-545-4021*
  Cloudcroft: *Tel. 682-2733*
- **Bus Depot**: *Tel. 437-3050*
- **Hospital**: *Tel. 439-2100*
- **Police** (non-emergency): *Tel. 437-2505*

19. THE SOUTHEAST

- DESERT LANDSCAPES & NATURAL WONDERS -

New Mexico's **southeast** is a vast region of remarkable contrasts. The northern portion is an extension of the High Plains where a few rivers combined with modern irrigation have created some of the best ranching country in the American Southwest. As you head further south it gives way to the deserts of Otero and Eddy Counties.

These aren't the types of desert you've pictured from seeing them in the movies – it isn't the Sahara. The White Sands aren't here either. It's a combination of dull-colored rocky terrain, desert shrubs, some areas of greater vegetation, including cactus, and even some surprisingly colorful rock formations. There are many deep gullies and the undulating land will gently rock you as you travel along its sparsely used roadways. The southwestern fringes of the region contain the high **Guadalupe Mountains** and even have some thickly forested areas. Mountains and forest are even more dramatic in the northwest part of the region centered around **Ruidoso** and the **Mescalero Apache Reservation**.

Yes, there are a variety of landscapes and sights to be seen in the southeast. But none can compare to the star attraction – **Carlsbad Caverns National Park**. I have always felt that a trip to New Mexico would be worthwhile even if it were only to see this amazing natural wonder.

ARRIVALS & DEPARTURES

If you're going to be coming to the southeast from Albuquerque the most logical route to follow would be to take I-25 south to Exit 139 at San Antonio and then east on US 380 as if you were going to Alamogordo.

At that point you could continue to Alamogordo to follow the same route or you could begin with the Ruidoso area and work it in reverse, ending at Alamogordo. It doesn't really matter as the total mileage and time would be very similar.

ORIENTATION/GETTING AROUND

If you draw a line on a New Mexico road map along US 380 from the Texas border over to Carrizozo and then down US 54 to the Texas border again, the area inside those lines conforms to my southeast region (except for the Alamogordo area described in the preceding chapter).

You can use Alamogordo as a good jumping off point for a tour through the southeastern quarter of the state. That's what I'm going to do here as we follow a route that takes us through Artesia, Carlsbad, the Carlsbad Caverns, Hobbs, Roswell and the Ruidoso area.

The extent of public transportation in the region is **Mesa Airlines**, *Tel. 1/800-MESA-AIR*, with service from Albuquerque to Carlsbad, Hobbs, and Roswell. Those three locations also have bus service either by Greyhound or under contract with Greyhound through the Texas, New Mexico, and Oklahoma Bus Lines. But again, you're pretty much forced to have a rental car to get from one place to another.

WHERE TO STAY

ARTESIA

Budget

BEST WESTERN PECOS INN, *2209 West Main. Tel. 748-3324, Fax 748-2868. Rates: $35-49. 80 Rooms. Major credit cards accepted. Toll-free reservations 1/800-528-1234. Located a mile west of the center of town on US 82.*

Artesia doesn't have a lot of places to stay that merit discussion, but the Pecos Inn is, at least, a good example of a modern motor inn where travelers can get attractive accommodations at an excellent price. The large rooms, located in a two-story building, feature queen size beds, refrigerator/wet bar, and coffee makers. Some upper level rooms have balconies, although the view is nothing special. Several two-room units are available for large families or couples traveling together. There's an indoor swimming pool with sauna and an on-premise restaurant with cocktail lounge.

CARLSBAD (see also White's City)

Moderate

HOLIDAY INN, *601 South Canal Street. Tel. 885-8500, Fax 887-5999. Rates: $75. 100 Rooms. Major credit cards accepted. Toll-free reservations 1/800-HOLIDAY. Located in the center of town on US Highways 62/180/285 at the intersection of Lee Street.*

A modern low-rise structure in modified Southwestern style, this inn has won numerous awards for quality from the Holiday Inn chain. Of course, one has to take such self-serving awards with at least a grain of salt. On the other hand, the building and rooms are quite attractive. Some rooms have coffee makers and whirlpools. There's a heated pool, spa, sauna, and well equipped exercise room. For dining and drinking, the Ventana Restaurant and the Phenix Bar and Grill are two of the better places in town.

Budget

BEST WESTERN STEVENS INN, *1829 South Canal Street. Tel. 887-2851, Fax 887-6338. Rates: $55-65. 202 Rooms. Major credit cards accepted. Toll-free reservations 1/800-528-1234. Located a mile south of the city center on US Highways 61/180/285.*

Carlsbad's largest lodging establishment has been a popular place to stay for about a half century. Newly renovated, the inn's rooms are diverse as to size and furnishings. Almost 40 rooms are efficiencies for those who want to cook in, while the upper price range rooms may have microwaves, refrigerators, or even a whirlpool bath. A couple of bridal suites are the top of the line at the Stevens Inn. Recreational facilities include a swimming pool and, for the children, a wading pool and playground.

The Flume Restaurant is also one of Carlsbad's better dining spots, or you can choose to eat at the coffee shop. The inn also has a cocktail lounge.

CONTINENTAL INN, *3820 National Parks Highway. Tel. 887-0341, Fax 885-0508. Rates: $40-45. 60 Rooms. Major credit cards accepted. Located in the southwestern part of town on the road to Carlsbad Caverns (which is US 61/180/285).*

A very basic facility, the Continental Inn is in a location that makes it a good jumping off point to get to Carlsbad Caverns. Otherwise, there's nothing special to mention except that for the money you get a clean and comfortable room so you can get a good night's sleep. The Continental doesn't have any restaurant but quite a few are located within a very short drive.

HOBBS

Budget

BEST WESTERN LEAWOOD MOTEL, *1301 East Broadway. Tel. 393-4101, Fax is same number. Rates: $51 including full breakfast. 68 Rooms. Major credit cards accepted. Toll-free reservations 1/800-528-1234. Located about two miles east of the center of town on US 62/180.*

A nice, comfortable single-story motel, the Leawood has covered car ports in some rooms. Guest rooms feature mostly king or queen size beds, while some have refrigerators. There's an outdoor swimming pool. While the made-to-order breakfast is quite good, there is no restaurant for dinner, but one with a lounge is within walking distance.

RAMADA INN, *501 North Marland Boulevard. Tel. 397-7171, Fax 635-6639. Rates: $53-59. 75 Rooms. Major credit cards accepted. Toll-free reservations 1/800-2-RAMADA. Located about 3 miles east of the center of town on US 62/180.*

Formerly the Hobbs Motor Inn and newly affiliated with the Ramada chain, the hotel features rooms with either two queen beds or king beds in "mini-suites." All rooms have coffee makers while some have microwave ovens. You can take a dive into the heated pool or use the nearby tennis courts or golf club. For dining, the Ramada features a full service restaurant called the Saxony Supper Club as well as a coffee shop. Live entertainment is available nightly in the lounge.

ROSWELL

Moderate

BEST WESTERN SALLY PORT INN, *2000 North Main Street. Tel. 622-6430, Fax 623-7631. Rates: $63-95. 124 Rooms. Major credit cards accepted. Toll-free reservations 1/800-528-1234. Located about 1 1/2 miles north of town on US 70/285.*

Better than average rooms are to be found in this modern and attractive facility. Some rooms have refrigerators and there are several suites with kitchenettes. Extensive recreational facilities include a heated swimming pool, sauna, whirlpool, one lighted tennis court, and an indoor recreation area. The coffee shop serves full meals as well as sandwiches, but for more atmosphere you'll have to try other restaurants in town.

Budget

ROSWELL INN, *1815 North Main Street. Tel. 623-4920, Fax 622-3831. Rates: $63. 121 Rooms. Major credit cards accepted. Toll-free reservations 1/800-323-0913. Located about 1 1/2 miles north of town on US 70/285.*

A two-story motor inn built around a nicely landscaped central courtyard, Roswell Inn features nice large rooms. Some have refrigerators or coffee makers. There's a decent dining room as well as a coffee shop and a cocktail lounge with entertainment. A swimming pool with whirlpool rounds out the picture.

SUPER 8 MOTEL, *3575 North Main Street. Tel. 622-8886, Fax 622-3627. Rates: $44-47. 63 Rooms. Major credit cards accepted. Toll-free reservations 1/800-800-8000. Located about three miles north of town on US 70/285.*

So you think I'm going mad recommending a Super 8? Not actually. Although many members of this chain are certainly hard pressed to meet "tourist class" level, some are far better than that and this is certainly one of them. (It's been given the "Pride of Super 8" designation by chain management.) All of the rooms are large and comfortable, even if the furnishings are a bit on the motel industrial side, and you'll find coffee makers. There's also a heated indoor pool with whirlpool. The two-story motor inn doesn't have a restaurant but there are several that are close by.

RUIDOSO (including Ruidoso Downs & Mescalero)
Expensive

INN OF THE MOUNTAIN GODS, *Carrizo Creek Road in Mescalero. Tel. 257-5141, Fax 257-6173. Rates: $90-145. 253 Rooms. Major credit cards accepted. Toll-free reservations 1/800-545-9011. Located three miles south of Ruidoso via Sudderth Drive (US 70) to Carrizo Creek Road.*

While the gorgeous mountain scenery of the Ruidoso area and the accompanying recreational opportunities bring lots of visitors to this region, the numbers are still far lower than the main tourist pathway through New Mexico: Albuquerque–Santa Fe–Taos. The result is that you can stay at world class resorts like Inn of the Mountain Gods for far less money than you might expect. The savings apply to every lodging category.

Run by the Mescalero Apache tribe, the Inn is magnificently situated at the 7,200-foot elevation on a nearly 150 acre site that's part of the much larger Mescalero Apache Reservation. Sitting astride the shore of a mountain lake amid colorful wildflower meadows and surrounded by dramatic vistas of towering snow-covered peaks, the Inn of the Mountain Gods is truly a place to enjoy nature as well as the all of the comforts of a fine hotel. The chalet-style building is in itself a work of art, especially the huge lobby with its massive beams and high vaulted ceiling. To remind you that you are on an Indian reservation, colorful tepees are scattered along the lake shore.

The large guest rooms, fully renovated in 1993, also are built in a style similar to a ski or country lodge. Rooms have private balconies overlooking the serene surroundings and all have fine views. Besides the comfortable and attractive standard rooms, there are 23 suites in three different categories of luxury.

Public facilities are quite extensive. Visitors can choose from one of three restaurants to dine in. There are also five separate bars, several with entertainment. An outdoor swimming pool, sauna, six tennis courts and one of the state's best 18-hole golf courses provide recreational diversions for almost everyone. If they aren't enough for you, then try horseback riding, skeet and trap shooting, fishing and boating on the lake or just walking or jogging through the expansive grounds. A casino and cardroom are also part of the complex, but at press time were temporarily closed.

Selected as one of my Best Places to Stay (see Chapter 12 for more details).

Moderate

BEST WESTERN SWISS CHALET, *1451 Mechem Drive. Tel. 258-3333, Fax 258-5325. Rates: $56-90. 82 Rooms. Major credit cards accepted. Toll-free reservations 1/800-528-1234 or 1/800-47-SWISS. Located about three miles north of central Ruidoso. Take NM 48 north from US 70 to NM 37, which is Mechem Drive.*

Another attractive chalet-style structure, as one would expect from the name, this Best Western boasts very big rooms with either king or queen-size beds. Many have balconies and the view from most rooms is excellent. There are also several suites (prices ranging from $140-200) that have all the comforts of home plus a private steam bath. The Swiss Chalet has a good restaurant on premises as well as a lounge with entertainment. A large swimming pool enclosed behind glass walls provides year-round swimming. There's also a Jacuzzi.

VILLAGE LODGE, *1000 Mechem Drive. Tel. 258-5442, Fax 258-3127. Rates: $59-89. 32 Rooms. Major credit cards accepted. Toll-free reservations 1/800-722-8779. Located two miles north of the center of town, take NM 48 into NM 37 (Mechem Drive).*

Nicely situated in a resort area called Innsbruck Village (it doesn't really look like the Austrian Alps but is beautiful in its own right), this contemporary two-story structure represents a real bargain in first-class accommodations. All of the guest units are large one-bedroom suites featuring either one king or two full size beds. The living room has a wood burning fireplace (free wood is furnished to guests) with a sofa that opens into a queen-size bed. A full kitchen, including microwave, gives you the opportunity to eat in and save money (I especially like to have breakfast in). Every suite has two televisions, so there shouldn't be any arguments over what to watch, and 1 1/4 baths.

The Lodge has an outdoor swimming pool. Within the Innsbruck Village area are extensive recreational facilities including golf and fishing. It's adjacent to the Ski Apache ski area for those coming in winter. Many restaurants, including several that are highly regarded, are located within the resort community.

Budget

INN AT PINE SPRINGS, *Highway 70 East. Tel. 378-8100, Fax 378-8215. Rates: $45-80, including Continental Breakfast. 100 Rooms. Most major credit cards accepted. Toll-free reservations 1/800-237-3607. Located on the east side of Ruidoso along the main highway directly opposite the Ruidoso Downs race track..*

While the rooms and facilities here don't match the Inn of the Mountain Gods or even the Village Lodge, I must say that the Inn At Pine Springs represents an excellent value. And if you're going to be taking in the races, no hotel could be more conveniently located. Guest rooms surround an attractive garden. All of the rooms are very spacious, many having oversized beds. Both restaurants and lounges with entertainment are located within walking distance of the Inn or, for a far bigger selection, within a short ride.

WHITES CITY (Carlsbad Caverns National Park)

Whites City isn't really a city or even a town. Rather, its a complex of business establishments providing food, lodging, and other services to visitors to Carlsbad Caverns. It's conveniently located at the park entrance. Since most visitors to this corner of New Mexico will spend more time at Carlsbad Caverns than in the city of Carlsbad, you might find it desirable to avoid the approximately 40-mile round trip from the park to Carlsbad. This is especially true if you're going to be staying in the park (or returning to it) for the evening bat flight.

Moderate

BEST WESTERN CAVERN INN/BEST WESTERN GUADALUPE INN, *17 Carlsbad Caverns Highway. Tel. 785-2291, Fax 785-2283. Rates: $60-80. 105 Rooms (total for both facilities). Major credit cards accepted. Toll-free reservations 1/800-CAVERNS. Located at the entrance to Carlsbad Caverns National Park at the junction of US 62/180 and NM 7.*

Also known as the Whites City Resort, these two inns (on opposite sides of the street) are actually the same thing – there's only one office and lobby. The two motels are about equal in quality, having nice comfortable rooms, although many rooms in the Guadalupe feature whirlpools. The resort complex features two swimming pools, two spas, and a playground.

Also located along either side of the street, in at atmosphere reminiscent of the old west, are a couple of restaurants (Fast Jack's Buffet for quickie meals and the Velvet Garter Steak House for more "formal" dining), and several shops. The gift shop off of the hotel lobby is huge and has practically any type of souvenir you may want – from junk to expensive. A game arcade is a good place to amuse the children. At night the entire "village" is lit up like a Christmas tree, creating a Disney-like atmosphere.

CAMPING & RV SITES

- **Carlsbad Campgrounds**, *Carlsbad. Tel. 885-6333*
- **Circle B Campground**, *Ruidoso Downs. Tel. 378-4990*
- **K.L. Towle Park**, *Hobbs. Tel. 393-4362*
- **Recreation Village RV & Mobile Home Park**, *Ruidoso. Tel. 258-3145*
- **Safe Haven RV Park**, *Ruidoso. Tel. 1/800-387-7701*
- **Twin Spruce RV Park**, *Ruidoso Downs. Tel. 257-4310*

- **White's City Resort RV Park,** *White's City/Carlsbad Caverns National Park. Tel. 785-2291 or 1/800-CAVERNS*
- **Windmill RV Park,** *Carlsbad. Tel. 885-9761*

WHERE TO EAT

ARTESIA

Budget – $10 or less

LA FONDA, *206 West Main Street. Tel. 746-9377. American Express, Discover, MasterCard and VISA accepted. Lunch and dinner served daily.*

Primarily offering Mexican cuisine, La Fonda also has a small selection of American dishes. The food and surroundings are surprisingly good for the low price. The waterfall in the lobby is extremely attractive and inviting. The buffet lunch is an excellent bargain and there's a nice salad bar for dinner. Children's menu available.

CARLSBAD (see also Whites City)

Moderate – $11-20

THE FLUME RESTAURANT, *1829 South Canal Street, in the Best Western Stevens Inn. Tel. 887-2851. Most major credit cards accepted. Reservations suggested.*

An American restaurant offering pleasant surroundings and good food. The prime rib is the special of the house and is worth considering. There's a good salad bar. Cocktails are served. Children's menu.

VENTANAS', *601 South Canal Street, in the Holiday Inn. Tel. 885-8500. Major credit cards accepted. Dinner only served nightly except Monday. Sunday brunch. Reservations suggested.*

Southwestern and new American cuisine are the specialties of the house, which offers strictly fresh ingredients prepared in a health-conscious way. While to me that often means you're going to leave the table hungry, it's not the case here where the portions are more than ample. Every entree is cooked to order and served by an attentive and excellent staff. The dining room is contemporary Southwestern and is quite attractive.

HOBBS

Moderate – $11-20

CATTLE BARON STEAK AND SEAFOOD, *1930 North Grimes, located a block off Turner Boulevard, the main US highway through town. Tel. 393-2800. Major credit cards accepted. Lunch and dinner served daily.*

Part of a regional chain, the Cattle Baron offers pretty standard fare as suggested by its name. You won't rave about it but the food, atmosphere, and service are all adequate. The salad bar is very good. What's said here also goes for any other branches of this outfit that you may find scattered throughout New Mexico. I list only this one because Hobbs is a little short on good eateries.

LA FIESTA RESTAURANT, *604 East Broadway. Tel. 397-1235. Most major credit cards accepted.*

The Morris family has owned and operated this nice comfortable family style restaurant since 1957. The menu is American but sprinkled with a number of Southwestern entrees as well. Good food and friendly service.

ROSWELL

Budget – $10 or less

EL TORO BRAVO, *102 South Main Street. Tel. 622-9280. American Express, Discover, MasterCard and VISA accepted. Lunch and dinner served daily except Sunday.*

Serving a nice variety of Mexican dishes, El Toro Bravo is a very attractive looking restaurant where the walls are decorated with colorful pictures of Mexico and bull fights. (The pictures aren't of the type that may make you lose your appetite if you're turned off by the sport.) Everything represents a good value, particularly the lunch buffet. The chimichangas are especially good.

THE ESTABLISHMENT, *118 East 3rd Street, off of Main. Tel. 623-5006. MasterCard and VISA accepted. Lunch and dinner served daily except Sunday.*

Both Mexican and American fare are served either indoors in a dining room decorated with stained glass depictions of the west or on the quaint outdoor patio. Also represents a good value, especially if you're looking for something other than strictly Mexican or Southwestern.

RUIDOSO

Expensive – $21-30

ANNA-MICHELLE'S RESTAURANT, *1451 Mechem Drive, in the Swiss Chalet Inn. Tel. 258-3333. Major credit cards accepted. Lunch and dinner served daily. Reservations suggested.*

An excellent restaurant featuring fine food and service as well as spectacular views of the beautiful Sierra Blanca, or White Mountain in English. The cuisine is expertly prepared Swiss and Italian, except that there is a wonderful German buffet on Friday night and a Prime Rib Buffet on Saturday night. Regardless of the theme or menu, the food is top-notch. Old Barry's Tavern, adjacent, provides the drinks.

LA LORRAINE, *2523 Sudderth. Tel. 257-2954. American Express, MasterCard and VISA accepted. Lunch served daily except Sunday and Monday; dinner served nightly except Sunday. Reservations accepted.*

Ruidoso's status as a resort means, like in the case of Anna-Michelle's, that you have a good choice of more sophisticated dining places. La Lorraine services distinctive and classic French cuisine in very elegant surroundings. Veal, seafood, beef, and fowl dishes are all on the menu, but the rack of lamb is extra special. There's a fine wine list (no other alcoholic beverages are served). During the summer guests can dine on the lovely patio.

Moderate - $11-20

CAFE CARRIZO, *Carrizo Canyon Road at the Carrizo Lodge. Tel. 257-3607. Discover, MasterCard and VISA accepted. Lunch and dinner served daily.*

This is another very attractive restaurant and features a Southwestern menu with dishes of beef, poultry, or seafood. Both indoor and outdoor dining is available in summer. Warm fireplaces provide a cozy and intimate atmosphere. There's a full service bar. Children's menu.

FLYING J RANCH, *on NM 48 north of town. Turn right 1 1/2 miles past the turnoff for Ski Apache. Tel. 336-4330. Most major credit cards accepted. Dinner only served nightly except Sunday from late May through Labor Day. Reservations suggested.*

If you pick only one chuck wagon supper during your stay in New Mexico, make it the Flying J, which is absolutely the best in the state. The dinner bell rings and guests line up to get generous helpings of beef or chicken in a special sauce along with all the fixin's associated with a western cowboy supper. It's simply amazing how more than 600 people can be served in a matter of minutes! This isn't gourmet cooking but is "real" food, and no one will ever be able to say they left hungry. After dinner you'll be treated to an evening of western entertainment, including stage show and gunfights. The western village has gift shops, pony rides, and gold panning. Kids will love it but so will adults. Gates open at 6:00pm and dinner is served at 7:30pm. I promise you'll have a good time.

INCREDIBLE RESTAURANT AND SALOON, *on NM 48 at Ski Run Road, about four miles north of town. Tel. 336-4312. Most major credit cards accepted. Lunch and dinner served daily. Reservations suggested.*

Serving visitors to Ruidoso for more than 30 years, what may be most incredible about Incredible is its diverse menu. You'll find prime rib (the specialty of the house), steaks, seafood, fish, chicken, lamb, veal, pasta and even fondues! They're all good, too. There's a lively lounge as well as another bar with a more subdued and quiet atmosphere. Good service and a lot of fun.

Budget - $10 or less

TEXAS FAJITA PATIO CAFE, *1009 Mechem Drive. Tel. 258-4432. Discover, MasterCard and VISA accepted. Lunch and dinner served daily.*

If you're on a budget and still want to get a lot of good food to eat for your money, the Texas Cafe is a wise choice. Besides the fajitas in the name of the place, the cafe has some of the best burgers around. They come in many varieties and are named for different cities in Texas. The patio is open for dining year-round. Beer, wine, and margaritas are served.

WHITE'S CITY (Carlsbad Caverns National Park)
Moderate – $11-20

VELVET GARTER SALOON AND RESTAURANT, *at the entrance to Carlsbad Caverns National Park, adjacent to the Best Western motel complex. Tel. 785-2291. Major credit cards accepted.*

A bit of the old west right next door to the grandeur of nature. The attractive restaurant is decorated with stained glass that depicts the splendor of the caverns. Steaks and other American dishes are available but a big part of the menu is excellent Mexican cuisine. Wine and other alcoholic beverages are served. If you're looking for fast food, Fast Jack's is located next door and is good for either breakfast or lunch. It's the same owners.

SEEING THE SIGHTS

Through the Desert to Carlsbad

Having left Alamogordo by US 82 and passed through Cloudcroft, the road continues for another 25 miles through the Lincoln National Forest, slowly descending into lower elevations and much more arid country for the next 65 or so miles until **Artesia**. There are few towns along the route, although you will see some farms or prairie land, especially on the north side of the road.

The ground beneath Artesia is laced by a network of natural subterranean rivers. So it seemed right to name the town for the numerous artesian wells that were dug in the area to bring water to the many farms that were established in the early part of the century. Another underground resource, namely oil, is the basis for most current economic activity in Artesia. The **Historical Museum and Art Center**, *505 W. Richardson Avenue, Tel. 748-2390*, consists of two early 20th century houses. One has displays on local history and economic development and a collection of western items. The adjacent house is an art gallery that features works by local artists. *The museum is open Tuesday to Saturday from 10:00am to noon and again from 1:oo-5:00pm. It's closed on holidays and there is no admission charge.*

Take US 285 south from Artesia for the 36-mile trip through rather desolate desert terrain to reach **Carlsbad**. However, you have to make a decision two-thirds of the way through that short ride. A 39-mile detour (and you have to come back the exact same way) via NM 137 and Farm

Route 206 leads to the **Sitting Bull Falls** in a semi-arid region of the Guadalupe Mountains. A lovely waterfall, rare in this part of the world, spills 180 feet over the beautiful canyon walls. A short trail leads to this hidden oasis. At the bottom are a couple of pools where some visitors like to take a refreshing dip. The mineral content of the water is so high that evaporation of the spray has resulted in odd rock formations near the falls. (That same mineral content can leave a residue on your body, so if you do go swimming towel off thoroughly because some people find it irritating to their skin.) It really is quite nice but you have to make a judgment whether it's worth the time and mileage of the side trip. I would go for it as long as you have a couple of hours to spare.

Upon reaching the northwestern edge of Carlsbad, take Skyline Drive to the excellent **Living Desert Zoological and Botanical State Park**, *Tel. 887-5516*. It's a long name but this park has a big task – to educate visitors on the entire spectrum of Southwestern desert flora and fauna. The park

DESERT WILDLIFE

When most people think of a desert they usually think that it is devoid of life or, at best, has a scarce animal population. In the case of many desert areas of the Southwest, nothing can be further from the truth. The Chihuahuan Desert especially supports a wildlife population that is surprisingly abundant and quite varied in the number of different species. In a completely natural setting it is fairly rare to see most animals during the daytime. However, a visit to Carlsbad's ***Living Desert*** *gives you the opportunity to see them close up during the day. Almost all of the desert's animals are represented.*

Among the animals in the Chihuahuan desert, besides the usual snakes and lizards, are mountain lions, bobcats, badgers, skunks, deer, elk, foxes, wolves and even bears. Two of the most unusual animals you're likely to see are the javelina and the prairie dog. The javelina is very quick afoot but is a rather ugly animal. It's grayish in color and looks something like a wooly, disheveled pig. The much cuter looking prairie dog is not a dog at all. It's a small brown or golden colored rodent that burrows under the ground and builds its community out of the heat of the sun. There's an excellent display of these animals at the park and you can see how industrious they are as they go about their business.

There's also plenty of bird life in the desert, including quails and owls and such birds of prey as hawks. Bats are frequent residents, too, but you'll learn more about them a little later. The funny looking roadrunner is the New Mexico state bird. These fast creatures have been known to kill rattlesnakes. Beep-beep!

is located on a hillside overlooking the Pecos Valley. A 1 1/3-mile long trail leads past exhibit areas that display more than 50 different desert animals and hundreds of types of desert plants. There's also an indoor visitor center with exhibits on minerals and paleontology. The natural terrain of the park is well suited to display the wildlife of the **Chihuahuan Desert**, which stretches from Mexico through parts of southern New Mexico and Texas. Although some of the plants in the greenhouses and other areas are from other desert zones, most of the park is devoted to the Chihuahuan region. Take a look at the sidebar on the preceding page if you want to learn more about the wildlife.

The park is open daily from 8:00am to 6:30pm from May 15 through Labor Day and from 9:00am to 3:30pm the remainder of the year. It's closed on Christmas. Admission is $3 for those age 8 and older. If you're vacationing in the heat of summer, I suggest that you time your visit for the morning. Unless you have to rush through, allow close to a couple of hours for this attraction.

Downtown Carlsbad has a couple of attractions. The **Carlsbad Museum and Art Center**, *located off of Canal Street (which is US 285), Tel. 887-0276*, has bones from prehistoric animals which once roamed this area. Apache Indian relics and items from pioneer days tell you about Carlsbad's more recent history. The Art portion of the museum is known as the McAdoo collection and features works of some members of the Taos Society of Artists. *The museum is open Monday to Saturday from 10:00am to 6:00pm and is closed on holidays. Admission is free.*

The **Pecos River**, which runs through Carlsbad and is the source of several recreational lakes within the city and in surrounding areas, is bordered by more than 2 1/2 miles of paths called the **Riverwalk**. While not overly scenic, it does make for a good way to relax for a while. It parallels Riverside Drive and can be reached from US 285 at either end.

It's 16 miles from Carlsbad to the town of **White's City**, gateway to Carlsbad Caverns National Park, by US 62/180. Actually, I don't know why they call it White's City – it doesn't even qualify as a town. It has one street with a motel on either side and a row of shops built like an old western town. It's there solely to serve visitors to the park. Now, don't let that make you think that I have a negative view of White's City. I don't. It may be tacky but it's really kind of quaint and even fun. At night it's lit up like a mid-west town at Christmas time.

And you would be missing something unique if you passed up the opportunity to visit the **Million Dollar Museum**, *Tel. 785-2291*, which is housed in a couple of those western style buildings. Containing ten rooms, the "museum" is one of the most eclectic collection of items you'll find no matter where you travel. You'll discover everything from dolls to furniture, from barbed wire to typewriters, from pioneer items to a mummified Indian. I'm not sure what the theme is or where the name comes from, but the bottom line is a very interesting mixture. *The museum is open daily from 7:00am to 9:00pm from the middle of May through the middle of September and until 8:00pm the rest of the year. Admission is $2.50 for adults and $1.50 for children under 13. The long hours make it convenient to schedule it in along with a visit to the Caverns.*

Carlsbad Caverns National Park

Covering almost 47,000 acres of the southwestern desert just a few miles north of Texas, **Carlsbad Caverns**, *Tel. 785-2232,* is one of the most beautiful and unique places in all the world. While most of the beauty is underground, you will be surprised at the good scenery above ground as well. It begins almost immediately after you pass through the entrance gate and take the seven mile drive on NM 7 that leads from White's City to the park's Visitor Center. The excellent road traverses a narrow canyon, rising by a series of easy switchbacks (some with pullouts providing great views) to the top of a plateau where the cave entrance is located.

The modern and large visitor center building has exhibits on the cave and the rest of the park, including a three dimensional model of the cave, films, and literature and information on your visit. All admission tickets to the cave are sold in the visitor center. Before getting to the heart of your visit – the unforgettable journey through the caverns – let's take a little while to list some of the other things you can do while in Carlsbad Caverns National Park.

The **Scenic Drive** is a nearly 10-mile long one-way gravel loop road through Walnut Canyon that provides more wonderful vistas of the mountain desert. You don't need four-wheel drive, but because it's a very narrow road trailers are not a good idea. There are also a couple of short trails in the vicinity of the visitor center and more than 50 miles of primitive back-country trails throughout the park. These are for the more experienced hiker. Finally, **New Cave** (or **Slaughter Canyon Cave**) is located 25 miles from the visitor center. You have to go back out of the park and follow US 62/180 to County Route 418. Guided tours are offered, but this is an undeveloped cave and should *not* be attempted by those who are not experienced in the art of spelunking (that's caving to the uninitiated).

Now for the big event – the main caverns of Carlsbad. This is a beautiful, eerie, and almost indescribable world of gigantic underground rooms, formations ranging from the small and delicate to the colorful and massive. It's all the result of some five million years of seepage of groundwater into the soft underlying limestone rock. The caverns cover more than 30 miles of surveyed corridors and passages which can still be reached by the natural entrance that measures 90 feet across and 40 feet high. Your tour of the caverns can last as little as a couple of hours if you're pressed for time or don't really dig being underground. More likely, it will comprise more than one of the available tours and last anywhere from a half to a full day. It takes a complete day to see everything below ground properly. There are three tours available, and I'll briefly describe each one separately.

The **Big Room Tour** is reached by elevator and portions of it are even wheelchair accessible. The tour is self-guided at your own pace and is recommended for those who have only a limited amount of time available. You can cover it in 90 minutes. The 755 foot elevator ride takes only a minute and leaves you at the entrance to the Big Room, which measures 1,800 feet long and 1,100 feet wide at its greatest dimensions. Portions of the room are as much as 255 feet high. It is an underground world unto itself and is one of the largest natural chambers of its kind in the entire world. The Big Room is filled with thousands of formations. Some of the highlights are the 62-foot high **Giant Dome**, the biggest stalagmite in the cave, and the 42-foot high **Twin Domes**. These are both in an area known as the **Hall of Giants**. **Mirror Lake** and the 140-feet deep **Bottomless Pit** are other popular features. Return to the surface is also by elevator.

The **Natural Entrance Tour**, of course, goes through the entrance I described previously. It's just a short walk from the visitor center. Upon entering, you spiral down a sloped path, occasionally glancing upward as the light of day slowly disappears. The paved path continues downward for a distance of about a mile, descending a total of 750 feet in the process. While the route along the so-called **Main Corridor** is not as beautiful as the Big Room, there are several advantages to coming this way. First of all, you get a better feel for how the early cave explorers must have felt – they didn't have an elevator to get down into the cave. Second, there are some interesting sights along the way, including the **Devil's Den** and the **Witch's Finger** to name but a couple of the formations. The route is not particularly difficult, although it is quite a bit more strenuous than taking the Big Room Tour. It's not for the physically challenged or elderly, but if you're in decent shape it doesn't present any problem.

For either of the first two tours you can rent portable radio receivers with commentary on the features you are passing.

The third tour is guided by Park Rangers and is called the **King's Palace Tour**. This used to be a part of the Big Room Tour and was also self-guided but, unfortunately there are a lot of thoughtless people – complete idiots who were damaging the delicate formations because they wanted a real cave "souvenir." This tour covers about a mile and involves some narrow passages and steps but isn't overly difficult. It visits several especially beautiful areas of the cave, including the **King's Palace**, the adjacent **Queen's Chamber**, and the **Papoose Room**. It leaves from the elevator lobby in the cave. The commentary of the experienced guides on this slower paced tour is very informative.

All three tours converge where the elevator reaches the cavern floor, which makes it very convenient if you're doing two or three tours. It isn't necessary to return to the surface each time to begin another tour. (The Natural Entrance Tour should definitely be done first if you're doing more than one tour.) Also, the subterranean lunchroom is located in this spot. The choice and quality of the food isn't great – strictly boxed cafeteria stuff – but it's convenient and what would a cave experience be without eating down there as well?

Once you do return to the surface, I hope you don't think that you're done. One of the best reasons for visiting Carlsbad Caverns is yet to come – the nightly **Bat Flight**. This is the final touch on what will certainly be one of your most unforgettable vacation memories. Every evening around sunset hundreds of thousands of bats leave the cave to look for food (insects) in the surrounding desert. Seated in an amphitheater carved out of the rock, park visitors watch the unparalleled sight of the bats emerging, almost as if on cue soon after hearing a ranger describe the process.

Everyone has an image of bats from all those horror movies we've been subjected to. The fact is, however, that they have been the victim of bad press. In general, they won't attack people unless threatened, and the bats at Carlsbad are especially gentle in that respect. The majority of bats who make Carlsbad their summer home are known as **Mexican freetail bats**. They are quite small, weighing only 1 1/2 ounces each and having a maximum wingspan of 11 inches. They "see" at night by means of a sophisticated radar-like system. Emitting ultrasonic pulses that are beyond the ability of human ears to hear, these pulses bounce off other objects in their path. The bats are capable of distinguishing between the echoes of stationary objects as opposed to the insects on which they feed.

Living about a half-mile inside the cave (in an area that's off limits to visitors for your safety and theirs), they emerge around sunset each night in continuous groups at the rate of about 5,000 bats per minute. Because of the steepness of the cave entrance they cannot fly straight out. The bats have to spiral out, always in a counter-clockwise direction.

Visitors sit on stone benches carved out from the rocky hillside adjacent to the natural entrance. It's especially weird to see the bats come out of the same place that you walked down hours earlier. The exact time of the start of the bat flight is an estimate based on sunset and the bats behavior over the past few days. The rangers will post the time each day at the Visitor Center, telling you when the bat talk begins at the amphitheater. They usually have it timed pretty well, so that by the time they're finished talking, the bats are almost ready to come out. You must remain within the confines of the amphitheater during the bat flight. Also, flash photography is not permitted because it can disturb the bats.

Most visitors watch for about 30 minutes until the darkness makes it difficult to see the small creatures. You can watch them return in the morning around sunrise, but few people seem to get up that early, except on the occasion of the Park Service's annual **Bat Breakfast**. Whenever you see them, though, it's a unique and thrilling experience.

The bats stay at Carlsbad from early **May through October** before heading down to Mexico for the winter. However, the best time to view the bat flight is in August and September. That's when the greatest number of bats emerge because the younger bats born in the early summer are then big enough to join the bat flight.

The park is open all the time. However, visitor center hours are daily 8:00am to 7:00pm from Memorial Day to Labor Day and until 5:30pm the remainder of the year. It is closed only on Christmas. Guided tours and self-guided tours into the cave via the natural entrance begin at 8:30am with the last admission being at 3:30pm, and 2:30pm during the winter season. Last admission to the Big Room Tour is at 5:00 during the summer season and until 3:30 the rest of the year. There is no admission charge to enter the park itself. However, cave tour prices are as follows: Guided tour of King's Palace, natural entrance tour and Big Room tour are $5 each for adults and $3 for children. The Slaughter Canyon Cave tour is $8. Holders of any NPS passport receive a 50 percent discount on all cave admissions. The fee for renting the interpretive radio receiver is 50 cents per tour.

HOW MANY BATS ARE THERE AT CARLSBAD CAVERNS?

Most people want to know how many bats there are. There used to be several million, but a variety of factors (all caused by man) depleted the number to around 300,000 in the 1980s. They've made quite a comeback in the past few years and on some nights the number can now approach almost a million. Sometimes it can take as much as two hours for all the bats to emerge.

They come out in small numbers at first but the pace quickly accelerates until the whole massive rock above the cave entrance is blocked by their thick swarm. Rising into the beautiful desert sky at sunset, it looks almost like a tornado moving away from you. Some children (and grown women) deliberately scream to add to their enjoyment but it isn't necessary. The bats are oblivious to the hundreds of people who come nightly to watch them go off on their journey. But, if you're in the first few rows of the amphitheater, you can actually feel the breeze from their collective flapping of wings.

Hobbs

From the city of Carlsbad, you can reach **Hobbs** by traveling east on US 62/180 for 69 miles. The road is good, crossing a rather uninteresting section of desert and then cattle country before arriving in town. Like Artesia, Hobbs is built upon a foundation of underground water and oil. In fact, the area contains New Mexico's largest oil field and is the major employer in this town of 30,000 people.

There are several things to see in Hobbs. However, if you don't feel particularly intrigued by the sightseeing possibilities, you can save a little over a hundred miles of driving from Carlsbad to Roswell by taking US 285 north from Carlsbad, back through Artesia, and then on into Roswell. Whichever way you choose to go, should you find yourself a bit bored by the lack of good scenery along some stretches of New Mexico's southeastern highways, look at the bright side – it's a whole lot better than being stuck in traffic and probably a lot safer, too. Anyway, I'll leave it that and give you an opportunity to review Hobbs.

The **New Mexico Wing of the Confederate Air Force** is located in an old hangar at the Lea County Airport on US Highway 62/180 (known as Maryland Boulevard) on the way into town. If the name sounds funny to you, just think about the fact that there are almost 80 aircraft collections in the United States that go under the banner of the Confederate Air Force. This is a collection of B-25s and other mainly World War II vintage planes and engines. *The free museum has variable hours, so call 397-3202 for information.*

Two similar museums are located on the north side of town via Turner Boulevard, which is also NM 18. The **Lea County Cowboy Hall of Fame and Western Heritage Center** is four miles north on the New Mexico Junior College campus, *Tel. 392-1275*. Plaques and artifacts honor New Mexico cowboys, rodeo stars, ranchers, and pioneers. There's also an exhibit on Native Americans. A bit further north on the other side of NM 18 is the **Thelma Webber Southwest Heritage Room**, part of the library at the College of the Southwest, *Tel. 392-6561*. It's smaller than the Hall of Fame and covers a lot of the same ground, but does have a lot of exhibits dealing with the oil industry. *The Lea County Cowboy Hall of Fame is open Monday to Friday from 8:00am to 5:00pm and on Saturday from 1:00-5:00pm. It's closed on all holidays and is free of charge. The Heritage Room is open on weekdays (except holidays) from 8:00am to 5:00pm. It also has no admission charge.*

For those making the loop through Hobbs, leave town via NM 18 northbound to Lovington, then north on NM 206 to the tiny town of Tatum at the junction of US 380. Go west on the latter route to Roswell. The total distance from Hobbs to Roswell is about 115 miles through an area of mediocre scenery.

Roswell

With a population of about 45,000, Roswell is the largest city in southeastern New Mexico. Located at the crossroads of several major US highways, Roswell is supported by a diversified agricultural economy. Several sights in town and a couple of others nearby are worth at least a brief stop. US 70/285 runs through town north to south as Main Street while another portion of US 70 and US 380 go east to west as 2nd Street. All of the in-town attractions are located close to where they intersect.

The **Chaves County History Museum**, 2nd Street west of Main Street, *Tel. 622-6744*is in a house built in 1910 by one of Roswell's earliest farmers and civic leaders. The house has literally hundreds of artifacts from those days and thus presents an accurate picture of what life was like in Roswell during the early 20th century. *The museum is only open on Fridays through Sundays from 1:00-4:00pm. There is no admission charge.*

The nearby **Roswell Museum and Art Center**, 11th and Main Streets, has a more diversified collection that deals with many different aspects of Southwestern culture. There are many fine portrait and landscape paintings by New Mexico artists. The famous rocket scientist, Robert Goddard, did a lot of his research in the surrounding desert and a wing of the museum is devoted to his work. There's a re-creation of his Roswell laboratory. *The museum's hours are Monday to Saturday from 9:00am to 5:00pm and Sunday and holidays from 1:00-5:00pm. It is closed on Thanksgiving and Christmas. Admission is free.*

Several blocks north on Main Street at College Boulevard is the **Douglas McBride Museum**, located on the attractive campus of the New Mexico Military Institute, *Tel. 624-8220*. McBride was a New Mexican who reached the rank of Lieutenant General and was a graduate of the Institute. Displays on the science of warfare as well as the role of the military in maintaining peace are quite interesting. Special attention is given to the role of New Mexico's residents and graduates of the Institute in America's armed forces. *The museum is open Tuesday through Thursday from 8:30am to 3:00pm but closes for lunch between 11:30 and 1:00. It's also closed on holidays and does not charge any admission.*

If you're a UFO-groupie (or maybe have just seen too many episodes of the *X-Files* on television) you probably know that there are a lot of people who believe that an alien spacecraft crashed in the desert near Roswell in 1947 and that our government has been covering up the whole affair (for shame!) since that time. I dunno. However, for the believers out there and anyone else who might have an interest in such things, Ruidoso has two museums dedicated to UFOs and related topics. These are the **International UFO Museum and Research Center**, *Tel. 625-9495* – sure sounds official, doesn't it? – and th**e OutaLimits UFO Enigma Museum**. Both are on Main Street. I hope you can find your way back to Earth.

Now I turn your attention to nearby attractions. The first is the **Bitter Lake National Wildlife Refuge** located northeast of town via US 380. More than 300 different species of birds numbering in the thousands inhabit the nearly 25,000 acres of marsh and grassland. Only the southern portion of the refuge can be visited without a special permit. In that section you can take a self-guiding auto tour that covers eight miles and has many opportunities to view birds and other wildlife.

While the winter months present the best time to visit, there's usually something to be seen at any time, especially from the overlooks that surround the refuge's many lakes. *The refuge is open every day of the year from an hour before dawn to an hour after dusk, except in times of very bad weather. There is no charge. Pick up a tour leaflet at the refuge headquarters.*

A final point of interest near Roswell is the **Bottomless Lakes State Park** reached by US 380 east to NM 409 and then south. It's only a few miles past the Wildlife Refuge. The park is named for the seven natural sinkholes caused by the collapse of small underground caverns and which have been filled with rainwater over the years. Early residents thought they were "bottomless" but in reality they're only up to about 90 feet deep. Some are only about a hundred feet across as well, but the largest covers 13 acres and even has a sand beach. There's a small visitor center explaining the geologic forces which created the sinkholes, and you can take a nature trail to pretty **Mirror Lake** and pass by a lake "in the making." Most people come to the park to partake of the recreational opportunities, but if you're coming in from Hobbs or have visited the Wildlife Refuge, it's close enough to be worth stopping for just to take a look.

Ruidoso

A little under 50 miles west of Roswell via US 70/380 you'll come to the small town of Hondo near the edge of the Lincoln National Forest. By this time you've climbed quite a bit and the desert has given way to views of mountain and forest as well as cooler air. The two US highways split at this point, US 70 heading slightly to the southwest while 380 goes to the northwest. Hondo, together with the towns of Capitan and Ruidoso, form a triangle that has become a year-round resort and scenic destination. National forest lands encompass a good portion of the triangle. I'll first take you up US 380 for a few miles to tiny Lincoln.

First settled in the mid 1800s, **Lincoln** came to be a sizable farming community for its day (with more than a thousand people). It is best known as the place where Bill the Kid was convicted and sentenced to hang. Of course, he escaped from jail, an event that is celebrated each August during the **Last Escape of Billy the Kid Annual Pageant**. The highlight is a reenactment of his escape from the Lincoln County Courthouse.

Today, Lincoln is far smaller. Its main street contains about 40 or so historic buildings and represents a walk through the past. You can visit portions of it in the **Lincoln National Historic Tour**. There's a Historical Center which presents a history of Lincoln through artifacts and a brief slide presentation. Then you can walk through five of the historic structures including a store, church, and several homes, as well as the infamous Lincoln County Courthouse. *You can walk around the historic district at any time. However, in order to go into the buildings you have to purchase an admission ticket at the Historic Center for $4.50 for those age 17 and older. Guided tours are offered at 10:30 and 2:30, but you can enter the Courthouse between 9:00am and 5:00pm on your own. The historic buildings are closed on New Year's, Easter, Thanksgiving and Christmas.*

Another famous event in the history of Lincoln is the so-called "Lincoln County War" that occurred in 1878. It had to do with personal power, greed, revenge and a lot of other things that make great books and motion pictures. Involving Billy the Kid and others, quite a few people were killed before it ended. The **Lincoln State Monument** commemorates the event.

After visiting Lincoln, head back to Hondo and then west on US 70 for 24 miles through the forested mountain terrain to **Ruidoso**, heart of one of the most popular resort areas in all of New Mexico and the Southwest. And why not? The scenery is simply beautiful. Located at an altitude of about 7,000 feet in the Sacramento Mountains, the adjacent towns of Ruidoso and Ruidoso Downs run alongside the Ruidoso River for about ten miles. The magnificent green carpet of trees covers the lower slopes of the mountains and 12,003-foot high **Sierra Blanca Peak** hovers above the rest, perpetually covered by snow. The towns themselves, with a combined population of about 6,000, are home to dozens of art galleries, shops, restaurants, and resort hotels. As an art colony, the Ruidoso area is second only to the Taos-Santa Fe corridor.

Any time of the year is beautiful in Ruidoso, so it's crowded year round, whether with skiers in winter or people just gazing at the tranquil scenery in the summer. The climate is certainly agreeable as well. The mountain meadows are filled with wildflowers from spring through the early fall and the Aspen forests, worth seeing at any time, are especially magnificent in the fall. You'll also find world-class golf and America's highest horse racing track. Those interested in the recreational aspects of Ruidoso should look for details in the *Sports & Recreation* section below.

You'll reach **Ruidoso Downs** first, so let's begin seeing the sights there. On US 70, about a quarter of a mile east of the racetrack, is the fabulous **Museum of the Horse**, *Tel. 378-4142*, housing the 10,000-item Anne C. Stradling Collection. Outside the building is one of the world's largest equine monuments – the larger than life bronze "Free Spirits at

Noisy Water," a magnificent sculpture of three wild horses galloping towards the wild, their life-like manes seemingly blowing in the breeze. The museum has many life-size models of different types of horses as well as saddles, harnesses, Indian artifacts, and other things related to horses. There's even a Russian sleigh and a real stagecoach from the middle of the 19th century. It's a large museum and you should plan on spending at least an hour there. *The museum is open daily from 9:00am to 5:30pm. The adult admission price is $4 but senior citizens and children age 5-18 get in for $3.*

RACING AT RUIDOSO DOWNS

The resort area of Ruidoso really got started with the opening of the ***Ruidoso Downs Racetrack****. While racing was held in an earlier track as far back as the 1930s, it wasn't until the name of the town was changed to Ruidoso Downs and the construction of a major track was completed that it became a big-time operation. The two-level grandstand is traditional in design. It, along with the meticulously manicured track, is in a setting par-excellence. Where else could you possibly enjoy watching horses race surrounded by a ring of magnificent mountains?*

There are two types of horse races held, the first being quarter horses and the second thoroughbreds. The season runs from Memorial Day weekend through Labor Day. The track is known as the venue with the greatest and richest events in quarter horse racing. This includes all three legs of the ***Quarter Horse Triple Crown****, culminating with the season-ending* ***All-American Futurity****, which has the single biggest purse in quarter horse racing.*

There is, of course, para-mutuel betting at the track during the season. In the off-season you can still gamble on the horses as major races from other parts of the country are simulcast. If you wish to get a complete schedule of racing activity at Ruidoso Downs, call ***378-4431*** *or* ***378-4140*** *for further information.*

NM 48 is known as Sudderth Drive as it goes into the heart of town off of US 70 and is the historic portion of Ruidoso. Besides the shops and galleries here, the **Old Mill** is of interest. No longer a mill, the historic building now houses the Chamber of Commerce and some gift shops.

One of the state's best resorts is the beautiful **Inn of the Mountain Gods** (take Sudderth into Carrizo Creek Road), run by the Mescalero Apache tribe. Although you may not wish to stay here at the luxury prices charged (see *Where to Stay*), it's definitely worth coming just to see the magnificent setting. Covering several acres of mountain meadow, it provides dramatic views of the surrounding mountains. There's even a small lake with tepees along the shoreline. The huge rustic lobby is also a work of art.

It's been awhile since we visited any Indian reservations. So if you're feeling the need to browse through some more shops filled with authentic Native American crafts, the Ruidoso area has the answer. Take US 70 west for about 17 miles to the town of Mescalero, center of the **Mescalero Apache Indian Reservation**. Visitors are welcome and the choice of goods is excellent. There are ceremonial dances held during the Fourth of July weekend that are open to the public.

When you're ready to leave Ruidoso, drive north along NM 48. You're heading toward Capitan, a distance of about 22 miles from Ruidoso. However, the more adventurous among you might want to take a detour at Ski Area Road and follow the route as it steeply curves through the aspen and evergreen forest to a wonderful lookout at around the 10,000 foot elevation of **Sierra Blanca**, or in English, White Mountain. The view is most rewarding. Sierra Blanca is the heart of the scenery that has made Ruidoso famous. The road through this area as well as much of the surrounding region is known as the **Apache Trail**. In the 19th century the Mescalero Apaches used the many canyons and other good natural hiding places as both a defensive and offensive weapon.

Capitan is a quiet town of 800 people beautifully nestled in the high Lincoln National Forest. It was here that the story of "**Smokey the Bear**" began. In 1950, a terrible forest fire struck the area around Capitan, burning more than 17,000 acres. Amid the devastation firefighters found a five-month old bear cub who they affectionately dubbed "Hot Foot Teddy." Somehow his name got changed to Smokey after a period of medical rehabilitation in Santa Fe. After it was decided not to return him to the wild, Smokey went to a zoo in Washington to live the rest of his life except when he was in parades or on tour as a "spokesbear" for forest fire prevention. The rest is history.

The people of Capitan built the **Smokey Bear Historical State Park**, *Tel. 354-2748*. The exhibits explain how to prevent forest fires as well as how forest fires are fought. There's also an exhibit that traces the life of Smokey. Appropriately, Smokey was returned to Capitan upon his death in 1976 and his grave site located behind the visitor center is a local shrine. A short nature trail representing the different vegetation zones of New Mexico completes your visit to the park. *The park is open daily 9:00am to 5:00pm. It is closed only on New Year's, Thanksgiving and Christmas. Admission is a nominal 25 cents.*

Once you've paid your respects to old Smokey, go west on US 380 as it descends from the mountains during a 20-mile ride to **Carrrizozo**, a small town at the junction of US highways 380 and 54. Four miles west of the town on US 380 is the 463-acre **Valley of Fires Recreation Area**, *Tel. 648-2241*. The entire area is within a large ancient lava flow, a *malpais* (you remember – badlands) and named by the Apaches when Little Black Peak erupted about 1,700 years ago and covered an area of almost 50 miles with hot magma. There's a small visitor center with exhibits on the geologic history of the area and information on visiting the site.

You can see the extensive lava flow in one of two ways. First, a road runs for a couple of miles along the flow with frequent pullouts from which you can clearly see the black rock. Or, you can take the Malpais Nature Trail and actually walk out on the lava flow. The trail is kind of rough and the rocks can be sharp if you're not careful. Stay on the trail as the surrounding area contains fissures, pits, and caves that you can fall into. *Valley of Fires is open every day from dawn to dusk. There is a $5 admission charge per vehicle. NPS passports are not valid here as the area is administered by the Bureau of Land Management, not the National Park Service.*

Those readers returning to Albuquerque can continue on US 380 to the junction of I-25. If you're going back to Alamogordo (or want to take a detour before heading back to Albuquerque), take US 54 south (the markers will read west) to Three Rivers where a short side road will take you to the **Three Rivers Petroglyph Site**. This is one of the most outstanding examples of prehistoric Native American rock art. A low ridge rises from the Three Rivers Valley and contains about 20,000 different carvings. That number ranks it as one of the largest such sites in the Southwest. The inscriptions, made with stone tools about a thousand years ago and whose meanings often still elude archaeologists, can be seen by taking a trail which climbs the ridge and then runs along the top. It's about three-quarters of a mile long and not overly difficult but should not be attempted by anyone with a handicap. There are few facilities at the site. I suggest you carry water if visiting during the heat of a summer day.

US 54 will take you on to Alamogordo in less than a half hour.

NIGHTLIFE & ENTERTAINMENT

While some of the larger hotels in Carlsbad have lounges, the nightlife in this region is headquartered in the **Ruidoso** area. Among the best places:

FARLEY'S FOOD, FUN & PUB, *1200 Mechem, in town.*

Also serves lunch and dinner, but I don't recommend it as a restaurant. Outdoor beer garden, big screen TV, and plenty of games such as billiards and such board games as chess and backgammon.

SCREAMING EAGLE BAR, *at the Enchantment Inn (Highway 70).*

A nice looking place with a large dance floor and a good variety of live entertainment.

SPORTS & RECREATION

Fishing

• **Bonito Lake**, *Ruidoso*. Trout.

Golf

- **Artesia Country Club**, *Artesia. Tel. 746-6732*
- **Lake Carlsbad Golf Course**, *901 N. Muscatel, Carlsbad. Tel. 885-5444*
- **Clovis Municipal Golf Course**, *Clovis. Tel. 762-4775*
- **Hobbs Country Club**, *Hobbs. Tel. 393-5212*
- **New Mexico Military Institute Golf Course**, *201 W. 19th, Roswell. Tel. 622-6033*
- **Cree Meadows Country Club**, *Ruidoso. Tel. 257-5815*

Horseback Riding

- **Buddie's Stables**, *Ruidoso. Tel. 258-4027*
- **Grindstone Stables**, *Ruidoso. Tel. 257-2241*
- **Inn of the Mountain Gods**, *Ruidoso area (Mescalero Apache Reservation). Tel. 257-5141*

Horse Racing

- **Ruidoso Downs**, *Tel. 378-4431*. May through Labor Day.

Skiing

- **Ski Apache**, *Ruidoso. Tel. 336-4356*. Late November through early April.

PRACTICAL INFORMATION:

- **Tourist Office/Visitors Bureau**
  - **Artesia**: *Tel. 746-2744 or 1/800-658-6251*
  - **Carlsbad**: *Tel. 887-6516 or 1/800-221-1224*
  - **Hobbs**: *Tel. 397-3202 or 1/800-658-6291*
  - **Roswell**: *Tel. 623-5695*
  - **Ruidoso**: *Tel. 257-7395 or 1/800-253-2255*
- **Bus Depot**
  - **Carlsbad**: *Tel. 887-1108*
  - **Roswell**: *Tel. 622-2510*
- **Hospital**
  - **Carlsbad**: *Tel. 887-6633*
  - **Hobbs**: *Tel. 392-6581*
  - **Roswell**: *Tel. 622-8770*
  - **Ruidoso**: *Tel. 257-7381*
- **Police** (non-emergency)
  - **Carlsbad**: *Tel. 885-3137*
  - **Hobbs**: *Tel. 397-2431*
  - **Roswell**: *Tel. 624-6770*
  - **Ruidoso**: *Tel. 257-7365*

20. THE SOUTHWEST

- THE RUGGED WILDERNESS -

If any area of New Mexico best represents the great diversity of this vast state, it is the **southwest** quarter. Aside from **Las Cruces** and a few other major towns along the Interstate corridors, it is sparsely populated. Even fewer tourists come to this part of the state, perhaps because of the lack of a "big name" to grab travel headlines. There's no Santa Fe, Taos, or Carlsbad Caverns. The advantage of fewer visitors is that things remain in a more pristine form, untrampled by the masses. On the other hand, those who don't make it to this part of the state are missing something very special – there's plenty to see and do.

Barren deserts in the southern portion of the region give way to thickly forested mountains as you travel further to the north. There are plenty of geologic oddities to go along with the beautiful high country, such as the **City of Rocks** and the fantastic gorge traversed by the **Catwalk**. It isn't only the land forms that are diverse. So, too, is the region's history and cultural traditions. Ruins of ancient Indian civilizations and ghost towns from the mining boom days survive along with contemporary communities. The life-style is typical New Mexico – laid back and friendly.

ARRIVALS & DEPARTURES

Socorro is located only 75 miles south of Albuquerque along I-25, allowing easy access to Albuquerque's airport or either of the two major Interstates for those driving in from other parts of the country or state.

There's also four-times daily service via "Roadrunner" to Albuquerque airport from Socorro. Amtrak's southern line has a station in Deming, and Las Cruces is served by **Mesa Air**, *Tel. 1/800-MESA-AIR*, from Albuquerque.

ORIENTATION/GETTING AROUND

The best way to take a journey through southwest New Mexico is in a roughly circular route beginning and ending in the town of Socorro. As mentioned above in *Arrivals & Departures*, Socorro is only 75 miles from Albuquerque. From Socorro, the suggested southwest route follows I-25 further south to Truth or Consequences and then on to Las Cruces before heading west to Deming and then north to Silver City. After a detour from that point to the Gila Cliff Dwellings, the route returns to Socorro via a wilderness route (US 180, NM 12, and US 60) through portions of the Gila, Apache-Sitgreaves, and Cibola National Forests.

If you want to tour the southwest from Alamogordo (or, by extension, from the southeast), you can join the loop at Las Cruces. You would only miss a small portion of the attractions around Truth or Consequences.

Public transportation is limited to four locations within the southwest quadrant. Greyhound bus service reaches Socorro, Truth or Consequences, Las Cruces, and Deming. You will, however, be hard-pressed to make convenient connections from one part of the southwest to another. Within the greater Las Cruces area, **Roadrunner Transit**, *Tel. 525-2500*, provides municipal bus service on several routes. Call them for current information and schedules.

WHERE TO STAY

DEMING

Budget

GRAND MOTOR INN, *1721 East Spruce Street. Tel. 546-2632, Fax 546-4446. Rates: $46-48. 60 Rooms. Major credit cards accepted. Located about 1 1/2 miles east of the center of town on the I-10 business loop, which is US 70.*

You would never know that the Grand Motor Inn is a "budget" motel by the way it looks. The classic looking entrance, complete with tall white columns, fronts the two-story glass wall of the main building. Guest rooms, which are spacious and attractively furnished, were refurbished in 1991 and are in one of two sturdy red brick buildings in an L-shape around the large heated pool and smaller wading pool. Some rooms have refrigerators. The Grand Restaurant is the best place to eat in Deming.

HOLIDAY INN, *I-10 Service Road. Tel. 546-2661, Fax 546-6308. 85 Rooms. Rates: $54-64. Major credit cards accepted. Toll-free reservations 1/800-HOLIDAY. Located at Exit 85 of I-10.*

A small notch above the run-of-the-mill roadside Holiday Inns. You won't, as the advertising for the chain goes, find any surprises. Decent accommodations along with a heated swimming pool. Some rooms have refrigerators and/or microwaves. The restaurant, Fat Eddies at the Inn, is better than the normal Holiday Inn fare and is one of Deming's better eateries.

LAS CRUCES
Moderate

HOLIDAY INN DE LAS CRUCES, *201 East University Avenue. Tel. 526-4411, Fax 524-0530. Rates: $72-81. 110 Rooms. Major credit cards accepted. Toll-free reservations 1/800-HOLIDAY. Located about three miles south of the center of Las Cruces on US 80/85/180 at the junction of I-10, Exit 142.*

This is one of my favorite Holiday Inns in New Mexico. Attractive Southwestern architecture is carried through to the rooms. You'll even encounter some authentic antiques. All of the recreational facilities are in the enclosed Holidome and include pool, wading pool, and jogging track. A nice gift shop is on the premises as well as a good restaurant and lounge. The lounge, which they refer to as a saloon, features lively entertainment and is frequented by students from New Mexico State University (located across the road from the Inn). Friendly employees are costumed in Southwestern style to add to the atmosphere.

LAS CRUCES HILTON INN, *705 South Telshor Boulevard. Tel. 522-4300, Fax 521-4707. Rates: $75. 203 Rooms. Major credit cards accepted. Toll-free reservations 1/800-HILTONS. Located near the Mesila Valley Mall on the east side of town. Take Exit 3 off of I-25 (Lohman Avenue) and go one block east to Telshor Boulevard.*

A modern seven-story first-class hotel built in adobe style manages to still capture the spirit of Old New Mexico. An elegant lobby with graceful arches, huge potted palm trees, and old fashioned wooden ceiling fans will make an immediate impression. The guest rooms are beautifully decorated in Southwestern fashion and overlooks the city and Mesilla Valley on one side and the East Mesa on the other. Some rooms have refrigerators and the few suites have whirlpools.

Ventana Terrace Restaurant features fine cuisine and service. There's a piano lounge that has a very happy Happy Hour. Recreational facilities include a heated swimming pool, Jacuzzi, and exercise room with weights.

LUNDEEN INN OF THE ARTS, *618 South Alameda Boulevard. Tel. 526-3327, Fax 526-3355. Rates: $62-95, including full breakfast. 20 Rooms. Most major credit cards accepted. Located in the center of town. Use Exit 3 from I-25 and take Lohman west to Alameda Boulevard.*

This historic inn is rather large for a Bed and Breakfast facility. The adobe style building dates from 1865 and was renovated and converted into a B&B exactly a hundred years later. Further renovations took place a few years ago. The atmosphere is of New Mexico in the 19th century, which fits in perfectly with the surroundings of the old town area where the inn is located.

Spacious accommodations (which include several suites and even larger villas) are each named after a famous artist with New Mexico connections. Seven units have kitchens and quite a few have microwave ovens. The decor is Southwestern, but no two rooms are decorated alike. There are fireplaces in many units and most of the second story rooms have balconies. You'll also find more modern amenities here than is usually the case with B&Bs. For example, all rooms have television and air conditioning.

While there is no restaurant, guests will receive a lavish breakfast and there is a charming late afternoon "Merienda" hour where beverages and hors d'oeuvres are served. Another interesting regular event at Lundeen are frequent workshops given by local and regional artists. That is the source of the Inn's name, but people without any artistic talents are just as welcome. The entire inn is a smoke-free zone. Several good restaurants are located within walking distance.

Budget

BEST WESTERN MESILLA VALLEY INN, *901 Avenida de Mesilla. Tel. 524-8603, Fax 526-8437. Rates: $58-62. 167 Rooms. Major credit cards accepted. Toll-free reservations 1/800-528-1234. Located by Exit 142 of I-10. The area is a commercial zone about half-way between downtown Las Cruces and the historic adjacent village of Mesilla.*

This is a modern two-story motor inn that features big rooms. Some rooms have full kitchens while others have refrigerators and microwaves. You'll also find a heated pool as well as a whirlpool. A full service restaurant is located on the premises as well as a piano bar and lounge with entertainment. Nothing special here, but the Mesilla Valley Inn represents the best of the budget class accommodations in Las Cruces.

SILVER CITY

Moderate

BEAR MOUNTAIN GUEST RANCH, *2251 Bear Mountain Road. Tel. 538-2538. Rates: $60-100. 15 Rooms. Most major credit cards accepted. Toll-free reservations 1/800-880-2538. Located three miles north of downtown via NM 15 towards the Gila Cliff Dwellings.*

This is a traditional guest ranch of the style found in the late 19th and early 20th centuries, although it was built in 1928. All of the guest rooms are very spacious. In addition to regular rooms, whose prices are quoted above, there are several cottages, multi-room ranch houses, and even a 5-bedroom house. Prices for these range from $115 to over $200 but are relatively inexpensive for larger groups traveling together.

The ranch lies adjacent to the Gila National Forest at an altitude of more than 6,200 feet. The setting is refreshing and tranquil. The dining rooms, available to guests only, are known for serving humongous portions of home-style meals.

CARTER HOUSE, *101 North Cooper Street. Tel. 388-5485. Rates: $58-69, including full breakfast. 5 Rooms. MasterCard and VISA accepted. Located downtown next to the County Courthouse.*

Another historic Bed and Breakfast inn, the main house was built in 1905 and boasts rich oak trim throughout. The rooms are nicely furnished and are smoke-free (as are the entire premises). Like so many B&Bs, the accommodations are a throwback to a more simple time and do not include such modern amenities as telephones, TVs, or air conditioning. A popular place for guests is on the stately front porch, providing a fabulous view of the nearby mountains.

In a separate wing is a 22-room hostel that has much more basic accommodations. I don't myself ever go for this type of lodging, but mention it simply as a service to those who might be interested.

Budget

HOLIDAY MOTOR HOTEL, *3420 US Highway 180 East. Tel. 538-3711, Extension 300, Fax 388-3711. Rates: $45-60. 80 Rooms. Major credit cards accepted. Toll-free reservations 1/800-828-8291. Located on the main highway into town (US 180) about two miles east of the center.*

You won't find the usual national chains represented in Silver City. Accommodations tend to be either of the guest ranch or B&B variety, as above, or small independent motels of dubious quality. The Holiday Motor Hotel is definitely the pick of the lot if you're looking for a regular roadside motel in the area. Rooms are of a nice size and are reasonably modern looking. There's a swimming pool for recreation and a couple of restaurants are very close by.

SOCORRO

Budget

BEST WESTERN GOLDEN MANOR, *507 North California Avenue. Tel. 835-0230, Fax 835-1993. Rates: $52 including full breakfast. 41 Rooms. Major credit cards accepted. Toll-free reservations 1/800-528-1234. Located one mile south of I-25, Exit 150 on US 60/85/I-25 business route.*

Socorro lies on a long stretch of I-25 between Albuquerque and points of interest in the southwestern portion of the state. As such, there's always the chance you may need to park here for the night. It's the type of town with undistinguished properties. Besides this Best Western, which I think is the best of the lot and the best value, there are several other major chains represented.

The newly refurbished rooms all include mircowaves and mini-refrigerators and are decorated in Southwestern style. There's a restaurant on the premises (open for breakfast and dinner only) and a heated swimming pool.

TRUTH OR CONSEQUENCES

Budget

BEST WESTERN HOT SPRINGS MOTOR INN, *2270 North Date Street. Tel. 894-6665, Fax is same number. Rates: $50. 40 Rooms. Major credit cards accepted. Toll-free reservations 1/800-528-1234. Located at Exit 79 of I-25.*

Another standard roadside motel offering, again, what I deem to be the best of its category if you want to stay within Truth or Consequences. Conveniently located, the one-story motel features good sized rooms with either king or queen beds. A variety of restaurants are located within a five minute ride and there's a heated pool on the premises.

"SEMI-ROUGHING IT" IN THE WILDS OF SOUTHWEST NEW MEXICO

The return to Socorro from Silver City travels through the very sparsely populated area along the western border of New Mexico and through several national forests. Although there a few small towns, none of them have what I would call "first class" accommodations. The choice below, in ***Glenwood****, should meet most people's minimum standards, but don't expect too much. I include it here in this sidebar for the convenience of those who need to find lodging in this region. It wouldn't otherwise qualify to appear in this book.*

LOS OLMOS GUEST RANCH*, US Route 180, Glenwood. Tel. 539-2311. Rates:$70-80 including full breakfast. 13 Rooms. American Express, Discover, MasterCard and VISA accepted. Los Olmos offers basic accommodations in individual stone cottages, and is located in a nice setting.*

On the other hand, if this prospect doesn't appeal to you, there is a simple way to avoid it. The distance from Silver City to Socorro by this route is approximately 250 miles. Even allowing time for seeing the sights enroute and lunch (there are acceptable places to get a mid-day meal), you could avoid having to stay overnight by leaving Silver City first thing in the morning. Most people should have no trouble reaching Socorro by six in the evening. So, take a look at the places to stay and at your itinerary. Then decide the way to go.

ELEPHANT BUTTE INN, *NM Highway 195 (Elephant Butte). Tel. 744-5431, Fax is same number. Rates: $59. Major credit cards accepted. Located in the community of Elephant Butte, about three miles north of I-25's Exit 83 on NM 195. It's about ten minutes from Truth or Consequences.*

This is a very attractive and modern two-story motor inn situated right near the shore of picturesque Elephant Butte Lake. It's close enough to town to make it the best choice in the vicinity. Very decent rooms are complemented by more facilities than at the Best Western. In addition to the almost mandatory swimming pool there are two tennis courts and an outdoor barbecue area with grilles. There's also an on-premise restaurant joined to a cocktail lounge that offers nightly entertainment.

CAMPING & RV SITES

- **Center Court RV Park**, *Truth or Consequences. Tel. 744-5453*
- **Continental Divide RV Park**, *Pinos Altos, north of Silver City. Tel. 388-3005*
- **Gila Hot Springs Vacation Center**, *Silver City. Tel. 536-9551*
- **KOA Campgrounds**, *Silver City. Tel. 388-3351*
- **Lakeside RV Park & Campground**, *Elephant Butte, Tel. 744-5996*
- **Monticello Point RV**, *Truth or Consequences. Tel. 894-6468*

WHERE TO EAT

DEMING

Moderate – $11-20

GRAND RESTAURANT, *1721 East Spruce Street, in the Grand Motor Inn. Tel. 546-2632. Most Major credit cards accepted.*

Although it may be the "fanciest" restaurant in a town of very simple tastes, the Grand is still a casual family-style restaurant. The chef cooks up a variety of entrees, although the emphasis is on authentic Mexican. Cocktails are available. The children can select from their own menu.

Budget – $10 or less

SI SENOR RESTAURANT, *Silver and Pine Streets, downtown. Tel. 546-3958. No credit cards accepted. Closed on Sunday.*

Basic Mexican fare at very reasonable prices. Better for lunch than for dinner, although if you're looking for Mexican the way they eat it south of the border than you'll definitely find it here. The dishes have not been influenced by New Mexican variations.

LAS CRUCES/MESILLA

Moderate – $11-20

DOUBLE EAGLE RESTAURANT, *in Mesilla on the old town Plaza. Tel. 523-6700. Most major credit cards accepted. Lunch and dinner served daily; Sunday brunch. Reservations suggested.*

One of several historic restaurants that dominate the dining scene in the Las Cruces/Mesilla area, the Double Eagle is located in a large adobe building constructed in 1848. It has a lot of atmosphere and fits in nicely in the historic Plaza setting. There are several small and intimate dining rooms done in various Victorian styles with a lot of antiques. You can also dine outside on the patio which features an attractive fountain. Steak and seafood are the main staples on the menu although there are quite a few

Southwestern dishes. The food is very good, the portions generous, and the service efficient. Cocktails are served and there is a separate lounge.

LA POSTA, *in Mesilla center, near the Plaza. Tel. 524-3524. Most major credit cards accepted. Lunch and dinner served daily except Monday. Reservations accepted.*

Another old adobe building that goes back to the earlier part of the 19th century. The decor is Southwestern and although it's quite nice, the atmosphere doesn't do as much for me as does the Double Eagle. The food, which is almost entirely Mexican, is very good. Beer and wine are served but no cocktails. A children's menu is available.

MAMA MARIE'S, *2190 Avenida de Mesilla in Mesilla. Tel. 524-0701. MasterCard and VISA accepted. Lunch and dinner served daily except Tuesday.*

An attractive Italian restaurant which, at first glance, seems to be another Southwestern style place. Mediterranean styles don't really differ that much. You can get veal, fish, and poultry dishes, but the very best at Mama Marie's is the excellent fettucine. Beer and wine are served.

Budget – $10 or less

MY BROTHER'S PLACE, *336 South Main Street in Las Cruces Tel. 523-7681. No credit cards accepted.*

A busy place, especially at lunchtime, the restaurant consists of two separate rooms, one of which has an old-fashioned soda fountain style set-up. You can get anything from a burger to a full dinner, all at very reasonable prices. For dinner the menu features steak and several types of chile dishes.

SILVER CITY

Moderate – $11-20

BLACK CACTUS CAFE, *107 West Yankie Street, about a half mile south of US 160 and NM 90 via College Boulevard and Bullard Street. Tel. 388-5430. MasterCard and VISA accepted. Dinner only served Tuesday through Saturday. Reservations suggested*

Definitely the most eclectic and interesting dining spot in the entire area. Very casual atmosphere – it doesn't have any particular style but is very bohemian in nature. Silver City's residents are said by some to be a breed apart – independent and detached. That may well describe the Black Cactus. I don't, however, mean to imply that attitude to the service which is quite acceptable.

The menu changes very often and usually features entrees from different countries. The common thread is that most can be described as for the health-conscious eater. No alcoholic beverages other than beer or wine or served. The restaurant has only on-street parking but it's usually not a big problem.

BUCKHORN SALOON AND OPERA HOUSE, *on Main Street in Pinos Altos, north of Silver City. Tel. 538-9911. Most major credit cards accepted. Dinner only. Reservations suggested.*

Within the confines of 18-inch thick adobe walls, the historic Buckhorn has an interior that can best be described as a combination of Victorian and rustic western. The menu is decidedly American in flavor. The saloon is a popular spot with visitors and locals. It's a lively place where the atmosphere and fun is ahead of the food quality, which is average. But if you're looking for something that exemplifies the Silver City area (without going as far as the Black Cactus), than the Buckhorn is the place to go.

DOUBLE EAGLE STEAK HOUSE AND SALOON, *2310 East US Highway 180. Tel. 538-0100. Most major credit cards accepted. Lunch and dinner served daily.*

Not to be confused with the Double Eagle in Mesilla (which is not related to this in any way), this Eagle doesn't fly nearly as high. However, the steaks are very good and cooked correctly to your specifications, and the bar serves up some mean drinks. Very western in atmosphere.

Budget – $10 or less

ST. PAUL'S ESPRESSO AND COFFEE SHOP, *925 North Hudson Street. Tel. 388-5358. No credit cards accepted.*

Especially good for lunch, St. Paul's serves a variety of sandwiches, Southwestern, and Mexican dishes. You'll get the food hot, fast, and at a very low price. Not the place to go, however, if you're looking for a quiet charming dinner. No alcoholic beverages served.

SOCORRO

Budget – $10 or less

ARMIJO'S MEXICAN RESTAURANT, *California and Vigil Streets (US 60 and 85). Tel. 835-1686. Most major credit cards accepted. Lunch and dinner served daily.*

A rather small and basic looking restaurant, Armijo's does offer excellent authentic Mexican dishes served either mild or hot. The food is plentiful and filling but won't take a big chunk out of your pocketbook. Armijo's serves beer and wine.

TRUTH OR CONSEQUENCES

Moderate – $11-20

LOS ARCOS STEAK HOUSE, *1400 North Date Street, on the I-25 business loop. Tel. 894-6200. Major credit cards accepted. Lunch and dinner served daily.*

Easily the best restaurant in town. Some entrees edge into the Expensive price category. The attractive decor is reminiscent of a Mexican restaurant, but the cuisine is mostly American. The steaks will be prepared exactly to your requirements on a fiery open grill visible to all diners. Los Arcos also features lobster, something you don't see on the menu nearly as often in the Southwest as you do in many other parts of the country. Alcoholic beverages are served.

Budget – $10 or less

BAR-B-QUE ON BROADWAY, *308 Broadway. Tel. 894-7047. Most major credit cards accepted. Lunch and dinner served daily.*

Nicely done ribs, chicken, and other dishes, including some Mexican in an attractive casual setting. The prices are very low and there's plenty to eat for the money. The home-made barbecue sauce is flavorful and tangy. It's okay to eat with your fingers; you're among friends here. Children's portions are also served.

HODGE'S FAMILY RESTAURANT, *on US Highway 195 in Elephant Butte, north of Truth or Consequences. Most major credit cards accepted.*

Hodge' serves a wide variety of American and other fare at reasonable prices in a very comfortable setting. Similar in style to many "chain" family restaurants, I think that the food quality and selection here are a notch above most of the chains, especially considering the modest prices. A good place to go when everyone in your party has said "enough Mexican, enough Southwestern," etc., etc.

SEEING THE SIGHTS

Traveling South on I-25

The approximately 90 minute drive from Albuquerque to Socorro is an easy one. All on I-25, the super-highway follows the course of the Rio Grande, passing a number of small towns and within view of distant mountains to both the east and west.

Socorro was at one time one of the biggest cities in New Mexico – during the silver boom of the 1880s. It was also one of the most lawless and wildest places in the west. A collapse in silver prices ended the boom and those who remained turned largely to farming. That holds true today, although mining technology is still important, as evidenced by the **New Mexico Institute of Mining and Technology** being located here. Socorro is today best known for being the nearest major town to the super-high tech Very Large Array radio telescope. However, it's over 50 miles to the west, so I'll defer on the VLA for now and wait until you pass right by it on the way back to Socorro.

For now, leave I-25 at Exit 150 and follow California Street for about a mile to the junction of College Street. Turn right and you'll soon reach the Institute of Mining campus, home to the **Mineral Museum** in the Workman Center complex, *Tel. 835-5420.* The collection of mineral samples is one of the largest in the world, numbering more than 12,000 pieces. Many are from the region and other parts of New Mexico, but samples from around the world can also be found. A number of displays relate to the mining of minerals. While this may not seem all that exciting, it's actually quite interesting to see a lot of names that you're familiar with and find that the mineral in its natural state is much different in appearance than you thought. Many of the minerals are also very colorful. *The museum is open weekdays from 8:00am until 5:00pm. It's closed on Thanksgiving and from Christmas through New Year's Day. There is no admission charge.*

You can leave the campus via the School of Mines Road side and follow that street as it cuts an angle across town, ending at Socorro's old **Central Plaza**. This is the heart of the town's historic district. Things will be a little easier to find if you pick up a map of the historic area at Socorro's **Chamber of Commerce**, *located in the plaza vicinity at 103 Francisco de Avondo*. Among the highlights of the historic district are the **San Miguel Mission**, *Tel. 835-1620*, a couple of blocks north of the Plaza on Camino Real, which was built in 1819 to replace an earlier mission built in the 1620s, and the old **Garcia Opera House** dating from 1886. The Opera House is on Terry Avenue a block northeast from the Plaza.

Continuing south from Socorro on I-25, it's another 74 miles to the next big town, which is Truth or Consequences. On the way, get off the highway at Exit 139 (San Antonio) and follow signs for NM 1 that will lead back to the Interstate 20 miles down the road. The reason is that NM 1 passes through the **Bosque del Apache National Wildlife Refuge**, home to many species of birds but especially known as a stopping place for cranes, including the endangered **whooping crane**. You can get a good view of the wildlife areas from the road, but even better from some of the marked viewing areas and short nature trails scattered along the 15-mile road that runs through the Refuge. There's also a small visitor center with exhibits and information.

Truth or Consequences

Just before reaching **Truth or Consequences** (referred to simply as "T or C" by New Mexicans, so I'll do the same from now on), you'll get a good view of a large lake called Elephant Butte Reservoir. It's the primary recreation area for the T or C area and if you wish to see it better or go for some recreational activities yourself, take Exit 83 off of I-25 right into **Elephant Butte Lake State Park**. The name comes from a large volcanic promontory that vaguely resembles an elephant. Construction of a dam that impounds the Rio Grande has created a narrow lake that stretches for more than thirty miles. The brilliant blue water and the interesting rock formations amid the surrounding desert make for a very pleasant sight.

On the recreation side, the state park features swimming, boating (including water skiing), and fishing.

Exit 79 off of I-25 will lead you into the downtown area of T or C. The town was built right over a number of **thermal springs**, eight of which are still visible within the community. The water averages about 110 degrees and has been claimed to be curative of all sorts of ills for centuries. Many bath houses were built in the late 19th and early 20th century. The ones that are still open are well past their glory days, but some people still come to take the "cure."

THE WHOLE TRUTH ABOUT A TOWN'S NAME

The first thing that most people think about when they hear ***Truth Or Consequences, New Mexico*** *is how in the world did they ever name a town that? Well, there is a story behind it, so here goes: T or C was originally called Springs of Palomas, but that was changed to simply Hot Springs when the Elephant Butte Dam was built. Many of you are probably too young to remember that in 1950 there was a popular radio show (yes, radio, not television) called "Truth or Consequences," hosted by a man named Ralph Edwards.*

Mr. Edwards was apparently very proud of the widespread following his program had. So he offered the enticement of a barrel of free publicity to any town that was willing to change its name to Truth or Consequences, since the prize would be a live broadcast of his program from the town on April Fool's Day of 1950. I don't know how many American towns seriously considered the proposal but a majority of Hot Springs residents voted in a special election to make the change. The show was broadcast from the newly renamed Truth or Consequences as promised and the rest, as they say, is history. Perhaps more surprising than the fact that the townspeople took up the challenge is that they haven't ever considered changing the name back. Maybe that's because New Mexico has so many towns with unusual names. Mr. Edward's legacy lives on in a municipal riverfront park bearing his name and in a wing of the Geronimo Springs Museum.

The town's greatest attraction (other than its name, the springs, and the nearby recreation areas) is the **Geronimo Springs Museum**, *325 Main Street (US 85), Tel. 894-6600*. The museum has an excellent collection of Native American artifacts and crafts, especially the fine examples of prehistoric Mimbres pottery. There are also exhibits on area history and the Ralph Edwards Wing which displays mementos of the radio show's creator. *The museum is open Monday through Saturday from 9:00am until 5:00pm. It is closed on New Year's, Thanksgiving, and Christmas. The admission charge is $2 for adults and $1 for students with a valid identification card.*

It seems almost too convenient that all of the major towns between Albuquerque and Las Cruces are approximately 75 miles apart. Just long enough to make some mileage and not long enough to get tired of driving. The final leg on I-25 from T or C to Las Cruces is just such a trip. However, you can make one stop before getting there. About 15 miles north of Las Cruces via Exit 19 is **Fort Selden State Monument**, *Tel. 526-8911*. The fort was on active duty from 1865 through 1891 and was one of a series of frontier posts to protect settlers from Indian attacks. The father of Gen. Douglas MacArthur was one of the post's commanders and little Doug lived here for a couple of years.

More important, however, is the fact that much of the adobe fort is still standing and you can take a self-guided walking tour that visits many of the fort's buildings. One of the buildings has been converted into a museum that documents the fort's history as well as that of the surrounding region. Uniformed guides give demonstrations of the weapons and equipment used during the fort's active period on weekend afternoons. *The fort is open from May 1st through September 15th daily from 9:30am to 5:30pm and closes an hour earlier the rest of the year. It is closed on most major holidays. Admission is $2 for those age 16 and up.*

A number of wineries are located in the Truth or Consequences area. The most convenient to visit is the **Domaine Cherulin**, *500 Main Street*. Let me know what you think of New Mexico's wines!

Las Cruces

The largest city in the southwestern quarter of the state and one of the biggest in all of New Mexico, **Las Cruces** has 65,000 residents. It's located less than 50 miles north of El Paso, Texas and sits at the junction of I-25 and I-10. It was part of the Camino Real, the royal Spanish road that cut through New Mexico on the way to Mexico City.

The name means "the crosses" and stems from the markers planted on the graves of a wagon train that was ambushed by the Apaches on this spot. The water of the Rio Grande has provided adequate irrigation for crops for several centuries and is the reason that the **Mesilla Valley** is one of New Mexico's prime agricultural areas. Las Cruces is also home to **New Mexico State University**, the state's second largest institution of higher education.

As you approach Las Cruces, you have to notice the nearby mountains to the east that form a beautiful backdrop for the city. Rising a mile above the valley floor, the **Organ Mountains** are a series of jagged peaks that do look a lot like the spires of a pipe organ. Anyone coming from Alamogordo will pass through the Organ Mountains on their way into Las Cruces. If you are coming from the north or south, however, it's worth a short detour on US 70 east (use Exit 6 off of I-25) to reach the 5,700-foot high **San Augustin Pass**. There's a turn-out at the summit where you can park and walk about 300 feet to a fantastic overlook. Stretched out beneath you to the west is the Rio Grande and the Mesilla Valley, with Las Cruces shining in the center. In the other direction you can see as far as the Tularosa Basin and maybe, depending upon the weather, even catch a glimpse of the distant White Sands.

Returning to the Interstate, take it south a couple of miles to Exit 3 which will lead you onto University Avenue alongside the campus of New Mexico State University. On the grounds of the school is the **University Museum**, *Tel. 646-3739*, which features rotating exhibits on the region's history, culture, and archaeology. Also on the campus is the **Southwest Residential Experiment Station**, a project studying the use of solar energy for domestic power supply. There's a visitor center that explains the work being done. *The university's museum is open Tuesday through Saturday from 10:00am to 4:00pm and on Sundays from 1:00-4:00pm. Donations are requested. The Experiment Station visitor center is open during weekdays from9:00am to noon and again from 1:00-5:00pm. Guided tours can be arranged. There is no admission charge.*

At the west end of the campus, turn right off of University Avenue onto El Paseo and take that to where it intersects like an "X" with Main Street. Bear right into Main and take that a couple of blocks to the central plaza area that is the core of downtown. The area is known as the **Downtown Mall**. The Chamber of Commerce is located on the Mall and can provide brochures on walking tours of two adjacent historic districts in the downtown area. These are the **Alameda District** located to the west of Main Street and the **Mesquite District** just east of Main. The Alameda dates from the late 1800s and features many beautiful homes in a variety of architectural styles. The Mesquite goes back to the town's early years in the mid-19th century and has many small adobe structures known for their vibrant colors. Pink, blue, and green dominate the attractive scene.

Among other things to see downtown are the **Branigan Cultural Center**, *Tel. 524-1422,* that features works by local artists (in the Downtown Mall); the **Bicentennial Log Cabin** on North Main Street, a well preserved pioneer dwelling and furnished with antiques that's open for inspection during the summer; and **Our Lady at the Foot of the Cross Shrine** (Lohman and Water Streets), a reproduction of Michelangelo's Pieta.

From downtown head east on Lohman Avenue, going past the Interstate for a block to Telshor Boulevard. Turn right into the Mesilla Valley Mall. Now, I'm not sending you shopping. The modern mall is an unusual place to put a museum, but the **Las Cruces Museum of Natural History**, *Tel. 522-3120,* is located here. Since opening a few years ago, the museum has put together a good reputation for its collection of permanent and changing exhibits on the region's natural history - both flora and fauna as well as geologic. *The museum is open from Monday to Friday, noon to 5:00pm (extended to 9:00pm on Fridays), Saturday from 10:00am to 6:00pm and on Sunday from noon to 6:00pm. It is closed on holidays and requests donations in lieu of an admission charge.*

The small town of **Mesilla** is located about three miles from the center of Las Cruces to the southwest. You can use the University Avenue Exit of I-25 once again, but continue past I-10 and into Mesilla. Turn right on NM 28 and in a few blocks you'll reach the **La Mesilla Central Plaza**. Mesilla was originally a stagecoach stop. It has largely been restored to its 19th century appearance and is home to many fancy shops, galleries, and restaurants. It has often been compared to Albuquerque's Old Town and, indeed, the similarities are quite striking. In some ways it seems more authentic. While Albuquerque's is a well preserved area surrounded by a big city, Mesilla's still functions as the heart of town. The Mesilla Valley is one of the prime areas for growing chile peppers and many of the eateries in the old village feature it served in every way imaginable, some of it extremely hot!

Once you've finished exploring the quaint streets of the village, continue north on NM 28 for a short distance until you reach the intersection of I-10. Take the highway westbound for about 60 miles until you reach the town of Deming (Exit 82).

Deming

Another agricultural community, **Deming** has 11,000 residents and lots of motels and tacky shops for people passing through on I-10 on their way to and from Arizona and California. I have to be honest and say that Deming is rather drab and undistinguished looking. However, there are a few bright spots, especially one fine museum and some of the natural sights to the north and south. One can only say good things, however, about Deming's most famous event - the **Great American Duck Race**.

The main street in Deming is Gold Avenue (NM 11). It can be reached from the Interstate exit by following Cedar Street to the center of town. Near the center of town is the **Deming Luna Mimbres' Museum**, *301 South Silver, Tel. 546-2382*, a block east of Gold and Hemlock Street. The building was once a national guard armory and was turned into a museum by the Luna County Historical Society in 1977. The large museum has a varied collection of artifacts and exhibits dealing with just about every aspect of the Southwest.

On display are a full size chuck wagon, ten different street scenes with vintage cars depicting the history of Deming, an Indian kiva featuring the art of the ancient Mimbres people, military artifacts, and even a collection

SOUTH OF THE BORDER

A little less than half of New Mexico's southern frontier (170 miles) borders on ***Mexico****. So a lot of visitors think about taking a short trip south of the border. This area, however, has only one road leading directly into Mexico (south of the town of Columbus), a sparsely populated region with nothing to see. On the other hand, the bigger portion of the New Mexico border is shared with Texas. Texas, at its extreme western end, comes to a triangular point where the city of* ***El Paso*** *is located. On the other side of the Rio Grande, which turns southeasterly at El Paso, is the large Mexican city of* ***Ciudad Juarez****. As it's only about 45 miles via Interstate highway from Las Cruces to El Paso, you can make a day trip to both Texas and Mexico!*

It's beyond the scope of this book to provide detailed sightseeing and other information on places not in New Mexico, but since it is so close (and some visitors may be using El Paso as their gateway into New Mexico) I'll provide a list of the highlights in those two cities.

EL PASO

- ***Magoffin Homestead*** *(an 1875 hacienda)*
- ***Chazimal National Memorial*** *(commemorating a peaceful solution to a border dispute)*
- ***El Paso Museum of Art*** *and* ***El Paso Museum of History***
- ***Fort Bliss Museum***
- ***Scenic Drive*** *(above El Paso through the Franklin Mountains)*
- ***Sierra del Cristo Rey*** *(huge statue of Christ the King on the international border)*

CIUDAD JUAREZ

- ***Chazimal National Park***
- ***Juarez Chazimal Park*** *(beautiful floral displays)*
- ***Guadalupe Mission***
- ***Lincoln Statue***
- ***City Market***
- ***Pueblito Mexicano***

United States citizens need not have any special documentation to visit Ciudad Juarez so long as you return within 72 hours and do not venture into the interior of Mexico. However, it can get complicated if you intend to drive into Mexico. My advice is to either walk across the short international bridge near Chazimal National Memorial or take the convenient ***El Paso/Juarez Trolley Company, Tel. (915) 544-0062****. Call for details and schedules.*

of more than 1,200 liquor decanters. The main exhibit room is dominated by a colorful 53-foot long mural that illustrates the history of Luna County. The museum also has an excellent shop that sells quality Southwestern items. *The museum is open Monday to Saturday from 9:00am to 4:00pm and on Sunday afternoons from 1:30-4:00pm. It is closed only on Thanksgiving and Christmas. There is no set admission charge but donations are expected.*

Returning to Gold Avenue, take NM 11 south from Deming for five miles and then follow along a marked road for another nine miles to the popular **Rockhound State Park**, *Tel. 546-6182*. The 250 acre park is on the slopes of the Little Florida Mountains and the jagged peaks rise impressively above the park. The park is a mineral treasure trove of agate, jasper, quartz, perlite and many, many others. The unique feature of the park is that you are encouraged to take the rocks with you. In fact, up to 15 pounds per person per trip is allowable.

The park attracts both the casual visitor and the serious rockhound. You'll be able to tell the latter by their well-equiped regalia – heavy boots, pick axe, and shovel. It isn't necessary to do that, though, if you're just coming to look or perhaps pick up a few small souvenir rocks that are always lying around. *The park is open daily from 7:30am to dusk. There is a $3 per vehicle charge to enter. If you intend to actually dig for rocks and are coming in the summer, it is best to do so early in the day before the heat sets in.*

Whether or not you take the short excursion south from Deming to Rockhound State Park, you also have another sightseeing option in that direction, but somewhat farther away. About 35 miles south of Deming via NM 11 (an arrow straight, flat, and unexciting road) is the sleepy border town of **Columbus**. With a population of 600 people, it isn't that different than it was on March 9, 1916, when the infamous Pancho Villa and approximately a thousand of his guerilla followers raided the small military outpost, killing 18 Americans. The raid provoked a now famous response – General John Pershing's military expedition into Mexico to track down Villa.

All of this is commemorated at the 38-acre **Pancho Villa State Park**, *Tel. 531-2711*. Some of the remaining buildings of Camp Furlong have been restored and many items from that era are on display. The park also has several interesting nature trails and one of the best cactus gardens in the Southwest, with more than 500 varieties on display. Some more mementos of the Pancho Villa days are also on display at the local historical society's museum located across the road from the park entrance. They are housed in an old Souther Pacific Railroad depot. *The park is open daily from 8:00am until 5:00pm and there is a $3 entrance fee per vehicle. The adjacent museum is free.*

THE GREAT AMERICAN DUCK RACE

*Deming's unpretentious exterior doesn't apply to the year's major event – **the Great American Duck Race** – held during the fourth weekend of August. The story goes that back in 1979 a couple of local businessmen thought it would be a good idea to bring some notoriety to Deming and one of them had a brainstorm: why not race ducks? There's some question as to whether the good gentleman was sober at the time of his suggestion but, nevertheless, the others thought it made sense and so the first race was held.*

Things have been just ducky with the race since then. The popular event has grown to the point where more than 30,000 visitors come to watch close to 500 ducks participate in the competition. What's more, it's not just for fun. The prize money has reached almost $10,000. The whole town seems to get involved. A young woman is selected to preside as the Duck Queen, while a Deming youngster is chosen as the Darling Duckling (ugly ducklings need not apply). Obviously, the parents of the Darling aren't concerned about their child having to grow up facing schoolmates with the moniker of Darling Duckling.

I think the whole thing is just swell. If all of this doesn't make you want to come to Deming in August, then how about one of the race's most important annual participants – a duck "trainer" and "coach" with the real name of Robert Duck! Honest, folks, I didn't make that up. Would I lie to you about something so important?

Upon returning to Deming, stay on NM 18 as it goes beneath the Interstate and then follow US 180, heading towards Silver City. That's about a 50 mile drive through mostly barren desert terrain, except for the last stretch where the altitude is higher and you're on the edge of the forested mountains. But before you get there, a very unusual natural area awaits your inspection. About 25 miles from Deming and then three more miles on NM 61 brings you to the fascinating **City of Rocks State Park**, *Tel. 536-2800*. Unlike at Rockhound State Park, you have to leave the rocks here. But then again, with many of the rocks reaching 50 feet in height, you'd probably have some trouble getting them in your car anyway.

The 680-acre park is highlighted by a central area covering about 40 acres which are covered by hundreds of these monolithic rocks. Geologists tell us that they aren't really rocks. They're **welded tuff**, a highly compressed form of volcanic ash that remained from eons ago while softer ash that once buried the tuff eroded away. You can wander around and through the boulders in a series of narrow passages that seem to be like streets in this most unusual city. There's also a small desert botanical garden at the edge of the rocks. For a great overall view of the "city," drive to the top of a nearby hill within the park from which you get the big picture. *The state park is open daily from 7:00am until dusk and there is a $3 admission charge per vehicle.*

From the City of Rocks, it's only about a half-hour drive into Silver City.

Silver City

The town's name gives away its origins. The silver boom that swept a large portion of southwest New Mexico began in the 1860s. By 1893, the mining of silver had seriously declined and many boom towns had already faded into oblivion. **Silver City** managed to survive owing to a combination of factors, including the foresight of some of its founders who saw the need to diversify the economy early on. Timber operations in the nearby forests were one reason that Silver City made it through the silver fall, and the addition of ranching also helped. Other types of mining also picked up some of the slack and these mining operations continue to this day. So, Silver City, far from becoming a ghost town, has continued to prosper. The town, however, still looks a lot like it would have a hundred years ago – a combination of Victorian architecture along with a wild west appearance. It does represent what southwest New Mexico is all about.

The history of the Silver City area isn't only about mining and the old west. The ancient **Mimbreno Indians** occupied the area from about 750AD until well into the 12th century. They had an advanced culture. Archaeological finds have yielded many examples of their beautiful pottery, which feature fine paintings of both geometric and nature designs. This so-called Mimbres style pottery is still produced today by tribes descended from the Mimbreno and is actively sought by many art lovers.

Several copper mining operations can be viewed within a short distance of Silver City. One is the Phelps-Dodge Corporation's **Tyrone open pit mine** about five miles from town. An overlook is located on NM 90. The biggest mine operation is the **Chino Mine**, about 15 miles east of Silver City on NM 152. A visitor center explains the mining process seen from the viewing platform.

It's natural to think of mining as damaging the beauty of the earth, and it's certainly true in some respects. But the open pit mine is extremely impressive and can also be said to have its own type of beauty. The thousand foot deep pit measures about 1 3/4 miles across, with many tiers having been carved to allow access to the bottom by huge trucks that are simply dwarfed by the size of the mine. The colorful rock strata makes it almost seem as if this giant hole is part of nature. The mining companies do a great deal to restore the landscape once mining operations cease. Of course, despite their pleas to the contrary, such efforts weren't usually voluntary on their part. *The free visitor center is open from Memorial Day weekend through Labor Day from 10:00am to 4:00pm. The viewing area is available during daylight hours all year long.*

Within Silver City itself you can spend some time wandering through the old town. Two museums of interest are the **Silver City Museum**, *312 West Broadway, Tel. 538-5921*, and the **Western New Mexico University Museum**, located at 10th and West Streets on the WNMU campus on the west side of town, *Tel. 538-6386*. The Silver City Museum is housed in a mansion built in 1881 and contains two main collections. The first relates to the mining days and includes many artifacts from the original Tyrone Mine while the second gallery has changing exhibits, still mostly themed to the area's history. The college's museum concentrates on Native American pottery, especially Mimbres pottery dating from the 8th century. It's the foremost collection of such pottery in the nation and many pieces from the museum have been displayed in famous museums throughout the United States and Europe. *The Silver City Museum is open Tuesday through Friday from 9:00am to 4:30pm and on weekends from 10:00am to 4:00pm. It is closed on New Year's, Thanksgiving, and Christmas and is free of charge. The University Museum has the same hours but requests donations.*

The isolated region surrounding Silver City makes it popular with people who are trying to get away from it all. In keeping with that effort a large number of dude and guest ranches are within a short distance from town. While I don't highly recommend any of them as a place to stay for the average visitor, those readers who might be interested in learning more should contact the local chamber of commerce for further information.

New Mexico's Ghost Town Country

While Silver City, along with quite a few other mining era communities, still exist, there are dozens of boom towns that weren't so fortunate. Some have virtually been obliterated while others remain in various states of disrepair in the form of "ghost towns." The majority of ghost towns don't offer a great deal for the average visitor to see. There are the partial remains of a few buildings, sometimes just a bunch of foundations. Only a handful have been even partially restored or have facilities for visitors. I've been disappointed with most ghost town visits. However, I'm sure that many of you would like to make that judgment for yourself. Silver City lies in about the center of the region that has the most of these towns, so here's a list that might make it easier for you to pick out one or two to visit.

Santa Rita is the closest to Silver City, just a couple of miles east and on the way to the Chino Mine. Two other towns that are either on or near to soon-to-be described sections of the southwest regional tour are one in **Mogollon** (75 miles northwest of Silver City) and **Kelly**, about 29 miles west of Socorro. There are also a couple of ghost towns about 40 miles northwest of Truth or Consequences: these are **Kingston** and **Chloride**.

There are two ghost towns that have had significant restoration work and even offer guided tours in the **Lordsburg** area. These are **Shakespeare** (two miles south of Lordsburg) and **Steins** (19 miles southwest of Lordsburg). Among the many buildings still standing in Shakespeare are the Stratford Hotel, which once employed a young man named William Bonney. He left the hotel industry after a short time and became known in another vocation as Billy The Kid. The interiors of Shakespeare's buildings are only open by guided tours which are given on an irregular schedule. However, its interesting to just walk around. Steins' ghost town looks too much like a tourist attraction. However, about 15 pioneer structures are open for your inspection, including the local bordello. *The Steins Railroad Ghost Town is open daily from 9:00am until 7:00pm from late may through October and from 8:00am to 5:00pm during the remainder of the year. It is closed on Thanksgiving and Christmas. Guided tours are offered. Admission is $2.50 for those over the age of 12.*

Guided tours of the town are available daily throughout the summer season. For your information, Lordsburg can be reached by I-25. It's 60 miles west of Deming and can be seen on a longer alternative route to Silver City if you prefer the ghost towns to the City of Rocks. This route follows NM 90 from Lordsburg to Silver City. Besides missing the City of Rocks (unless you like backtracking on the same roads a lot) this routing adds up to 90 miles of driving depending upon whether you visit both Lordsburg area ghost towns.

Gila Cliff Dwellings

Here's a wonderful excursion from Silver Springs – a 90-mile round-trip that you can do in a half day or up to a full day. It will most certainly be a highlight of any visit to New Mexico's southwest or even the entire state. It combines magnificent scenery with some of the best ancient dwellings to be found anywhere.

The route to and from Silver City is by NM 15. Although it isn't particularly far, allow at least three hours for the complete ride because the road is constantly winding and quite narrow. Trailers and very large motor homes are permitted on the road, but I definitely would advise against it. Whether you're traversing scenic narrow canyons, riding alongside towering mountain peaks, or sweeping through thick green forests of pine and fir, the road provides breathtaking vistas at just about every turn. Except for the first seven miles from Silver City, all of the route lies within the **Gila National Forest and Wilderness Area**, a portion of the rugged **Mogollon Mountains** and a hiker's delight. This was once Apache country, and the likes of Geronimo and Cochise spent much time in this area.

At an elevation of more than 6,800 feet, the town of **Pinos Altos** is the first stop on the route. It began in 1860 when someone accidentally discovered gold in a creek. Eventually more than 700 miners would set up shop in Pinos Altos, but today only a small population remains, mostly descendants of those miners along with some artistic types. The town has been carefully restored and appears much as it did during the boom days, making it a splendid place for the visitor.

One of the successful miners was George Hearst, who made enough money so that his son, William Randolph Hearst, could begin his publishing empire. An old church has been converted into the **Hearst Museum** and displays works by local artists. Items from the town's early days are on display in a restored log cabin, now going by the name of **Pinos Altos Historical Museum**, *Tel. 388-1882*. But the best part of Pinos Altos is just wandering about the small town.

The exciting ride along NM 15 ends abruptly upon reaching the **Gila Cliff Dwellings National Monument**, *Tel. 536-9461*. On this site near a fork in the **Gila River**, the ancient Mogollon culture built their homes in seven natural cavities located 175 feet above the valley floor in the very face of the cliff. After stopping at the visitor center, drive to the parking area at the base of the cliff where a mile long trail (moderately difficult) leads to the cliff dwellings. The sight of the 42 rooms sculpted into the cliff is hard to forget, as is the view looking out from the dwellings. The state of preservation is quite good, certainly good enough for visitors to get an excellent idea of how the Mogollon lived ten centuries ago. After visiting the dwellings retrace your route back to Silver City.

The monument is open daily from 8:00am to 6:00pm between Memorial Day and Labor Day and from 9:00am to 4:00pm the rest of the year. At the present time there's no charge, but that will likely change unless you have an NPS passport.

The Wilderness Route

Upon leaving Silver City for the last time we're ready to embark on a 250-mile trip back to Socorro. This route passes through some of the least developed areas of New Mexico. You'll have wonderful scenery provided by several mountainous national forests and a few scattered towns that barely qualify for that term. However, this wilderness route is more than just a pleasant ride. There are a couple of excellent attractions, both natural and man-made, along the way.

Take US 180 westbound from Silver City for about 60 miles to Glenwood. Just east on Forest Route 95 is scenic **Whitewater Canyon** (no relationship to an Arkansas land deal, by the way) a very rugged, narrow, and steep gorge. The Forest Service has constructed a walking route through the canyon known as **The Catwalk**. The name comes from an earlier (and dangerous) walkway that was built above a water pipeline that was needed for a no-longer existent mill. The narrow walkway is suspended on a series of trestle-like structures jutting out from the rocky canyon walls. Sunlight, even at mid-day, only reaches small portions of the canyon at a time, making the experience more unusual. The route takes you over the swirling river and at one point crosses a short swinging bridge.

The canyon's rugged beauty can be taken it at your own pace along the walk, which is very steep in some places. (The walk is not accessible to the handicapped. If you have any health problems, don't attempt it either as it is quite strenuous in some sections.) The Catwalk extends for almost 2 1/2 miles and you have to return the same way. As most visitors won't want to devote either the time or energy for a five mile hike, I suggest you walk as far into the canyon as your interest carries you and then turn around.

Also located in Glenwood is the **Glenwood State Trout Hatchery**, where this popular and delicious fish is raised to keep New Mexico's lakes and streams adequately stocked. A small population of **bighorn sheep** is often visible from the hatchery. Public hours can vary.

A few miles up the road by the town of Alma, NM 159 leads ten miles into the mountains and to the ghost town of **Mogollon**. Perhaps more interesting than the ghost town is the magnificent mountain and forest scenery. However, only experienced mountain drivers should attempt the trip because the steep road climbs for almost the entire distance through a nearly continuous series of precarious looking switchbacks. If that prospect doesn't bother you (or maybe even entices you), then go for it – the views of the Mogollon Mountains are fantastic.

Don't feel bad if you chickened out on the side trip to Mogollon. The scenery along the next stretch of US 180 is also excellent, especially in the vicinity of the 6,400-foot **Saliz Pass** where the Mogollon and San Francisco Mountains adjoin. Several miles after the pass, get onto NM 12. The road will now generally descend through the **Apache-Sitgreaves National Forest**. The landscape is attractive, with colorful mountains on either side of the road until you suddenly reach the much flatter **Plains of San Augustin**. NM 12 ends at the small town of Datil. Pick up US 60 in an easterly direction and in about eight miles you'll come to the space-age **Very Large Array**, *Tel. 835-7000*. This is the largest and one of the most important radio telescopes in the world.

The Array (or VLA as it is more commonly known) is a series of 27 dish-shaped antennas arranged along railroad tracks in the shape of the letter "Y." Each dish is 82 feet in diameter and weighs about 230 tons.

That's why they're on tracks. One branch of the Y is almost 13 miles long and the other is more than 11. You can see the array from miles away and its quite fascinating as these small specks keep growing in size until you get close and realize how big they are. The whole scene is rather unreal – almost as if you are in some sci-fi movie or about to take part in an invasion from Mars.

The array is designed to photograph light and radio waves from all sorts of interstellar sources. It's all explained in the visitor center where self-guided tours begin. You can get right up close to the antennas, the computer and control rooms, and even a building where antenna dishes are assembled.

A fascinating and educational experience for all ages, there's even something beautiful about the sight of the massive array of steel glistening on the Plains of San Augustin. Perhaps it is the stark contrast of modern technology surrounded by a vast natural area that has been touched only lightly by mankind. *The complex is open to visitors daily from 8:30am to dusk. There is no admission charge.*

Some 20 miles to the east of the VLA is the town of **Magdalena**, named after Mary Magdalena because of a natural rock formation on the side of Magdalena Mountain. Called the **Lady on the Mountain**, there is some resemblance if you use your imagination. I've seen many other natural formations which resemble other people or things much more vividly but, of course, it's all in the eyes of the individual beholder. There's also a very small museum on local history located in a rail car in the Atchinson, Topeka, and Santa Fe railroad depot. It's called, appropriately enough, the **Box Car Museum**, *Tel. 854-2261.*

It's only about 30 miles further east from Magdalena to I-25 and access to your return to Albuquerque.

NIGHTLIFE & ENTERTAINMENT

Once again the small and usually quiet towns of the southwest quadrant of the state don't provide for much excitement during the evening hours. In most places the lounges in the larger hotels are your best bet.

There is one exception, however, and that is in **Las Cruces**. A combination of more people and the presence of a major university make things in this town more lively. This is especially true in the area along South Main Street immediately to the south of Old Town.

Among the better nightspots you'll find here are:

COWBOYS, *2205 South Main, Las Cruces.*

Features a lively bar and excellent country music entertainment. Caters to a crowd of fairly diverse age groups so you probably won't feel out of place.

THE RAIN FOREST, *1765 South Main, Las Cruces.*

Despite its name, it's Southwestern all the way. A lively atmosphere and a mostly young clientele make this one of the most popular places in town. There's a live show on Friday and Saturday evenings featuring Tejano music.

SPORTS & RECREATION

Fishing

- **Caballo Lake State Park**, *Truth or Consequences.* Bass, catfish, crappie, walleye.
- **Elephant Butte Lake State Park**, *Truth or Consequences.* Bass, catfish, crappie, striper, walleye.

Golf

- **Rio Mimbres Country Club**, *Deming. Tel. 546-9481*
- **Las Cruces Country Club**, *Las Cruces. Tel. 526-8731*
- **New Mexico State University Golf Course**, *Las Cruces. Tel. 646-3219*
- **Scott Park Memorial Municipal Golf Course**, *Silver City. Tel. 538-5041*
- **Oasis Golf and Country Club**, *located in Elephant Butte, Truth or Consequences. Tel. 744-5224*
- **Truth or Consequences Golf Course**, *685 Marie Street, Truth or Consequences. Tel. 894-2603*

Horseback Riding

- **Circle S Stables**, *Las Cruces. Tel. 382-7708*

Horse Racing

- **Sunland Park**, 45 miles south of Las Cruces near El Paso, Texas. Fall through Spring.

Swimming

- **Elephant Butte Lake State Park**, *Truth or Consequences.*

PRACTICAL INFORMATION

- **Tourist Office/Visitors Bureau**

  Deming: *Tel. 562-2674 or 1/800-848-4955*
  Las Cruces: *Tel. 524-8521 or 1/800-FIESTAS*
  Silver City: *Tel. 538-3785 or 1/800-548-9378*
  Socorro: *Tel. 835-0424*
  Truth or Consequences: *Tel. 894-3536 or 1/800-831-9487*
- **Bus Depot**

  Deming: *Tel. 564-3881*

Las Cruces: *Tel. 524-8518*
Socorro: *Tel. 835-0236*

- **Municipal Transit Information** –Las Cruces only: *Tel. 525-2500*
- **Hospital**
  Deming: *Tel. 546-2761*
  Las Cruces: *Tel. 522-8641*
  Silver City: *Tel. 388-1591*
  Socorro: *Tel. 835-1140*
  Truth or Consequences: *Tel. 894-2111*
- **Police** (non-emergency)
  Deming: *Tel. 546-8848*
  Las Cruces: *Tel. 526-0795*
  Silver City: *Tel. 538-3723*
  Socorro: *Tel. 835-1150*
  Truth or Consequences: *Tel. 894-7111*

INDEX

THINGS CHANGE!

Phone numbers, prices, addresses, quality of food, etc, all change. If you come across any new information, we'd appreciate hearing from you. No item is too small! Write us at:

New Mexico Guide
Open Road Publishing, P.O. Box 20226
Columbus Circle Station, New York, NY 10023